London
for Children

timeout.com

Time Out Guides Limited
Universal House
251 Tottenham Court Road
London W1T 7AB
Tel + 44 (0)20 7813 3000
Fax + 44 (0)20 7813 6001
Email guides@timeout.com
www.timeout.com

Contributors
Introduction Emma Perry. **Trips & Tours** Elizabeth Winding. **My London** Emma Perry. **City of Discovery** Nick Coleman. **Festivals & Events** Alex Brown. **Attractions** Ronnie Haydon, Tom Howard, Emma Perry (*Great Days Out: Westminster* Elizabeth Winding; *Great Days Out: South Bank, Covent Garden* Emma Perry; *Three Thames tasters* Rose Catt). **Museum & Galleries** Nick Coleman, Meryl O'Rourke, Emma Perry, Peter Watts, Elizabeth Winding (*Great Days Out: Bloomsbury, South Kensington* Elizabeth Winding; *Great Days Out: Docklands, Bold as brass* Emma Perry; *Planes, trains and automobiles, Go to town on school projects* Rose Catt; *The jet set* Jessica Cargill Thompson). **Parks & Gardens** Emma Perry (*Great Days Out: Camden, Off the rails* Emma Perry; *Great Days Out: Hampstead Heath* Nick Coleman; *Great Days Out: Greenwich* Elizabeth Winding; *Field of dreams* Meryl O'Rourke). **Meet the Animals** Emma Perry (*Great Days Out: Marylebone* Elizabeth Winding; *Animals that won't bite* Emma Perry. **Parties** Meryl O'Rourke (*Ask the organiser* Fiona Barrows & Heather Welsh; *Acting up* Sally Harrild. **Arts & Entertainment** Meryl O'Rourke, Elizabeth Winding (*Funny Business* Sarah Labovitch; *Rock-a-bye baby* Bruce Dessau; *Meet the musicians* Heather Welsh; *Clowning around* Jessica Cargill Thompson). **Sport** Peter Watts (*One giant leap, On your marks... Peter Watts; *Anyone for a paddle?* Bruce Dessau. **Eating** Fiona Barrows, Bruce Dessau, Sarah Labovitch, Anna Leach, Meryl O'Rourke and contributors to Time Out Eating & Drinking guide (*Field day* Fiona Barrows; *Perfect pizza* Jenni Muir; *Send in the clowns* Emma Perry). **Shopping** Fiona Barrows, Alex Brown, Emma Perry, Heather Welsh, Elizabeth Winding (*Purls of wisdom, From beans to bar* Lisa Mullen; *Pick and mix* Heather Welsh). **Directory** Alex Brown, Elizabeth Winding.

The Editor would like to thank Flora and Polly Maxwell, Jenny Perry, Deirdre Maxwell Scott, Liz Boulton, Sarah Moore and all the contributors to previous editions of *London for Children*, whose work forms the basis for parts of this book.

Maps john@jsgraphics.co.uk
Cover art direction by Nicola Wilson
Cover Photography by Rob Greig, iStock, Jonathan Perugia
Illustrations by Nicola Wilson
Photography by pages 3, 15, 27, 29, 35, 57, 75, 112, 121, 125 Elisabeth Blanchet; pages 5, 67, 118, 136, 137, 144, 152, 156, 158, 188, 201, 204, 207, 262, 271, 280, 281, 285 Christina Theisen; pages 7, 117 (right), 149 Jonathan Perugia; page 8 Christine Boyd; page 21 Tricia de Courcy Ling; pages 40, 123 Olivia Rutherford; pages 48, 49, 72, 76, 81, 103, 107, 130, 141, 171, 177, 180, 182, 183, 184, 192, 193, 245, 254, 268, 273, 279 Heloise Bergman; pages 68 (bottom), 94, 122, 168 Susannah Stone; pages 69, 74, 79 (top), 134, 135, 164, 174 Tove K Breitstein; pages 73, 85, 102, 117 (left), 133, 165, 187 Andrew Brackenbury; pages 78, 79 (bottom), 246 Alys Tomlinson; page 89 The Royal College of Surgeons of England; page 95 arsenalpics.com; page 100 Britta Jaschinski; pages 111, 265 Jael Marschner; page 157 Susan Porter-Thomas Photography; page 178 Nina Large; page 214 Ashley Grainger; pages 219, 224, 234, 237 Jitka Hynkova; pages 222, 228 (top right) Rogan Macdonald; page 226, 250 Michelle Grant; page 228 Scott Wishart; page 240, 248 Ming Tang-Evans; page 242 Britta Jaschinski; page 266 Marzena Zoladz.

The following pictures were supplied by the featured establishments/artists: pages 9, 18, 19, 25, 43, 51, 54, 60, 68 (top), 99, 146, 147, 179, 196, 211, 217, 258, 277, 283.

Printer St Ives (Web) Ltd, Storeys Bar Road, Eastern Industrial Estate, Peterborough, PE1 5YS
Time Out Group uses paper products that are environmentally friendly, from well managed forests and mills that use certified (PEFC) Chain of Custody pulp in their production.

ISBN 978-1-905042-36-4

Distribution by Seymour Ltd (020 7429 4000)
Distributed in US by Publishers Group West
Distributed in Canada by Publishers Group Canada
For further distribution details, see www.timeout.com

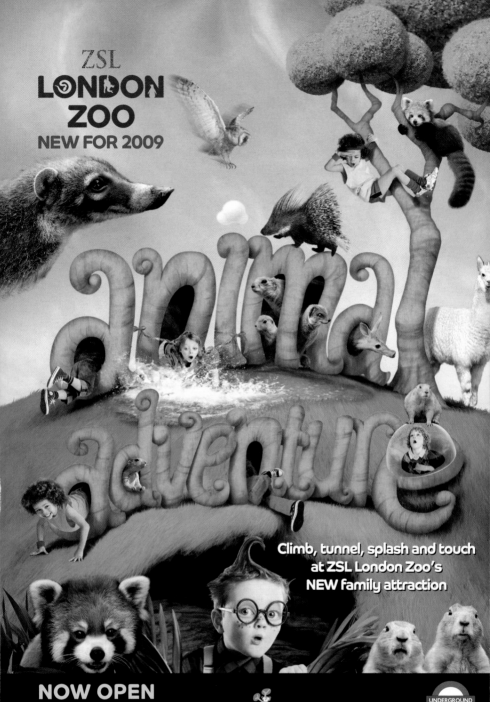

Contents

Introduction

Even if you're lucky enough to call London home, it's all too easy to stay local when you've got a family, enjoying the same tried and tested venues time and again. We hope this book will inspire you to venture further afield for days of intrepid exploration around the capital. Why not start with our **Great Days Out** series, which gives you the lowdown area by area, with lunch destinations included?

If you're looking for something more specific, each chapter is brimming with ideas. Try **Museums & Galleries** for London's phenomenal range of cultural venues, or take a closer look at iconic buildings such as the Tower of London and Buckingham Palace, listed in **Attractions**. For glorious greenery and playgrounds, consult **Parks & Gardens**. Want to get a bit closer to nature than a picnic rug allows? How about exploring one of London's zoos or city farms, detailed in **Meet The Animals**? **Arts & Entertainment** suggests shows and concerts for all the family, as well as workshops and classes for budding performers. For the more sportily-inclined, **Sports & Leisure** advises what to join and where. Got a birthday coming up? **Parties** does the hard work for you, listing venues, suppliers and entertainers to make the big day go off with a bang. **Eating** is full of child-friendly establishments for every occasion, while **Shopping** should take care of all your material needs. Happy hunting!

TIME OUT LONDON FOR CHILDREN GUIDE

This is the ninth edition of the Time Out *London for Children Guide*, produced by the people behind the successful listings magazines and travel guide series. It is written by resident experts to provide you with all the information you'll need to explore the city, whether you're a local or a first-time visitor.

THE LOWDOWN ON THE LISTINGS

Addresses, phone numbers, websites, transport information, opening times, admission prices and credit card details are included in the listings. Details of facilities, services and events were all checked and correct as we went to press.

Before you go out of your way, however, we'd advise you to phone and check opening times, ticket prices and other particulars. While every effort has been made to ensure the accuracy of the information contained in this guide, the publishers cannot accept any responsibility for any errors it may contain.

FAMILY-FRIENDLY INFORMATION

Having visited all the places with our children, we've added essential information for families. Where we think it's important, we've stated whether a building can accommodate buggies, or if there's a place to change a nappy. We've also listed the nearest picnic place.

Attractions are required to provide reasonable facilities for disabled visitors, although it's always best to check accessibility before setting out.

PRICES AND PAYMENT

We have noted where venues accept the following credit cards: American Express (AmEx), Diners Club (DC), MasterCard (MC) and Visa (V).

THE LIE OF THE LAND

Map references are included for each venue that falls on our London street maps (starting on page 310. We would recommend that you also use a standard A-Z map of the city.

PHONE NUMBERS

The area code for London is 020. All phone numbers given in this guide take this code unless otherwise stated, so add 020 if you're calling from outside London; otherwise, simply dial the number as written. The international dialling code for the UK is 44.

LET US KNOW WHAT YOU THINK

We hope that you enjoy this book and we'd like to know what you think of it. Email us at guides@timeout.com.

Out & About

My London

Smarties Award winner **SF Said** has lived in London all his life and believes the city is a huge part of his identity.

SF Said's first novel *Varjak Paw*, about a Mesopotamian Blue cat with special powers, won him the Gold Award Smarties Book Prize in the six- to eight-year-olds category in 2003. After following up the book with a sequel, *The Outlaw Varjak Paw*, Said began a different novel entirely. This one is about a boy who has the power of a star inside him – both powerful and dangerous – and a girl who is the fiercest warrior in the universe. Together they must save a galaxy.

Three and a half years later, Said is on draft 'seven b'. 'If you want to make something really good it takes time. I write every day and set achievable targets. Lots of small things eventually add up to something big before you notice. One of my favourite things in *Varjak Paw* is the black cats at the beginning who set up the whole story. I didn't think them up until the 15th draft. I'm lucky in that my editor believes a story takes as long as it takes.

I think it's an old-fashioned way of publishing, but I'm glad it still exists.'

As well as the new sci-fi novel, Said is also some way down the line with an animated film version of *Varjak Paw*. The novel has already been made into an opera that was put on at the Royal Opera House in 2008. 'Not long after the first Varjak book came out, Dave McKean (the book's illustrator) did his first feature film. We talked about an animated version of the story, and the Jim Henson Company optioned it. We're hoping that a French animation house is going to make it. If only someone would just give us the $20 million we need…'

In between writing, Said likes to prowl around London at night. 'I wander around with my large collection of antiquated cameras. The Polaroid is my favourite. I love the glow of neon on wet pavements. I suppose the low angle of Varjak's view of the city is my view.' When Said finishes the new book, his present to himself is going to be a Hasselblad camera. 'Many people think it's the best camera ever made,' Said says longingly.

Said grew up in west London, where his family lived in a flat directly above Quentin Blake's. 'We leaked on his flat one day and he was incredibly nice about it (luckily it didn't go anywhere near his artwork). When I was first trying to get *Varjak Paw* published, I took a draft to him and he was incredibly positive about it. I feel very privileged to know him'. Apart from his university years in Cambridge, Said has never left London for more than three months, when he went off to live with the Inuits (no really, he did).

'If people ask me where I'm from, "London" is the first thing to come out of my mouth rather than a country. It's a huge part of my identity, and I love just how diverse it is and how inclusive. There are parts of London where every language is spoken, where there's every food in the world and someone who knows how to cook it. Very few cities I've been to are like that. Perhaps New York and Toronto to a certain extent, but not as much as London. It's important to me.'

He thinks the cultural infrastructure is incredible, although worries that the next generation won't experience this resource. 'I spend a lot of time in Soho and the West End in shops and cinemas. Music is very important to me and I always have it on when I'm writing. I used to spend hours in record shops, but there are fewer of them around now. I really miss them because I like to browse. I download to try things, but I like owning a physical object.' He also believes there are some amazing independent bookshops around the city. 'I'm worried they are going to go the same way as the record shops. Foyles is one of my favourite places in London. Everyone likes a bargain but that doesn't mean you should buy a book just because it's 1p on the internet. If you like to be able to interact with knowledgeable staff who might be able to point you in the direction

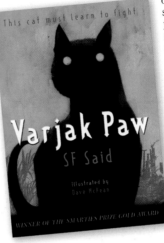

of something that will change your life… well, I think that's worth paying more for. It's important that we continue to spend money in shops. When you can walk around and pick books off the shelves, you stumble across things you would never find online – how can you search on Amazon for something you don't know exists?'

His relatively recent interest in photography takes him to scour the camera shops around Tottenham Court Road and towards Russell Square. 'Everyone's obsessed with digital cameras now, so you can buy second-hand film cameras much more cheaply.' He's often to be found in the Photographer's Gallery in Soho. 'It has a fantastic shop that sells rare photography books, cameras and accessories. I've put together a massive record collection over my lifetime, and now I've got an almost equally large collection of photography books,' he says.

Favourite eats around town

Café *1st Floor, Foyles Bookshop, 113-119 Charing Cross Road, WC2H OEB (7437 5660/www.foyles.co.uk).* 'This used to be Ray's Jazz Café, and now is just called the Café. It does great juices. I'm very happy about the explosion of fruit juices, smoothies and herbal teas in recent years. I drink a lot of different kinds of tea when I'm writing; Chai, mint tea, rooibos. Smoothies are a great way to get kids to eat fruit.'

Electric Brasserie *191 Portobello Road, W11 2ED (7908 9696/www.electric house.com).* 'The Electric Cinema has really luxurious, comfortable seats and then there's a brilliant brasserie next door that does great brunches.'

Grain Shop *269A Portobello Road, W11 1LR (7229 5571).* 'The Grain Shop sells freshly made, delicious vegetarian food

incredibly cheaply. You go there and think "why doesn't everywhere in London have one of these?" It's one of the nicest lunches you can have.'

Shampan *79 Brick Lane, E1 6QL (7375 0475).* 'Of all the Bangladeshi places on Brick Lane, I seem to keep going back to the Shampan. Maybe it's partly to do with the big sign saying "Welcome to Bangla" when you go down there.'

VitaOrganic *74 Wardour Street, W1F OTE (7734 8986).* 'An amazing, 100 per cent vegan place where they have lots of great, huge salads, and incredible juices and smoothies with names like Pink Mermaid Tonic. It's a fantastically unusual place with good cakes too; although it's not super cheap, it is incredibly relaxed. The chairs and tables are not of this world. They're quite strange.'

City of Discovery

An itinerary for a very full day, by **Nick Coleman**.

There's this four-year-old kid, and his dad takes him to London for the first time. Dad is about to jack in his job at the Shellmex building and relocate the family to East Anglia, so he wants to show his son his kingdom before he leaves it. They make a day of it, all the way from the end of the tube line in Buckinghamshire. First they go up the Shell tower to Dad's office. Then they go to Buck House to see the Queen. She isn't in. Then there's the Tower of London, the Monument and tea in a posh tea room in Fleet Street, near the Inns of Court. Everything is teeming and fast and loud. So as dusk falls, father and son make their way down through the warren of City backstreets to the river, where it's quiet. There is no one about.

The sun is sinking and a milky orange-pink bloom softens every surface, especially the surface of the water, which is moving slowly like oil. The boy is tired and he feels as if he is in a dream. At the end of the street a flight of stone steps continues the line of the road down to the water and keeps on going, through the surface of the water, down and down. The steps look as if they might go on for ever. There is nothing to stop them. Only oily water with the disc of the sun settled on it like a plate. The boy decides that when he grows up he will live in London.

Forty-five years later, he cannot remember going to the Palace or the Tower, or tea or the ladies in the Shell building. But he still finds himself thinking sometimes about the steps down through the water. Somehow it is the most vivid memory of his early childhood.

London is like that. It is the most exciting city in the world, but not always in the way you think it's going to be. The secret to getting the most out of it is to be a kid. So in the light of that thought, allow me to make a suggestion: why not introduce your children to their capital by dropping them right in it? The river has been the lifeblood of London since London began. It's why London is where it is and how it is. And because the river is, by definition, always in a state of flux, it is the place where new things are always taking shape, or being revealed. So take your children out to the middle of it.

I recommend London Bridge. Get halfway across and look upstream, then downstream. Regard the little beaches which, dependent on the tide, may or may not be baring themselves. Drink in one of the great views. Gazing east, marvel at the symbols of prestige that are the **Tower of London** (*see p39*), **Tower Bridge** (*see p29*), **HMS Belfast** (*see p101*) and, in the distance, the shiny protuberances at Canary Wharf. In a westerly direction, look upon the majesty of **St Paul's Cathedral** (*see p41*), **Tate Modern** (*see p66*) and the

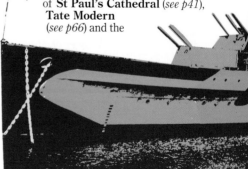

Millennium Bridge, which conjoins those two great, contrasting cathedrals like an umbilicus. Beyond them, now poking up rather self-consciously into the 21st-century skyline, stands the BT Tower. This is London as it is in books.

Meanwhile, your children won't be bothering with any of that. They will be clocking something else altogether; something smaller than St Paul's Cathedral but of greater consequence. A sweet wrapper twisting in an updraft, a man with a funny walk, a refuse launch making figures of 88, a one-legged pigeon with an unblinking evil eye, a flight of steps leading straight down into the water. They will be thinking... Well, who knows what they will be thinking? The art of being in London with children is all about giving them their head: letting them soak it up in their own terms, while they abide by the rules you have set with a view to your own peace of mind and your own stimulation – there is nothing worse than a parent cranky with boredom.

So while you're on the bridge you may as well freak them out. Behind London Bridge Station in St Thomas's Street you'll find a doorway leading up a tiny spiral staircase to the **Old**

Operating Theatre (*see p89*), which is exactly as it sounds: a galleried Victorian house of gore, equipped with a full complement of tools of the trade, bottled bits of real Victorians and the occasional live demonstration of how the tools were used. There have been no fatalities reported this century, but there's always a first time. The children will now be thoroughly cowed – or excited beyond endurance – so if it's a Friday or Saturday morning, yank them over the road and under the arches to **Borough Market**. Though it's far from cheap, it is the most spectacularly endowed farmer's market in the country, as well as a brilliant one-stop shop for all your healthy fast-food needs. There's now a skeleton market operating on the site on mornings throughout the week, so even if it's Wednesday you can stock up on meat, fish and veg. Then, assuming you haven't lost the tinies in the seething throng, it is barely a toddle from the market to the **Clink Prison Museum** (*see p94*), which attempts rather dustily to replicate the conditions of the unsavoury prison which once stood on

City of Discovery

the site, and the replica of that great totem of piratical discovery, Drake's **Golden Hinde**, now berthed in her permanent dock (*see p32*). Both of them lurk in the shadow of beautiful, soothing **Southwark Cathedral** (*see p41*).

If you do all those things you will be knackered, as will they. So change the pace. If London is a place of discovery, time should be allowed for it to reveal itself. Give yourself some space. London is endowed with hundreds of spaces, green ones as well as the more conventional metropolitan sort – it is the greenest major city in the world. Go to Trafalgar Square if you must, although you won't find much grass. **Hyde Park** (*see p123*), on the other hand, has lots, not to mention a terrific little modern art gallery parked pavilion-style right next to the Serpentine. Alternatively, play among the fountains in the handsome court at **Somerset House** – and if it's wintertime, skate about on top of them (*see p211*).

Virtually every quarter of the city has a recreational lung of some description, an open space whose only purpose is to promote well-being. The biggest and best lung of them all is the magnificent **Hampstead Heath** (*see p113*) in north London, a tube or bus ride away from just about anywhere north of Clapham Common. The Heath is to Londoners what the high seas are to sailors: the place where they breathe. It is so big you can forget that it is bounded by traffic; it is so uncultivated that your children can forget they're in the middle of a city. So when they've finished falling out of trees, take them up

Parliament Hill, give them the long view of London and whet their appetite for getting in among it again.

Heading south from that outpost, I'd be tempted to take a shot at the **Wellcome Collection** (*see p92*) opposite Euston Station, which is one of London's newer sepulchres of discovery; in this case, dedicated to the worship of all things medical. Some of the collection is rather unsavoury – but what kind of a museum of the human body would it be if it didn't disturb lunch just a little? The kids will love it. And if they don't, why not scoot down the road into Bloomsbury to the **Foundling Museum** (*see p71*) at Brunswick Square, close to **Coram's Fields** (*see p113*). There is no more heartbreaking institution in London. It is all that remains of Captain Coram's 18th-century Hospital for the Maintenance and Education of Exposed and Deserted Children. Some of the remains are tiny. You will not forget going there. And the children might, for once, feel gratitude for the fullness of their own estate. Or not, as the case may be.

At all events, the experience may have sobered them just a tad, so now is the moment to stick them on a bus and head west through the consumer hell that is London's Throbbing West End, where the pavements teem with lost souls, and out to Sloane Square and the King's Road – which isn't what it was when you were a young thing but, well, time is like that. What is new

phil&teds®

First Class travel for the streets of London

adapt & survive!™

For your nearest stockists
visit www.philandteds.co.uk
or call: 01234 344 230

Head northwards and you will find yourself in the midst of Museumville, aka Exhibition Road. This is the destination to which all proper parents take their children, whether the children like it or not. And for very good reason. The **Natural History Museum** (*see p87*), the **Science Museum** (*see p92*) and the **V&A** (*see p67*) are fabulous, not at all dusty and so very thoughtful in siting themselves right next door to each other. If you're very lucky, you might find yourselves there on the annual Exhibition Road Music Day in June, on which every institution for hundreds of yards in every direction (including the Goethe Institute, Institut Français and the Serpentine Gallery) give themselves over to musical activities of every type and specification. Just think – dinosaurs, space rockets, the Great Bed of Ware and bluegrass/be-bop/zydeco/Mozart all in exactly the same spot, give or take. It really doesn't get any better than that.

Best of all, having convinced yourselves that you are proper parents after all, you are then entitled to drag the posse in a north-westerly direction, beyond the park and Bayswater, to Portobello Road. Despite the unpleasant gentrification of recent years, it's still home to a more than decent market, Friday through to Sunday, and you can always park the posse in a recently tarted-up café and play the splendid family game of Spot The Former Member Of The Clash. The kids will love you for it. Especially when you reward every successful 'spot' with a potted lecture on the history of punk, with footnotes. Like I say: London, it's the city of discovery.

and delightful there is the **Saatchi Gallery** (*see p65*), which is architecturally attractive, just the right size and, best of all, free. It also has a decent record over its first year or so for mounting interesting exhibitions of contemporary art from all over the world (once more, sensitive souls are advised first to read up on what they're letting themselves in for). It is my children's favourite gallery – and not only because there's a Pret A Manger just over the road with window seats from which you can play the family favourite game of Spot The Person With More Money Than Taste.

From there, you have to decide whether to head north or south (King's Road is no longer worth the time it would take to do a full exploratory wander, even for nostalgia's sake). If you go towards the river, don't expect to find an awful lot apart from thickets of Chelsea footballer-owned Mercedes and the **National Army Museum** (*see p103*), which is gravely underrated both as a museum and as a place of unexpected soul. If you don't have boys in your entourage, perhaps there are more sensible destinations though.

Trips & Tours

Seeing the sights by road, rail and river.

Duck Tours. *See p16.*

Getting around

For speed, it's generally best to hop on the tube (*see p287*), but taking the bus is far more scenic. Good routes for city sightseeing are the 7, 8, 11 and 12 (all double-deckers) and, along the South Bank, the single-decker RV1. A couple of old-style Routemaster buses – numbers 9 and 15 – now run as Heritage Routes; the 9 runs from the Aldwych via the Strand, Trafalgar Square and Piccadilly Circus to the Royal Albert Hall, and the 15 from Trafalgar Square to Tower Hill, allowing passengers to get a glimpse of the Strand, Fleet Street and St Paul's Cathedral. Normal fares apply.

Tourist information

To get the most from the city, a tourist information office is an essential port of call. **Visit London** (7234 5800, www.visit london.com) is the city's official tourist information service, with its main office in Lower Regent Street. There are also outposts in Greenwich, Leicester Square and just by St Paul's Cathedral.

If your programme takes in some of the city's pricier sights, a **London Pass** (01664 485020, www.londonpass.com) gives you pre-paid access to more than 50 attractions. Check the website for prices.

In our listings, the initials 'EH' means English Heritage members, and their kids, get in free. 'NT' means National Trust members get free admission.

Britain & London Visitor Centre *1 Lower Regent Street, SW1Y 4XT (8846 9000/ www.visitbritain.com). Piccadilly Circus tube.* **Open** *Apr, May* 9.30am-6.30pm Mon; 9am-6.30pm Tue-Fri; 10am-4pm Sat, Sun. *June-Sept* 9.30am-6.30pm Mon; 9am-6.30pm Tue-Fri; 9am-5pm Sat; 10am-4pm Sun. *Oct-Mar* 9.30am-6pm Mon; 9am-6pm Tue-Fri; 10am-4pm Sat, Sun.
London Information Centre *Leicester Square, WC2H 7BP (7292 2333/www.londontown.com). Leicester Square tube.* **Open** *Phone enquiries* 8am-10pm Mon-Fri; 9am-8pm Sat, Sun. *In person* 10am-6pm daily.

Moving experiences

See also p43 **Three Thames tasters.**

On the river

City Cruises *7740 0400/www.city cruises.com.* **Credit** MC, V.
City Cruises' handy Rail River Rover ticket (£13.50; £6.75 5-16s, reductions; free under-5s) combines hop-on, hop-off travel on any of its regular cruises (pick-up points: Westminster, Waterloo, Tower and Greenwich piers) with unlimited travel on the DLR.
London Duck Tours *7928 3132/www.london ducktours.co.uk.* **Tours** phone for details. *Pick-up* Chicheley Street, behind the London Eye. **Fares** £20; £16 reductions; £14 1-12s; £58 family (2+2). **Credit** AmEx, MC, V.
There's no missing these bright yellow amphibious vehicles, which tour the City of Westminster. The thrilling road and river trip, lasting 75 minutes, starts at the London Eye and plunges into the Thames at Vauxhall.
London RIB Voyages *7928 8933/www. londonribvoyages.com.* **Tickets** £32.50-£45. **Credit** AmEx, MC, V.
Sightseeing is fast and furious with RIB's speedboat trips, which power passengers from the London Eye to Canary Wharf (£32.50; £19.50 under-17s, 50mins) or the Thames Barrier (£45; £28 under-17s, 80mins). Book in advance.
London Waterbus Company *7482 2660/ www.londonwaterbus.com.* **Tours** check website for departure details. **Fares** *Single* £6.50; £5 3-15s. *Return* £9; £6 3-15s. Free under-3s. **No credit cards.**
Navigate Regent's Canal in a narrowboat. Trips run between Camden Lock and Little Venice, stopping off at London Zoo.
Thames Clippers *0870 781 5049/ www.thamesclippers.com.* **Departures** 10am-5pm Mon-Fri; 9am-midnight Sat, Sun. **Credit** MC, V.
Equipped with a River Roamer ticket (£12; £6 5-15s; free under-5s) you can hop-on and hop-off along the banks of the Thames between Millbank Pier and Royal Arsenal Woolwich pier, with stops at Waterloo, Embankment, Tower, Canary Wharf, Greenwich and the O2. The Family Roamer costs £25 (2+3).

On the buses

Big Bus Company *0800 169 1365/7233 9533/www.bigbustours.com.* **Departures** every 10-20mins. *Summer* 8.30am-6pm daily. *Winter* 8.30am-4.30pm daily. *Pick-up* Green Park (near the Ritz); Marble Arch (Speakers' Corner); Victoria (outside Thistle Victoria Hotel, 48 Buckingham Palace Road, SW1W

0RN). **Fares** £24; £10 5-15s; free under-5s. Tickets valid for 24hrs, interchangeable between routes. **Credit** AmEx, MC, V.
These open-top buses, with commentary, stop at the major tourist sights, where customers can hop on and off at will. Big Bus also runs cruises and walking tours.
Original London Sightseeing Tour *8877 1722/www.theoriginaltour.com.* **Departures** *Summer* every 5-10mins, 9am-10pm daily. *Winter* every 10-25mins, 9am-5pm daily. *Pick-up* Grosvenor Gardens; Marble Arch (Speakers' Corner); Haymarket (Piccadilly Circus); Embankment tube; Trafalgar Square. **Fares** £24; £12 5-15s; free under-5s. **Credit** AmEx, MC, V.
Another open-top bus operation, taking a circuit of the sights. The Kids' Club tours include a special activity pack.

Pedal power

London Bicycle Tour Company *1A Gabriel's Wharf, 56 Upper Ground, SE1 9PP (7928 6838/www.londonbicycle.com).* Waterloo tube/ rail. **Open** 10am-6pm daily. **Hire** £3/hr; £19/1st day, £9/day thereafter. **Credit** AmEx, MC, V.
Bike and tandem hire; children's bike seats are free with an adult bike. Guided tours covering major sights in central London start at 10.30am.
London Pedicabs *7093 3155/www.london pedicabs.com.* **Fares** from £3 per person per mile. **No credit cards.**
Hard-working cycle rickshaws, based in Covent Garden and Soho.

Take a hike

Guided walking tours are also offered by **And Did Those Feet** (8806 4325, www.chr.org.uk), **Performing London** (01234 404774, www.performing london.co.uk) and **Silver Cane Tours** (07720 715295, www.silvercanetours.com).

Original London Walks *7624 3978/www. walks.com.* **Tours** £7; £5 reductions; 1 free under-15 per adult. **No credit cards.**
These themed walks criss-cross the capital, revealing all sorts of fascinating facts along the way. Plenty appeal to kids, not least the Harry Potter walk (5pm Sun) and Ghosts of the Old City walk (7.30pm Tue, Sat).

'Taxi!'

Black Taxi Tours of London *7935 9363/ www.blacktaxitours.co.uk.* **Cost** £100-£110. **No credit cards.**
A tailored two-hour tour for up to five people.

Festivals & Events

A city with plenty to celebrate.

There's no doubt about it, Londoners love a good knees-up. Whether it's cheering the **London Marathon** runners on (*see p26*), getting down to the steel bands and sound systems of the **Notting Hill Carnival** (*see p20*) or staring skywards as fireworks usher in **Chinese New Year** (*see p25*), there's something to suit all ages and tastes: what's more, most of it won't cost you a penny.

While we've included the regular events and festivals that keep the city in a giddy social whirl, there's always more going on: check *Time Out* magazine for the latest one-off celebrations and cultural happenings. We've given exact dates for events where possible; phone or check websites nearer the time for unconfirmed timings.

SUMMER

Coin Street Festival

Bernie Spain Gardens, next to Oxo Tower Wharf, SE1 9PH (7021 1686/www.coinstreet festival.org). Southwark tube/Waterloo tube/rail. **Date** June-Sept 2009. **Map** p318 N7.

This welcoming, family-friendly summer shindig brings a series of culturally themed weekday and weekend events that celebrate different communities in the capital. Festivities take place in the open spaces around Bernie Spain Gardens, Gabriel's Wharf and the South Bank and include music, dance and performances, as well as craft and refreshment stalls and workshops. Check the website for more information nearer the time.

Story of London

Various venues (www.london.gov.uk/story oflondon). **Date** June 2009.

The Mayor's office has collaborated with institutions all over the capital to put together this new, month-long festival of events and activities, celebrating the city's past, present and future. The ambitious programme incorporates music, history, film, walks and architecture. Check online for the full list of events.

Beating Retreat

Horse Guards Parade, Whitehall, SW1A 2AX (booking 0844 847 2435). Westminster tube/Charing Cross tube/rail. **Date** 3-4 June 2009. **Map** p317 K8.

Held on two June evenings, this spirited, stirring ceremony kicks off at 9pm, with the 'Retreat' beaten on drums by the Mounted Bands of the Household Cavalry and the Massed Bands of the Guards Division.

Trooping the Colour

Horse Guards Parade, Whitehall, SW1A 2AX (7414 2271). Westminster tube/Charing Cross tube/rail. **Date** 13 June 2009. **Map** p317 K8.

The Queen was actually born on 21 April, but this is her official birthday celebration, for practical reasons. At 10.45am, Her Majesty makes the journey from Buckingham Palace to Horse Guards Parade, then scoots home to watch a Royal Air Force flypast and receive a formal gun salute from Green Park.

Open Garden Squares Weekend

Various venues (www.opensquares.org). **Date** 13-14 June 2009.

For one weekend a year, the London Parks & Gardens Trust opens locked and gated green spaces to one and all. Tickets (£8, £6.75 in advance, free under-12s) allow entry to all participating gardens, which range from secret 'children-only' play areas to allotments and exclusive garden squares. Many are wheelchair-accessible and host activities and plant sales; if you're lucky, there might be home-made cakes to munch on as you admire the greenery. Check online for the full list of gardens taking part.

City of London Festival

Venues across the City, EC2-EC4 (7583 3585/www.colf.org). St Paul's tube/Bank tube/DLR/Cannon Street, Farringdon or Moorgate tube/rail/Blackfriars rail. **Date** 19 June-9 July 2009.

Founded in 1962, with the aim of revitalising the City's cultural life, this summer festival stages indoor ticketed concerts and free outdoor events in and around some of the Square Mile's finest historic buildings. Outdoor events, including walks, street theatre, jazz concerts and dance performances, run until 7 August.

Wimbledon Lawn Tennis Championships

All England Lawn Tennis Club, PO Box 98, Church Road, SW19 5AE (8944 1066/info 8946 2244/www.wimbledon.org). Southfields tube/Wimbledon tube/rail. **Date** 22 June-5 July 2009.

To nab tickets for this prestigious tennis tournament, you'll need to plan ahead. For Centre Court and Court Number One seats, request an application form from the All England Lawn Tennis Club between August and mid December the year before; you'll then be entered into the public ticket ballot. Queuing on the day should gain you entry to the outside courts. In the afternoon, returned show-court tickets are available from the booth opposite Court One, so it may be worth hanging about to see the stars slicing, serving and mopping their perspiring brows on one of the world's most famous courts.

Greenwich & Docklands International Festival

Various venues (8305 1818/www.festival.org). **Date** 25-28 June 2009; 24-27 June 2010.

With its vibrant mixture of theatre, music and spectacle, this free festival looks set to make a big splash in 2009, when an aquatic theme is planned. A contemporary celebration of Handel's 'Water Music', marking the 250th anniversary of the composer's death, and French outfit Ilotopie's bizarre, water-based performance art are among the highlights.

Young Pavement Artists Competition

www.muscular-dystrophy.org/pavementart. **Date** Awards ceremony takes place July 2009

Over 5,000 schools and community and youth groups take part in this national competition, which aims to raise awareness of muscular dystrophy and generate funds for the Muscular Dystrophy Campaign. The theme for 2009 is Endangered Species of the World; children aged four to 19 can compete at events across the country, with pitches costing a pound per entrant. Photos of the day's winners are then entered into the national competition, judged by members of Tate Britain and the Royal Academy of Arts, which is followed by a prestigious awards ceremony.

Henley Royal Regatta

Henley Reach, Henley-on-Thames, Oxon RG9 2LY (01491 572153/www.hrr.co.uk). Henley-on-Thames rail. **Date** 1-5 July 2009; 30 June-4 July 2010.

First held in 1839, and under royal patronage since 1851, Henley is still going strong; it's now a five-day affair. Boat races range from open events for men and women through club and

Great River Race. *See p20.*

In 2008 this mini-Olympics attracted 27,000 sporting hopefuls, all of them under 17, representing their London borough in 30 different sports – including archery, fencing, canoeing, cycling, rugby and athletics. The finals weekend takes place at Crystal Palace Sports Ground, while other competitions are held at venues around the capital throughout the summer. Extra entertainments include dance performances, DJs, street sport demonstrations and graffiti art.

Streatham Festival
Various venues (www.streathamfestival.com). **Date** 4-12 July 2009.
From humble beginnings in 2002, this local festival has blossomed into a week-long community arts jamboree. More than 50 events are held in all sorts of locations, from churches and youth centres to parks and bars. There are family heritage walks and talks, garden parties and parades, along with poetry workshops, theatre, dance, comedy and film. Check the online programme for details.

Chap & Hendrick's Olympiad
Bedford Square Gardens, WC1 (www.hendricks gin.com). Tottenham Court Road tube. **Date** mid July 2009. **Map** p315 K5.
Expect a surreally splendid afternoon out at this terribly silly, terribly English event, where children can watch adults engage in all manner of tomfoolery. Events kick off with the lighting of the Olympic Pipe, with 'sports' including umbrella hockey (with a bowler hat for a ball) and the three-trousered limbo.

BBC Sir Henry Wood Promenade Concerts
Royal Albert Hall, Kensington Gore, SW7 2AP (box office 7589 8212/www.bbc.co.uk/proms). Knightsbridge or South Kensington tube/ 9, 10, 52 bus. **Date** 17 July-12 Sept 2009. **Map** p313 D9.
While plenty of the concerts are broadcast on the radio or TV, there's nothing like seeing them in person. Choose carefully and you should find something in the main programme that will appeal to children; there are also special family events, and a young composers' competition. Under-16s get half-price tickets to every prom, bar the legendary Last Night.

Lambeth Country Show
Brockwell Park, SE24 0NG (7926 7085/ www.lambeth.gov.uk). Brixton tube/rail, then 2, 3, 68, 196 bus/Herne Hill rail. **Date** 18-19 July 2009.

student crews to the Princess Elizabeth race for juniors (boys under the age of 19). Straw boaters and blazers are *de rigueur*, as is bringing a picnic.

Watch This Space
Theatre Square, outside the National Theatre, South Bank, SE1 9PX (7452 3400/www. nationaltheatre.org.uk/wts). Waterloo tube/ rail. **Date** 1 July-27 Sept 2009. **Map** p318 M7.
This superb free festival brings all manner of entertainment to an artificial lawn laid out on the South Bank. Lounge in the sunshine and catch the best street theatre, circus, cinema, music, art and dance from all over the world.

Big Dance
Various venues (www.london.gov.uk/bigdance). **Date** 3-11 July 2010.
The next instalment of this week-long, biennial celebration of all styles of dance will be in summer 2010. Hundreds of jumping, jiving free events and performances take place in parks, museums, theatres and streets across London. Various dance-related records were broken at the 2008 event, including the biggest number of streetdance moves performed in one minute, and the biggest Bollywood dance class.

London Youth Games
Various venues (7717 1570/www.londonyouth games.org). **Date** (finals) 4-5 July 2009.

Hankering for the countryside, and an escape from the urban grind and grime? No need to leave town; instead, head down to Brockwell Park's free country show. Aside from meeting and greeting assorted farmyard beasts, children can cheer on horse and dog shows, watch sheep-shearing and birds of prey demonstrations and have fun on numerous bouncy castles and fairground rides. An international array of food stalls keep the masses well-fed (don't miss the jerk chicken), while the strains of brass bands fill the air.

Sundae on the Common

Clapham Common, SW4 (www.benjerry.co.uk/ sundae). Clapham Common tube. **Date** 25-26 July 2009.
A family-friendly mix of fairground activities and live music, this year's Sundae will feature banana jousting (fair-trade of course) and toe wrestling – not to mention free ice-cream all day. You can pet farm animals, make cookies, scoot down the helter-skelter, pelt the coconut shy and have your fortune told by Mystic Moo. Check the website for ticket prices, and the latest musical line-up; in previous years, headline acts have included the Charlatans, Badly Drawn Boy and Ash.

Innocent Village Fete

Gloucester Green, north-east corner of Regent's Park, NW1 (8600 3939/www. innocentdrinks.co.uk). Baker Street or Regent's Park tube. **Date** 1-2 Aug 2009 (tbc). **Map** p314 G3.
This enjoyable weekender is all about summer's gentler pastimes: picnics on the grass, enthusiastic Morris dancing displays and trying your luck on the tombola. Music and comedy acts do feature, but you'll also find arts and crafts, plus fancy dress games for children and, possibly, a spot of snail racing and welly wanging. Tickets go on sale a few weeks before the event; check the website for details.

Carnaval del Pueblo

Burgess Park, SE5 (7686 1633/www.carnaval delpueblo.co.uk). Elephant & Castle tube/ 12, 25, 36, 68, 68A, 100, 172 bus. **Date** 2 Aug 2009.
The UK's largest Latin American celebration kicks off at noon with a colourful parade from Elephant and Castle, which makes its way to Burgess Park. Here, the entertainment runs until around 9.30pm, and includes over 100 food and crafts stalls, a children's zone and four stages; the live Brazilian samba, Latin hip hop, Mexican mariachi and Colombian salsa soon gets everyone dancing.

Underage

Victoria Park, Old Ford Road, E3 (tickets 0844 477 2000/www.underagefestivals.com). Mile End tube/Cambridge Heath or Hackney Wick rail/8, 26, 30, 55, 253, 277, S2 bus. **Date** 2 Aug 2009. **Tickets** £23.
Strictly for 14- to 18-year-olds, Underage attracts an enviable line-up of alternative, rock and electro bands. This year's hipper-than-thou acts include the Horrors, Santigold, Little Boots and Ladyhawke. The ban on alcohol (and adults) is firmly enforced.

Notting Hill Carnival

Notting Hill, W10 & W11 (7727 0072/ www.lnhc.org.uk). Ladbroke Grove, Notting Hill Gate & Westbourne Park tube. **Date** 30-31 Aug 2009.
The carnival's as colourful and chaotic as they come – and the August Bank Holiday Sunday is traditionally decreed to be children's day. Masquerades, steel bands, decorative floats and ground-shaking sound systems take over the streets of Notting Hill, and there's curried goat, roti and fried plantain to sample. Its reputation for bringing short, sharp spikes to the annual crime rate continues to court controversy, but increasing commercialism and a strong police presence have made the carnival safer than ever.

AUTUMN

Great River Race

River Thames, from Island Gardens, Greenwich, E14 to Ham House, Richmond, Surrey (8398 9057/www.greatriverrace.co.uk). **Date** 5 Sept 2009.
Vessels of every shape and size compete over a 22-mile (35km) course in this traditional boat championship, from Viking longboats to Hawaiian war canoes. The race begins at 11am and reaches the finish at around 4.30pm. The best viewing points are at Richmond Bridge, along the South Bank or on the Millennium and Hungerford Bridges; due to tides, the race will go from east to west in 2009.

Regent Street Festival

Regent Street, W1 (7287 9601/www.regent streetonline.com). Oxford Circus or Piccadilly Circus tube. **Date** 6 Sept 2009. **Map** p316 J7.
All traffic is banned from Regent's Street in honour of this annual event; in its place, fairground rides, storytellers, street entertainers and musicians take over the tarmac. There's usually plenty of input from Regent Street's resident toy emporium extraordinaire, Hamleys.

Discover Dogs. *See p24.*

Mayor's Thames Festival

*Between Westminster & Tower Bridges
(7983 4100/www.thamesfestival.org). London
Bridge or Waterloo tube/rail/Blackfriars rail.*
Date 12-13 Sept 2009.

This jolly celebration of the Thames brings a
weekend of riverside stalls, performers, sand
sculptures, environmental activities and creative
workshops – plus the chance to milk a cow in
the middle of Southwark Bridge. An
atmospheric lantern procession and dramatic
fireworks display bring proceedings to a close
on Sunday evening.

Spitalfields Show & Green Fair

*Allen Gardens & Spitalfields City Farm, Buxton
Street, E1 (7375 0441/www.alternativearts.
co.uk). Whitechapel tube.* **Date** 13 Sept 2009;
12 Sept 2010. **Map** p319 S5.

Oodles of own-made produce, handicrafts,
Fairtrade goods and healing therapies are on
offer at this east London horticultural show,
along with advice on growing-your-own,
composting, and other ways to go green.

City Harvest Festival

*Capel Manor Gardens, Bullsmoor Lane,
Enfield, Middx EN1 4RQ (0845 612
2122/www.capel.ac.uk). Turkey Street rail
(closed Sun)/217, 310 bus.* **Date** 19 Sept 2009.

Every year, London's city farms and community
gardens gather in the grounds of Capel Manor
College to hold a harvest festival. Events and
activities include an animal show (with entrants
from various city farms), milking and shearing
demonstrations, vegetable and plant sales,
crafts displays and food stalls.

Horseman's Sunday

*Church of St John's Hyde Park, Hyde Park
Crescent, W2 2QD (7262 1732/www.stjohns-
hydepark.com/horsemans). Edgware Road
or Lancaster Gate tube/Paddington tube/rail.*
Date 20 Sept 2009. **Map** p313 E6.

The first Horseman's Sunday was held in 1967,
when local stables, threatened with closure, held
an outdoor service to protest. Since then, it's
become an equine institution: at noon, after
morning service, the vicar of St John's rides out
to bless and present rosettes to a procession of
horses and riders, then delivers a short service
with hymns and occasional guest speakers.
There are children's activities, games and face-
painting in the church grounds.

Big Draw

*Venues across London & nationwide (www.
thebigdraw.org.uk).* **Date** 1-31 Oct 2009.

Pencils at the ready – this brilliant annual event
aims to bring out the inner artist in everyone,
with imaginative free events running in
libraries, community centres, shopping centres,
gardens and cultural institutions across the
country. London's big museums and galleries
always come up with some excellent offerings.

Punch & Judy Festival

*Covent Garden Piazza, WC2 (0870 780 5001/
www.coventgardenmarket.co.uk). Covent Garden
tube.* **Date** early Oct 2009. **Map** p315 L6.

That's the way to do it! Slapstick humour and
violent altercations between Punch and his
missus hold kids enthralled, with performances
taking place around the market building. Call
nearer the time to confirm this year's date.

Children's Book Week

8516 2977/www.booktrust.org.uk.
Date 5-11 Oct 2009.

This festival aims to encourage children of
primary school age to get reading – and enjoy
it. Hands-on activities and author visits take
place across the country, and there's always
plenty going on in London's schools and
libraries. National Poetry Day (www.national
poetryday.co.uk) is on 8 October.

Pearly Kings & Queens Harvest Festival

*St Paul's Church, Bedford Street, WC2E 9ED
(8778 8670/www.pearlysociety.co.uk). Covent
Garden tube.* **Date** 11 Oct 2009. **Map** p317 L7.

Pearly kings and queens – so named because of
the shiny white pearl buttons sewn in elaborate
designs on their dark suits – have their origins
in the 'aristocracy' of London's early Victorian
costermongers, who elected their own royalty to
look after their interests. Now charity
representatives, today's pearly monarchs gather
in their resplendent garb an hour before the
11am thanksgiving service.

The Baby Show

*Earl's Court Exhibition Centre, SW5 9TA
(booking 0870 122 1313/www.thebabyshow.
co.uk). Earl's Court tube.* **Date** 16-18 Oct 2009.

Earl's Court overflows with all manner of baby-
related paraphernalia, with a mind-boggling
array of pregnancy gear, nursery equipment
and stimulating toys. Consult the website to
search for your area of interest.

Trafalgar Day Parade

*Trafalgar Square, WC2 (7928 8978/www.ms-
sc.org). Charing Cross tube/rail.* **Date** 25 Oct
2009. **Map** p401 K7.

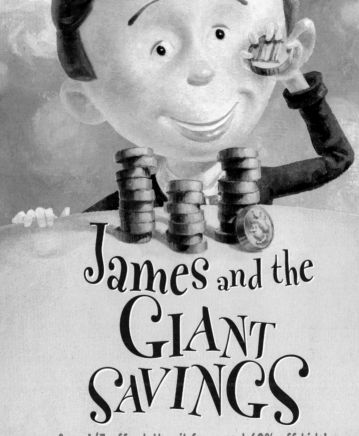

FAMILY & FRIENDS RAILCARD PRESENTS

Kids +

James and the GIANT SAVINGS

Save 1/3 off adult rail fares and 60% off kids'

JUST £26 FOR A WHOLE YEAR A RAILCARD GIVES YOU EPIC SAVINGS

AS YOU TRAVEL THE LENGTH AND BREADTH OF GREAT BRITAIN

Save 10% – Buy Online
www.familyandfriends-railcard.co.uk

Formerly Family Railcard

 National Rail

Epic Savings with Family & Friends Railcard

Over 500 sea cadets parade with marching bands and musical performances, in celebration of the British victory at Trafalgar. Events culminate in a wreath-laying at the foot of Nelson's Column, in honour of the mortally wounded admiral.

London to Brighton Veteran Car Run

Start at Serpentine Road, Hyde Park, W2 (01327 856024/www.lbvcr.com). Hyde Park Corner tube. **Date** 1 Nov 2009. **Map** p311 F8.
There's no time for lie-ins if you want to see this parade of gleaming vintage motors leaving London, or join the crowds lining the route. The buffed-up fleet sets off from Hyde Park at 7am, with the first cars reaching Brighton around 10am. The rest arrive by 4pm; bear in mind that the average speed is a stately 32kmph (20mph). The handsome vehicles are on display in Regent Street the day before (11am-3pm, Saturday 31 October).

Bonfire Night

Date 5 Nov.
Numerous public pyrotechnic displays to commemorate Guy Fawkes and his ill-fated Gunpowder Plot are held on the weekend nearest 5 November. Those at Battersea Park, Alexandra Palace and Crystal Palace are among London's best; for an overview, book a late ride on the London Eye.

Lord Mayor's Show

The City EC2-EC4 (7332 3456/www.lord mayorsshow.org). Mansion House, St Paul's or Temple tube/Bank tube/DLR/Blackfriars rail. **Date** 14 Nov 2009.
This is the day when, under the conditions of the Magna Carta, the newly elected Lord Mayor is presented for approval to the monarch, or his or her justices. Amid a procession of around 140 floats, the Lord Mayor leaves the Mansion House at 11am and travels through the City to the Royal Courts of Justice on the Strand, then receives a blessing at St Paul's Cathedral before returning to Mansion House. The procession takes around 75 minutes to pass by. At around 5pm, fireworks are set off from a barge moored on the Thames between Waterloo and Blackfriars Bridges; anywhere along the Embankment affords a good vantage point.

Discover Dogs

Earl's Court 2 Exhibition Centre, entrance on Lillie Road, SW5 9TA (7518 1012/www. discoverdogs.org.uk). West Brompton tube/ rail. **Date** 14-15 Nov 2009. **Map** p312 A11.

They say every dog has its day – and this is a chance for mutts that don't quite fit Crufts' criteria to take centre stage. Visitors can meet around 190 pedigree pooches and their breeders, watch Heelwork to Music displays and see husky team and police-dog agility demonstrations. Competition categories range from 'dog that looks most like a celebrity' to Scruffts (family crossbreed dog of the year).

Children's Film Festival

Main venue: Barbican Centre, Silk Street, EC2Y 8DS (Barbican box office 7638 8891/ www.londonchildrenfilm.org.uk). Barbican tube. **Date** 21-29 Nov 2009. **Map** p318 P5.
This annual festival proves that kids are interested in more sophisticated film fare than big blockbusters. The line-up features foreign language films, documentaries and animations; seven- to 12-year-olds are invited to join a jury and become film critics. Check online for workshops and events, many of which are free.

State Opening of Parliament

House of Lords, Palace of Westminster, SW1A 0PW (7219 4272/www.parliament.uk). Westminster tube. **Date** Nov/Dec 2009 (exact date to be confirmed). **Map** p317 L9.
In a ceremony that has changed little since the 16th century, the Queen reopens Parliament after its summer recess. Watch Her Majesty arrive and depart in her Irish or Australian State Coach, attended by the Household Cavalry.

Christmas Lights & Tree

Covent Garden (0870 780 5001/www.covent gardenmarket.co.uk); Oxford Street (7462 0680); Regent Street (7152 5853/www.regent-street.co.uk); Bond Street (www.bondstreet association.com); Trafalgar Square (7983 4234/www.london.gov.uk). **Date** Nov-Dec 2009.
The glittering lights on St Christopher's Place, Marylebone High Street, Bond Street and Kensington High Street add a magical touch to grey winter's days. The giant fir tree that stands in pride of place in Trafalgar Square is an annual gift from the Norwegian people, in gratitude for Britain's role in liberating their country from the Nazis during World War II.

WINTER

London International Horse Show

Olympia Exhibition Centre, Hammersmith Road, W14 8UX (01753 847900/www.olympia horseshow.com). Kensington (Olympia) tube/ rail. **Date** 15-21 Dec 2009.

Enthusiasts of all things equestrian can enjoy dressage, show-jumping, mounted military displays, dog agility contests and a Shetland Pony Grand National. The grand finale features Father Christmas (with a sledge pulled by horses) and there are over 200 trade stands, so you can also do some seasonal shopping.

Bankside Frost Fair

Bankside Riverside, next to Tate Modern, SE1 9TG (7928 3998/www.visitsouthwark. com). Southwark tube/rail/Blackfriars rail. **Date** Dec 2010. **Map** p318 O7.
In centuries gone by, the Thames regularly froze over – whereupon enterprising Londoners set up 'Frost Fairs' on the ice, with skating, puppet shows, mulled wine and roast meat stalls. This wonderfully festive revival of the tradition takes place by the river, rather than on it; in previous years it has involved food and craft stalls, ice sculptures, children's shows and a lantern parade, although changes are afoot for 2010.

Peter Pan Swimming Race

The Serpentine, Hyde Park, W2 (7298 2000/ www.royalparks.gov.uk). Hyde Park Corner tube. **Date** 25 Dec.
Established in 1864 by *Peter Pan* author JM Barrie, this chilly 100-yard race draws intrepid swimmers (Serpentine Swimming Club members only) and spectators every Christmas morning, competing for the Peter Pan cup. However mild the weather is, the Serpentine always looks less than inviting.

New Year's Eve Celebrations

Date 31 Dec.
London's New Year revelry has traditionally been concentrated around Trafalgar Square; the spectacular fireworks on the South Bank are a more recent draw. Both attract huge crowds, and can be nightmarish with younger children in tow.

London International Mime Festival

Various venues (7637 5661/www.mimefest. co.uk). **Date** 16-31 Jan 2010.
An international array of companies and artists perform visual theatre of every genre: circus skills, mask, mime, clown and visual theatre shows appeal to audiences of all ages.

Chinese New Year Festival

Around Gerrard Street, Chinatown, W1, Leicester Square, WC2 & Trafalgar Square, WC2 (7851 6686/www.chinatownchinese.co.uk). Leicester Square or Piccadilly Circus tube. **Date** 14 Feb 2010 (to be confirmed). **Map** p317 K7.

Riotous celebrations to mark Chinese New Year begin at 11am with a children's parade that weaves its way from Leicester Square Gardens to Trafalgar Square, where lion and dragon dance teams entertain the masses. Firework displays at lunchtime and 5pm fill the sky with colour (and loud bangs, which might alarm unwary tinies).

National Storytelling Week

Various theatres, museums, bookshops, arts centres, schools, libraries & pubs (Del Reid 8866 4232/www.sfs.org.uk). **Date** 30 Jan-6 Feb 2010.
Now in its tenth year, this annual celebration of the art of storytelling sees theatres, bookshops, community centres and schools across the country hosting events for tellers and listeners. Events cater to all ages, with stories drawn from an array of global cultures.

Great Spitalfields Pancake Day Race

Dray Walk, Old Truman Brewery, 91 Brick Lane, E1 6QL (7375 0441/www.alternative arts.co.uk). Aldgate East tube/Liverpool Street tube/rail. **Date** 16 Feb 2010. **Map** p319 S5.

May Fayre & Puppet Festival. *See p26.*

Relay teams of four toss pancakes as they race along Dray Walk, with heats starting at 12.30pm and all proceeds going to the London Air Ambulance charity. Register in advance if you fancy taking part and bring your own frying pan (pancakes are provided); everyone races together, so it isn't suitable for younger children. It's fun to go along as a spectator though, as fancy-dress clad teams get flipping and pancakes hit the pavement.

SPRING

National Science & Engineering Week
Various venues (www.britishscience association.org). **Date** 12-21 Mar 2010.
A week of scientific shenanigans, hosted by the British Association for the Advancement of Science. From hands-on shows, workshops and guided nature walks for youngsters to in-depth discussions for adults, each event celebrates different aspects of science, engineering and technology. Events take place at various London venues, so check online for further information.

St Patrick's Day Parade & Festival
Trafalgar Square, Leicester Square & Covent Garden (7983 4000/www.london.gov.uk). **Date** around 17 Mar 2010. **Map** p317 K7.
This good-natured, raucous parade departs from Hyde Park Corner at noon and continues to romp through the streets until 6pm. Expect lively performances of traditional Irish music in Trafalgar Square, a Covent Garden food market, ceilidh dancers in Leicester Square and lots of other activities for all ages.

Kempton Park Family Fun Day
Kempton Park, Sunbury-on-Thames, Middx TW16 5AQ (01932 782292/www.kempton. co.uk). Kempton Park rail. **Date** 28 Mar, 11 Apr, 4 May 2009.
Take the train from Waterloo for a family-friendly day at the races. Free entertainment (simulator rides, crafts, a soft play area, face-painting, balloon-modelling) is laid on, while 2009 also sees a *High School Musical*-themed concert (24 August) to keep the youngsters happy after you've blown their university fees on the gee-gees.

Shakespeare's Birthday
Various venues around South Bank & Bankside. **Date** 23 Apr 2010.

Celebrations of the Bard's birth date are concentrated around Shakespeare's Globe and Southwark Cathedral, when performances, music, readings and walks mark the great man's contribution to literature.

London Marathon
Greenwich Park to the Mall via the Isle of Dogs, Victoria Embankment & St James's Park (7902 0200/www.virginlondonmarathon.com). **Date** 25 Apr 2010.
Completing this 26.2 mile (42km) course is no mean feat, so the runners need all the support they can get along the way. Energetic 11 to 17s can compete in the three-mile Mini London Marathon – check online for details of the time trials held in every London borough. *See p214* **On your marks…**

Canalway Cavalcade
Little Venice, W9 (01494 783453/www. waterways.org.uk). Warwick Avenue tube/ Paddington tube/rail. **Date** 1-3 May 2010.
Decked out in bunting and flowers, more than 130 colourful narrowboats assemble in the pool of Little Venice to celebrate this three-day Bank Holiday boat bash. Events include craft, trade and food stalls; a teddy bears' picnic, Punch and Judy shows, music and (of course) boat trips. The beautiful lantern-lit boat procession on Sunday evening is a must-see.

May Fayre & Puppet Festival
St Paul's Church Garden, Bedford Street, WC2E 9ED (7375 0441/www.alternative arts.co.uk). Covent Garden tube. **Date** 9 May 2010. **Map** p317 L7.
Marking the first recorded sighting of Mr Punch in England (by Pepys, in 1662), this free event offers puppetry galore from 10.30am to 5.30pm. A brass band procession around Covent Garden is followed by a service at 11.30am in St Paul's Church, with Mr Punch in the pulpit. Then there are puppet shows, booths and stalls, plus workshops for puppet-making and dressing-up. Folk music and maypole dancing, clowns and jugglers add to the mayhem.

Kew Summer Festival
Royal Botanic Gardens, Kew, Richmond, Surrey TW9 3AB (8332 5655/www.kew.org uk). Kew Gardens tube/rail/Kew Bridge rail. **Date** May-Sept 2009.
Each season at Kew Gardens brings its own programme of events and family activities but 2009 is its 250th anniversary, so expect something a little bit special. Phone or check the website for details.

Out and About

Sightseeing

Attractions

School holidays need never be boring again.

The more you learn about London's history, the greater the city becomes. In this chapter, we've listed London's most iconic, beautiful and unusual buildings, plus where to see the best cityscapes. Some of it is educational (although most attractions try their hardest to make learning fun), all of it should be interesting, and there's a Thrills & Chills section at the end for pure physical excitement.

Being one of London's top tourist attractions means a licence to charge high entry fees, so pick and choose carefully so that your child gets the most out of each experience. To help parents out, we've marked our recommended age range in green. Some attractions offer free entry to under-fives – but that doesn't necessarily mean they'll enjoy it.

ASTRONOMY

Royal Observatory & Planetarium

Greenwich Park, SE10 9NF (8312 6565/www. rog.nmm.ac.uk). Cutty Sark DLR/Greenwich DLR/rail. **Open** 10am-5pm daily (last entry 4.30pm). *Tours* phone for details. **Admission** free. *Starlife* £6; £4 1-16s, reductions; free under-1s. *Tours* free. **Credit** MC, V. 3+ (5+ for shows)

This is a World Heritage Sight, and it's easy to see why. In the courtyard is the Greenwich Meridian Line, where visitors can stand with one foot in the Western Hemisphere and one in the Eastern; every place in the world is measured in terms of longitudinal distance from this point. The Observatory, originally built for Charles II by Wren in 1675, underwent a £15m refurbishment in 2007. The Peter Harrison Planetarium is the impressive result. Inside, shows about the stars are presented by a Royal Observatory astronomer who enjoys fielding knotty nipper questions. The shows are full of awesome facts: did you know there are more stars in the galaxy than the total number of heartbeats in the history of human existence?

Neighbouring galleries chart timekeeping since the 14th century, and the Observatory's dome houses the largest refracting telescope in the country. In the Observatory Courtyard is a small summerhouse, home to London's only public camera obscura. The moving, real-time view of Greenwich and the Thames is best seen on a bright day. *See also p126* **Great Days Out**.

Buggy access (courtyard only). Café. Nappy-changing facilities. Nearest picnic place: Greenwich Park. Shop.

BIRD'S EYE VIEWS

London Eye

Riverside Building (next to County Hall), Westminster Bridge Road, SE1 7PB (0870 990 8883/www.londoneye.com). Westminster tube/Waterloo tube/rail. **Open** Oct-Apr 10am-8pm daily. *Apr-Sept* 10am-9pm daily. **Admission** £17; £14 reductions (not offered at weekends, or July & Aug); £8.50 5-15s; free under-5s. Fast Track tickets £27. **Credit** AmEx, MC, V. **Map** p317 M8. All ages

This shining circle of pods has become such a defining point on London's skyline, it's hard to believe it was originally only supposed to be here for five years. No one wants to see it come down, and it's very near the top of every child's must-do list. Some kids, expecting a more white-knuckle affair, express disappointment that it turns so slowly, but there's no other view in London like it. Each ride (or flight, as the ticket office has it) is one complete revolution and takes half an hour – long enough to have a good look at the Queen's back garden and trace the silvery snaking of the Thames.

You can queue for tickets on the day, but there are often monumental tailbacks to the booth, especially on clear days. Better to book a Fast Track ticket online from 10am on the day. Night flights provide a twinkly experience, and the Eye gets festive with fairy lights at Christmas; other holiday specials include Hallowe'en and Easter. Visit the website for special Eye and river cruise packages.

Buggy access. Café. Disabled access: toilet. Nappy-changing facilities. Nearest picnic place: Jubilee Gardens. Shop.

Monument

Monument Street, EC3R 8AH (7626 2717/ www.cityoflondon.gov.uk). Monument tube. **Open** 9.30am-5pm daily. **Admission** £2; £1 5-15s; free under-5s. **No credit cards.** **Map** p319 Q7. 6+

A year late in reopening after an extensive refurbishment, Monument is once again open to the public. The tallest freestanding stone column in the world was designed by Christopher Wren and is a monument to the Great Fire of London of 1666. It is 61m (202ft) high, and located 61m (202ft) west of the exact location of the bakery in Pudding Lane where the fire broke out. The stone has been cleaned, the golden orb re-gilded and there's an improved viewing gallery at the top (although we're not sure we like the talking telescopes). Children who make it to the top of the 311 steps can expect two treats: the spectacular view from the top and a commemorative certificate for the climb. At ground level, you can admire relayed views from the top.

Nearest picnic place: riverside by London Bridge.

Tower Bridge Exhibition

Tower Bridge, SE1 2UP (7403 3761/www. towerbridge.org.uk). Tower Hill tube/Tower Gateway DLR. **Open** *Apr-Sept* 10am-6.30pm daily (last entry 5.30pm). *Oct-Mar* 9.30am-6pm daily (last entry 5pm). **Admission** £7; £5 reductions; £3 5-15s; free under-5s; £15.50 family (2+2). **Credit** AmEx, MC, V. **Map** p319 R8. 6+

This soaring structure is London's most iconic bridge, partly because of the bascules that raise when a ship needs to come through. It took eight long years to build, finally opening in 1894. At first, it was painted an unexciting shade of brown: only in 1977, in celebration of the Queen's Silver Jubilee, was it painted in jaunty red, white and blue. A lift transports you to the walkway foyer, 42m (138ft) above the Thames, where you watch a short film on the history of the bridge, then pass through both walkways to catch the stupendous views to the east and west. Large aerial photographs pinpoint famous landmarks (kids can take a playsheet and tick them off), and there are photo points where you can slide open the windows to get an unimpeded shot. Ring for details of occasional school-holiday storytelling events and for when the famous bascules will next be raised. From the walkways, it's a short stroll to the south tower and the Victorian engine rooms, for a more thorough explanation of the hydraulics involved.

Buggy access. Disabled access: lift, toilet. Nappy-changing facilities. Nearest picnic place: Potters Field, Tower of London Gardens. Shop.

Nautical yarns aboard the **Golden Hinde**. *See p32.*

Sightseeing

Great Days Out
South Bank & Bankside

For 2,000 years, the Thames was the working heart of London, but in the last half century its primary function has become leisure and pleasure. Many of London's great cultural institutions, old and new, nestle along its banks. The South Bank is a great place for a family day out whatever the weather, offering so much more than organised activities.

Its wide, riverside promenade provides great scope for wheels of any sort (scooters, bikes or skates), while the sculptural landscaping is good for climbing expeditions; children of all ages will want to gawp for hours at the skateboarders' pit underneath the Hayward Gallery. Beyond that, Bankside's attractions stretch off towards the east.

The arts

The iconic **Royal Festival Hall** (see p164) often has free dance, music and poetry performances and events for families in the foyer or out on the terrace; check online for details.

Jeppe Hien's playful outdoor water sculpture *Appearing Rooms* is back by popular demand until October 2009 – walk inside the rooms as one wall of water disappears, then hide inside when it shoots up again. Endless fun. The summer of 2009 (May to July) also sees a large purple cow squatting just the other side

of Hungerford Bridge from the RFH. Called the E4 Udderbelly, it's a new seasonal venue – planned as an annual pre-Edinburgh treat – offering comedy, music, circus, theatre and lots of children's shows and workshops.

The light, bright **Hayward Gallery** (see p58) is free for under-12s. Whatever the current exhibition, it's an intriguing place to explore, with its visually confusing space created by curved two-way mirrors. Further east is the **BFI Southbank** (see p166); on Saturday mornings, junior film screenings bring a mix of current and classic hits. You can also book a viewing station in the mediathèque and choose from over 1,000 films and TV programmes from the BFI archive.

The **IMAX** (see p165) is just around the corner. Kids enjoy wearing the 3D glasses for special features, but the storylines can be secondary to the fantastic effects that seem to leap from the screen.

Strolling past the National Theatre – home to the **Watch This Space Festival** (see p19) every summer – will take you to Gabriel's Wharf, where arts and crafts shops sit alongside cafés and restaurants. This area is always bustling, but never more so than during the **Coin Street Festival** (see p17), when it's overtaken by performers celebrating different communities in the capital. All events are

free, taking place in and around the green spaces of Bernie Spain Gardens.

Head under Blackfriars Bridge, along Queen's Walk. Next stop for the arts is **Tate Modern** (*see p66*), once Bankside Power Station. Children absolutely love this vast gallery. Even the sloping entrance to the Turbine Hall is exciting to young eyes and, once inside, the sheer scale of the hall gives them pause for thought.

Further along Bankside is the distinctive **Shakespeare's Globe** (*see p191*), which offers guided tours of the building and seasonal performances.

History writ large

At Southwark Bridge, one wall is covered with an etching depicting the frost fairs in the days when the Thames was 'frozen o'er'. Walk as far as you can by the river until you are diverted past the Vinopolis wine museum, down Clink Street and straight to the **Clink Prison Museum** (*see p94*), where unsettling exhibitions reveal what life was like for the prisoners incarcerated here from 1247 to 1780.

Straight ahead, in Pickfords Wharf, is a replica of the **Golden Hinde** (*see p32*), the tiny vessel in which Sir Francis Drake circumnavigated the globe in the 16th century. Just around the corner is **Southwark Cathedral** (*see p41*); its gardens are great for a picnic. Turn left at the cathedral, taking the pavement studded with blue and green lights that goes under London Bridge (Montague Close). Keep walking until you emerge on Tooley Street, not far from the **London Dungeon** (*see p52*), where London's great disasters and grisly murders are brought garishly to life.

Those needing a pit stop and some 21st-century materialist diversions should follow the signs to **Hays Galleria**, a touristy enclave with shops and restaurants. It also houses a ship-like sculpture by David Kemp called *The Navigators*. A rather more substantial vessel looms up ahead, though. Rejoin

LUNCH BOX

Also in the area: Giraffe, Nando's, Pizza Express (four branches), Strada, Wagamama.

fish! *Cathedral Street, Borough Market, SE1 9AL (7407 3803/www.fishdiner. co.uk).* Posh fish and chips. *See p238.*

House of Crêpes *56 Upper Ground, SE1 9PP (7401 9816).* Flippin' lovely pancakes in sweet and savoury forms.

Riverside Terrace Café *Royal Festival Hall, Southbank Centre, SE1 8XX (0871 663 2501).* Arts centre café.

Table *83 Southwark Street, SE1 0HX (7401 2760/www.thetablecafe.com).* Superbly inventive salads, sarnies and hot meals, made from carefully-sourced ingredients.

Tate Modern Café 2 *2nd Floor, Tate Modern, SE1 9TG (7401 5014/www. tate.org.uk).* Highly recommended for children. *See p223.*

the Thames footpath to see **HMS Belfast** (*see p101*), a floating wing of the Imperial War Museum. Carry on eastwards until you reach City Hall, the odd-shaped, glass-sided headquarters of Mayor Boris Johnson, the London Assembly and the Greater London Authority. This is part of a 13-acre riverside development known as More London, which has some sculptural fountains that children love to play in. Potters Fields Park is next door, and a great place for a picnic with views of **Tower Bridge** (*see p29*) and the **Tower of London** (*see p39*), just across the river.

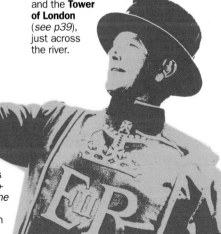

LIVING HISTORY

Age Exchange Reminiscence Centre

11 Blackheath Village, SE3 9LA (8318 9105/ www.age-exchange.org.uk). Blackheath rail. **Open** 10am-5pm Mon-Fri; 10am-4pm Sat. **Admission** free. Groups must book in advance; charges vary. **Credit** MC, V. 8+
Run by the charity Age Exchange, this living history centre comprises several different areas. A mock-up of a grocer's shop from about 60 years ago features drawers of comestibles; an old-fashioned sweetie shop stocks classics like rosy apples; and a 1940s sitting room features vintage toys, a stove and old-style furnishings. It's a low-key, cosy sort of place that aims to promote lively communication between the generations; there's also a small café and theatre space at the back. The Centre's programme of exhibitions is based on older people's memories, and recent events have included recreations of a VE Day street party and a wartime London Docks soundscape. The centre also organises a variety of workshops; check the website for dates of future attractions.
Buggy access. Café. Disabled access: toilet. Nearest picnic place: centre gardens. Shop.

Dennis Severs' House

18 Folgate Street, E1 6BX (7247 4013/ www.dennissevershouse.co.uk). Liverpool Street tube/rail. **Open** noon-4pm 1st & 3rd Sun of mth; noon-2pm Mon (following 1st & 3rd Sun of mth); Mon evenings (times vary; booking required). **Admission** £8 Sun; £5 noon-2pm Mon; £12 Mon evenings. No under-10s. **Credit** MC, V. **Map** p319 R5. 10+
Dennis Severs (1948-1999) was the artist son of a garage owner from California, who came to Spitalfields and fell in love with the area and this house. He restored the house to its original splendour (living day-to-day *sans* bathroom, electricity or modern cooking facilities), created a fictional Huguenot silk-weaving family to live in it and opened the doors to the public.
Each of the ten rooms is the scene of a drama, set between 1724 and 1914. Visitors make their way from the cellar to the kitchen, and on to the grander entertaining rooms above, hearing footsteps, whispers and doors closing, smelling the scent of pomanders and seeing strewn clothes and half-eaten meals. It's as if the inhabitants deserted the rooms seconds before; Severs himself called it a 'still life drama'. No museum can provide an experience quite like this.
Nearest picnic place: Broadgate Circus (Liverpool Street Station), Elder Street Gardens. Shop.

Golden Hinde

Pickfords Wharf, Clink Street, SE1 9DG (0870 011 8700/www.goldenhinde.org). Monument tube/London Bridge tube/rail. **Open** daily; times vary. Phone for details. *Tours* phone for times. **Admission** £6; £4.50 reductions; £4.50 4-16s; free under-4s; £18 family (2+3). **Credit** MC, V. **Map** p319 P8. 4+
The first thing that strikes visitors to this meticulous replica of Sir Francis Drake's 16th-century galleon is how small it is. The first ship to circumnavigate the globe (in a voyage that began in 1577) looks almost like an expensive model toy. This thoroughly seaworthy replica *Golden Hinde* was built in 1973 to mark the admiral-pirate's 400th birthday – after which it sailed to San Francisco.
Pirate Fun Days offer storytelling, a treasure hunt and prizes for the best pirate costume. Families can also attend sleepovers, in which participants dress in period clothes, eat Tudor food, learn ancient seafaring skills and sleep next to the cannons. These take place on Saturdays and cost £39.95 per person (the minimum age for would-be recruits is six years old). Costumes and entertainment are provided; book ahead and bring a sleeping bag. During the school holidays there are storytelling sessions, craft activities and special workshops every weekend. You can also have a party here; ring or check online for details.
Nearest picnic place: Southwark Cathedral Gardens, riverside benches. Shop.

Houses of Parliament

Parliament Square, SW1A 0AA (Commons info 7219 3000/Lords info 7219 3107/tours 7219 4206/www.parliament.uk). Westminster tube. **Open** (when in session) *House of Commons Visitors' Gallery* 2.30-10.30pm Mon, Tue; 11.30am-7.30pm Wed; 10.30am-6.30pm Thur; 9.30am-3pm Fri. Closed bank hols. *House of Lords Visitors' Gallery* 2.30-10pm Mon, Tue; 3-10pm Wed; 11am-7.30pm Thur; 10am until close of business Fri. Check website for debate times. *Tours* summer recess only; phone for details for other times. **Admission** *Visitors' Gallery* free. *Tours* £11.70; £7.80 reductions; £4.80 5-15s; free under-5s; £29.20 family (2+2). **Credit** MC, V. **Map** p317 L9. 10+
The building we see today, with its 1,100 rooms and three miles of corridors, was rebuilt by Charles Barry and Augustus Pugin. All that's left of the original Palace of Westminster that burned down in 1834 are the Westminster Hall (used for major ceremonial events) and the Jewel Tower. Tours only run in the summer, when Parliament is not sitting; for the rest of the year,

Sightseeing

THE ALL NEW
LONDON
SEA·LIFE
AQUARIUM
GET CLOSER THAN EVER BEFORE

sealifelondon.co.uk

visitors can attend debates and watch committees in session. Children are usually satisfied by the mere proximity of the big old bell known as Big Ben, but only UK residents over 11 can climb the Clock Tower to take a closer look; tickets must be booked ahead through your MP.

Buggy access. Disabled access: lift, toilet. Nappy-changing facilities. Nearest picnic place: Victoria Tower Gardens. Shop.

Linley Sambourne House

18 Stafford Terrace, W8 7BH (Mon-Fri 7602 3316/Sat, Sun 7938 1295/www.rbkc.gov.uk/ linleysambournehouse). High Street Kensington tube. **Open** *Tours* (groups only; maximum 12 people. Pre-booking essential) 11.15am, 2.15pm Weds; 11.15am, 1pm, 2.15pm, 3.30pm Sat, Sun; also by appointment. **Admission** £6; £4 reductions; £1 under-18s. **Credit** MC, V. **Map** p314 A9. 5+

Edward Linley Sambourne was a Victorian cartoonist, famous for his work in *Punch*. His great grandson married Princess Margaret and became the Earl of Snowden. His classical Italianate house has almost all its original fittings and furniture and can be visited only by eccentric (and terrific) pre-booked tours. On Saturdays and Sundays these are guided by costumed actors, which goes down well with children. Gossipy housekeeper Mrs Reffle shines a cheeky light into Victorian family life and tells jokes along the way. There's also a visitors' centre, where children can take part in craftwork sessions relating to objects in the house. *Shop.*

Shakespeare's Globe

21 New Globe Walk, Bankside, SE1 9DT (7401 9919/tour information 7902 1500/ www.shakespeares-globe.org). Mansion House tube/London Bridge tube/rail. **Open** *Box office theatre bookings* 10am-6pm daily. *Tours* 9am-5pm daily. May-Sept afternoon tours only visit the Rose Theatre, not the Globe. **Tickets** £5-£33. *Tours* £9; £7.50 reductions; £6.50 5-15s; free under-5s; £20 family (2+3). **Credit** AmEx, MC, V. **Map** p318 P7. 8+

There is no better way to see Shakespeare than standing up (without a roof over your head) at the Globe. A reconstruction of the Bard's own theatre, it was built less than 100m (328ft) from where the original stood. It opened in 1997, the brainchild of actor Sam Wanamaker (who, sadly, died before it was finished). Tours of the 'wooden O' take place all year, and include the UnderGlobe exhibition on the reconstruction, Elizabethan theatres and Shakespeare's London; the annual theatre season runs from late April

to early October. Historically authentic performances of Shakespeare's plays make up the bulk of the programme, but new theatre also gets a showing.

There's fun for all around the time of Shakespeare's birthday (23 April) and at the drama sessions for eight to 11s that accompany the theatre season; see the website or ring 7902 1433 for details. The remains of the Rose Theatre (www.rosetheatre.org.uk), where many of Shakespeare's works were staged, are around the corner in the basement of an office block. *Café. Disabled access: lift, toilet. Nappy-changing facilities. Nearest picnic place: South Bank benches. Restaurant. Shop.*

PALACES & STRONGHOLDS

Buckingham Palace & Royal Mews

SW1A 1AA (7766 7300/www.royalcollection. org.uk). Green Park or St James's Park tube/ Victoria tube/rail. **Open** *State Rooms* 26 July-30 Sept 9.45am-3.45pm daily. *Royal Mews* Mar-Oct 11am-3.15pm Mon-Thur, Sat, Sun (last entry 4.15pm when palace is open); 26 July-29 Sept 10am-5pm daily (last entry 4.15pm). *Queen's Gallery* 10am-4.30pm (closes 5.30pm) daily. Closed during Ascot & state occasions. **Admission** *State Rooms* £16.50; £9.59 5-16s; £15 reductions; free under-5s; £44 family (2+3). *Royal Mews* £7.50; £4.80 5-16s; £6.75 reductions; free under-5s; £20 family (2+3). *Queen's Gallery* £8.50; £4.25 5-16s; £7.50 reductions; free under-5s; £21.50 family (2+3). *Joint ticket* (Royal Mews and Queen's Gallery) £14.50; £8 5-16s; £13 reductions; £38 family (2+3). **Credit** AmEx, MC, V. **Map** p316 H9. All ages (Royal Mews). 5+ (Queen's Gallery).

Monarchs have used this building in one form or another since 1762, but Queen Victoria was the first to make it her home. While it's not the world's most beautiful palace, it is probably the most famous, drawing millions of visitors every year. The famous Changing of the Guard takes place daily in the palace forecourt at 11.30am from May to July, and on alternate days the rest of the year.

The State Rooms were first opened to the public in 1993 (the fire at Windsor Castle the previous year meant the Queen had to raise some cash for reconstructions) and can be seen during August and September, while the Queen is at Balmoral. There are 19 rooms to see in all, including the White Drawing Room. Designed by John Nash

Get lost in **Hampton Court Maze**. See p39.

and furnished in opulent luxury with treasures from the Royal Collection, this will set the children's imaginations spinning. The Queen's Gallery, open all year round, has paintings by Dürer, Rembrandt, Canaletto, Rubens and Van Dyck, as well as some exquisite Fabergé eggs.

There's a nature trail for children in the gardens and a family activity room, also open throughout August and September. At the Royal Mews, children can watch the horses being groomed, fed and exercised, and examine the royal Rolls-Royces and the Gold State Coach, last used for the 2002 Golden Jubilee. See also p36 **Great Days Out**.

Buggy access. Disabled access: lift, toilet (Buckingham Palace). Nappy-changing facilities (Buckingham Palace). Nearest picnic place: Green Park. Shop.

Eltham Palace

Court Yard, SE9 5QE (8294 2548/www. elthampalace.org.uk). Eltham rail. **Open** *Apr-Oct* 10am-5pm Mon-Wed, Sun. *Nov, Dec, Feb, Mar* 11am-4pm Mon-Wed, Sun. Closed week before Christmas-31 Jan. **Admission** *House & grounds* (incl audio tour) £8.30; £7.10 reductions; £4.20 5-15s; £20.80 family (2+3); free under-5s. *Gardens only* £5.30; £4.50 reductions; £2.70 5-15s; free under-5s. **Credit** MC, V. 5+

This magnificent abode was largely erected in 1936 by textiles heir Stephen Courtauld – like his more famous brother Samuel (who founded the Courtauld Institute of Art in 1932), a collector of the arts. Stephen and his wife Virginia created a masterpiece of Art Deco design in Eltham Palace, and the Great Hall was the scene of many a lavish party before World War II broke out and the building was commandeered by the War Office.

The furniture and fittings look like a film set – check out the pink leather chairs, ornate black and silver doors and moulded maple veneer in the dining room, or the onyx and gold-plated taps in Virginia's glamorous vaulted bathroom. The house was way ahead of its time when it came to mod cons, including underfloor heating, ensuite bathrooms and a quirky vacuum-cleaning system. Upstairs there's a chance to look at the Courtauld family's photos and artefacts and enjoy a home movie of Stephen and Virginia with their pet lemur, Mahjong (who had his own, specially designed quarters). But there's more to this Palace than its red brick façade, and the moat should give the kids a clue.

It was a full blown Tudor Palace until it fell out of favour in Henry VIII's reign; he was said to prefer nearby Greenwich. There's still a Tudor bridge over the moat, as well as evidence of earlier medieval ruins. The grounds are beautifully restored and hold various events in summer, like an Art Deco fair and Tudor trails for kids. The quaint tearoom and shop have a distinctly 1930s flavour.

Café. Disabled access: lift. Shop.

Fulham Palace & Museum

Bishop's Avenue, off Fulham Palace Road, SW6 6EA (7736 3233/www.fulhampalace. org). Hammersmith or Putney Bridge tube/ 220, 414, 430 bus. **Open** noon-4pm Mon, Tue; 11am-2pm Sat; 11.30am-3.30pm Sun. *Tours* phone for details. **Admission** *Museum* free; under-16s must be accompanied by an adult. *Tours* £5; free under-16s. **No credit cards.** 3+

This site was the official residence of the Bishops of London from 704 until 1975. The main house – more manor than palace – is Tudor (try out the echo in the courtyard), with significant Georgian and Victorian additions. Refurbishment has left the East Quadrangle looking beautiful, and the café (although no longer run by Peyton & Byrne, alas) is a particularly pleasant place to sit. The museum has plenty of new interactive features, lots more room to display treasures dug up in the grounds, and a brand new programme of theatre, exhibitions and activities for families: music

Sightseeing

Westminster

Walking through Westminster feels like stepping into the London of storybooks. Minor details may have changed over the years, but the iconic sights and sounds remain, from the sonorous peal of Big Ben to the squabbling pigeons in Trafalgar Square (although numbers were severely depleted under Mayor Ken), to the ramrod-backed, scarlet-clad Guards, stiffly wheeling and marching like clockwork automatons.

Nelson's patch

Though the official centre of London is just south of here (marked by a small plaque behind the equestrian statue of Charles I), **Trafalgar Square** is the city's symbolic heart. Its delights are timeless: the great lions at the base of Nelson's column are often overrun with children, who shelter between their massive paws or clamber astride their sun-warmed backs. Above the throng, Admiral Nelson gazes across the city from atop his granite column.

There's plenty going on at his feet, with all manner of protests, performances and free festivals held here throughout the year. Dance a jig to lilting Irish fiddles in celebration of St Patrick's Day, see the famous fountains filled with floating lanterns for Diwali, or gawp at a fiery-mouthed dragon, weaving its way through the revellers welcoming in Chinese New Year.

While military dignitaries and royalty occupy three stone pedestals around the square, the fourth plinth showcases daring contemporary artworks. For 100 days from July 2009, Anthony Gormley's *One & Other* will give members of the public the chance to occupy the plinth for an hour – doing whatever they please, so long as they're not breaking the law.

Art for all

At the northern edge of Trafalgar Square, follow the broad flight of stairs up to the splendid **National Gallery** (*see p60*). You can pick up various audio tours and trails around the artworks, or design and print out your own bespoke route in the Sainsbury Wing's ArtStart room. Sundays and school holidays are our favourite times to visit, with free art workshops for five to 11s and story sessions for under-fives; enquiring-minded toddlers can squeeze on to the magic carpet to learn about a selected painting. Alternatively, scoot up past the National Gallery and on to the **National Portrait Gallery** (*see p61*), where all sorts of famous faces peer down from the walls: after checking your heroes have been honoured (we're glad to see Roald Dahl has no less than three likenesses), you can head to the rooftop Portrait Restaurant for a posh afternoon tea and truly magnificent views.

For more down-to-earth grub and prices, take the kids to the excellent Café in the Crypt at nearby St-Martin-in-the-Field – also home to the low-key but lovely **London Brass Rubbing Centre** (*see p195*).

All the queen's horses

Another option is to head down Whitehall, keeping your camera at the ready. Why? Well for a start, the dashing chaps of the Household Cavalry – and their trusty steeds – are headquartered here. At Horse Guard Parade, you can watch the mounted regiment change the Queen's Life Guard at 11am (10am on Sundays). With their shiny coats and well-polished hooves, the horses are every bit as dapper and professional as their riders; for a glimpse of them when they're off duty, visit the **Household Cavalry Museum** (*see p102*), which offers a sneaky peek into the stables.

Halfway down Whitehall, Downing Street is guarded by a rather less photogenic phalanx of policemen. Though the road is closed to the public, you can peep through the heavy iron gates to see No.10. The road leads on to Parliament Square, **Westminster Abbey** (*see p42*), and the **Houses of Parliament** (*see p32*) – home, of course, to **Big Ben**.

A palatial park

The Abbey and the home of British politics are interesting for older children, but on a sunny day we'd be tempted to forgo its suits and seriousness in favour of a stroll and a nice ice-cream in **St James' Park** (*see p124*), and a quick peek at **Buckingham Palace** (*see p34*). The Changing of the Guard, as witnessed by Alice and Christopher Robin in AA Milne's famous ditty, takes place in the palace forecourt. The ceremony begins at 11.30am, and is held every day from May to July, then on alternate days for the rest of the year.

Crowds start to build behind the railings around half an hour before the start, and it can get very busy; if all you're really after is a spot of military marching and a gander at the famous bearskin hats, you might be better off mooching up to **St James' Palace** at elevenish. Here, you can get an unobstructed view of the Old Guard setting off along the Mall to Buckingham Palace.

A no less august ceremony in these parts is the daily feeding of the pelicans at St James' Park. At 2.30pm, the hungry pelicans gather by the lake to feast on fresh fish; in 2006 one swallowed a live pigeon, but hasn't been seen to repeat the alarming feat since. They're friendly creatures (so long as you're not a tasty-looking pigeon); if you sit on one of the benches by the lake, you might find one

LUNCH BOX

Also in the area: Pizza Express.
Café in the Crypt *St-Martin-in-the-Fields, Duncannon Street, WC2N 4JJ (7736 1158/www.smitf.org).* Wholesome comfort food and nursery puds, with child-sized portions of main courses available on request.
Inn the Park *St James's Park, SW1A 2BJ (7451 9999/www.innthepark.com).* Expensive but appealing back-to-British fare, in a sylvan setting; the self-service café area is cheaper than the proper restaurant. See p230.
Jom Makan *5-7 Pall Mall East, SW1Y 5BA (7925 2402).* Noodles, curries and Malaysian street food for daring eaters, plus bite-sized side dishes and satay for cautious kids to try.
National Café *East Wing, The National Gallery, WC2N 4DN (7747 5942/www. thenationalcafe.com).* Classic brasserie fare in smart but unstuffy surrounds, plus a simple kids' menu. See p222.
Thai Square *21-24 Cockspur Street, SW1Y 5BL (7839 4000/www.thai square.net).* Hot and spicy fare, just off Trafalgar Square.

alighting next to you. Afterwards, take the bridge across the lake for a fairytale view of Buckingham Palace, beautifully framed by the trees.

workshops for nippers between two and five, for example, or craft sessions where over-fives turn out hobby horses or soldier skittles. All must be pre-booked; most cost £5-£10 a head. Leave time to admire the gorgeous gardens and make sure the children look out for the Bishop's Tree, a sculpture on one of the cedar of Lebanon trees on the North Lawn. *Buggy access. Café. Disabled access: toilet (in palace). Nearest picnic place: grounds. Shop.*

Hampton Court Palace

East Molesey, Surrey KT8 9AU (0844 482 7777/www.hrp.org.uk). Hampton Court rail/ riverboat from Westminster or Richmond to Hampton Court Pier (Apr-Oct). **Open** *Palace* Mar-Oct 10am-6pm daily. Nov-Feb 10am-4.30pm daily. Last entry 1hr before closing. *Park* dawn-dusk daily. **Admission** *Palace, courtyard, cloister & maze* £14; £11.50 reductions; £7 5-15s; free under-5s; £38 family (2+3). *Gardens only* £4.60; £4 reductions; free under-16s. *Maze only* £3.50; £2.50 5-15s; free under-5s; £10 family (2+3). **Credit** AmEx, MC, V. 6+

You can get here by boat from Westminster (*see p43*), but it will take you a couple of hours. This spectacular palace is worth the trek, though, and you can always come by train instead – a mere half-hour's journey from the centre of town. Henry VIII is always a favourite monarch with children, who are fascinated by his large girth, eccentric ways and habit of having his wives executed. This palace was his home, and positively oozes with historical drama. Elizabeth I was imprisoned in the tower by her elder sister Mary; Shakespeare performed here; and Cromwell made it his home after the Civil War. The ghost of Henry's fifth wife, Catherine Howard, who was executed for adultery at the Tower of London, is said to shriek around in the Haunted Gallery.

The various Tudor and Baroque buildings sprawl over six acres, with costumed guides adding a lively dimension to the state apartments, courtyards and cloisters. The world famous gardens are truly wonderful, with the maze taking centre stage in any child's itinerary. It's the oldest in the country, having been planted between 1689 and 1694 – though it's virtually impossible to get lost in.

Themed activities are plentiful during the school holidays, but expect 2009 – which marks the 500th anniversary of Henry VIII's accession to the throne – to be a bit special. Events will reflect Henry's favourite entertainments, with jousting, archery, hunting, shooting and jesters. On selected bank holidays and weekends, Tudor cookery demonstrations take place in the huge kitchens, where children love the bubbling cauldrons and game bird carcasses (see the website for dates). This year, Henry VIII's Council Chamber will be opened to the public for the first time, with a special exhibition on Henry's ill-fated wives. *Buggy access. Café. Disabled access: lift, toilet. Nappy-changing facilities. Nearest picnic place: palace gardens/picnic area. Restaurant. Shops.*

Kensington Palace

Kensington Gardens, W8 4PX (0844 482 7777/www.hrp.org.uk). Bayswater or High Street Kensington tube/9, 10, 49, 52, 70 bus. **Open** *Mar-Oct* 10am-6pm daily. *Nov-Feb* 10am-5pm daily. Last entry 1hr before closing. **Admission** (incl audio guide) £12.50; £11 reductions; £6.25 5-15s; free under-5s; £34 family (2+3). **Credit** MC, V. **Map** p310 B8. 7+

This Jacobean Mansion has, over the years, been closely associated with various Royal females. Queen Victoria loved it so much she pronounced the whole borough 'Royal'. Princess Margaret lived here, as did Princess Diana (an exhibition of her clothes runs until January 2010). The original mansion was turned into a palace by Christopher Wren, as commissioned by William III and his wife Mary when they came to live here in 1689. They moved from Whitehall Palace to escape the smoggy air, which played havoc with William's asthma.

The palace is open for tours of the State Apartments (which you enter via Wren's lofty King's Staircase), the King's Gallery and the Queen's Apartments, where William and Mary lived quite simply. Family trails begin in the dressmakers' workshop, where children can begin an interactive quiz; there are special activities here during the school holidays. 'The Last Debutantes' exhibition, which runs until January 2010, marks the 50th anniversary of the last ever formal presentation of well bred young ladies at court. *Buggy access. Disabled access: toilet. Nappy-changing facilities. Nearest picnic place: grounds. Restaurant. Shop.*

Tower of London

Tower Hill, EC3N 4AB (0844 482 7777/www. hrp.org.uk). Tower Hill tube/Tower Gateway DLR/Fenchurch Street rail. **Open** *Mar-Oct* 10am-5.30pm Mon, Sun; 9am-5.30pm Tue-Sat (last entry 5pm). *Nov-Feb* 10am-4.30pm Mon, Sun; 9am-4.30pm Tue-Sat. *Tours* (outside only, weather permitting) every 30mins until 3.30pm. **Admission** £17; £9.50 5-15s; £14.50 reductions; free under-5s; £47 family (2+3). Audio guide £4; £3 reductions. *Tours* free. **Credit** AmEx, MC, V. **Map** p319 R7. 5+

Sightseeing

There's a lot to see at the Pool of London here on the Thames, including Tower Bridge and HMS *Belfast*. But few tourist attractions can top this centuries-old fortress, palace, prison and execution ground (two of Henry VIII's wives got the chop here) for sheer historical bounty. You can easily spend a whole day exploring. The Medieval Palace, where kings and queens stayed until the reign of Elizabeth I, has recently been restored, and uses smells and sound effects to whisk you back in time. Interactive displays reveal the ordeals of life as a prisoner, while outside on Tower Green is the place where unfortunates such as Anne Boleyn and Lady Jane Grey were beheaded; a glass pillow sculpted by artist Brian Catling marks the spot. Battle nuts love the gleaming armoury in the White Tower, and can learn about what it was like to be a soldier in medieval times; there are also replicas of two fearsome-looking siege engines (a special half-term event usually centres on the collection).

The crown jewels are the Tower's biggest draw, with 23,578 gems on display. Highlights include a model of the uncut, fist-sized Cullinan I – the largest diamond in the world – and an illustrated description of how it was cut into nine smaller diamonds. You can't miss the two-metre-wide Grand Punch Bowl – it's big enough to bathe in.

The beautiful vaulted chamber of the Bowyer Tower has been open to visitors since Easter 2007. Legend has it the Duke of Clarence met a grisly fate here in 1478, drowning in a barrel of malmsey wine. The most entertaining way to hear such stories is to join one of the highly entertaining free tours, led by a Yeoman Warder (Beefeater). The Warders, photogenic in their black and red finery, are genial hosts and a mine of information.

Children's trails and quizzes tackle different themes, including Knights and Princesses and the Peasants' Revolt. Check the website for details of daily special events.
Buggy access (Jewel House). Café. Nappy-changing facilities. Nearest picnic place: riverside benches, Trinity Square Memorial Gardens. Shops.

PLACES OF WORSHIP

London Central Mosque
146 Park Road, NW8 7RG (7724 3363/www. iccuk.org). Baker Street tube/13, 82, 133 bus. **Open** 9.30am-6pm daily. **Admission** free. All ages
If you've ever wondered about the golden dome that you can see from Regent's Park, here's your answer: it belongs to the imposing London Central Mosque. Around a central courtyard, the Islamic Cultural Centre holds regular lessons, lectures and seminars (phone for details); there's also a library, bookshop and information booth.

Shri Swaminarayan Mandir Temple.

Visitors entering the prayer area must remove their shoes, while women are asked to wear a headscarf at all times. Tours can be arranged, but must be booked in advance. *Buggy access. Café. Disabled access: ramp, toilet. Nappy-changing facilities. Nearest picnic place: Regent's Park. Shop.*

Shri Swaminarayan Mandir Temple

105-119 Brentfield Road, NW10 8LD (8965 2651/www.swaminarayan.org). Wembley Park tube, then BR2 bus/Neasden tube, then 15min walk. **Open** 9am-6pm daily. **Admission** free. Exhibition £2; £1.50 6-15s; free under-6s. **Credit** AmEx, MC, V. 5+

This extraordinary temple is otherwise known as the Neasden Temple. Most of the stone used to build the incredibly decorative and intricate white structure was shipped from the quarries of Italy and Bulgaria to India, where it was carved by 1,500 master sculptors before being shipped to London. The temple has a permanent exhibition (with a video) called 'Understanding Hinduism', which is especially useful for children studying world religion. It also holds family seminars, and there's colourful kite flying for all the family every year on January 14, to mark the festival of Uttarayan. *Buggy access. Café. Disabled access: lift, toilet. Nappy-changing facilities. Shop.*

Southwark Cathedral

London Bridge, SE1 9DA (7367 6700/tours 7367 6734/www.dswark.org/cathedral). London Bridge tube/rail. **Open** from 8am daily (closing times vary). *Restaurant* 8.30am-6pm Mon-Fri; 10am-6pm Sat, Sun. Closed 25 Dec, Good Friday, Easter Sunday. *Services* 8am, 8.15am, 12.30pm, 12.45pm, 5.30pm Mon-Fri; 9am, 9.15am, 4pm Sat; 8.45am, 9am, 11am, 3pm, 6.30pm Sun. **Admission** *Audio tour* £2.50; £2 reductions; £1.25 under-16s, students. Donations appreciated. **Credit** MC, V. **Map** p319 P8. 5+

This beautiful Anglican cathedral began life on this site more than eight centuries ago; the retro-choir and lady chapel and the north transept are the remaining medieval sections. The church fell into disrepair after the Reformation (one part was used as a bakery, another as a pigsty), but in 1905 it became a cathedral; it now has an Education Centre, a shop and a refectory. Memorials are devoted to the 51 people who drowned in the 1989 *Marchioness* accident; Shakespeare (and Sam Wanamaker who persevered for over 20 years to get the Globe Theatre built nearby); John Gower; and John Harvard. The windows show images of Chaucer, who set off on pilgrimage to Canterbury from a pub in Borough High Street, and John Bunyan, who preached locally. In the churchyard, hunt for the flattish, ribbed stone monument to Mahomet Weyomon, a Mohegan chief buried in the churchyard in 1735. He died of smallpox after travelling to London to state his case in the Mohegan Land Dispute.

The cathedral choir is one of the UK's best, and families cram inside to hear it at Christmas when the charismatic Dean indulges his love of theatre. You can also hear the choir sing evensong on Mondays and Thursdays (girls) and Tuesdays, Fridays and Sundays (boys). An all-male choir usually sings morning Eucharist, except on high days and holidays. Joining the choir gives kids a fantastic musical education; phone for audition dates. *Buggy access. Disabled access: lift, ramp, toilet. Nappy-changing facilities. Nearest picnic place: gardens. Restaurant. Shop.*

St Paul's Cathedral

Ludgate Hill, EC4M 8AD (7236 4128/www.stpauls.co.uk). St Paul's tube. **Open** 8.30am-4pm Mon-Sat. *Galleries, crypt & ambulatory* 9.30am-4.15pm Mon-Sat. Closed for special services, sometimes at short notice. *Tours* 10.45am, 11.15am, 1.30pm, 2pm Mon-Sat. **Admission** *Cathedral, crypt & gallery* £11; £3.50 7-16s; £8.50-£10 reductions; free under-7s; £23.50 family (2+2). *Tours* £3; £1 7-16s; £2.50 reductions; free under-7s. Audio guide £4; £3.50 reductions. **Credit** MC, V. **Map** p318 O6. 5+

Despite the high-rise buildings crowding around it, St Paul's remains an iconic feature on the London skyline. It sits on top of Ludgate Hill, the highest point in the City. The world-famous cathedral was thoroughly cleaned for its 300th birthday in 2008, as part of a £40 million restoration project that also included a complete rebuild of the organ and the creation of a new set of ecclesiastical robes by Royal College of Art designer Marie Brisou. The present building is the fourth to sit on the site, and was designed by Sir Christopher Wren after the previous incumbent was burned down in the Great Fire of London. Wren had to campaign vociferously to get it built to his specifications – it was nearly vetoed on several occasions as being too ambitious and expensive.

The audioguide recounts quirky facts about everything from the organ pipes (some big enough to crawl through) to Nelson's corpse (they had a hell of a time getting it back to England for the funeral) to enliven the tour. During Christmas and Easter holidays, there are trails that are rewarded at the end with a small

Sightseeing

prize; parents who need ideas for a self-guided tour can download the activity sheets for schools. The most fun of all is the Whispering Gallery, whose acoustics simply have to be heard to be believed. From there, it's a few more steps up to the Stone Gallery for an amazing 360° view of London. If you're likely to have the energy to ascend still further to the Golden Gallery, go early, or you may find yourself jostled by boisterous teens on the cramped balcony.

Down in the crypt are tombs of historical figures such as Nelson, Wellington and Wren; Lawrence of Arabia and Florence Nightingale are honoured with memorials. At the back is the shop and the Crypt Café. And if you want to experience the true spirit of St Paul's, come for evensong, held every day at 5pm.

Buggy access. Café. Disabled access: lift, ramp, toilet. Nappy-changing facilities. Nearest picnic space: garden. Restaurant. Shops.

Westminster Abbey

20 Dean's Yard, SW1P 3PA (7222 5152/tours 7654 4900/www.westminster-abbey.org). St James's Park or Westminster tube/11, 12, 24, 88, 159, 211 bus. **Open** *Westminster Abbey* June-Sept 9.30am-3.30pm Mon, Tue, Thur, Fri; 9.30am-6pm Wed; 9.30am-3.30pm Sat. Oct-May 9.30am-3.30pm Mon, Tue, Thur, Fri; 9.30am-6pm Wed; 9.30am-1.30pm Sat. *Abbey Museum & Chapter House* 10.30am-4pm daily. *Cloisters* 8am-6pm daily. *College Garden* Apr-Sept 10am-6pm Tue-Thur. Oct-Mar 10am-4pm Tue-Thur (last entry 1hr before closing). *Tours* phone for details. **Admission** £15; £6 11-15s, reductions; free under-11s with adult; £30 family (2+1). *Chapter House* free. *Abbey Museum* free (audio guide free). *Tours* £3. **Credit** AmEx, MC, V. **Map** p317 K9. 5+ Westminster Abbey has always had close links with royalty, not least because it has been the Coronation Church since 1066. The Queen was also married here. The body of Edward the Confessor, who built the first church on the site, is entombed in the abbey, though no one knows exactly where: it was removed from its elaborate shrine and reburied in an unmarked spot during the Reformation. Henry III was responsible for the Gothic splendour of the current building, which was heavily influenced by the French architectural style of the period. Poets' Corner is the final resting place of Geoffrey Chaucer, and you can also see the graves of Dickens, Dryden, Johnson, Browning and Tennyson. Statues of several 20th-century martyrs (including Martin Luther King) occupy 15th-century niches above the west door.

You can escape the crowds in the 900-year-old College Garden, one of the oldest cultivated gardens in Britain. The Abbey Museum (Broad Sanctuary; free if you have a ticket to the Abbey, £1 otherwise) is in the vaulted area under the former monks' dormitory, in one of the oldest parts of the Abbey. Here you'll find a collection of effigies and waxworks of British monarchs such as Edward II and Henry VII, wearing the robes they donned in life; the Queen's Coronation robes are also on show. The Choir School is the only school in Britain exclusively for the education of boy choristers from eight to 13; voice trials are held twice a year. Its Christmas services are magnificent. Next door is St Margaret's Church, where the weddings of Samuel Pepys and Winston Churchill (in 1655 and 1908 respectively) took place; Sir Walter Raleigh is buried here.

Buggy access. Café. Disabled access: toilet. Nearest picnic place: college gardens (10am-6pm Tue-Thur), St James's Park. Shop.

SCIENCE

Centre of the Cell

64 Turner Street, E1 2AB (7882 2562/ www.centreofthecell.org). Whitechapel tube. **Open** *Sessions* 10-11.30am, noon-1.30pm, 2-3.30pm, 4-5.30pm, 6.30-8pm daily. Session times may vary; phone to check. **Admission** free. 9+ The medical centre inside the RIBA award-winning Blizard Building was always supposed to include an educational resource for school-age children. It's a year late in opening (doors should now open in September 2009), but looks to be pretty exciting. A glass-walled walkway takes visitors over the labs and their 400 white-coated occupants to a large multimedia 'pod' (designed to take 40 people), which is where the fun takes place. A film introduces children to the amazing work going on around them, then a huge silver tube opens up to reveal more audio-visual magic and interactive jollies illustrating different aspects of biomedical science for key stages 2, 3 and 4. One game compares the size of a cell to a five-pence piece (a quarter of the size of one of the little dots around the coin edge), another charts the growth of an embryo. Other features show how to repair a damaged spinal cord, or grow real skin for grafts; there are even (oo-er!) real body organs. The pod is intended to be regularly updated in line with the discoveries of the boffins in the labs below.

The whole experience lasts around 90 minutes; thanks to the unique setting and the theatricality of the presentation, young 'uns will be entertained throughout – and hardly aware that they're learning things.

Three Thames tasters

London RIB Voyages.

Speed fiends

London RIB (rigid inflatable boat) Voyages runs thrilling speedboat rides, setting off from London Eye Millennium Pier. Donning waterproofs, lifejackets and science goggle-style visors is fun in itself, and that's before the real adventure starts. Guide Nick (think Russell Brand without idiotic hair: result all round) keeps kids and adults entertained with fun facts and celebrity stories. Once the boat gets past Tower Bridge it really speeds up. The cry goes out: 'Put your hand up if you want us to slow down.' If a small hand shoots up, they steady the boat. The next – 'Hold up a £20 note if you want to go faster' – has imploring young eyes answered with a collective parental 'No'. The boat zigzags excitingly, then turns around by Canary Wharf and speeds back to base.

Book online at londonribvoyages.com or ring 7928 8933. Tickets cost from £32.50 for adults and £19.50 for under-16s.
Perfect for: A unique and thrilling encounter with the Thames – you can't get any closer without going in.
Remember: Wear a jumper and gloves, and another jumper. Take a flask of hot chocolate. Hold on tight!

Tate to Tate

Two art galleries in one day may OD even the most dutiful junior – but a boat trip in the middle could sell the idea. Running every 40 minutes, the boat service connecting London's two Tates, Tate Modern and Tate Britain (*for both, see p66*), takes you through the heart of London, with plenty to see on both banks; there's no commentary, so take a map.

As well as offering tired art-gazers a sit-down, the boat is the quickest way to flit from Tate to Tate – a painful journey any other way. Pick your favourite gallery first, as masterpiece-fatigue kicks in much faster second time around. Both galleries have a lawn outside for a little fresh air before more artistic scrutiny.

The journey costs £5 for adults and £2.50 for children (free under-5s), with a third off for travelcard holders. Call 7887 8888 or visit www.tate.org.uk/tatetotate.
Perfect for: Impecunious art-lovers – both galleries are free, so it's a cheap day out.
Remember: It's only a 20-minute journey, and there's no outdoor deck on the boat.

Slow cruise

From the Palace of Westminster, Thames River Boats sail all the way to Hampton Court Palace. It's a long, leisurely 22-mile journey; 90 minutes to Kew, then another 90 to Hampton Court. That's a long time on a boat, but perfect for a breather from sightseeing. Clued-up skippers take their Thames history seriously, but it's quite grown-up stuff. As you head west, under the bridges and past Battersea Power Station, it's incredible how quickly buildings shrink, the banks get greener and rowers replace river buses. From Kew it's even prettier as you pass through Richmond and Teddington Lock, before disembarking at Hampton Court Pier.

Westminster to Hampton Court one-way is £13.50 for adults, £6.75 for children or £33.75 for a family, with a third off for travelcard holders. Visit www.thamesriver boats.co.uk or ring 7930 4721 for details.
Perfect for: Seeing city and countryside London in one trip, and taking a breather.
Remember: It's a long trip. Younger ones can get antsy, so take plenty of colouring books. Arrival times mean you don't have long at Hampton Court.

Sightseeing

Buggy access. Disabled access: lift; toilet. Café. Nearest picnic place: Whitechapel hospital grounds. Shop.

STATELY HOMES

Chiswick House

Burlington Lane, W4 2RP (8995 0508/ www.chgt.org.uk). Turnham Green tube, then E3 bus/Hammersmith tube, then 190 bus/ Chiswick rail. **Open** *Easter-Oct* 10am-5pm Mon-Wed, Sun. Last entry 30mins before closing. Closed Nov-Mar. *Tours* by arrangement; phone for details. **Admission** *House (EH)* (incl audio guide) £4.40; £3.70 reductions; £2.20 5-16s; free under-5s; £11 family (2+3). *Gardens* free. **Credit** MC, V. 5+

This grand villa was modelled on Palladio's Villa Rotonda at Vicenza, and commissioned by the fifth Duke of Devonshire to sit on the site of an old Jacobean mansion. Illustrious house guests included Alexander Pope and Jonathan Swift; in more recent times, the Beatles filmed the video for *Paperback Writer* in its gardens. The house was built more as a private art gallery than a home, and exhibits aren't especially child-friendly – although eagle-eyed kids could look out for two sculptures of the Green Man and a lead Sphinx.

Ordinarily, a walk through the gardens makes you feel as if you've stepped into a classical landscape painting – there are obelisks among the trees, an exquisitely domed temple, a lake and a cascading waterfall – but extensive work on the grounds is in progress, which interrupts the fantasy somewhat. The usual kitchen garden activities for children and the House Festival have also been cancelled for 2009. The old café has shut, although a temporary kiosk will be serving refreshments near the cricket pavillion next to the Staveley Road entrance until the new one opens in spring 2010. Despite being a work in progress, the garden is still a great place for family picnics.

Buggy access. Disabled access: stairlift, toilet. Nearest picnic place: Chiswick Park. Shop.

Fenton House

3 Hampstead Grove, NW3 6RT (7435 3471/ information 01494 755563/box office 01494 755572/www.nationaltrust.org.uk). Hampstead tube/Hampstead Heath rail. **Open** *Mar* 2-5pm Sat, Sun. *Apr-Oct* 2-5pm Wed-Fri; 11am-4.30pm Sat, Sun, bank hols. *Tours* phone for times. **Admission** (NT) £5.70; £2.80 5-15s; free under-5s; £14.20 family (2+2). **No credit cards.** 5+

This 17th-century house dominated Hampstead when it was still a country village. Today, it's best known for the impressive Benton Fletcher collection of early keyboard instruments (including harpsichords, clavichords, virginals and spinets), which were donated on the condition that professional musicians be allowed to play them; check the website for details of lunchtime and evening concerts.

There is also a collection of paintings and drawings by the Camden Town Group and many fine examples of English and Continental porcelain from George Salting (who donated his amazing Chinese pottery collection to the V&A). Children particularly enjoy the Meissen Harlequins and the 'curious grotesque teapot'. Outside, they can run around the carefully tended vegetable garden, herb garden, lawns and orchard, whose 30 varieties of old English apples can be sampled on Apple Day (celebrated every year on 21 October). Occasional garden trails are available.

Buggy access. Disabled access: ramp. Nappy-changing facilities.

Guildhall

Corner of Gresham Street & Aldermanbury, EC2P 2UJ (7606 3030/tours 7606 3030 ext 1463/www.corpoflondon.gov.uk). St Paul's tube/Bank tube/DLR/Moorgate tube/rail. **Open** *May-Sept* 9.30am-5pm daily. *Oct-Apr* 9.30am-5pm Mon-Sat. Last entry 4.30pm. Closes for functions; phone ahead to check. *Tours* by arrangement; groups of 10 or more only. **Admission** free. **Map** p318 P6. 8+

The Guildhall is one of the few structures in the City built before 1666, having survived the Great Fire of London. Now it's the seat of local government: the Court of Common Council meets at 1pm on selected Thursdays each month in the vast, 15th-century Great Hall (visitors are welcome; phone for dates). The Hall is also open when it's not being used for official business. The impressive space has a vaulted ceiling, marble monuments, and banners and shields of 100 livery companies on the walls; every Lord Mayor since 1189 is named on the windows. Two large wooden statues of Gog and Magog, carved in 1953 to replace the pair destroyed in the Blitz, stand in the West Gallery. They represent the mythical conflict between Britons and Trojan invaders; the result of this struggle was the founding of Albion's capital city, New Troy, on whose site London is said to stand. On the north wall hangs a fascinating list of trials and grisly executions.

You can only nose round the Guildhall's enormous medieval crypt on a pre-booked group tour; tours last half an hour and are free.

Covent Garden

For three centuries, Covent Garden was famous for its fresh produce and flower market. Now Londoners have to travel to Vauxhall for the pleasure. The move was made in 1973, when unfashionable historic buildings were being knocked down in their droves to make way for new planning. Developers wanted to clear the area for hotels and conference centres, but the locals campaigned, and Covent Garden became a des res shopping centre instead. Like nearby Leicester Square, Covent Garden is generally overrun with tourists, but it is worth a trip.

The name Covent Garden is most likely drawn from the 'convent garden' that once surrounded the historic abbey of St Peter. The land that belonged to the Convent of St Peter at West Minster was handed over by the Crown to John Russell, the first Earl of Bedford, following Henry VIII's dissolution of the monasteries. In the 1630s, the Earl commissioned master architect Inigo Jones to design a series of Palladian arcades. These wonderfully elegant, stately terraces, opening on to a central courtyard, constituted the first public square in the country and proved popular with wealthy tenants, until the fruit and vegetable market expanded on to their exclusive patch.

Going underground

Weekdays in term time are best for exploring this area. Head straight down James Street from the tube exit, cut through the market, and start off at one of London's most fun museums: the **London Transport Museum** (see p84). Inside, children tend to steam past the historic timeline that puts London's travel achievements in context with other major cities, straight on to the interactive rooms. For the under-sixes, the All Aboard! Gallery has climb-on model vehicles and soft play. For older children (seven to 11s), there are train carriages and buses to explore (from the horse-drawn Shillibeer's model to a sliced-through modern bus), tricky computerised driving games, costumes to try on, mystery objects to guess at and – the ultimate excitement – the possibility of driving a bus. There's also a fantastic shop with imaginative themed gifts.

If all that travelling has made you rather peckish, nip upstairs to the friendly Upper Deck café (see p235), overlooking Covent Garden Piazza. In addition to the Upper Deck, the Museum also has a modest picnic area where visitors can eat their packed lunches.

The Piazza and beyond

Designed by architect Charles Fowler, the **covered central market** (7836 9136, www.coventgardenmarket.co.uk) is a mix of cool and quirky shops (toy shop Eric Snook, antiques seller Nauticalia) and upmarket chains (Culpeper, Monsoon and the like). The Apple Market in the North Hall is where you'll find antique stalls on Mondays, a general market Tuesday to Friday and hand-made crafts at weekends. Jubilee Hall Market is a bit tackier, flogging novelty T-shirts and other tat.

Outside in the Piazza, usually in front of the portico of St Paul's Church, comedians, musicians and living statues perform for the amusement of tourists and families. It was under this portico that Samuel Pepys observed what is thought to have been Britain's first Punch and Judy show ('an Italian puppet play', as he described it) on 9 May 1662; fittingly, the **Punch & Judy Festival** (see p22) is held here on the first Sunday in October. You can also catch Punch and Judy's slapstick at the annual May Fair in St Paul's churchyard.

Every summer there are open-air operatics courtesy of the **Royal Opera House** (see p173). The ROH itself is a beautiful space, and has an upstairs café with wonderful views over the Piazza. Guided tours give the curious a glimpse into working dressing rooms and rehearsal studios; if you have enough time to take in a performance, there are free lunchtime recitals on Mondays.

Out of the market, head towards the river and down to the Strand. In the 14th century, this was a swanky residential street that stood right on the riverbank. Gradually, the overflow of hoi polloi from Covent Garden threatened to overwhelm the narrow strip; by 1600 the wealthy folk had run away, and the Strand had a reputation for poverty and bawdiness.

Sir Christopher Wren suggested the creation of a reclaimed embankment to ease congestion and house the main sewer, and by the mid-19th century the area's respectability was restored. At the Strand's

LUNCH BOX

Also in the area: Pizza Express, Strada, Wagamama.

Café Pasta *2-4 Garrick Street, WC2E 9BH (7497 2779/www.cafepasta. co.uk).* Straightforward pasta, pizza and grills are rustled up at this Italian mini-chain.

Christopher's *18 Wellington Street, WC2E 7DD (7240 4222/www. christophersgrill.com).* A smart, upmarket restaurant with American cuisine and hearty brunches.

Upper Deck Café *London Transport Museum, WC2E 7BB (7379 6344/ www.ltmuseum.co.uk).* Enjoyable museum café. *See p235.*

Wahaca *66 Chandos Place, WC2N 4HG (7240 1883/www.wahaca.co.uk).* Delicious Mexican street food at affordable prices. *See p247.*

World Food Café *1st Floor, 14 Neal's Yard, WC2H 9DP. (7379 0298/www. worldfoodcafenealsyard.co.uk).* Homespun, tasty vegetarian platters.

eastern end is the Aldwych, a grand crescent that dates to 1905 – although the name, 'ald wic' (old settlement), has its origins in the 14th century. On its south side stands the imposing bulk of **Somerset House** (see p65).

Guildhall. *See p45.*

In the absence of an on-site café, packed lunches can be scoffed in the cloakroom area, which is equipped with a water cooler.
Buggy access. Disabled access: lift, ramp, toilet. Nappy-changing facilities. Nearest picnic place: grassy area by London Wall. Shop.

Ham House

Ham Street, Ham, Richmond, Surrey TW10 7RS (8940 1950/www.nationaltrust.org.uk). Richmond tube/rail, then 371 bus. **Open** *House* Mid Feb noon-4pm Mon-Wed, Sat, Sun. Early Mar noon-4pm Sat, Sun. Mid Mar-Oct noon-4pm Mon-Wed, Sat, Sun. *Gardens* Early Feb, Late Dec 11am-4pm Mon-Wed, Sat, Sun. Mid Feb-Dec 11am-5pm Mon-Wed, Sat, Sun. Closed 1 Jan, 25, 26 Dec. *Tours* Wed (pre-booking essential); phone for details. **Admission** (NT) *House & gardens* £9.90; £5.50 5-15s; free under-5s; £23.30 family (2+2). *Gardens only* £3.30; £2.20 5-15s; free under-5s; £8.80 family (2+2). **Credit** AmEx, MC, V.
5+ (house). All ages (gardens)
This is a Sleeping Beauty of a house, with very little changed since it was built and furnished in the 17th century by William Murray (whipping boy to James I) and his descendants. It sits on the river in gorgeous landscaped grounds, which include the Cherry Garden, with its central statue of Bacchus and lavender parterres, and the maze-like Wilderness, as well as the oldest thorn bush and orangery in the country. Many of the original interiors have been lavishly restored, offering a rare chance to see the bold colour schemes of the day – strong, contrasting colours in damask, velvet and satin. Television drama *Elizabeth* was filmed here, and there are extensive collections of period furniture, art and textiles.

Children tend to get more excited by Ham House's reputation as one of the most haunted buildings in Britain: ghostly visitors are said to include William's daughter, the Duchess of Lauderdale, and her pet dog. Regular family events include entertaining Ghost Tours, which are suitable for over-fives; a torch-lit adult version is also available.

Open-air theatre takes place in the garden in summer, and there are egg trails for Easter, art and craft days for the August bank holiday weekend, more spooky tours for Hallowe'en and all manner of carols, feasts and craft events for Christmas. A ferry crosses the river to Marble Hill House (*see below*) at weekends year round, and daily during the summer.
Café. Disabled access: lift, toilet. Nappy-changing facilities. Shop.

Marble Hill House

Richmond Road, Middx TW1 2NL (8892 5115/www.english-heritage.org.uk). Richmond tube/rail/33, 90, 290, H22, R70 bus. **Open** *Apr-Oct* 10am-2pm Sat; 10am-5pm Sun. Closed Nov-Mar. **Admission** (EH) £4.40;

£3.70 reductions; £2.20 5-15s; free under-5s; £11 family (2+2). Price includes tour. **Credit** MC, V. 5+

A superb Palladian villa, Marble Hill House was constructed in the 1720s for Henrietta Howard, mistress to King George II when he was Prince of Wales. In those days Twickenham was a country retreat, fashionable for weekend salons. The mansion is packed to the brim with Georgian antiques and paintings, but the star of the decorative show is the Honduran mahogany staircase, whose construction nearly sparked a war with Spain. Marble Hill House hosts special events throughout the year, including Easter trails and open-air concerts; guided tours can be taken of the house and its surrounding parkland, and there's a ferry across the Thames to Ham House (*see left*).
Café. Nearest picnic place: Marble Hill Park. Shop.

19 Princelet Street

19 Princelet Street, E1 6QH (7247 5352/ www.19princeletstreet.org.uk). Aldgate East tube/Liverpool Street tube/rail. **Open** check website or phone for occasional open days. *Tours* groups by appointment. **Admission** free; donations appreciated. **Map** p319 S5. 3+

For decades, this house was in danger of collapsing, but now it's Grade II listed and the home of Europe's only museum devoted to immigration and cultural diversity. Extensive restorations are planned, although until the £3 million funding is raised, it's quite difficult to visit the house because of its fragility. Still it's worth making an effort to experience the haunting atmosphere, rickety staircase and fascinating stories of its past inhabitants.

The house was first home to exiled Huguenot silk weavers (you can still see a big bobbin hanging above the door), then to Irish dockers. In 1869, Polish Jews converted it into an Ashkenazi synagogue; in the 20th century, it hosted English lessons for Bangladeshi women. It's also the site where Jewish scholar David Rodinsky simply disappeared one day (Iain Sinclair and Rachel Lichtenstein wrote *Rodinsky's Room* based on the story).
Buggy access. Nearest picnic place: Christ Church grounds.

Osterley Park & House

Osterley Park, off Jersey Road, Isleworth, Middx TW7 4RB (8232 5050/www.national trust.org.uk). Osterley tube. **Open** *House* Mar-Nov 1-4.30pm Wed-Sun. Nov-Dec 12.30-3.30pm Sat, Sun. *Gardens* Mar-Nov 11am-5pm Wed-Sun. *Park* Feb, Mar, Nov-Jan 8am-6pm daily. Apr-Oct 8am-7.30pm daily. *Tours* by arrangement; minimum 15 people. **Admission** (NT) *House & garden* £8.40; £4.20 5-18s; free under-5s; £21 family (2+3). *Garden only* £3.70; £1.85 5-18s; free under-5s. *Park* free. **Credit** MC, V. 3+

In the 18th century this Tudor mansion became a no-expense-spared country retreat for the family of self-made banking magnate Sir Francis Child, remodelled at their behest by architect Robert Adam. Its setting is decidedly more suburban these days, but Mrs Child's flower garden is still delightful, and the rest of the grounds are currently being restored to their former glory.

The house was largely unchanged by Childs' descendants before being donated to the National Trust in 1949, and the splendour of the state rooms alone makes the house worth a visit. Children will enjoy exploring the 'below stairs' areas and discovering what life was like as a servant, before visiting the horses in the Tudor stables; there's also a resident spectre, said to lurk in the basement. Regular events include tours of the house, bluebell walks, outdoor performances and the annual (free) Osterley Day, full of arts and fun.

Buggy access (not when busy). Café. Disabled access: stair climber, toilet. Nappy-changing facilities. Nearest picnic place: front lawn, picnic benches in grounds. Shop.

PM Gallery & House

Walpole Park, Mattock Lane, W5 5EQ (8567 1227/www.ealing.gov.uk). Ealing Broadway tube/rail/65 bus. **Open** *May-Sept* 1-5pm Tue-Fri, Sun; 11am-5pm Sat. *Oct-Apr* 1-5pm Tue-Fri; 11am-5pm Sat. Closed bank hols. *Tours* by arrangement; phone for details. **Admission** free. Audio guide £1. **Credit** AmEx, MC, V. 5+

Anyone who has visited Sir John Soane's Museum in Lincoln's Inn Fields (*see p80*) will know about the architect's wonderfully eccentric use of light and space. Soane built Pitzhanger Manor (pitshanger means 'wooded slope frequented by kites') as his weekend country retreat, and it is now, along with the PM Gallery, Ealing's flagship cultural centre.

Among the exhibits is the Hull Grundy Martinware pottery collection, and there's a workshop programme for all ages; special events for kids include half-term craft sessions and 'clay play'. Soane's ornamental gardens are now known as Walpole Park, Ealing Borough's rose-scented pride and joy, which hosts jazz and comedy in summer.

Buggy access. Disabled access: lift, ramp, toilet. Nappy-changing facilities. Nearest picnic place: Walpole Park.

Syon House

Syon Park, Brentford, Middx TW8 8JF (8560 0881/Tropical Forest 8847 4730/Snakes & Ladders 8847 0946/www.syonpark.co.uk). Gunnersbury tube/rail, then 237, 267 bus/ Kew Bridge rail. **Open** House mid Mar-late Oct 11am-5pm Wed, Thur, Sun, bank hol Mon (last entry 4pm). *Gardens* Mar-Oct 10.30am-5pm daily. Nov-Feb 10.30am-4pm daily. *Tours* by arrangement; phone for details. *Snakes & Ladders* 10am-6pm daily (last entry 5.15pm). **Admission** *House & gardens* £9; £8 reductions; £4 5-16s; free under-5s; £20 family (2+2). *Gardens only* £4.50; £3.50 5-16s; free under-4s; £10 family (2+2). *Tropical Forest* £5.50; £4.50 3-15s; free under-3s; £18 family (2+3). *Snakes & Ladders* £3.90 under-2s; £4.90 under-5s; £5.90 over-5s; free over-16s. Reduced rate after 4pm. **Credit** MC, V. 5+

Looking out across the Thames to Kew, this turreted Tudor mansion has been the seat of the Duke of Northumberland for over 600 years. It was built on the site of a medieval abbey that was brutally dissolved by Henry VIII, and it was here that Henry's fifth wife Catherine Howard awaited her execution. Henry's coffin was later brought here in transit to Windsor Castle; as if by divine retribution, it mysteriously burst open during the night and the king's remains were found being licked by dogs. It was here, too, that the doomed Lady Jane Grey reluctantly accepted the crown and became queen for nine days. In short, it's bursting with history.

The rooms, designed by Robert Adam, are positively breathtaking (John Betjeman described Syon as 'the grand architectural walk'), from the grand Roman hallway in black and white marble to the Red Drawing Room, with its crimson silk walls and Roman statues. Its magnificently-preserved grandeur has made it a popular filming location: *The Madness of King George* was filmed here, as were scenes from *Gosford Park*.

Outside, children will love the restored 19th-century Great Conservatory, with its huge iron and glass dome – and if the extensive Capability Brown-landscaped gardens aren't enough for a run around, there's also indoor adventure playground Snakes & Ladders (an extra charge applies). Then there's the London Tropical Zoo enclosure, full of endangered animals that live in or near water, such as piranhas, snakes, crocs and poison tree frogs.

A programme of family-friendly events includes demonstrations, re-enactments and after-dark walks in winter, when the woods are illuminated with dazzling light displays (check the website for details). In summer, movies are screened in the gardens; bring a picnic to consume on the lawns before the film begins. *Café. Nappy-changing facilities. Nearest picnic place: Syon House Gardens, Syon Park. Shop.*

Legoland.

THRILLS & CHILLS

Chessington World of Adventures

Leatherhead Road, Chessington, Surrey KT9 2NE (0870 444 7777/www.chessington.com). **Getting there** *By rail* Chessington South rail, then 71 bus or 10-min walk. *By car* J9 off M25. **Open** Check website for timetables. **Admission** (online advance price) £23; £16 3-15s; annual pass £68; £50 3-15s. Free under 1m tall. Check website for on-the-day prices & other annual passes. **Credit** AmEx, MC, V. All ages

Chessington has two things to offer: animals and rides. The zoo has gorillas, tigers, lions and leopards as well as smaller animals; keep an eye out for its latest residents, the pygmy marmoset monkeys. It has also taken a leaf out of London Zoo's book and introduced child-friendly animal antics presentations (2pm & 4pm). At the new Sea Life aquarium, a walk-through ocean tank offers a chance to get close to the sharks, while the Amazonian display includes piranhas.

Many of the adventure rides are geared towards families with young children, unlike the more extreme offerings at nearby stablemate Thorpe Park (*see p55*). There's lovable Beanoland with dodgems and foam ball firing, a large soft play area for younger tots, plus an extreme games area and more challenging white-knuckle rides for older kids, like the Vampire rollercoaster and Rameses Revenge water plunge. Guides dressed up as fun characters help families on their way around. *Buggy access. Café. Car park (free). Disabled access: toilet. Nappy-changing facilities. Restaurant. Shops.*

Chislehurst Caves

Old Hill, Chislehurst, Kent BR7 5NB (8467 3264/www.chislehurstcaves.co.uk). **Getting there** *By rail* Chislehurst rail. **Open** 9am-5pm Wed-Sun. *Tours* phone for details. **Admission** £5; £3 5-15s, reductions; free under-5s. **Credit** MC, V. 8+

Twenty miles of caves sit beneath Chislehurst, carved out of the chalk by Druids, Saxons and Romans. Since then, the caves have been turned to all sorts of purposes, including an ammunition dump in World War I and a mushroom farm; during World War II, they acted as Britain's largest bomb shelter. Most of the underground scenes in the TV series *Merlin* were filmed here. The 45-minute lamplit tour covers about a mile of the tunnels; children will enjoy locating the Druid Altar, the Caves Church and the Haunted Pool. *Restaurant. Shop.*

Legoland

Winkfield Road, Windsor, Berks SL4 4AY (0870 504 0404/www.legoland.co.uk). **Getting there** *By rail* Windsor & Eton Riverside or

Windsor Central rail, then shuttlebus. *By car* J3 off M3 or J6 off M4. **Open** *Mid Mar-early Nov* times may vary, check website for timetables. **Admission** *One-day ticket* £36; £27 3015s, reductions. *Two-day ticket* £71; £53 3-15s; free under-3s. Shuttlebus £3.50; £2 3-15s, reductions. Free under-3s. **Credit** AmEx, MC, V. All ages

What immediately strikes first-time visitors to this shrine to the famous brick is the sheer size of the car park; once you're in, it's the impressive view of the park, which cascades, ride after ride, down a steep hill with Berkshire's rolling countryside in the distance. Legoland remains an incredibly popular family day out – though while it's suitable for all ages, even hard-to-please early teens, adults may occasionally struggle to see the appeal. That's largely because of the queues, which can be particularly testing for toddlers' tempers. The best advice is to come early and make a beeline for the rear of the site first, thus avoiding the worst waits.

Queues aside, there are some brilliant rides. Driving School puts six to 13s behind the wheel of whizzy electric cars, amid roundabouts, traffic lights and much confusion; there's also a scaled-down version for tots. Other star turns include the park's biggest and wettest ride, Vikings' River Splash, the twisting Dragon rollercoaster, Miniland's scaled-down London landmarks and the Imagination Theatre – with a brand-new *Bob the Builder* 4D show that holds unruly toddlers spellbound.

There's plenty to see while you wander from queue to queue, but those with preschool children should seize the chance to go in term time. It's also a good idea to take activities to keep the kids amused while they're waiting, and to draw up a hit list of the rides your children particularly want to try: call the day before to check your chosen attractions will be running. *Buggy access. Cafés. Disabled access: toilet. Nappy-changing facilities. Nearest picnic place: grounds. Restaurants. Shops.*

London Bridge Experience

2-4 Tooley Street, SE1 2SY (0800 043 4666/ www.londonbridgeexperience.com). London Bridge tube/rail. **Open** 11am-5pm Mon-Fri; 10am-6pm Sat, Sun. **Admission** £21.95; £17.95 reductions; £16.95 under-16s; free under-5s; £64.95 family (2+2). **Credit** MC, V. All ages (Bridge Experience). 11+ (London Tombs)

The experience is a split-level one. The first part is a fun-for-all-the-family history lesson that engages all five senses and serves the choicest cuts from the crossing's 2,000-year history. The second takes you underground to the 'London Tombs', and frightens the pants off you. We like the first bit best, where actors appear at every turn: in a cobwebbed replica of a Victorian study, we meet the ghostly portrait of Sir John Rennie, who designed the 1831 bridge, and whose ravings are translated by a dusty butler; through heavy doors and along dank passages we're shown Boudicca's sacking of London, narrated by a bloodied Roman soldier amid disembowelled corpses. Next up is the Russell Crowe-like viking, who asks his guests to help pull down the bridge's wooden piers. After that, we're introduced to William Wallace's ghost, and taken into a chamber of gore run by the chap in charge of heads on sticks, once proudly displayed on London Bridge. Each period involves interaction with the key players, who also include a garrulous lighterman's widow, the American who bought the bridge in 1970 (it's a myth that he thought he was buying Tower Bridge, he insists), and the Queen. It's all quite kitsch and entertaining; the shocks and horrors come downstairs in the dark and threatening Tombs, where zombie actors show little mercy. *Buggy access. Café. Disabled access: lift; toilet. Nearest picnic place: South Bank. Shop.*

London Dungeon

28-34 Tooley Street, SE1 2SZ (7403 7221/ www.thedungeons.com). London Bridge tube/ rail. **Open** times vary, phone or check website for details. **Admission** £21.95; £19.95 reductions; £15.95 5-14s; £2 reduction for registered disabled; free carers, under-5s. **Credit** AmEx, MC, V. **Map** p319 Q8. 10+

In thrillingly dark and smelly surrounds, the London Dungeon leads its visitors through the more gruesome episodes of London's history. Costumed actors bring the city's characters and disasters to life, often pretending to be one of the waxwork models and frightening kids into delighted squeals by suddenly moving. There's a gruesome section devoted to Jack the Ripper, and another for demonic 18th-century barber Sweeney Todd; new for 2009, Surgery – Blood and Guts is a reconstruction of the operating room of Tooley Street's butcher surgeon.

Guaranteed to provoke even more high-pitched exclamation is 'Labyrinth of the Lost', the largest horror mirror maze in the world. If that's not enough depravity for you, there's the Traitor Boat Ride to Hell (visitors play the part of condemned prisoners, death sentence guaranteed), and Extremis: Drop Ride to Doom, which aims, charmingly, to recreate at least part of the experience of being hanged.

The Dungeon is clearly on to a winner, judging from the length of the weekend queues outside the Victorian railway arches that are its home.

5 HUGE FLOORS OF FUN!
WEIRD, WACKY & WONDERFUL!

NEW FOR 2009 THE WORLD'S SMALLEST CAR!

The p-50 holds the record for being the smallest road-legal car ever produced and you can now see it at Ripley's!

Ripley's
Believe It or Not!®

Welcome to the world of Ripley's Believe It or Not! London's Biggest New Attraction Situated in the heart of the West End at 1 Piccadilly Circus, the attraction houses over 800 authentic, original and unbelievable exhibits spread over 5 floors, from a four-metre long model of Tower Bridge made out of matchsticks and an upside-down tea party to the world's tallest man and a Mini Cooper encrusted with 1,000,000 Swarovski crystals. Ripley's Believe It or Not! presents a unique mixture of entertainment, education and fun for the entire family - appealing to anyone with a basic sense of curiosity.

YOU WON'T BELIEVE YOUR EYES!
OPEN UNTIL MIDNIGHT EVERYDAY!

RIPLEYSLONDON.COM | 1 PICCADILLY CIRCUS | LONDON W1J 0DA | 020 3238 0022

London Dungeon. See p52.

There are always plenty of small children standing in line, where gorily made-up Dungeon staff work the crowds, but we'd advise against taking anyone younger than ten – our eleven-year-old tester came out rather whey-faced, but said he loved it. Tours last around 90 minutes; you can purchase fast-track tickets on the website to beat the queues.

Buggy access. Disabled access: toilet. Nappy-changing facilities. Nearest picnic place: Hay's Galleria. Shop.

Madame Tussauds

Marylebone Road, NW1 5LR (0870 400 3000/www.madame-tussauds.co.uk). Baker Street tube/13, 27, 74, 113, 159 bus. **Open** 9am-6pm daily (last entry 5.30pm). Times vary during holiday periods. **Admission** £25; £21 4-15s; free under-4s. £85 family (2+2 or 1+3). **Credit** AmEx, MC, V. **Map** p314 G4. **3+**
We're still not entirely sure why this is quite so popular with tourists, especially at these prices. But if one of your children wants a picture of themselves with their arm around cricket legend Sachin Tendulkar (new in April 2009), this is probably the surest means of getting it. Adults may find it hard to escape the fact that they're among a bunch of static waxwork models – although Madame Tussauds works hard to ramp up the excitement. As you enter the first room, you're dazzled by paparazzi flashbulbs; starry-eyed kids can then take part in a 'Divas' routine with Amy Winehouse and Justin Timberlake. Robbie Williams, meanwhile, has a kiss sensor that activates a twinkle in his eye. New figures are constantly added and old favourites updated: Kylie Minogue and the Queen have been recast no less than four times. There's a *Pirates of the Caribbean* diorama in the hull of the Black Pearl, staffed by Keira, Orlando and Johnny; the World Stage hall is an interactive room split into zones for sports, culture, politics, popular music, royals and history. Holographs and touch screens add pizzazz. Nobody prevents visitors hugging the stars (or pinching their bottoms, if so inclined).

Elsewhere, the kitsch Spirit of London ride takes you through 400 years of London life in a taxi pod. Children love this, and always want to ride again to spot the historic figures around them. Below stairs lurks Scream – the Chamber of Horrors, which isn't child-friendly at all. It surrounds you with corpses and eviscerated victims of torture, with a truly terrifying 'live' experience (actors dressed up as psycho killers jump out and stalk you; unsurprisingly, it's over-12s only). Such morbid thrills chime with the work of Marie Tussaud (1761-1850), who made death masks out of wax in the French Revolution. Her cast of the mask of Marie-Jeanne du Barry, Louis XV's mistress, is the oldest work on display: it's now used as the peaceful face of the reclining, animatronic *Sleeping Beauty. See also p138* **Great Days Out.**

Café. Disabled access: lift, toilet. Nappy-changing facilities. Nearest picnic place: Regent's Park. Shop.

Ripley's Believe It or Not

1 Piccadilly Circus, London, W1J 0DA (0203 238 0022/www.ripleyslondon.com). Piccadilly Circus tube. **Open** 10am-10.30pm daily. **Admission** £19.95; £17.95 reductions; £15.95 4-15s; free under 4s. £65 family (2+2). **Credit** MC, V. All ages

Robert LeRoy Ripley opened his first odditorium in Chicago, in 1930. He's long gone, but the 31 museums that bear his name march weirdly (some say wonderfully) on. The five-floor London one, ominously located in a high-rental part of town where many tourist attractions have come and gone, has attracted mixed reviews. There are plenty of oddities to make your eyes pop; we particularly enjoyed the two-way gurning mirror, which has unsuspecting visitors trying out seemingly impossible facial contortions, unaware they're being watched by everyone else. The matchstick Tower Bridge fascinates children, as do the freakshow exhibits, like two-headed calves and shrunken skulls.

A more dizzying delight is the Topsy Turvy Tunnel, which is like a bridge through a kaleidoscope that has you staggering drunkenly about while attempting to cross it. It's near the Mirror Maze, which engendered mutiny in the ranks when we learned you had to pay £3.95 extra to get lost in it. The admission price is high enough, without hidden extras. After all, there are all sorts of free museums in town where you can see some pretty freaky stuff – pickled tumours in the Hunterian (*see p88*), anyone? Still, Ripley would no doubt say you have to go past a load of boring stuff in a regular museum before meeting things that make you say 'I don't believe it!' every time, which is what we said when we saw Leonardo da Vinci's *Last Supper* painted on a grain of rice. You'd better believe it.

Thorpe Park

Staines Road, Chertsey, Surrey KT16 8PN (0870 444 4466/www.thorpepark.com). **Getting there** *By rail* Staines rail, then 950 shuttlebus. *By car* J11 or J13 off M25. **Open** times vary, check website for timetables. Height restrictions vary, depending on rides. **Admission** £35; £21 under-12s; free under-1m tall. £92 family (2+2); £115 (2+3). Check the website or phone for advance bookings; allow 24hrs for processing. **Credit** MC, V. 5+

If it took all the strength you had to face up to the horrifyingly fast Stealth (standstill to 80mph in two seconds, plus a hideous vertical drop), you may be defeated by the latest white-

knuckler, Saw. It's quite shockingly awful, but you're a wuss if you don't give it a go: this is, after all, Europe's most extreme G-Force experience. Unless you make a beeline for Saw on entering the park at 10am, be prepared to queue for up to two hours to experience the dark, blood-stained slasher movie build-up, the initial drops in pitch blackness, the climb to the top of the mountainous loop that has you looking at the sky dry-mouthed while you wait for the vertical downward rush. The track is concave (they call it 'beyond vertical'), the screams are in earnest and the eyes are best kept tight shut; unsurprisingly, it's not recommended for under-12s (you have to be over 1.4m tall too).

Our favourite ride on a hot day is the exhilarating Tidal Wave, which hits the water at such speed that wet pants are inevitable. It's a perfect place for adolescents to wander free, bonding good-naturedly in the long, long queues (coming in wet weather and on school days is one way to avoid them).

The staff, for the most part, are young and extremely friendly, so the atmosphere in the park is pleasant. Parents with young, or short children – the scary rides require you to be 1.4m tall – will find plenty to do at Neptune's Beach (a big paddling and sunbathing spot), Octopus Garden (little, friendly rides) and the delightful Mr Monkey's Banana Ride, with its slightly sinister commentary. The family can get together again for a soaking in the Rumba Rapids, another favourite of ours. Perhaps we're just wet.

Buggy access. Café. Disabled access: toilet. Nappy-changing facilities. Restaurants. Shops.

Trocadero

Coventry Street, W1D 7DH (7439 1791/ www.londontrocadero.com). Piccadilly Circus tube. **Open** 10am-midnight Mon-Thur, Sun; 10am-1am Fri, Sat. **Admission** free; individual attractions vary. **Credit** varies. **Map** p317 K7. 5+

Most Londoners avoid this part of town, particularly in summer. At its heart, this pulsating indoor complex houses a vast arcade of coin-in-the-slot video games, simulator rides and dance machines. The noise and disorientating lights are a fast track to tantrums and headaches – and still they come to spend all their pocket money. There's a seven-screen cinema, a dodgem track, a ten-lane bowling alley and various fast-food outlets. The sports bar is grown-ups only.

Buggy access. Cafés. Disabled access: lift, toilet. Nappy-changing facilities. Nearest picnic place: Leicester Square, Trafalgar Square. Restaurants. Shops.

Sightseeing

Museums & Galleries

Fill budding minds with fascination.

It was 1759 when the **British Museum** (*see p73*) first opened its doors to the public. That's 250 years ago. Just pause to think about that. And although the British Museum holds an infinitely vast and varied collection of wonderful artefacts, it's just one tiny corner of London's jaw-dropping historical and cultural tableaux. A child can learn more from one well-structured day at a museum or gallery than they could during hours of lessons in the classroom, so take your pick and encourage them to learn on family excursions.

Most of the capital's museums and galleries put considerable effort into making their exhibits accessible to children. The **Science Museum** (*see p92*) and **Natural History Museum** (*see p87*) are perhaps the leaders in interactive exhibits, but if you're organised and check ahead, you'll find all kinds of imaginative activities and workshops going on at venues listed in this chapter that will make a big impression on small minds. We've done our best to alert you to the possibilities in each individual review.

Children with particular interests are also incredibly well served. From the **Charles Dickens Museum** (*see p76*), the **Fashion & Textile Museum** (*see p57*) and Wimbledon's **Lawn Tennis Museum** (*see p98*) to the **Imperial War Museum** (*see p102*), there's something for absolutely everyone. To get the most out of your day, leave plenty of time for looking round, plan your refreshment stops and, most of all, set off early to avoid the crowds, especially during school holidays.

ART & DESIGN

Camden Arts Centre

Corner of Arkwright Road & Finchley Road, NW3 6DG (7472 5500/www.camdenartscentre. org). Finchley Road tube/Finchley Road & Frognal rail. **Open** 10am-6pm Tue, Thur-Sun; 10am-9pm Wed. **Admission** free. **Credit** MC, V. 7+ (parental advisory)
The three galleries at this stylish contemporary arts centre host exhibitions, and there's a state-of-the-art ceramics studio. Half terms bring four-day courses in clay or mixed media for five to sevens and eight to 11s (£148; £100 reductions). The café is a gem, with its lavender-planted terrace, chunky granary sandwiches and frothy babycinos.
Buggy access. Café. Disabled access: lift, toilet. Nappy-changing facilities. Nearest picnic place: gallery garden. Shop.

Design Museum

Shad Thames, SE1 2YD (0870 833 9955/ 7403 6933/www.designmuseum.org). Tower Hill tube/London Bridge tube/rail/47, 100, 188 bus. **Open** 10am-5.45pm daily. **Admission** £8.50; £6.50 reductions; free under-12s. **Credit** AmEx, MC, V. **Map** p319 S9. 5+
Inspiring design of all kinds is showcased in this sleekly converted Thameside warehouse. It's a surprisingly child-friendly sort of place: young visitors are given a Family Trail worksheet to doodle on, while acclaimed Get Creative! sessions run on the first and last Sunday of the month. Here, creative five- to 11-year-olds can dabble in arty activities: the monthly-changing themes range from modern millinery to furniture design and architecture. The cost is £4 per child, though participants must be accompanied by a paying adult (£8.50); fees also cover admission to the museum's current crop of exhibitions.
Buggy access. Café. Disabled access: lift, toilet. Nappy-changing facilities. Nearest picnic place: Butler's Wharf riverside benches. Shop.

Dulwich Picture Gallery

Gallery Road, SE21 7AD (8693 5254/www. dulwichpicturegallery.org.uk). North Dulwich or West Dulwich rail. **Open** 10am-5pm Tue-Fri;

Make your own masterpiece at **Dulwich Picture Gallery**.

11am-5pm Sat, Sun, bank hol Mon. **Admission** £5; free-£4 reductions; free under-18s. **Credit** MC, V. 6+

Founded in 1811, and housed in bijou premises built by the eccentric, energetic Sir John Soane, this tiny gallery punches well above its weight. Its outstanding collection of 17th- and 18th-century Old Masters includes the likes of Rembrandt, Tiepolo, Rubens, Van Dyck and Gainsborough, while temporary exhibitions romp across the centuries (in 2008, an exhibition of pieces by a Lambeth youth group won rave reviews). Thursday nights bring six-week art courses, devoted to different media (silk screen printing, paper cut-outs) for 11 to 14s, while Tuesday's Evening Art School gives 15 to 18s the chance to develop their portfolios; prices range from £65 and £70. Seven- to ten-year olds can attend half-day Saturday sessions, costing £15, or enrol on quirkily themed courses.

Holidays bring yet more activities, with topics such as Creepy Creatures and Life in a Box; Art in the Garden gatherings are on Wednesdays in the summer hols and cost £2 per child. Artplay afternoons, held on the first and last Sunday of the month from April to October, invite parents and over-fours to partake in artist-led activities, from making sock puppets to designing African masks (£2; free with gallery ticket). Check online for details and fees of all courses and classes; booking is generally essential.

Buggy access. Café. Disabled access: toilet. Nappy-changing facilities. Nearest picnic place: gallery gardens. Shop.

Fashion & Textile Museum

83 Bermondsey Street, SE1 3XF (7407 8664/ www.ftmlondon.org). London Bridge tube/rail. **Open** 11am-6pm Wed-Sun (last entry 5.15pm). **Admission** *Museum* free. *Temporary exhibitions* £5-£7; £3-£4 reductions; free under-12s. **Credit** MC, V. 8+

There's no missing the Fashion & Textile Museum, whose bright orange premises (with flashes of take-no-prisoners pink and electric blue) were designed by Mexican architect Ricardo Legorreta. Founded by flamboyant British fashion designer Zandra Rhodes and now run by Newham College, it showcases fashion, textiles and jewellery, with temporary exhibitions to supplement the permanent collection. Inexpensive, inspiring children's workshops run in half term and the summer holidays, often led by industry professionals; perfect for fledgling fashion mavens.

Buggy access. Café. Disabled access: lift, toilet. Nearest picnic place: Bermondsey Square.

Geffrye Museum

136 Kingsland Road, E2 8EA (7739 9893/ www.geffrye-museum.org.uk). Liverpool Street tube/rail, then 149, 242 bus/Old Street tube/

rail, then 243 bus. **Open** 10am-5pm Tue-Sat; noon-5pm Sun, bank hol Mon. **Admission** free; donations appreciated. *Almshouse £2; £1 reductions; free under-16s.* **Credit** MC, V. 5+
Walking through the Geffrye Museum is like entering an odd series of timewarps. Set in attractive 18th-century almshouses, its rooms recreate interiors from different historical periods, from the Elizabethan era to the present day. Visitors walk past in a roped-off corridor, admiring – or deploring – the tastes and styles of past generations. On the first Saturday of the month, there are free quizzes and craft activities for five to 16s, while half terms bring hands-on workshops for all ages. In summer, there's an eclectic array of garden parties and family days; kids might learn bhangra dancing, make masks or listen to a Caribbean steel band. Events often spill into the glorious gardens, so bring a picnic to eat on the grass. In winter, the Christmas Past exhibition sees each room decorated for the festive season according to its period; the museum also holds an outdoor Twelfth Night ritual, with singing, holly-and ivy-burning and a taste of traditional Twelfth Night cake for the kids (and mulled wine for grown-ups). Temporary exhibitions are housed in the second, newer, half of the museum, along with the airy, inviting restaurant.
Buggy access. Disabled access: lift, toilet. Nappy-changing facilities. Nearest picnic place: museum grounds. Restaurant. Shop.

Guildhall Art Gallery
Guildhall Yard, off Gresham Street, EC2V 5AE (7332 3700/www.guildhall-art-gallery. org.uk). Mansion House or St Paul's tube/Bank tube/DLR/Moorgate tube/rail/8, 25, 242 bus. **Open** 10am-5pm Mon-Sat; noon-4pm Sun. **Admission** £2.50; £1 reductions; free under-16s. Free to all after 3.30pm daily, all day Fri. **Credit** (over £5) MC, V. **Map** p318 P6. 6+
Along with unenthralling portraits of stuffy politicians, the City of London's gallery has some gems, with works by Constable, Reynolds and the Pre-Raphaelites, and absorbing depictions of London through the ages. Up in the Main Gallery is the vast *Defeat of the Floating Batteries at Gibraltar* by John Singleton Copley, the largest painting in Britain; down in the basement lie the scant remains of London's sole amphitheatre. Although only the foundations of the walls and entrance survive, the slick presentation of the site does an excellent job of suggesting how the amphitheatre would have looked, with the staggered seats printed on a screen, dynamic illustrations of gladiators and sound effects. In October the gallery takes part in the annual Big Draw *(see p22)*, and there are pre-bookable half-

term workshops; every Friday, four free tours (hourly from 12.15pm, no booking needed) take in the highlights of the collection.
Buggy access. Disabled access: toilet. Nappy-changing facilities. Nearest picnic place: Finsbury Circus.

Hayward Gallery
Belvedere Road, SE1 8XX (7921 0813/www. hayward.org.uk). Embankment tube/Waterloo tube/rail. **Open** 10am-6pm Mon-Thur, Sat, Sun; 10am-10pm Fri. **Admission** £9; £5.50-£8 reductions; £4.50 12-16s; free under-12s. Prices vary; phone for details. **Credit** AmEx, MC, V. **Map** p318 M8. 7+ (parental advisory)
Its position within the Southbank Centre makes this gallery popular with families on a day out. The light, bright pavilion by Daniel Graham was added in 2003; children enjoy watching cartoons on the touch screens or just wandering around the visually confusing space created by curved, two-way mirrors. There are no permanent collections on display; instead, three or four major temporary exhibitions are staged through the year. Walking In My Mind (23 June-9 Sept 2009) explores the inner workings of the artist's thoughts with wonderfully surreal, large-scale installations, which will occupy the galleries and outdoor terraces; check the website for details of family workshops linked to the exhibition (sevens and overs, free with exhibition ticket). *See also p30* **Great Days Out**.
Buggy access. Café. Disabled access: lift. Nappy-changing facilities. Nearest picnic place: Jubilee Gardens/riverside benches. Shop.

Kenwood House
Hampstead Lane, NW3 7JR (8348 1286/ www.english-heritage.org.uk). Archway tube, then 210 bus. **Open** 11.30am-4pm daily. **Admission** free. **Credit** MC, V. 5+
A 17th-century mansion on the northern perimeter of Hampstead Heath, substantially remodelled the following century by Robert Adam. Not that your children are likely to give two hoots about that. They will enjoy the great rolling sward of the estate in front of the house, the posh ice-creams, lunch or (especially) breakfast in the Brew House *(see p223)*, and the fact that the site provides a superb jumping-off point for all things Heathly. Adults will enjoy all of the above, plus the very decent collection of paintings: Gainsborough, Vermeer, Reynolds, Van Dyck, Hals, Turner and a great Rembrandt self-portrait. *See also p114* **Great Days Out**.
Buggy access. Café. Disabled access: toilets. Nappy-changing facilities. Nearest picnic place: House grounds, Hampstead Heath. Restaurant.

Museum of Brands, Packaging & Advertising

2 Colville Mews, Lonsdale Road, W11 2AR (7908 0880/www.museumofbrands.com). Ladbroke Grove or Notting Hill Gate tube/ 23 bus. **Open** 10am-6pm Tue-Sat; 11am-5pm Sun. Last entry 1hr before closing. **Admission** £5.80; £2 7-16s; £3.50 reductions; free under-7s; £14 family (2+2). **Credit** MC, V. **Map** p310 A6. 6+

When Robert Opie was 16 years old, he decided to keep a Munchies wrapper rather than throw it in the bin. He went on to become a consumer historian, and this museum contains his vast collection of packaging. Spanning some 200 years of brands, it covers Victorian leisure pursuits, the advent of the radio, the chirpy thrift of wartime Britain and the liberal revolution of the swinging '60s. The displays are geared towards nostalgic adults, but historically-minded children may be amused by the antiquated toys, magazines and comics on show – not to mention old versions of all their favourite chocolate wrappers. Maltesers once looked quite different, you know. Temporary exhibition 'Waste Not, Want Not' runs until 29 November 2009, looking at World War II efforts to make the most of limited resources, and asking how they can inform contemporary packaging for a sustainable future.

Buggy access. Café. Disabled access: toilet. Nappy-changing facilities. Nearest picnic place: Kensington Gardens. Shop.

National Gallery

Trafalgar Square, WC2N 5DN (7747 2885/ www.nationalgallery.org.uk). Charing Cross tube/rail/24, 29, 176 bus. **Open** 10am-6pm Mon-Thur, Sat, Sun; 10am-9pm Fri. *Tours* 11.30am, 2.30pm daily. **Admission** free. *Temporary exhibitions* prices vary. *Tours* free. **Credit** MC, V. **Map** p317 K7. 5+

Children can become guides at the National Gallery, thanks to the 'Teach your grown-ups about art' audio tour, which equips kids with a map and audioguide, then asks them to relay choice snippets to their elders. Other audio guides ask children to follow secret agents or hunt for kings and queens, learning about various paintings as they go. Printed trails also help families navigate the immense collections, which include many a masterpiece: Van Gogh's *Sunflowers*, Cézanne's *Bathers* and Velàzquez's curvaceous *Rokeby Venus* among them.

Pick up a plan at the information desk before you set off, or make for the touch-screen terminals in the Sainsbury Wing's ArtStart Room or the East Wing's espresso bar; here, you can plan and print out your own tour. Family events include magic carpet storytelling sessions for under-fives on Sunday mornings,

Works in progress at the **Whitechapel Gallery**. *See p69.*

plus two-hour art workshops for five to 11s; you can't book ahead, so turn up well in advance of start times (detailed on the website). The school holidays also bring a healthy spread of free activities, led by painters and sculptors.

Come lunchtime, Oliver Peyton's National Café (*see p222*) offers simple, sustaining fare to fuel the kids' creativity: a boiled egg with soldiers, say, or creamy macaroni cheese. *See also p36* **Great Days Out**.
Buggy access. Café. Disabled access: lift, toilet. Nappy-changing facilities. Nearest picnic place: Trafalgar Square. Restaurant. Shop.

National Portrait Gallery
2 St Martin's Place, WC2H 0HE (7306 0055/ tours 7312 2483/www.npg.org.uk). Leicester Square tube/Charing Cross tube/rail/24, 29, 176 bus. **Open** *10am-6pm Mon-Wed, Sat, Sun; 10am-9pm Thur, Fri. Tours times vary, phone for details.* **Admission** *free. Temporary exhibitions prices vary. Audio guide £2. Tours free.* **Credit** MC, V. **Map** p317 K7. 5+
Likenesses of Britain's great and good make up the NPG's tremendous collection, from Tudor royalty to modern-day thespians, writers, politicians and academics. The chronologically-arranged collection comprises paintings, photographs and sculptures, while temporary exhibitions include the annual BP Portrait Award. The third Saturday of the month brings free storytelling for over-threes and crafts activities for over-fives, while school-holiday workshops might range from making Regency bonnets and top hats to sketching oil-pastel portraits. *See also p36* **Great Days Out**.
Buggy access. Café. Disabled access (Orange Street entrance): lift, toilet. Nappy-changing facilities. Nearest picnic place: Leicester Square, Trafalgar Square. Restaurant. Shops.

Orleans House Gallery
Riverside, Twickenham, Middx TW1 3DJ (8831 6000/www.richmond.gov.uk/orleans_ house_gallery). St Margaret's, Richmond or Twickenham rail/33, 490, H22, R68, R70 bus. **Open** *Apr-Sept 1-5.30pm Tue-Sat; 2-5.30pm Sun, bank hols. Oct-Mar 1-4.30pm Tue-Sat; 2-4.30pm Sun, bank hol Mon.* **Admission** *free; donations appreciated.* **Credit** MC, V. 5+
After a Lottery cash injection in 2008, this elegant riverside gallery is on top form (and nominated for a prestigious Art Fund prize). Three galleries host an engaging assortment of contemporary and historical exhibitions; outside, the woodland gardens are open until dusk. Upbeat children's workshops run year-round: the after-school Art Club caters for five-

to ten-year-olds, while 10:15 entertains tens to 15s. All need to be booked via the website. The Coach House education centre hosts holiday art workshops, using the gallery's exhibitions as a starting point. The team also co-ordinates the annual summer Larks in the Park children's theatre festival (28 June-27 Aug in 2009), with performances in parks across the borough.
Buggy access. Café. Disabled access: toilet. Nappy-changing facilities. Nearest picnic place: Orleans House Gallery grounds, Marble Hill Park or riverside benches. Shop.

Queen's House
Romney Road, SE10 9NF (8312 6565/www. nmm.ac.uk). Cutty Sark DLR/Greenwich DLR/ rail. **Open** *10am-5pm daily (last entry 4.30pm). Tours noon, 2.30pm daily.* **Admission** *free; occasional charge for temporary exhibitions. Tours free.* **Credit** *(over £5)* MC, V. 4+
A grand, Palladian-style villa, Queen's House was designed in 1616 by Inigo Jones. It's now home to the National Maritime Museum's art collection, which includes all sorts of pictures of naval heroes, battles, uncharted lands and stormy seascapes. For a cherry-picked selection of its treasures, explore the second-floor Art for the Nation exhibition. An exhibition on the ground floor charts the house's former life as a naval boarding school (the timetable revolved around lessons in seafaring and lashings of cocoa), while first floor galleries are devoted to the Tudors and early polar photography. On the Trail of the Stuarts is a 'detective notebook' that leads children around the building, while a trail for younger children tests their observational skills; download them from the website before you go.

The Tulip Stairs was the first self-supporting spiral staircase in the country: while adults admire its elegant lines and wrought iron fleurs-de-lys, children are advised to keep a watchful eye out for the resident ghost. It was supposedly captured on film by a couple of Canadian visitors in 1966 as it ascended the staircase, and spotted again in 2002 by a spooked gallery assistant, who saw it vanish through a wall. A colonnade connects the building to the National Maritime Museum (*see p104*).
Buggy access. Cafés. Disabled access: lift, toilet. Nappy-changing facilities. Nearest picnic place: picnic area on grounds, Greenwich Park. Shop.

Royal Academy of Arts
Burlington House, Piccadilly, W1J 0BD (7300 8000/www.royalacademy.org.uk). Green Park or Piccadilly Circus tube. **Open** *Temporary exhibitions 10am-6pm Mon-Thur, Sat, Sun;*

Sightseeing

Great Days Out
Bloomsbury

In years gone by, Bloomsbury was the stamping ground of the literati (Virginia Woolf, TS Eliot and the rest of the 'set'), whose presence has left a legacy of blue plaques affixed to its stately Georgian townhouses. It remains a pleasantly bookish, cultural sort of place, thanks to its fine clutch of museums – headed up, of course, by the mighty British Museum – and specialist book and art supply shops.

Bloomsbury is also home to Lamb's Conduit Street; a Dickensian-looking thoroughfare that's become a bastion of independent traders. The bike shop, grocer's, bookshops and boutiques ooze character; happily, it's too compact to strike fear into shop-resistant children's souls. The perfect reward for good behaviour is just around the corner: the park, pets' corner and playground at Coram's Fields.

Welcome to the Ancient World

Step into the **British Museum** (*see p73*), and you're whisked into all sorts of weird and wonderful ancient civilisations. Pick up activity backpacks and trails from the Paul Hamlyn Library, or take a wander and prepare to be astonished. In one room, graceful Grecian youths strike nonchalant poses; in the Africa gallery on the floor below, you might find a defiantly-bristling two-headed dog named Kozo (room 23). On the upper floor, the Egyptian mummies in rooms 62 and 63 will send a delicious thrill down your spine, as the unseeing eyes of long-dead priests and pharoahs stare back at you; the first century AD mummified cat looks far friendlier.

Don't try to cram it all into one visit – and if the kids need a break from statues and sarcophagi, head to the light-flooded Great Court. Below here, the Clore Education Centre and Ford Centre for Young Visitors host weekend and holiday activity sessions: mummy-making is an eternally popular offering. For earnest Egyptologists, the **Petrie Museum of Egyptian Archaeology** is also close by (*see p74*). It's a dimly lit, delightfully old-fashioned sort of establishment, run by enthusiastic staff; thrillingly, you can request a torch with which to explore the murkier recesses. Peek at the skeleton in a pot, write your name in hieroglyphs, and admire the eclectic array of beads, tools, pots and textiles, displayed in rows of Victorian glass cabinets.

Have a field day

Seven acres of lawns, football pitches, sandpits, swings and slides await at **Coram's Fields** (*see p113*) – sheer heaven for space-starved city kids, who run circuits around the grass like giddy spring lambs. As a sign on the gate firmly states, unaccompanied adults are banned, giving parents extra peace of mind. Older kids can swoop along the flying fox or zoom down the helter-skelter while tinies potter in the sandpit or fearlessly ascend the climbing frame. Smell a certain fruity something in the air? That'll be the petting zoo – a whiffy but happy home to goats, geese, ducks, guinea pigs and other docile mini-beasts.

Bring a picnic to spread out on the grass, or eat at the on-site café. It's run by the Kipferl team, who also own a great little Austrian deli/café in Smithfield, so expect bretzels and sachertorte alongside open sarnies, hot dishes and soups.

In addition to Coram's Fields, Bloomsbury is dotted with more sedate squares. Just north of Coram's, the tranquil, plane tree-shaded **St George's Gardens** (www.friendsofstgeorgesgardens. org.uk) were a burial ground in the 18th and 19th centuries. Children can decipher the crumbling inscriptions on the tombs that dot the gardens, or hunt for the final resting-place of Oliver Cromwell's granddaughter, Anna Gibson; those who like their history dark and gory may be interested to learn that this was the site of the first recorded attempt at body-snatching, in 1777.

Past the uncompromising, concrete bulk of the Brunswick Centre (home to a massive Waitrose that's good for picnic provisions, along with various shops) lies **Russell Square** – a jewel among Bloomsbury's garden squares. It's a sun-dappled, quietly dignified expanse, with a water-jet fountain at the centre that cries out to be scampered through; at its northern end, the café has a lovely terrace and does a fine trade in ice-cream cornets as well as more substantial sustenance.

Find out about the foundlings

In the 18th century, Coram's Fields was the site of the Foundling Hospital. A home for abandoned and destitute children, it was established by a kindly sea captain, Thomas Coram. Though the orphanage was demolished in the 1920s, its small inhabitants – and the adults who campaigned on their behalf – are remembered at the **Foundling Museum** (*see p71*) on Brunswick Square, overlooking Coram's Fields. The little love tokens left by the poverty-stricken mothers who abandoned their babies at the hospital would touch the hardest of hearts: a key; a button; a scrap of poetry; letters; a hazelnut shell. Look out for special family days, when activities might include making a Victorian jumping-jack or a pop-up street scene.

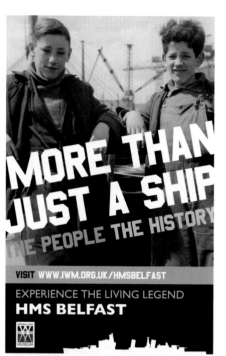
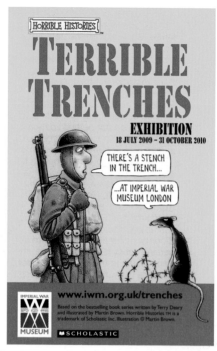

10am-10pm Fri. *John Madejski Fine Rooms*
1-4.30pm Tue-Fri; 10am-6pm Sat, Sun.
Admission *Fine Rooms* free. *Exhibitions*
prices vary; free under-7s. **Credit** AmEx,
DC, MC, V. **Map** p316 J7. **7+**
There's a real sense of occasion on arriving at the
Royal Academy, walking under the arches into
its impressive courtyard. George III established
Britain's first art school in 1768, which moved to
its present location at Burlington House a century
later. Works by British artists from the 18th
century to the present day (Constable, Reynolds,
Turner, Millais, Waterhouse, Hockney) are on
permanent, free display in the John Madejski Fine
Rooms – but the main focus is on the major
temporary exhibitions. Who could forget Charles
Saatchi's 1997 YBA show 'Sensation'?

The annual Summer Exhibition, held from June
to August, is incredibly popular; children will
probably find the endless and unstructured
rooms of work submitted by the general public
overwhelming, although there are some
interactive family workshops and gallery talks
on offer. At other times, grab an activity sheet for
'art detectives' from reception.
*Buggy access. Café. Disabled: lift, toilet. Nappy-
changing facilities. Nearest picnic place: Green
Park, St James's Square. Restaurant. Shop.*

Saatchi Gallery
*Duke Of York's HQ, Duke of York Square,
King's Road, SW3 4SQ (7811 3085/www.
saatchi-gallery.co.uk). Sloane Square tube.*
Open 10am-6pm daily. **Admission** free.
7+ (parental advisory)
The Saatchi moved to its current home off the
King's Road a few years ago, and immediately
struck a resonant note with its inaugural
exhibition: emerging young artists from China.
The gallery's self-ascribed brief is to exhibit
work by innovative, as-yet-unrecognised artists
or by international artists with no real profile in
this country. You'll need to do your 'suitability'
homework before you go (best achieved through
the Saatchi's extensive website as well as
independent reviews). When you get there you'll
find an open, airy, elegant set of conjoined
spaces, which amount to just the right size for
small legs to manage. An adventure in art – and
best of all it's free.
*Buggy access. Disabled access: lift, toilets.
Nappy-changing facilities. Nearest picnic place:
Duke of York Square.*

Serpentine Gallery
*Kensington Gardens (near Albert Memorial),
W2 3XA (7402 6075/www.serpentinegallery.
org). Lancaster Gate or South Kensington*
tube. **Open** 10am-6pm daily. **Admission** free;
donations appreciated. **Credit** AmEx, MC, V.
Map p311 D8. **7+ (parental advisory)**
If this 1930s park building looks conservative
from the outside, its exhibitions are anything
but. The bonus of a day trip here is the gallery's
location; as soon as the fidgets set in, families
can decamp to the park. The gallery maintains
a high profile in the art world with a rolling two-
monthly line-up of exhibitions (children will
enjoy *Jeff Koons: Popeye Series* running until
mid September 2009, which explores everyday
objects and children's toys in imaginative ways).
The best time to visit is in summer, when the
annual Serpentine Pavilion architectural
commission is on site. This year's construction
is by Kazuyo Sejima and Ryue Nishizawa of
SANAA. The events programme includes
family days, artist-led drawing and painting
courses, and trails relating to the current
exhibitions; check the website for dates.
*Buggy access. Disabled access: toilet. Nappy-
changing facilities. Nearest picnic place: Hyde
Park. Shop.*

Somerset House & Galleries
*Strand, WC2R ORN (7845 4600/www.
somersethouse.org.uk). Embankment or Temple
tube/Charing Cross tube/rail.* **Open** 10am-6pm
daily. *Courtyard* 7.30am-11pm daily. *River
terrace* 8am-6pm daily (extended hours apply
for restaurant). *Embankment Galleries* 10am-
6pm Mon-Wed, Fri-Sun; 10am-9pm Thur.
Courtauld Gallery 10am-6pm daily. *Tours*
1.30pm, 2.30pm, 3.45pm 1st Sat of mth; free.
Admission *Parts of South building, courtyard
& river terrace* free. *Exhibitions* prices vary;
phone for details. **Credit** MC, V. **Map** p317 M7.
8+ (galleries), 5+(courtyard)
The north bank of the Thames was once the
preferred spot for the nobility to build their
opulent houses. This one-time Tudor palace
became a royal residence (Elizabeth I often
stayed here before she was crowned) before it
was remodelled into neo-classical splendour and
used as offices by various public bodies (all
gone, bar the Inland Revenue). These days it
houses some of the UK's finest galleries. The
Courtauld Gallery has a huge collection of
Impressionist and post-Impressionist paintings
and stages exhibitions throughout the year,
while the Embankment Galleries, which opened
in April 2008, focus on photography, design,
fashion and architecture. London Fashion Week
will relocate here for the first time in 2009, and
an accompanying SHOWstudio exhibition will
run until late December.

But Somerset House isn't just about the exhibits.
The enchanting courtyard is an attraction in its

own right, with an ice rink in winter and a play fountain in the summer; on hot days, children love running down the ever-shifting corridors of water as the jets dance up and down. There are imaginative free family workshops on Saturdays for six to 12s (2-3.30pm) and occasional Studio Days for 13- to 18-year-olds, themed around the art in the galleries; these must be booked ahead and cost £12.
Buggy access. Cafés. Disabled access: lift, toilet. Nappy-changing facilities. Nearest picnic place: courtyard. Restaurant. Shops.

South London Gallery
65 Peckham Road, SE5 8UH (7703 6120/ www.southlondongallery.org). Peckham Rye rail/12, 36, 171, 345 bus. **Open** noon-6pm Tue-Sun. **Admission** free. **Credit** AmEx, MC, V. 5+ (parental advisory)
This Camberwell gallery is known for its forward-thinking approach. In the 1990s, it was one of the main showcases for Young British Artists, giving shows to Marc Quinn, Gavin Turk and Tracey Emin; this was the first gallery to exhibit Emin's famous appliquéd tent. It remains one of the capital's foremost contemporary art galleries, with exhibitions that comprise installations, performance pieces and film, as well as paintings and sculpture. Inventive family workshops tie in with the current exhibitions: check online for details.
Buggy access. Disabled access: lift, toilet. Nappy-changing facilities. Nearest picnic place: gallery garden.

Tate Britain
Millbank, SW1P 4RG (7887 8888/www.tate. org.uk). Pimlico tube/77A, 88, C10 bus. **Open** 10am-5.50pm daily; late opening 6-10pm first Fri of mth. *Tours* 11am, noon, 2pm, 3pm Mon-Fri; noon, 3pm Sat, Sun. **Admission** free. *Temporary exhibitions* prices vary. *Tours* free. **Credit** MC, V. **Map** p317 L7. 5+
Downriver from its younger sister, Tate Britain possesses a princely collection of British fine art, sweeping from 1500 to the present day. It's an extraordinary spread, with something for everyone: from Constable's placid landscapes to Blake's apocalyptic visions; the Turner collection is magnificent. Every year, four shortlisted contenders for his namesake award (the Turner Prize) exhibit here, in a flurry of controversy and media hype.
A children's discovery trail, available any time from the information desks, explores the 'secret' Tate, while the venerable art trolley is wheeled out at weekends and during school holidays (11am-5pm), laden with activities. Check the

website for more family and kids' goings-on. When you've finished here, you can cruise swiftly to Tate Modern for another art fix, on the Damien Hirst-decorated Tate to Tate boat (*see p43* **Three Thames tasters**).
Buggy access. Café. Disabled access: lift, toilet. Nappy-changing facilities. Nearest picnic place: lawns, Riverside Gardens. Restaurant. Shop.

Tate Modern
Bankside, SE1 9TG (7887 8000/www. tate.org.uk). St Paul's tube/Blackfriars rail. **Open** 10am-6pm Mon-Thur, Sun; 10am-10pm Fri, Sat. Last entry 45mins before closing. **Admission** free. *Temporary exhibitions* prices vary. **Credit** AmEx, MC, V. **Map** p318 O7. 5+
Even before you set foot inside, visiting this place feels like an adventure. The dramatic slope leading down to the entrance could be straight out of a playground, and the sheer scale of the Turbine Hall is enough to give most children a sensory hit. This is where, each year, a large-scale, specially commissioned work is installed in the autumn and stays until April. The permanent collections are shown in four wings on Levels 3 and 5, guided by themes such as Cubism, Futurism and Vorticism, Surrealism, Abstract Expressionism and European Informal Art and Minimalism.
Early art appreciation is encouraged by the family activity packs available from Level 3. The Start team will help you choose which art materials, puzzles or architectural trails are suitable for your brood (available at weekends, 11am-5pm, and in school hols). There's a kids' audio tour too. On Level 5, the Bloomberg Learning Zone offers educational attractions for over-fives, including games, multimedia activities and a short film. A major expansion is scheduled for completion in 2012, which will incorporate a new building from architects Herzog de Meuron and a former electricity substation, the Switch House, both on the south side of the current gallery. *See also p30* **Great Days Out**.
Buggy access. Café. Disabled access: lift, toilet. Nappy-changing facilities. Nearest picnic place: grounds. Restaurant. Shops.

Vestry House Museum
Vestry Road, E17 6HZ (8509 1917/www. walthamforest.gov.uk). Walthamstow Central tube/rail. **Open** 10am-5pm Wed-Sun. *Tours* groups only, by prior arrangement. **Admission** free; donations appreciated. **No credit cards.** 6+
Vestry House was once a workhouse; look out for the stone plaque above the entrance, which decrees 'if any would not work, neither should

he eat' – one to remember when the kids won't tidy their rooms. It's now an engaging little museum devoted to local history. One room displays vintage toys and games; another is done up as a Victorian parlour. On the ground floor you can see a reconstructed police cell (the building served a stint as a police station in the late 19th century), complete with amusing wax figures dressed as village bobby and drunkard. You can also walk through the workhouse garden, admire a reconstructed Bremer Car (London's first petrol-driven vehicle), and discover the housewife's lot with a display of labour-intensive domestic paraphernalia (carpet beaters, flat irons, and other antiquated devices). *Buggy access (ground floor). Disabled access: toilet (ground floor). Nappy-changing facilities. Nearest picnic place: museum garden. Shop.*

Victoria & Albert Museum

Cromwell Road, SW7 2RL (7942 2000/www. vam.ac.uk). South Kensington tube. **Open** 10am-5.45pm Mon-Thur, Sat, Sun; 10am-10pm Fri. Tours daily; phone for details. **Admission** free; charges apply for special exhibitions. **Credit** AmEx, MC, V. **Map** p313 E10. 5+
Sculpture, ceramics, textiles, jewellery and decorative arts of every description fill the V&A's lofty galleries. The British Galleries are particularly good for hands-on exhibits: kids can squeeze into a corset and crinoline, try on an armoured gauntlet or construct the Crystal Palace; other interactive displays are marked on the museum's floorplan with a special symbol. Family trails (designed for seven to 12s) can also be picked up from the information desk. On Saturdays and school holidays, over-fives can take their pick of various activity backpacks, then delve in to find puzzles, games and challenges linked to the displays.
There's also lots going on in the art studios and media labs at the new Sackler Centre. Sunday's Drop-in Design events bring all sorts of arts and crafts, from making extravagant accessories to designing crazy cups for the Mad Hatter's tea party, and there are brilliant holiday sessions. The café (*see p235*) offers high chairs, and under-tens can order half-price portions of adult mains. Give the children a run around in the courtyard then check out the newly-installed Theatre and Performance galleries – a visual feast of costume, puppets and stage sets, which might inspire the kids to stage a show of their own back at home. *See also p96* **Great Days Out**. *Buggy access. Café. Disabled access: toilet. Nappy-changing facilities. Nearest picnic place: basement picnic room (weekends & school holidays), museum garden, Pirelli Gardens. Restaurant. Shop.*

Bold as brass

There is something new sitting on the pavement just north of St Martin-in-the-Fields – a sleek, gleaming glass box, glinting in the sunshine. Has Matt Smith's Doctor Who warranted a new Tardis? No, it's the new entrance to the revamped **London Brass Rubbing Centre**. Enter the futuristic lift and sink beneath the pavement…
The murky old vaults that once housed the Homeless Centre and the Chinese Community Centre have gone. In their place is a large, bright open space that leads on to the enlarged Café in the Crypt. Next to the new shop is the much improved brass rubbing area. Sure, there could be a few more tables for actual rubbing, given the vast space available, but it's a very pleasant atmosphere in which to create an artwork for the wall at home.
Children can choose from the smaller replica brasses: a dragon, a decorative elephant, a unicorn, or various historical figures, including William Shakespeare. The nice people at the counter will tape the paper to the block, lend out crayons and give instruction in the gentle art of brass rubbing.
Start with the side of the large block crayon to get the outline without tearing the paper, then press harder with the point for the detail. It sounds simple, but then things with that quality are often the best in life. It's curiously satisfying watching the gorgeous pictures come to life before your very eyes. Be warned, adults will want to have a go too – having started off intending to retire to the café for coffee and cakes, you'll likely find yourself getting stuck in alongside the kids.

Sightseeing

Planes, trains and automobiles

RAF Museum Hendon.

Zoom through the sky, splash into the Thames, pedal through a park then climb to the top deck. Kids love vehicles, and luckily London's full of them – and we're not just talking traffic.

For a fast take-off, head north to the free **Royal Air Force Museum Hendon** (*see p104*). Three huge hangars are packed full of fighters, bombers, jets, helicopters, boat planes and more. You can't climb on the historic planes, but you can sit in a few and the child-focused Aeronauts Centre has a sit-in plane and helicopter, plus fun hands-on experiments all about flight. The museum has two flight simulator rides (there's an extra fee to pay for these), while the newly refurbished self-service Wings Restaurant is good for lunchtime refuelling.

Moving to the Navy: World War II and Korea veteran **HMS Belfast** (*see p101*) is moored by Tower Bridge. It's brilliant to explore (though not for pushchairs). You can clamber into the deck guns, climb up and down ladders, see where the 750-strong crew lived and worked (it must have been cosy), and delve the engine rooms far below.

Is it a boat or is it a truck? A **Thames Duck Tour** (*see p16*) is a bit of both: a real World War II amphibious vehicle (used to take troops ashore at the D-Day landings) will give you a road tour around Westminster, then plunges into the river for an aquatic voyage.

Less splashy is a relaxing cruise on green-fringed **Regent's Canal**. Board a barge at pretty Little Venice or teenage-heaven Camden Lock for a 45-minute cruise past London Zoo (for which you can book an all-in ticket with London Waterbus, *see p16*). Jason's Trip (7286 3428, www.jasons.co.uk), meanwhile, has a commentary on the leg to Camden.

Horses were the main mode of transport in London up to the start of the last century. Today, over-fives can try a horse ride in **Hyde Park** and children aged three and up in **Richmond Park** (*for both, see p207*) – definitely one to book in advance. Adults can walk with the horses. Hyde Park also has the Serpentine Boating Lake, where in summer you can hire a

HMS Belfast.

London Transport Museum

rowing boat or pedalo. There's a roped-off lido for swimming (*see p214*) and a children's paddling pool too – ideal for cooling hot, tired feet when it's a scorcher. The **Diana Princess of Wales' Memorial Playground** (*see p121*) is just a short walk from the Serpentine; at its heart is a fantastic wooden pirate ship, perfect for inspiring *Peter Pan* adventures.

Cycling in London with kids takes a lot of nerve and insider knowledge, but the South Bank-based **London Bicycle Tour Co** (7928 6828, www.londonbicycle.com) offers bikes and guides for two- or three-and-a-half hour city tours on quieter roads and paths. It's recommended for confident cyclists from around ten years old.

Then, of course, there's **London Transport**. LT's dedicated museum in Covent Garden (*see p84*) is full of vintage buses, trams, horse-buses, tube carriages and other fun vehicles to explore. Less well known is the museum's big depot at Acton Town. Open just a few weekends a year (sign up online for email alerts), it offers rides on full-size heritage vehicles and mini trains and has a fabulously detailed model railway.

Once grumpy commuters are safely pen pushing, London Transport's huge network offers endless brilliant ways for kids to see London. And they ride free! Marvel/worry at how Docklands Light Railway trains have no driver, try a tram down south or hop (carefully) on and off waterbuses to explore the Thames. But the top deck of a shiny red London double-decker is still the best way to see London, and if you get the front seats... well it really doesn't get much better than that, whatever age you are.

Wallace Collection

Hertford House, Manchester Square, W1U 3BN (7563 9500/www.wallacecollection.org). Bond Street tube/2, 10, 12, 30, 74, 113 bus. **Open** 10am-5pm daily. **Admission** free. **Credit** MC, V. **Map** p314 G5. 6+

Set in a dignified 18th-century townhouse, the Wallace oozes grandeur – but its stately demeanour belies its welcoming, family-friendly approach. All sorts of trails and artist-led activity sessions help children relate to its priceless collections of paintings, porcelain and furniture, and small visitors often go home clutching their own masks, collages, hats and watercolours. Award-winning painter Sadie Lee is currently in charge of the Little Draw sessions, held on the first Sunday of the month.

Lush paintings by Titian, Velàsquez, Fragonard, Gainsborough and other greats adorn the galleries' walls, while a series of grand, irresistibly opulent rooms showcase Sèvres porcelain, Louis XIV and XV furnishings and other fabulously costly trinkets. The biggest draw for most youngsters, though, is the magnificent armoury; regular events invite kids to handle some of the collection's treasures, while would-be gallant champions can stagger under the weight of a replica suit of armour in the Conservation Gallery. In the glass-roofed courtyard is an Oliver Peyton-run French brasserie; children's mains feature organic meat and fish, but are commensurately pricey at £7.50 a throw. *See also p138* **Great Days Out**. *Buggy access. Disabled access: lift, toilet. Nappy-changing facilities. Nearest picnic place: courtyard benches. Restaurant. Shop.*

Whitechapel Gallery

77-82 Whitechapel High Street (7522 7888/ www.whitechapelgallery.org). Aldgate East tube. **Open** 11am-6pm Tue, Wed, Fri-Sun; 11am-9pm Thur. **Admission** free. **Credit** MC, V. 5+

The Whitechapel Gallery took two years to appropriate the space inside what used to be the Whitechapel Library next door. Whatever you think about the library having being relocated and renamed the 'Idea Store', the Gallery has certainly benefited. There are several new light and airy gallery spaces, the most beautiful of which are the Clore Creative Studios right at the top. This is where family workshops are to be held, along with the two-day courses planned for the summer holidays. Family art and poetry trails and activity packs are also on the agenda. See website for details.

Buggy access. Café. Disabled access: lift, toilet. Nappy-changing facilities. Nearest picnic place: Christ Church Spitalfields. Restaurant. Shop.

Sightseeing

William Morris Gallery

Lloyd Park, Forest Road, E17 4PP (8527 3782/www.walthamforest.gov.uk/wmg). Blackhorse Road tube, then 123 bus. **Open** 10am-5pm Wed-Sun. *Tours phone for details.* **Admission** free; donations appreciated. **Credit** MC, V. 5+

The tireless William Morris (artist, socialist and designer of all that flowery wallpaper) lived in this handsome, moated building as a child. It's now a gallery devoted to the man and his work, with a diverse range of exhibits: his satchel and coffee cup are on show alongside tiles, textiles, tapestries, furniture and glass designed by Morris and his Arts & Crafts movement contemporaries. Kids may enjoy the family trails, which encourage them to examine ceramic tile illustrations of stories like *Beauty and the Beast*, while activities run on the second Sunday of the month; call or check online for details. To the rear of the house, invisible from the road, is Lloyd Park. There's an aviary, a skateboard park, play areas and a moat with ducks and geese; plans are afoot for a major revamp. *Buggy access. Nearest picnic place: Lloyd Park. Shop.*

CHILDHOOD

Foundling Museum

40 Brunswick Square, WC1N 1AZ (7841 3600/www.foundlingmuseum.org.uk). Russell Square tube. **Open** 10am-5pm Tue-Sat; 11am-5pm Sun. *Tours by arrangement.* **Admission** £5; £4 reductions; free under-16s. **Credit** MC, V. **Map** p317 L4. 3+

This touching museum tells the story of London's Hospital for the Maintenance and Education of Exposed and Deserted Children – better known as the 'Foundling Hospital'. Founded in 1739 by retired sea captain Thomas Coram, it was largely funded by donations from the painter William Hogarth and the composer George Frideric Handel. For the next 250 years, the hospital provided education for babies who had been abandoned by their mothers.

As well as paintings by William Hogarth and other artists, the museum has a second-floor room dedicated to Handel. Kids love the 'musical chairs', with hidden speakers playing excerpts from the composer's works. The best time to visit the museum is on the first Saturday of every month, when activities are laid on for children: dressing up, listening to stories, becoming a curator for the day or designing cards might feature on the agenda. Extra family fun days and storytelling sessions take place on Tuesdays and Thursdays in the school holidays. Brilliant backpacks for three to fives and five to eights can be borrowed for free any time, and are stuffed with games, puzzles, dressing-up gear, finger puppets and more: themes include Costume, Food and Meet the Foundlings. *See also p62* **Great Days Out**. *Buggy access. Café. Disabled access: lift. Nappy-changing facilities. Nearest picnic place: Brunswick Square, Coram's Fields. Shop.*

London International Gallery of Children's Art

Waterlow Park Centre, Dartmouth Park Hill, N19 5JF (7281 1111/www.ligca.org). Archway tube. **Open** 10am-4pm Fri-Sun. **Admission** free; donations appreciated. **No credit cards.** 5+

LIGCA has moved from the O2 Centre to this much nicer location in Highgate's Waterlow Park (*see p120*), and celebrates the creativity of children all over the world with temporary exhibitions that change every few months. A display on Cuba runs until September 2009, after which the theme will be Refugees. Art materials are left out for any young visitor who might want to get creative; staff also offer children's birthday parties. The gallery is manned by volunteers, so phone before setting out. *Buggy access. Disabled access: lift, toilet. Nappy-changing facilities. Nearest picnic place: Waterlow Park.*

Pollock's Toy Museum

1 Scala Street (entrance on Whitfield Street), W1T 2HL (7636 3452/www.pollockstoy museum.com). Goodge Street tube. **Open** 10am-5pm Mon-Sat. **Admission** £5; £4 reductions; £2 3-16s; free under-3s. **Credit** MC, V. 5+

Set in a Georgian townhouse just behind Goodge Street station, this museum is a warren of wonderfully atmospheric rooms and creaky, narrow staircases. It's named after Benjamin Pollock, the last of the Victorian toy theatre printers: to see examples of his tiny tableaux, visit room six. Elsewhere, there are treasures gathered from nurseries across the world, from delicate china dolls to mechanical tin toys and dapper lead soldiers.

Adults are more likely to appreciate the nostalgia value of the old board games and playthings, but the museum shop has child appeal, with its reproduction cardboard theatres, wind-up music boxes, animal masks and tin robots. *Nearest picnic place: Crabtree Fields, Colville Place. Shop.*

The age of innocence: **Pollock's Toy Museum**. *See p71.*

Ragged School Museum

46-50 Copperfield Road, E3 4RR (8980 6405/ www.raggedschoolmuseum.org.uk). Mile End tube. **Open** 10am-5pm Wed, Thur; 2-5pm 1st Sun of mth. *Tours by arrangement.* **Admission** free; donations appreciated. **No credit cards.** 6+ (term time), 2+ (school holidays)

In Victorian times, ragged schools provided poor and destitute children with a basic education. This one, set by Regent's Canal, was London's largest. The buildings have now been converted into a fascinating museum, with gallery areas and a mock-up of a classroom. Here, lessons – complete with slates, dunce hats and a costume-clad teacher – are staged for schoolchildren, and are open to everyone on the first Sunday of the month. The 45-minute lessons start at 2.15 and 3.30pm; book on arrival at the museum, as places are limited. In the holidays, special events run on Wednesdays and Thursdays (call for details). There's also a Victorian kitchen and displays on local history and industry.

Buggy access. Café. Disabled access: toilet. Nappy-changing facilities. Nearest picnic place: Mile End Park. Shop.

V&A Museum of Childhood

Cambridge Heath Road, E2 9PA (8983 5200/ recorded information 8980 2415/www.vam.ac. uk/moc). Bethnal Green tube/rail/8 bus. **Open** 10am-5.45pm daily. **Admission** free. Under-12s must be accompanied by an adult. **Credit** MC, V. 1+

This beautiful iron building and its exhibits moved from South Kensington to Bethnal Green in 1866, but has remained an outpost of the V&A (*see p67*) ever since. As you walk inside, the well-stocked shop and Benugo café are on the ground floor; note the 19th-century black and white mosaic floor tiles, made by female prisoners in Woking jail. The mezzanine and upper floors are configured to house the permanent collections, alongside temporary and touring exhibitions: Snozzcumbers and Frobscottle (until September 2009) celebrates the combined creative forces of Roald Dahl and Quentin Blake. A lot of thought has gone into making this museum child-friendly; after all, it's a tease to see so many toys and not be able to play with them. To compensate, there are activity stations in each area with lego, stickle bricks, a sandpit, board games, rocking horses, a book corner and many other treats dotted throughout the display cases. In the high-ceilinged, open gallery space, the encouragement to play means the din inside is redolent of an indoor playcentre. It's not conducive to studying what's inside the cases, which is a shame; some of the exhibits – like the 1780s models of a Chinese Rock Garden and the 1825 Viennese model theatre – merit a bit of contemplation.

Buggy access. Café. Disabled access: lift, toilet. Nappy-changing facilities. Nearest picnic place: basement, museum grounds. Shop.

ETHNOGRAPHY

British Museum

Great Russell Street, WC1B 3DG (7323 8000/ 7323 8299/www.britishmuseum.org). Holborn, Russell Square or Tottenham Court Road tube. **Open** *Galleries* 10am-5.30pm Mon-Wed, Sat, Sun; 10am-8.30pm Thur, Fri. *Great Court* 9am-6pm Mon-Wed, Sun; 9am-11pm Thur-Sat. *Tours* Highlights 10.30am, 1pm, 3pm daily; phone for details. *Eye Opener tours* phone for details. **Admission** free; donations appreciated. *Temporary exhibitions* prices vary; phone for details. *Highlights tours* £8; £5 under-11s, reductions. *Eye Opener tours* free. **Credit** AmEx, DC, MC, V. **Map** p317 K5. 5+

The collections at the mighty British Museum span the centuries, with an incredible array of treasures from across the globe. In 2008, it was declared Britain's most popular museum, with six million visitors a year. Other museums would give their eye teeth for a fraction of its priceless relics, which include the Rosetta Stone, the Lewis Chessmen, the Anglo-Saxon helmet from Sutton Hoo and the Elgin Marbles. Rooms 62 and 63 of the Roxie Walker galleries are top of most children's agenda; it's here that the mummies reside, exerting an eerie spell over visitors. The Africa galleries, full of vivid colours and spooky masks, and Living & Dying – a surreal collection of tribal objects relating to death and mortality from the collection of the Wellcome Trust – are also atmospheric.

Norman Foster's two-acre covered Great Court was an inspired idea, and equals Tate Modern's Turbine Hall (*see p66*) for vast indoor spaces that children love to feel tiny in. The café at the far end is overpriced, but it's a lovely light place to sit. On a practical note, the baby changing room has no loo in it and giving your baby to a complete stranger in the queue for the ladies doesn't feel like a great option. So take a friend.

The museum opened its doors to the public in 1759 and celebrates its 250th anniversary in 2009, with plans to expand the building on the north-west side (due for completion in 2012). Inventive family events run on Saturdays, ranging from Greek theatre workshops to Ancient Egyptian storytelling, while digital photography-based sessions are held on selected Sundays at the Samsung Digital Photography Centre. *See also p62* **Great Days Out**.

Buggy access. Cafés. Disabled access: lift, toilet. Nappy-changing facilities. Nearest picnic place: Russell Square. Restaurant. Shops.

Horniman Museum

100 London Road, SE23 3PQ (8699 1872/ www.horniman.ac.uk). Forest Hill rail/122, 176, 185, 312, 356, 363, P4, P13 bus. **Open** 10.30am-5.30pm daily. **Admission** free; donations appreciated. *Robot Zoo* £5; £2.50 children; free under-3s. **Credit** MC, V. 3+

Victorian tea trader Frederick John Horniman was an inveterate collector, amassing all sorts of curios on his travels. His collection soon grew far too large for the family home in Forest Hill; undaunted, he commissioned a new museum to contain it, which opened to the public in 1901. The Natural History gallery has skeletons, fossils, pickled animals, stuffed birds and insects in glass cases, presided over by an overstuffed walrus (never having seen such a beast before, the taxidermist didn't realise it ought to have thick folds of skin).

Meanwhile, the atmospheric World Cultures section has a staggering 80,000 objects from across the globe, and the Music Room features

Victoria & Albert Museum. *See p67.*

Sightseeing

Horniman Museum. *See p73.*

hundreds of instruments and touch screens to unleash their sounds. A 'Hands-On' room gives young visitors carte blanche to bash away at world instruments – including little hollow wooden frogs from South East Asia to bang and scrape, Tibetan singing bowls and a 'flip-flop-o-fone'. Outside, the 16-acre gardens have an animal enclosure with rabbits, goats and chickens, an elegant conservatory and a picnic spot with superb views. Until November 2009, the Robot Zoo exhibition brings a marvellous menagerie of mechanical beasts, with plenty of opportunities to get hands-on. For the Horniman's Aquarium, *see p129*.
Buggy access. Café. Disabled access: lift, toilet. Nappy-changing facilities. Nearest picnic place: museum gardens. Shop.

Petrie Museum of Egyptian Archaeology

University College London, entrance through DMS Watson Library, Malet Place, WC1E 6BT (7679 2884/www.petrie.ucl.ac.uk). Goodge Street or Warren Street tube/29, 73, 134 bus. **Open** 1-5pm Tue-Fri; 10am-1pm Sat. Closed Easter hols. **Admission** free; donations appreciated. **No credit cards. Map** p317 K4. 7+
In this age of touch-screen technology and interactive bells and whistles, the Petrie's old-fashioned glass cabinets are practically a museum piece in their own right. Its eccentricity imbues it with an inimitable charm: some corners are so dimly lit, staff lend out torches. They're also endearingly keen, and happy to talk about the collection – based on a bequest from 19th-century collector Amelia Edwards. As one chap charmingly explained to us, she was 'more interested in how ordinary Egyptians lived from day to day than in bling' – which

means the collections are focused on everyday minutiae such as beads, tools, amulets and clothes. Children can write their name in hieroglyphs, make a pot, or dress like an Ancient Egyptian; it's simple stuff, but great fun. The skeleton in a pot, dating from around the third millenium BC, also enthrals saucer-eyed small fry, along with a mummified head and various fragmentary human remains. Plans for swanky new premises are on the cards, but not for a year or two yet. *See also p62* **Great Days Out**.
Buggy access. Disabled access: lift, toilet. Nearest picnic place: Gordon Square. Shop.

EMERGENCY SERVICES

London Fire Brigade Museum

Winchester House, 94A Southwark Bridge Road, SE1 0EG (8555 1200/www.london-fire.gov.uk). Borough tube/Southwark tube/rail/344 bus. **Open** by appointment 10.30am, 2pm Mon-Fri. **Admission** £3; £2 7-14s, reductions; £1 under-7s. **Credit** MC, V. **Map** p318 O9. 5+
Any child with a fire engine fixation will relish the chance to visit the London Fire Brigade's Museum. Visits are by appointment only – which means an expert guide will take you round the collection, comprising of memorabilia, photos, uniforms, paintings and equipment, showing how firefighting has changed since the Great Fire of 1666. Small children are most smitten with the shiny fire engines, ranging from an 1830s model to red and brass beauties. Although they're not allowed to touch the fire engines, kids are given fireman uniforms to try on, as well as colouring materials. Booking is essential.

Buggy access. Disabled access: toilet. Nearest picnic place: Mint Street Park. Shop.

Museum & Library of the Order of St John

St John's Gate, St John's Lane, EC1M 4DA (7324 4005/www.sja.org.uk/museum). Farringdon tube/rail/55, 63, 243 bus. **Open** (Closed until May 2010). 10am-5pm Mon-Fri; 10am-4pm Sat. Closed bank hol weekends. *Tours* 11am, 2.30pm Tue, Fri, Sat. **Admission** free; suggested donations for tours £5; £4 reductions. **Credit** MC, V. **Map** p318 O4. 5+

The museum devoted to the venerable organisation is closed until May 2010 for a major, Lottery-funded redevelopment. The order began with the crusaders in 11th-century Jerusalem, and its long history is told via all manner of exhibits: bandages printed with first aid instructions, first-aid kits and archaic-looking ambulances, along with archaeological finds, armour, coins and seals dating back to the Order's earliest years. The redevelopment plans include spacious new galleries, a children's trail and a learning space, along with improved access to the 16th-century Tudor gatehouse that houses the museum. Keep an eye on the website for the latest news.

Buggy access (ground floor). Disabled access: lift (limited access), toilet (ground floor). Nearest picnic place: Clerkenwell Close. Shop.

GREAT LIVES

Apsley House

149 Piccadilly, W1J 7NT (7499 5676/www. english-heritage.org.uk). Hyde Park Corner tube. **Open** *Apr-Oct* 11am-5pm Wed-Sun & bank hols. *Nov-Mar* 11am-4pm Wed-Sun. *Tours* by arrangement. **Admission** £5.40 (includes audio guide if available); £2.70 5-16s; £4.30 reductions; free under-5s. *Joint ticket with admission to Wellington Arch* £6.80; £3.40 5-16s; £5.40 reductions; free under-5s; £17 family (2+3). *Tours* phone for details. **Credit** MC, V. **Map** p316 G8. 5+

This imposing mansion is one of London's most impressive addresses, lording it over Hyde Park Corner. It was the family home of Arthur Wellesley, the first Duke of Wellington, who defeated Napoleon at Waterloo. His descendants still live in the building, but some of it has been given over to a museum about the duke, his campaigns and the fine art and precious antiques he brought back from his travels. Pieces include Canova's enormous marble statue of Napoleon in his birthday suit, as well as paintings by Rubens and Van Dyck. Families should pick up the 'Wellington Boot' pack with activities and puzzles for five to 11s. The anniversary of the battle of Waterloo, in June, brings a weekend of soldierly activities.

Buggy access. Nearest picnic place: Hyde Park.

Kitted-up fire-engine fans tour the **London Fire Brigade Museum**.

Taking a closer look at the **Sherlock Holmes Museum**. *See p80.*

Benjamin Franklin House

*36 Craven Street, WC2N 5NF (7930 9121/
bookings 7930 6601/www.benjaminfranklin
house.org). Embankment tube/Charing
Cross tube/rail.* **Open** 10.30am-5pm daily.
Admission £7; £5 reductions; free under-16s.
Tours noon, 1pm, 2pm, 3.15pm, 4.15pm
Wed-Sun. Booking advisable. **Credit** MC, V.
Map p317 L7. 6+

This 18th-century house was Benjamin
Franklin's home for 16 years before the
American Revolution, and opened to the public
in 2006 on Franklin's 300th birthday. It's not a
museum exactly, but more of a historical
experience, during which Franklin's landlady
speaks to her guests using sound and projected
imagery to conjure up the period in which the
great man lived.
*Buggy access (ground floor). Nearest picnic
place: Victoria Gardens, Embankment. Shop.*

Charles Dickens Museum

*48 Doughty Street, WC1N 2LX (7405 2127/
www.dickensmuseum.com). Russell Square tube.*
Open 10am-5pm Mon-Sat; 11am-5pm Sun.
Admission £5; £4 reductions; £3 5-15s; free
under-5s; £14 family (2+4). **Credit** AmEx, DC,
MC, V. **Map** p317 M4. 8+

Dickens has given us a vivid picture of
Victorian London in his writing. This was his
home for three years, and *Oliver Twist* and *A*
Christmas Carol were both written here. The
building is crammed with memorabilia and
artefacts; in the basement, visitors can see a 25-
minute film on Dickens's life in London. Weekly
children's 'handling sessions' let young visitors
write with Dickens's pen and hold various other
possessions. These take place most
Wednesdays, but call ahead as they are run by
volunteers. There are two mini-trails for
children, based on Dickens's stories, plus
walking tours of Dickensian London.
*Buggy access (ground floor). Nearest picnic
place: Coram's Fields, Russell Square. Shop.*

Dr Johnson's House

*17 Gough Square, off Fleet Street, EC4A
3DE (7353 3745/www.drjohnsonshouse.org).
Chancery Lane or Temple tube/Blackfriars
rail.* **Open** *May-Sept* 11am-5.30pm Mon-Sat.
Oct-Apr 11am-5pm Mon-Sat. *Tours* by
arrangement (groups of 10 or more).
Admission £4.50; £1.50 under-18s; £3.50
reductions; £10 family (2+ unlimited children).
Tours free. *Evening tours* by arrangement;
phone for details. **No credit cards.**
Map p318 N6. 6+

This solid, four-storey Georgian house was
home to Dr Samuel Johnson, author of the
Dictionary of the English Language. He lived
here with his cat, Hodge – described by his
master as 'a very fine cat indeed'. Johnson fed
his beloved moggie on oysters; hence the oyster

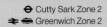

Go to town on school projects

Imperial War Museum.

It's easy to see Google as the school project genius and think Wiki full of wisdom, but taking a school project out into the real world turns a stressful undertaking into a stimulating day trip. And London has it all... What a relief.

Ancient Egyptians
Bury yourself in the incredible Egyptian galleries of the **British Museum** (*see p73*), where you'll find mummies in various states of unwrap and much more. (They can be nightmare inducing, so avoid *Scooby Doo* before bed.) **Cleopatra's Needle**, an 18-metre (59ft) high granite obelisk dating from 1450BC, stands on Victoria Embankment. Erected in 1878, it has a Victorian time capsule buried beneath it (whose peculiar contents include hairpins, a razor and snapshots of famous beauties of the day). The Needle's two guardian sphinxes face the wrong way (they should look outwards, like Nelson's lions), but Queen Victoria liked them as they are, and no one wanted to disagree.

Animals and plants
As well as the huge resources at **London Zoo** (*see p140*), there is also **Battersea Park Children's Zoo** (*see p140*), and city farms such as **Mudchute** (*see p134*) on the Isle of Dogs. For uncaged nature in all its glory, take a 'duck bus' (no.283) from Hammersmith to the superb 105-acre **London Wetland Centre** (*see p137*), head to **Kew Gardens** (*see p105*) for a lesson about plants, or visit **Camley Street Natural Park** (*see p104*), a small natural oasis near King's Cross. At the **Natural**

History Museum (*see p87*), the living Butterfly Jungle is open from from May to September. For aquatic life, there's the recently refurbished **Sea Life London Aquarium** (*see p129*) in County Hall with its new shark walk and whale skeleton tunnel. Another option is the aquarium at the **Horniman Museum** (*see p73*) in Forest Hill, which also has traditional (and eccentric) natural history exhibits.

Dinosaurs
Inevitably it's the **Natural History Museum** (*see p87*) that comes out on top, thanks to its fantastic dino fossils, interactive exhibitions and even a (really very scary for little ones) roaring T-Rex. **Crystal Palace Park** (*see p113*) has some Victorian dinosaur statues rearing out of the undergrowth, although scientific knowledge has progressed considerably since their construction, and they're not terribly accurate.

Great Fire of London
Standing at 61 metres (202ft), Christopher Wren's recently refurbished **Monument** (*see p29*) to the Great Fire of 1666 is the tallest stone column in the world. It also stands 61 metres from where the fire started, at a bakery in Pudding Lane. Find out about the fire at the **Museum of London** (*see p84*), the **London Fire Brigade Museum** (*see p75*) – for which you have to book – and **St Paul's Cathedral** (*see p41*).

How we lived yesterday
Visit the East End **Ragged School Museum** (*see p72*) to experience life in a poor school in Victorian times and sit through a Victorian lesson, taught by a suitably strict costumed teacher. **Dennis Severs' House** (*see p32*) in Spitalfields is a rich evocation of 18th-century domestic life, full of atmospheric sounds and smells, although it's only open occasionally. At the **Imperial War Museum** (*see p103*), the Children's War depicts World War II through children's eyes.

The Romans
It was the Romans that founded the glorious city of Londinium, back in 47AD. The **British Museum** (*see p73*) has

Sightseeing

artefacts from Roman Britannia, while the **Museum of London** (*see p84*) has room set-ups; outside it you can see pieces of the Roman London Wall, originally two miles long and six metres high. There are more bits of Wall outside the **Tower of London** (*see p39*), along with a statue of Emperor Trajan. Underneath **5 Strand Lane** (8232 5050, www.nationaltrust.org.uk) is a Roman bath 'run' by the National Trust; you can see it through a window from Surrey Street. Further afield, in Orpington, you can visit the genuine ten-room article at **Crofton Roman Villa** (8460 1442, www.bromley.gov.uk/leisure/museums/croftonvilla).

Space

Greenwich's **Royal Observatory** (*see p28*) has excellent new interactive astronomy galleries and London's only Planetarium, which runs daily children's shows. The **Science Museum** (*see p92*) has an Exploring Space gallery on the ground floor, with rockets, space suits, satellites and a fragile-looking lunar module. Go next door to see real space rocks: the **Natural History Museum** (*see p87*) has the country's largest collection of meteorites.

Toys

Introduce your offspring to the pre-Nintendo world (however did we cope?) at the **V&A Museum of Childhood** (*see p72*) in Bethnal Green. It's a huge place with

Science Museum.

quite a bit of hands-on fun. More eccentric is **Pollock's Toy Museum** (*see p71*), tucked away off Tottenham Court Road. In Wimbledon, the **Polka Theatre** (*see p180*) is a dedicated children's theatre that also houses a sweet teddy bear museum.

Tudors

Starting with Henry VII, the Tudors reigned from 1485 until 1603 when Elizabeth I died without having produced an heir. The Great Fire destroyed most of Tudor London, but you can still find glimpses – and admire Henry VIII's **Hampton Court Palace** (*see p39*). The **Tower of London** (*see p39*) is where Henry VIII's unfortunate wives were beheaded, and also has the king's armour on display. The **Golden Hinde** (*see p32*), a replica of Sir Francis Drake's ship, sits in Clink Street, near **Southwark Cathedral** (*see p40*).

Victorians

Hit the South Ken big three: the **Victoria & Albert** (*see p67*), **Science Museum** (*see p92*) and **Natural History Museum** (*see p87*) were established by the Victorians, and reflect their preoccupations and ambitions. You can also visit the **Charles Dickens Museum** (*see p76*) in Bloomsbury, where Dickens penned *Oliver Twist* and *Nicholas Nickleby*. The alleged Old Curiosity Shop isn't far away, in Portsmouth Street WC2. Visit the **Old Operating Theatre, Museum & Herb Garret** (*see p92*) to discover a sharper side of Victorian life. A guided walk is another way to explore Victorian London: www.walks.com has some child-friendly suggestions.

Victoria & Albert Museum.

shells at the foot of the bronze statue of Hodge outside the house. It's one of the few items that will really interest children, although they might enjoy trying on replica Georgian costumes in the garret.
Buggy access. Nearest picnic place: Lincoln's Inn Fields. Shop.

Florence Nightingale Museum
St Thomas's Hospital, 2 Lambeth Palace Road, SE1 7EW (7620 0374/www.florence-nightingale.co.uk). Westminster tube/Waterloo tube/rail. **Open** 10am-5pm daily. **Admission** £5.80; £4.80 5-18s, reductions; free under-5s; £16 family (2+2). **Credit** AmEx, MC, V. **Map** p317 M9. 5+
The Lady with the Lamp's important status in Key Stage One and Two of the National Curriculum means school holidays are always busy at the museum dedicated to her life. Mementoes and tableaux evoke the field hospitals of Scutari, where nurse Nightingale first came to public attention; details of her privileged life before then, and selfless life thereafter, are told in a 20-minute film.

Among the objects on display are her beloved, hand-reared pet owl, Athena (stuffed, and looking slightly wild of eye) and the medicine chest she took to Turkey. Trails for children are available, and art and history activities run during school holidays.
Buggy access. Disabled access: toilet. Nappy-changing facilities. Nearest picnic place: benches by hospital entrance, Archbishop's Park. Shop.

Sherlock Holmes Museum
221B Baker Street, NW1 6XE (7935 4430/ www.sherlock-holmes.co.uk). Baker Street tube/74, 139, 189 bus. **Open** 9.30am-6pm daily (last entry 5.30pm). **Admission** £6; £4 6-16s; free under-6s. **Credit** AmEx, MC, V. **Map** p311 F4. 6+
The famous address is set up as if the fictional master detective and his amiable sidekick are in situ. So too, is their long-suffering landlady, Mrs Hudson, who can tell you all you need to know about the great man. Nose about Holmes's study, take a seat in his armchair by the fireplace and investigate his personal effects: the deerstalker cap, pipe, violin and magnifying glass are all present and correct. Upstairs is the room belonging to his associate, Dr Watson, while the third-floor exhibit rooms contains wax models of scenes from the stories; Holmes and his dastardly arch-enemy, Professor Moriarty, can be seen in the same room.
Nearest picnic place: Regent's Park. Shop.

Sir John Soane's Museum
13 Lincoln's Inn Fields, WC2A 3BP (7405 2107/www.soane.org). Holborn tube. **Open** 10am-5pm Tue-Sat; 10am-5pm, 6-9pm 1st Tue of mth. *Tours* 2.30pm Sat. **Admission** free; donations appreciated. *Tours* £5; free under-16s. **Credit** AmEx, MC, V. **Map** p315 M5. 7+
This was the home of imaginative architect John Soane (1753-1837), whose house and collections reflect his passion for an eclectic mix of artefacts and paintings. The joy is not just in what is here, but also how Soane chose to present it; there are all sorts of ingenious nooks and crannies. It's particularly atmospheric if you visit on the first Tuesday of the month, when it stays open late and is lit by candlelight; there can be lengthy queues for admission.

The old kitchen is used for holiday workshops for children of seven and above (£10-£15 whole day/£5-£8 half day, book in advance): learn how mirrors increase light in a room and produce optical illusions, make a mosaic or get stuck into plaster moulding. There are also free drop-in family sessions on the third Saturday of the month (1.30-4.40pm). Children aged seven to 13 can sign up to the Young Architects Club, which meets on the first Saturday of the month. Note that buggies cannot be accommodated.
Nearest picnic place: Lincoln's Inn Fields. Shop.

LONDON & LOCAL

Bruce Castle Museum
Lordship Lane, N17 8NU (8808 8772/www.haringey.gov.uk). Wood Green tube, then 123 or 243 bus/Seven Sisters tube/rail then 123 or 243 bus/Bruce Grove rail. **Open** 1-5pm Wed-Sun. **Admission** free; donations appreciated. **No credit cards.** 4+
In an otherwise unremarkable-looking suburban street, the museum is a delightfully unexpected find: a splendid, Grade I-listed 16th-century mansion, whose grounds are now a public park. Its displays are devoted to the history and achievements of Haringey and its residents – more interesting than you might think, as the borough was home to both madcap illustrator William Heath Robinson and Rowland Hill, the inventor of the Penny Post.

The museum's 'Inventor Centre' has numerous buttons to press and levers to pull. There are black-and-white photos dating back to the days when the area was open countryside and White Hart Lane a sleepy country track. Football fans should keep an eye out for the displays on Tottenham Hotspur and read the surprising history of Walter Tull, one of the first black

Hackney Museum: a hands-on look at Hackney's heritage. *See p83.*

football players in Britain. There are free activity sheets for kids, including a nature trail that rambles around the pleasant park outside, plus free art and craft sessions for families from 2pm to 4pm on Sundays year-round, with extra school holiday sessions.
Buggy access. Disabled access: lift, toilet. Nappy-changing facilities. Nearest picnic place: museum grounds. Shop.

Brunel Museum
Brunel Engine House, Railway Avenue, SE16 4LF (7231 3840/www.brunel-museum.org.uk). Rotherhithe tube. **Open** 10am-5pm daily. **Admission** £2; £1 reductions; free under-16s. **No credit cards.** 5+
The Brunel father and son team (Sir Marc and Isambard Kingdom) worked from 1825 until 1843 to create a pioneering under-river tunnel, running from Rotherhithe to Wapping; young Isambard nearly drowned in the process. The story of what the Victorians hailed as 'the Eighth Wonder of the World' is told in this museum in the original engine house; the tunnel itself is now used by the East London tube line. There's plenty for children, not least the popular summer play-scheme in the sculpture garden. The giant figure of Brunel that is owned by the museum is always (and literally) a big player in the Bermondsey and Rotherhithe carnivals. A brand new café and activity centre are now open, following a major refurb, while the vast entrance hall to the Thames Tunnel, once the site of a shopping arcade and underground fairground, is due to open in late 2009; call for the latest updates.
Buggy access. Café. Disabled access: toilet. Nappy-changing facilities. Nearest picnic place: museum gardens & riverbank. Shop.

Crystal Palace Museum
Anerley Hill, SE19 2BA (8676 0700/www. crystalpalacemuseum.org.uk). Crystal Palace rail. **Open** 11am-4.30pm Sat, Sun, bank hol Mon. **Admission** free. 7+
To learn about the majestic, glittering exhibition hall that gave this area its name, visit this friendly museum, housed in the old engineering school where John Logie Baird invented television. The 'exhibition of an exhibition' includes Victorian artefacts from the original Hyde Park edifice, as well as video and audio presentations about the great glass building, which burnt to the ground in November 1936. A small Logie Baird display marks the birth of home entertainment; from June 1934 the Baird Television Company occupied four studios at Crystal Palace. Note that opening hours are limited, as the museum is run by volunteers.
Buggy access. Nearest picnic place: Crystal Palace Park. Shop.

Sightseeing

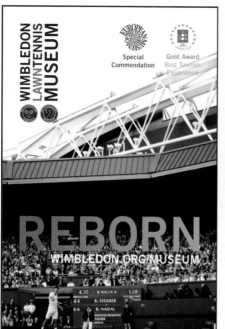

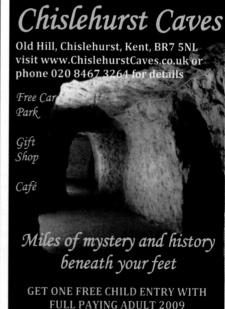

Hackney Museum

Technology & Learning Centre, 1 Reading Lane, off Mare Street, E8 1GQ (8356 3500/ www.hackney.gov.uk). Hackney Central rail. **Open** 9.30am-5.30pm Tue, Wed, Fri; 9.30am-8pm Thur; 10am-5pm Sat. **Admission** free. **No credit cards.** 3+

This community-focused museum is a vibrant affair, with plenty to keep kids busy. Displays include exhibits on immigration in the area and a recreation of Cooke's pie and eel shop, plus activity stations and touch-screen interactives that tie into the history of the borough. Other highlights include a recreated Saxon boat that kids can pile up with goods (the original is displayed under glass in the floor) and a section on the Matchbox car factory, founded in Hackney in 1952. Toddlers can settle into the reading corner while older kids dress up in Victorian clobber and try making matchboxes – an industry that employed countless children in Victorian times. Interactive art and role-playing workshops take place on Wednesday and Thursday afternoons, while the temporary exhibition changes every four months; until September 2009 the theme is Board Games. *Buggy access. Disabled access: toilet. Nappy-changing facilities. Nearest picnic place: benches in square, London Fields. Shop.*

Islington Museum

Finsbury Library, 245 St John Street, EC1V 4NB (7527 3235/www.islington.gov.uk). Angel tube/Farringdon tube/rail/153 bus. **Open** 10am-5pm Mon, Tue, Thur-Sat. **Admission** free. **No credit cards.** 5+

Reopened in May 2008, after a funding injection from the Heritage Lottery Fund, Islington Museum now occupies purpose-built premises underneath Finsbury Library. Its collection spans centuries of local history, from the days when Islington dairies provided the milk for medieval London (check out the centuries-old cow's skull) to World War II, and the rise of the mighty Arsenal. Children will enjoy the sections on Edwardian school life, and the special activity desks and quiz screens. Call or check online for half term and summer holiday events. *Buggy access. Disabled access: lift, toilet. Nearest picnic place: Northhampton Square. Shop.*

Kew Bridge Steam Museum

Green Dragon Lane, Brentford, Middx TW8 0EN (8568 4757/www.kbsm.org). Gunnersbury tube, then 237 or 267 bus/Kew Bridge rail/65, 391 bus. **Open** 11am-4pm Tue-Sun, bank hol Mon. **Admission** (annual ticket, allows for multiple visits) £9.50; £8.50 reductions; free under-16s. Under-16s must be accompanied by an adult. **Credit** MC, V. 5+

The golden age of steam is celebrated at this Victorian riverside pumping station. At weekends, selected steam engines – the pumping variety, as well as the locomotive sort – burst into life, powered by a 1920s Lancashire boiler. The fascinating Water for Life gallery saturates you with facts about the history of water supply and usage in London, including the spread of cholera, while Down Below takes you down the sewers to learn about the work of Bazalgette and the whiffy world of toshers (sewer scavengers). *Cloister*, the narrow-gauge steam locomotive, gives rides on Sundays between April and October; family activities are held during the school and bank holidays. *Buggy access. Café (Sat, Sun). Disabled access: lift, toilet. Nappy-changing facilities. Nearest picnic place: Kew Green. Shop.*

London Canal Museum

12-13 New Wharf Road, N1 9RT (7713 0836/www.canalmuseum.org.uk). King's Cross tube/rail. **Open** 10am-4.30pm Tue-Sun, bank hol Mon. Last entry 3.45pm. **Admission** £3; £2 reductions; £1.50 5-15s; free under-5s. **Credit** MC, V. **Map** p315 M2. 5+

Housed in the former ice warehouse of Italian-Swiss entrepreneur Carlo Gatti, this charming museum chronicles the history of everything canal-related, as well as exploring the once highly lucrative ice trade. Kids can clamber aboard the narrowboat, *Coronis*, and get a taste of life on the waterways; an activity corner has books and building blocks to create your own tunnel; and there's the chance to learn how to tie a sheepshank and clove hitch. Most atmospheric is the ice well, once used to store imported ice from Norway; it could be kept here for months before being delivered around London. Visitors have taken to tossing coins into the cool, dark space; extra points if you can hit the bucket. Upstairs, a life-size model horse makes convincing horsey noises in his stable, while there are four videos on canal life to watch and regular temporary exhibitions (a photographic display on England's waterways on our last visit). The back of the museum leads on to Battlebridge Basin, once a grimy industrial wharf, now lined with pretty residential canal boats and converted warehouses. For those with the energy, the shopping hubs of Camden and Islington are within walking distance along Regent's Canal. *See also p108* **Great Days Out.** *Buggy access. Disabled access: lift, toilet. Nappy-changing facilities. Nearest picnic place: museum terrace, canal towpath. Shop.*

Sightseeing

London Transport Museum

*The Piazza, WC2E 7BB (7379 6344/www.
ltmuseum.co.uk). Covent Garden tube.* **Open**
10am-6pm Mon-Thur, Sat, Sun; 11am-9pm
Fri. **Admission** £10; £6-£8 reductions; free
under-16s. **Credit** AmEx, MC, V. **Map** p317
L7. 2+
London would grind to a halt without its
sophisticated travel system. This much-loved
museum does a sterling job of presenting a
fascinating and entertaining history of
transportation in the capital, with 20 vehicles to
explore along the way. The posters are glorious
too – particularly the stylised, often marvelously
avant-garde designs of the 1920s and '30s. *See
also p46* **Great Days Out**.
*Buggy access. Café. Disabled access: lift, toilet.
Nappy-changing facilities. Nearest picnic place:
museum picnic room, Piazza. Shop.*

Museum of London

*150 London Wall, EC2Y 5HN (7001 9844/
www.museumoflondon.org.uk). Barbican or St
Paul's tube/Moorgate tube/rail.* **Open** 10am-
6pm daily. Last entry 5.30pm. **Admission**
free. **Credit** MC, V. **Map** p318 P5. 6+
An extensive redevelopment project means the
lower galleries of this excellent museum are
currently off-limits; if all goes according to
plan, they'll open in Spring 2010. There's plenty
to see in the meantime, though, with displays
charting London's history from prehistoric
times, when mammoths roamed where Regent
Street now lies, to the Great Fire of London in
1666. (The galleries under refurbishment cover
from 1700 to the present day.)
The 'London Before London' gallery is full of
stone tools and primitive weapons, with modern
recreations that kids can safely handle; there are
more objects to touch and costumes to play with
in the Roman and Medieval London galleries.
Computer stations throughout the museum offer
activities based on the displays, and activity
sheets for families are available from the
information desk.
Storytelling sessions and craft workshops
take place at weekends, and there are special
activities throughout the school holidays. At
least once a month, the museum runs a themed
walk through the City, visiting sections of the
Roman Wall, the Thames foreshore and other
relics of London's ancient history. Other events
include gallery tours; drop-in object handling
sessions and exhibition tours, led by curators;
check the website for details.
*Buggy access. Café. Disabled access: lift, toilet.
Nappy-changing facilities. Nearest picnic place:
Barber Surgeon's Garden. Shop.*

Museum of London Docklands

*West India Quay, Hertsmere Road, E14 4AL
(7001 9844/www.museumoflondon.org.uk/
docklands). Canary Wharf tube/West India
Quay DLR.* **Open** 10am-6pm daily.
Admission (annual ticket, allows for
multiple visits) £5; £3 reductions; free
under-16s. **Credit** MC, V. 4+
There's a wealth of absorbing exhibits at this
converted Georgian warehouse; luckily kids'
admission is free, while adult tickets remain
valid for a year. Displays devoted to migration
and river trade explore the history of how 'the
world came to the East End', with plenty of
nautical relics and atmospheric recreations.
Must-sees for kids include Sailortown, a murky,
full-size recreation of 18th-century Wapping
(look out for the wild animal emporium), the
gibbet cage (where captured pirates met their
end) and the Mudlarks Gallery, crammed with
interactive exhibits and with a soft play area for
under-fives. The galleries on the modern history
of the docks are more interesting than adults
children, but everyone can learn something from
the 'London, Sugar & Slavery' and 'Docklands
at War' exhibitions. Many of the displays come
with an entertaining audio commentary, voiced
by *Time Team's* Tony Robinson.
Costumed storytelling sessions and craft
workshops take place at the museum most
Saturday and Sunday afternoons, and there are
extra sessions during the school holidays. The
line-up has plenty for younger children, including
storytimes and Monday play sessions for under-
fives. There's a refectory, but the best place to
enjoy your sandwiches is out on the quayside,
beneath the giant loading cranes. *See also p90*
Great Days Out.
*Buggy access. Café. Disabled access: lift, toilet.
Nappy-changing facilities. Nearest picnic place:
quayside benches, refectory. Restaurant. Shop.*

Old Royal Naval College

*King William Walk, SE10 9LW (8269 4747/
tours 8269 4799/www.greenwichfoundation.
org.uk). Cutty Sark DLR/Greenwich DLR/rail.*
Open 10am-5pm daily. *Tours* by arrangement.
Admission free. *Tours* £4; free under-16s.
Credit MC, V. 5+
Sir Christopher Wren drew up the plans for this
show-stopping baroque masterpiece – all the
lovelier for its riverside location. Originally, it
was a shelter for retired seamen, who were given
bed and board, plus a shilling a week (about five
pence in modern-day money). In the late 19th
century, the buildings were occupied by the
Royal Naval College, before passing into the
hands of the Greenwich Foundation. The

University of Greenwich and Trinity College of Music are now in residence, but the exquisite neoclassical chapel and Painted Hall are open to the public. The hall is an outstanding feat of trompe l'oeil, 19 long years in the painting; see if the kids can spot the Pocahontas-like figure who represents the Americas on the Upper Hall's central ceiling panel.

The visitors' centre, café and shop are currently closed for an ambitious remodelling, and will open in early 2010 as Discover Greenwich, a new education centre exploring Greenwich's maritime history. In the meantime, check the website for seasonal events such as the Big Draw or the May Fair. *See also p126* **Great Days Out**.

Buggy access. Café. Disabled access: toilet. Nappy-changing facilities. Nearest picnic place: Naval College grounds. Restaurant. Shop.

Museum of Richmond

Old Town Hall, Whittaker Avenue, Richmond, Surrey TW9 1TP (8332 1141/www.museum ofrichmond.com). Richmond tube/rail. **Open** 11am-5pm Tue-Sat. **Admission** free. **No credit cards.** 4+

Leafy Richmond is an area with abundant royal connections, from the 12th-century Henry I to Elizabeth I, 400 years later; fittingly, the town's museum was opened by Queen Elizabeth II. There are permanent and temporary displays on its illustrious residents of days gone by, plus a gallery of work by local artists. Engaging family workshops run during the school holidays – trying on replica Tudor headgear, say, before creating your own resplendent hat. *Buggy access. Disabled access: lift, toilet. Nearest picnic place: Richmond Green, riverside. Shop.*

Wimbledon Windmill Museum

Windmill Road, Wimbledon Common, SW19 5NR (8947 2825/www.wimbledonwindmill museum.org.uk). Wimbledon tube/rail. **Open** *Apr-Oct* 2-5pm Sat; 11am-5pm Sun, bank hols. School groups by appointment only. **Admission** £2; £1 under-16s, reductions. **No credit cards.** 5+

One of Wimbledon Common's more unusual assets is its windmill. It was built in 1817 by carpenter Charles March, at the request of locals who wanted to grind their own wheat. These days it's a small museum, run by volunteers and open weekends-only.

On the ground floor, there's a film about how windmills work, a display showing how the windmill was built, and a collection of woodworking tools used in its restoration. The first floor is more hands-on, with a working model of the windmill in action, the chance for children to have a go at grinding wheat with a saddle-stone or hand quern, and commentaries at the push of a button. Climbing the ladder takes you up to the tower, where you can see the sails' operating machinery turning on blusterous days.

Buggy access (ground floor). Nearest picnic place: Wimbledon Common. Café. Shop.

Discover a musical genius at the **Handel House Museum**. *See p87.*

Sightseeing

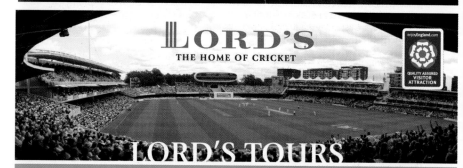

MUSIC

Handel House Museum

25 Brook Street (entrance at rear), W1K 4HB (7495 1685/www.handelhouse.org). Bond Street tube. **Open** 10am-6pm Tue, Wed, Fri, Sat; 10am-8pm Thur; noon-6pm Sun. **Admission** £5; £4.50 reductions; £2 6-16s (free Sat); free under-6s. **Credit** MC, V. **Map** p316 H6. **5+**
The legendary composer lived in this Georgian townhouse from 1723 until his death in 1759. Its interiors have been painstakingly restored, and the house now contains a museum devoted to the man and his work. The collection includes paintings, letters, scores and a reproduction of his harpsichord. Children are encouraged to visit, with free entry on Saturdays, plus the odd family-friendly musical event (the Thursday evening recitals are aimed more at adults). The child-friendly ethos extends to trails, quizzes and activities to go with the displays.
Buggy access. Disabled access: lift, toilet. Nappy-changing facilities. Nearest picnic place: Hanover Square. Shop.

Musical Museum

399 High Street, Brentford, Middx TW8 0DU (8560 8108/www.musicalmuseum.co.uk). Kew Bridge rail. **Open** 11am-5.30pm Tue-Sun, bank hol Mon. Last entry 4.30pm. **Admission** £7; £5.50 reductions; free under-16s. **Credit** MC, V. **5+**
Children who find themselves all thumbs when it comes to music lessons will be deeply impressed by the ingenious self-playing pianos and violins on display at this museum of automatic instruments. Other exhibits include clockwork musical boxes, orchestrions (a mechanical instrument that sounds like a large ensemble), musical toys and barrel organs. Most are in working order and are demonstrated by the staff, with their functions fully explained. Upstairs is a concert hall with an orchestra pit from which a Wurlitzer console slowly rises, as it did in cinemas in the 1930s; check the online events diary for performances.
Buggy access. Café. Disabled access: lift, toilet. Nappy-changing facilities. Nearest picnic place: riverside. Shop.

NATURAL WORLD

Garden Museum

Church of St Mary-at-Lambeth, Lambeth Palace Road, SE1 7LB (7401 8865/www.gardenmuseum.org.uk). Lambeth North tube/
Waterloo tube/rail, then 507 bus/C10, 77 bus. **Open** 10.30am-5pm daily (Closed 1st Mon of mth). **Admission** £6; free-£5 reductions; free under-16s. **Credit** MC, V. **Map** p317 L10. **6+**
Escape from the bustle of central London at this tranquil museum, set by the Thames in a deconsecrated church. Inside, the collection of tools and gardening paraphernalia has some unexpected oddities, including a weird-looking 'vegetable lamb' (believed for centuries to be half lamb, half plant) a set of pony boots (worn by lawnmower-pulling horses to prevent their hooves from marking the grass) and a cunning, cat-shaped bird scarer.
Outside, the old graveyard has some distinguished residents: the Tradescants, a pioneering family of gardeners and botanists; Captain William Bligh, of *Bounty* fame; and half a dozen Archbishops of Canterbury. The wild garden is awash with valerian, poppies, harebells and cow parsley, while the 17th century-style knot garden is a riot of colour in summer, enclosed in neat box-hedge borders.
Buggy access. Café. Disabled access: toilet. Nappy-changing facilities. Nearest picnic place: Archbishop's Park. Shop.

Natural History Museum

Cromwell Road, SW7 5BD (7942 5000/ www.nhm.ac.uk). South Kensington tube. **Open** 10am-5.50pm daily. **Admission** free; charges apply for special exhibitions. **Credit** AmEx, MC, V. **Map** p313 D10. **4+**
The cobalt blue and buff façade of this venerable museum is a true London landmark, and a mecca for streams of families. Inside, exhibits are split into four colour-coded zones, each with its own marvels.
The Blue zone is the one most younger visitors make a beeline for, thanks to the famous dinosaur gallery – presided over by a scary, animatronic T-Rex. In the mammals gallery, the sabre-toothed tiger skeleton also elicits a delicious shudder, while a life-size model of a blue whale is suspended from the ceiling.
The Green zone encompasses the child-friendly and fiendishly popular Creepy Crawlies exhibit: watching leaf-cutter ants at work, exploring a termite mound and gawping at the world's longest stick insect (a twiggy, leggy 56.7cm beast) are among its attractions. Geology takes centre stage in the Red zone, which you can access directly from the museum's Exhibition Road entrance. It's a dramatic, dark, escalator ascent through the centre of the earth. At the top you'll find the ground-shaking earthquake simulator – a reliable source of giggles (and a few shrieks of alarm). Finally, the Orange zone comprises the wildlife garden and the new

Sightseeing

Darwin Centre buildings, set to open in Autumn 2009. Visitors will be able to peek at scientists at work in the state-of-the-art laboratories, before exploring the massive plant and insect collections – housed in a sleek eight-storey cocoon, itself contained in a glass and steel box. If seeing the scientists at work inspires the kids to get hands-on, take them down to the Investigate Centre in the main museum's basement (open weekday afternoons and weekends; call ahead to check times). Here, seven to 14s can study specimens (some living) through a microscope, and note their findings. When lunchtime rolls round, the museum has a restaurant, a café and a sandwich bar, along with indoor and outdoor picnic areas if you'd rather bring your own grub. *See also p96* **Great Days Out**.
Buggy Access. Cafés. Disabled access: lift, toilet. Nappy-changing facilities. Nearest picnic place: basement picnic room, museum grounds. Restaurant.

RELIGION

Jewish Museum
129-131 Albert Street, NW1 7NB (www. jewishmuseum.org.uk). Camden Town tube. **Open/admission** check website for details. **Credit** MC, V. 4+
The Jewish Museum has been closed since late 2007, but is due to reopen in the winter of 2009/10. The old museum has been connected to a neighbouring building, with both undergoing complete refurbishment. When the doors finally open, there will be five shiny new galleries, the first of which is an introductory audiovisual exhibit about the Jewish community today. Permanent displays on the upper floors will explore Judaism as a living religion, the holocaust, and the history of Jews in Britain from 1066 to the present day. The first temporary exhibit will be 'Jews in the British Entertainment Industry'.
Buggy access. Café. Disabled access: toilets. Nappy-changing facilities. Nearest picnic place: Regent's Park. Shop.

Museum of Methodism & John Wesley's House
Wesley's Chapel, 49 City Road, EC1Y 1AU (7253 2262/www.wesleyschapel.org.uk). Moorgate or Old Street tube/rail. **Open** 10am-4pm Mon-Wed, Fri, Sat; 10am-12.30pm, 1.45-4pm Thur; 12.30-1.45pm Sun. **Admission** free, donations appreciated. **Credit** MC, V. **Map** p319 Q4. 8+

Just around the corner from the thunderous traffic of City Road sits this lovely chapel and its surrounding Georgian buildings. It was built by John Wesley in 1778, and is known as the cathedral of world Methodism. Wesley called it 'perfectly neat but not fine', although there are many more adornments now than in his day.
Down in the crypt, the museum has a permanent display charting the history of Methodism, while Hogarthian prints depict poverty, alcoholism and moral degradation in 18th-century England. Look out for the regular lunchtime recitals making use of the chapel's organ. Wesley's neighbouring house has been restored to 18th-century simplicity; much of the furniture is of the period, although the tiny four-poster in the bedroom is reproduction, as is the curious 'chamber horse' in the study – an early form of home-gym equipment.
Buggy access. Disabled access: lift, toilet. Nappy-changing facilities. Nearest picnic place: enclosed courtyard at entrance, Bunhill Fields. Shop.

SCIENCE & MEDICINE

Alexander Fleming Laboratory Museum
St Mary's Hospital, Praed Street, W2 1NY (7886 6528/www.st-marys.nhs.uk). Paddington tube/rail/7, 15, 27, 36 bus. **Open** 10am-1pm Mon-Thur; also by appointment. Closed bank hols. **Admission** £2; £1 5-16s, reductions; free under-5s. **No credit cards. Map** p313 D5. 8+
Explore a recreation of the laboratory where Alexander Fleming discovered penicillin back on 3 September 1928. Exhibits and a video celebrate Fleming's life and the role of penicillin in fighting disease. In the era of the superbug, this shrine to antibiotics is both increasingly relevant and a relic from a simpler time. Staff run tours for family and school groups; note that the museum is not accessible to the disabled.
Nearest picnic place: canalside, Hyde Park. Shop.

Hunterian Museum
Royal College of Surgeons of England, 35-43 Lincoln's Inn Fields, WC2A 3PE (7869 6560/ www.rcseng.ac.uk/museums). Holborn tube. **Open** 10am-5pm Tue-Sat. **Admission** free; donations appreciated. **Credit** MC, V. **Map** p318 M6. 4+
The Hunterian is quite possibly the weirdest museum in all of London – and the most wonderful, some would say. Its gleaming glass

Sightseeing

cabinets are filled with row upon row of specimen jars, containing human and animal remains of every description in various states of disease and dissection: brains, hearts, hernias, big toes, paws and jaws, all spookily suspended in formaldehyde. The museum's namesake, John Hunter (1728-93) was a pioneering surgeon and anatomist, appointed physician to King George III. He amassed thousands of medical specimens; after he died, the collection was enhanced and expanded by others. Children (and grown-ups) of a grisly bent will be gripped, but more sensitive souls and younger kids should probably steer clear.

The most famous pieces in the collection are the brain of mathematician Charles Babbage and the towering skeleton of 'Irish Giant' Charles Byrne, who stood a towering 2.2m (7ft 7in) tall in his socks. There are trails for kids to complete, along with a skeleton suit to try for size and a fabric body part game; medically themed events for fives to 12s take place during school holidays, led by costumed actors (booking is essential).

Buggy access. Disabled access: lift, toilet.
Nearest picnic place: Lincoln's Inn Fields. Shop.

Old Operating Theatre, Museum & Herb Garret

9A St Thomas's Street, SE1 9RY (7188 2679/ www.thegarret.org.uk). London Bridge tube/

rail. **Open** 10.30am-5pm daily. Closed 15 Dec-5 Jan. **Admission** £5.60; £4.60 reductions; £3.25 6-15s; free under-6s; £13.75 family (2+4). **No credit cards. Map** p319 Q8. 7+

Entry to this one-of-a-kind museum is via a narrow, rickety, wooden spiral staircase, which leads to a very different London from the one below. The Herb Garret smells pungently of fennel and other herbs and contains a jumble of ghoulish exhibits packed under its dark eaves. Nineteenth-century amputation kits and terrifying obstetric implements jostle with bits of Victorians preserved in jars and early anatomical charts.

Through a narrow antechamber lies Europe's oldest operating theatre, perched rather incredibly inside the roof of St Thomas' Church (St Thomas' Hospital was also on this site until it moved to Lambeth in 1862), where re-enactment demonstrations at 2pm every Saturday bring the traumas of pre-anaesthesia surgery gorily to life.

Nearest picnic place: Southwark Cathedral Gardens. Shop.

Royal London Hospital Museum

St Philip's Church, Newark Street, E1 2AA (7480 4823/www.bartsandthelondon.nhs.uk/ museums). Whitechapel tube. **Open** 10am-4.30pm Tue-Fri. **Admission** free. **Credit** (café) MC, V. 7+

Unearthly remains at the freakish but fascinating **Hunterian Museum**.

Great Days Out
Docklands

The Canary Wharf Tower, with its flashing beacon and wispy plume of steam at its apex, is the iconic symbol of this Thatcherite development. It's the tallest building in Great Britain and visible from all over London; unfortunately, (in true Thatcher style) you have to work in the building to enjoy the views.

Docklands is the semi-official name given to the massive redevelopment of this eastern stretch of the Thames. And here on the **Isle of Dogs** (supposedly named after some royal kennels in the area), where great ships once lined up in impressive docks, there are now shiny office blocks, luxury flats and the biggest cluster of high-rise buildings in Europe. That said, a day out here makes a surprisingly pleasant excursion.

These days, the area is easily accessible from the centre of town, thanks to the Jubilee line. Visitors disembark in the sleek, cavernous Canary Wharf underground station, which was designed by Norman Foster; the area around the curved entrances has been made into a pretty Japanese garden.

But perhaps the most scenic way to travel here is by taking the **Docklands Light Railway**, or DLR (7363 9700, www.tfl.gov.uk/dlr) which zips along raised tracks and gives great views over the area. Children will be fascinated by the driverless trains and can even pretend they're in control of the train, if you travel outside peak time and nab seats in the glass-fronted lead carriage.

If you want to combine Canary Wharf with some more traditional sightseeing, then consider buying a Rail & River Rover ticket (£13.50, £6.75 children, free under-5s, £33 family), which allows a day's travel on the DLR with unlimited trips on the City Cruises sightseeing boats that run between Greenwich pier, Tower, Waterloo and Westminster. But don't be too quick to leave… This centre of commerce has its tourist attractions too.

Trails and sails

With its clean lines and neat landscaping, Docklands is a bit like a model town, and children will enjoy exploring the bridges, pathways and open stretches of water.

To give some purpose to your roaming, tackle one of two walking trails available at www.canarywharf.com (click on the 'lifestyle' link). The first lists the area's many film location spots and will interest budding cinephiles, while the second leads you around Docklands' generous sprinkling of artworks and sculptures. Our favourites are Ron Arad's red spike *Windwand* and his *Big Blue* at Westferry Circus and Lynn Chadwick's *Couple on Seat* in Cabot Square.

Emma Biggs' wonderfully intricate mosaics, embedded into the floor of

Jubilee Place shopping centre, evoke the area's past ('London used to be a city of ships. A thousand vessels a week passed through the docks').

For some idea of what this city of ships once looked like, head for the surprisingly thorough and enjoyable **Museum of London Docklands** (see p84). Follow the bouncing bridge (it's supported on floats) from Cabot Square; the museum is in a row of converted warehouses on the edge of West India Quay. Inside, there are some fantastically evocative photographs, paintings, prints and models of the bustling docks as they would have been when this area was London's industrial heart. The museum's three jam-packed floors tell the story of the Thames, the port of London and its people, from Roman times up to the Docklands redevelopment.

The children will be rewarded for their learning when they get to the Mudlarks Gallery, with all its hands-on discovery games. It's so popular that entry is by timed ticket. There's also a great café where for every adult meal bought, a child eats for free.

Great escape

If all this talk of industry and business is making the children feel old before their time, it might be the moment to grab some fresh air. A short south-bound DLR ride from Canary Wharf takes you to Mudchute. Here, in the shadow of Docklands' high rises, lies **Mudchute City Farm** (see p134).

From Mudchute station, take the raised path past the parkland and allotments, where you can play spot-the-llama as you make your way towards the farm entrance. The closer you get, the more audible the resident ducks, chickens, pigs, goats, donkeys and horses become. Inside sprawl acres of fields and pastures; this is one of the largest city farms in Europe. If helping to feed the

LUNCH BOX

Also in the area: Nando's, Pizza Express, Wagamama.
1802 *Museum In Docklands, No.1 Warehouse, Hertsmere Road, West India Key, E14 4AL (7538 2702/www. museumindocklands.org.uk).* Great food and plenty of atmosphere.
Carluccio's Caffè *Reuters Plaza, E14 5AJ (7719 1749/www.carluccios.com).* Child-friendly and reasonably priced.
Gun *27 Coldharbour, E14 9NS (7515 5222/www.thegundocklands.com).* A smart gastropub that welcomes kids.
Mudchute Kitchen *Mudchute Farm, Pier Street, E14 3HP (7515 5901/ www.mudchutekitchen.org).* Fresh, flavoursome farm grub. *See p231.*
Smollensky's *1 Nash Court, E14 5AG (7719 0101/www.smollenskys.com).* Tasty steaks, popular with nippers. *See p250.*

animals makes you a bit peckish, head for the farm's acclaimed café, Mudchute Kitchen, for a scrumptious farmhouse breakfast or slab of cake.

If animals aren't the order of the day, there's always **Island Gardens** (cross the main road from the eponymous station), with its beautiful view of Greenwich (see p126) on the other side of the Thames. Cross via the spookily drippy Victorian foot tunnel that runs below the river; the attendant-operated lifts (7am-7pm Mon-Sat, 10am-5.30pm Sun) are big enough for a fleet of buggies. You're not allowed to cycle through the tunnel, though, so any bike-riders will have to dismount and push their trusty steeds.

Great Days Out

The entrance to this fascinating museum lies at the bottom of an unprepossessing staircase in a backstreet. Exhibits chronicle the history of what was once the biggest general hospital in the UK: the Royal London opened in 1740, so there's a lot of history to explore.

The museum devotes a section to each century, with special displays relating to the hospital's most famous patients and staff, including Thomas Barnardo, Florence Nightingale, John Merrick (the 'Elephant Man') and Edith Cavell. The development of nursing and childcare is traced through displays of starchy uniforms, and there's a forensics case with a copy of Jack the Ripper's notorious 'From Hell' letter. Most entertaining, however (and a welcome respite if you've been dragging children about all day), is the 1934 X-ray control unit that could have been created by a mad inventor from a sci-fi B-movie, and the plummily-narrated documentaries, which date from the 1930s to the '60s. These show, for example, children wearing pilot's goggles receiving doses of ultraviolet light at a time the London smog prevented the natural synthesis of vitamin D.

Buggy access. Café (in hospital). Disabled access: lift, toilet. Nappy-changing facilities (in hospital). Nearest picnic place: hospital garden. Shop.

St Bartholomew's Hospital Museum

West Smithfield, EC1A 7BE (7601 8152/ www.bartsandthelondon.nhs.uk/museums). Barbican or St Paul's tube. **Open** 10am-4pm Tue-Fri. *Tours* (Church & Great Hall) 2pm Fri. **Admission** free. *Tours* £5; £4 reductions; free under-16s accompanied by adult. **No credit cards. Map** p318 O6. **12+**

St Bart's was founded in the 12th century, and the museum here recalls the hospital's origins as a refuge for chronically sick people hoping for a miraculous cure. The exhibits include 19th-century watercolours and sketches of various diseases, leather lunatic restraints, a wooden head used by medical students to practise their drilling techniques on and photographs documenting the slow progress of nurses from drudges to career women. Don't miss the two huge paintings by local lad William Hogarth.

Café (in hospital). Nearest picnic place: hospital grounds.

Science Museum

Exhibition Road, SW7 2DD (7942 4454/ tickets 0870 870 4868/www.sciencemuseum. org.uk). South Kensington tube. **Open** 10am-6pm daily. **Admission** free; charges apply for special exhibitions. **Credit** AmEx, MC, V. **Map** p313 D9. **4+**

No one's too young or old to get a kick out of the Science Museum – a temple to scientific knowledge and discovery that welcomes inquisitive visitors. Icons of science (Stephenson's *Rocket* locomotive, Crick and Watson's DNA model) are treated with due respect, but this place couldn't be less stuffy: with its games, simulators and interactive exhibits, it feels like a giant playground.

The jewel in its crown is the Launchpad, where 50 hands-on exhibits and experiments keep kids agog; here, they can make a rainbow, check out their chilly noses on the thermal imaging screen, attempt to run a radio on pedal-power or take a dizzying turn on the rotation station. It's aimed at eight to 14s, but appeals to all ages. Other areas cater to younger children: five to eights can explore the Pattern Pod, while under-sixes race around the magical, multi-sensory Garden play areas, whose marvels include computerised flowers and giant building blocks. Extra charges apply for the IMAX cinema and the third-floor motionride simulator – though both are free for members. If you're planning to eat here, the Deep Blue Café is a reliable bet (*see p226*).

As you'd expect, the museum attracts hordes of visitors in the school holidays. Book ahead if you want to catch a film, and try to arrive at Launchpad at 10am to avoid lengthy queues. Held throughout the year, Science Night sleepovers (eight to 11s) are another big draw. It's £30 well spent, as kids take part in hands-on science activities and explore the galleries, before hunkering down for the night: you need to book well in advance, and the minimum group size is five children and one adult. *See also p96* **Great Days Out**.

Buggy access. Cafés. Disabled access: lift, toilet. Nappy-changing facilities. Nearest picnic place: Hyde Park, museum basement and 1st floor picnic areas. Restaurant. Shop.

Wellcome Collection

183 Euston Road, NW1 2BE (7611 2222/ www.wellcomecollection.org). Euston Square tube/Euston tube/rail. **Open** 10am-6pm Tue, Wed, Fri, Sat; 10am-10pm Thur; 11am-6pm Sun. Closed bank hol Mon. **Admission** free. **Credit** MC, V. **14+** (parental advisory)

Unlike many of London's medical museums, the Wellcome Collection displays its exhibits in modern, airy galleries that are well laid out and stuffed to the brim with eye-opening curios. The man behind the collection was Sir Henry Wellcome, a pioneering 19th-century pharmacist, philanthropist and entrepreneur, who amassed

1000 ways to entertain your kids

Only £12.99 from all good bookshops and **timeout.com/shop**

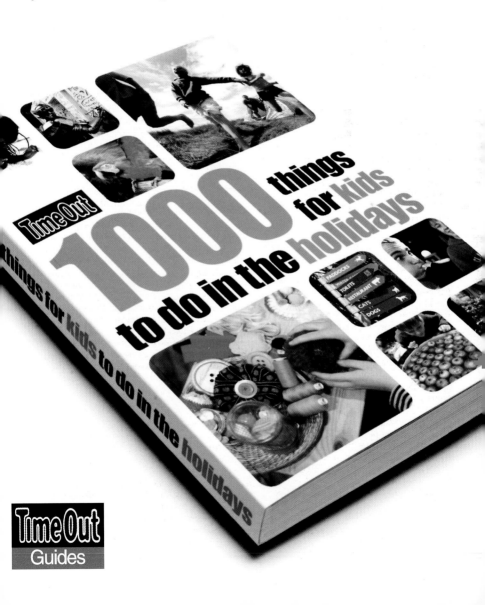

an idiosyncratic selection of artefacts relating to the medical profession, a tiny proportion of which is displayed in the permanent Medicine Man section. Sensitive children might find some of the items too grisly (the vicious, bladed torture chair, the slips of real human skin) or too saucy (Japanese sex aids, phallic amulets), but older children will get a kick out of seeing a religious mendicant's nail sole sandals, a mummified body from Peru, Napoleon's toothbrush and a lock of George III's hair.

Medicine Now presents exhibits on the themes of genomes, malaria, obesity and the body. The permanent sections are bolstered by a programme of excellent temporary exhibitions that examine various aspects of life and death; the events programme, suitable for teenagers, includes talks and microscopy workshops. There's also a good bookshop, and a superb Peyton & Byrne café on the ground floor, serving meals, fabulous cakes and a good selection of teas.

Buggy access. Café. Disabled access: lift, toilet. Nappy-changing facilities. Nearest picnic place: Gordon Square. Shop.

SPECIALIST

Bank of England Museum

Entrance on Bartholomew Lane, off Threadneedle Street, EC2R 8AH (7601 5491/ cinema bookings 7601 3985/www.bankof

england.co.uk). Bank tube/DLR. **Open** 10am-5pm Mon-Fri. Closed bank hols. **Admission** free. **Credit** MC, V. **Map** p319 Q6. 5+

The first room of the museum is Sir John Soane's beautiful 18th-century banking hall (restored to its original mahogany splendour) with bewigged and bestockinged mannequins appealing to younger visitors' imaginations. Permanent displays of notes, coins and early handwritten cheques illustrate a chronological history of banking, which is summed up in an educational film. There are lots of terribly impressive paintings, cartoons and pieces of furniture, but children will be much more excited by the everyday tools of the banking trade like calculators, weights, inkwells and the interactive foreign exchange desk.

One consistently popular exhibit is the gold bar: put a hand into a perspex case and try to lift the bar encased within. Its weight – 12.7kg (28lb) – will come as a shock to anyone who has ever fantasised about scarpering with a sack full of bullion. Activity sheets and quizzes for different age groups can be downloaded from the website before setting off.

Buggy access. Disabled access: toilet. Nappy-changing facilities. Nearest picnic place: St Paul's Cathedral Garden. Shop.

Clink Prison Museum

1 Clink Street, SE1 9DG (7403 0900/www. clink.co.uk). London Bridge tube/rail. **Open** *June-Sept* 10am-9pm daily. *Oct-May* 10am-6pm Mon-Fri; 10am-9pm Sat, Sun. **Admission** £5;

Inspire reluctant savers at the **Bank of England Museum**.

Arsenal Museum.

Sightseeing

£3.50 5-15s, reductions; free under-5s; £12 family (2+2). **Credit** MC, V. **Map** p318 P8. 6+ (parental advisory)
The clinking of inmates' manacles, fetters and chains is what gave this former prison its name. In operation from 1247 until 1780, it was the place where thieves, prostitutes, debtors and priests were incarcerated. The list of allowed punishments included scourging with rods, the rack, breaking on the wheel and being crushed under heavy weights. Jailers were not paid well, so provided small creature comforts to rich inmates, at a price, and allowed whorehouse madames to carry on the trade for which they were imprisoned, as long as they were given a cut of the takings. The museum tries to recreate the atmosphere of the prison with candlelight, sawdust on the floor and moans and groans coming from the waxwork prisoners. Brave visitors can 'try on' some of the torture devices, such as a scold's bridle or ball and chains. Children of a sensitive disposition may be scared – particularly at the entrance, where a waxwork man in a cage whimpers as you descend the stairs. *See also p30* **Great Days Out**. *Buggy access. Nearest picnic place: Southwark Cathedral Gardens. Shop.*

SPORT

London's big four – Arsenal, Chelsea, Tottenham and West Ham United – all offer stadium tours that take fans behind the scenes at their grounds. So does

Wembley Stadium (*see p204*), home of the England team and host of cup finals in several sports and of major pop concerts. Arsenal and Chelsea have also made space for club museums (*see below*). Largely speaking, these appeal to partisan supporters of the teams in question, but London's football scene has a fascinating history, and the museums have plenty to interest fans of rival teams as well.

Arsenal Museum

Northern Triangle Building, Drayton Park, N5 1BU (7704 4504/www.arsenal.com). Arsenal or Holloway Road tube/Drayton Park rail. **Open** 10am-6pm Mon-Sat; 10am-5pm Sun. *Match days* 10am until 30mins before kick-off. **Admission** £6; £3 under-16s, reductions; free under-5s. *Tour & museum* £12-£15; £6-£8 under-16s, reductions; free under-5s. *Legends tour* £35; £18 under-16s, reductions; free under-5s. No tours match days. **Credit** MC, V. 7+
The vast Emirates Stadium has plenty of room for a museum within its walls. Fans will find it housed in the North Triangle building, directly opposite the north entrances. It offers a lavish celebration of all things Arsenal. Club fans will be thrilled by all exhibits of course, but there's plenty to appeal to the visitor with a more general interest, particularly in the sections that deal with how the club developed. Visitors can pick up a phone to hear an account of the club's early days, initially as Dial Square FC, after its formation by workers at the Woolwich Arsenal munitions factory. The club's more recent

Great Days Out
South Kensington

When it comes to London days out, South Kensington's a classic. Over the years, hordes of children have taken the well-trodden route from the tube to its mighty triumverate of museums: the Science Museum, Natural History Museum and Victoria & Albert. Weather permitting, it's traditional to make for the green swathes of Hyde Park and Kensington Gardens after a morning's museum-strolling. In short, South Ken's jam-packed with things to see – just don't make the mistake of trying to do it all in a day.

Dem bones

The **Natural History Museum** (*see p87*) is a big place, so start by picking up a free map from one of the information desks. Upon production of a parental credit card (a £25 refundable deposit is required), under-sevens can be kitted out with an Explorer backpack, with a pith helmet and binoculars. Themed Discovery Guides for five to 12s, meanwhile, cost a pound. Now you're all set to go.

Generations of children have stood in the lofty central hall and gazed up at the mighty diplodocus cast, which has stood here for over a century. He was a vegetarian – unlike the animatronic T-Rex. Bravado runs high in the long, snaking queue that leads to his lair, though his swishing tail, baleful eyes and low growl strike fear into the stoutest of hearts – and can be too much for smaller children.

Solace can be found in the creepy crawlies gallery, where even toddlers can tower over the mini-beasts; watching the leaf-cutting ants toiling away is strangely therapeutic. If your offspring are more in the mood for destruction, head for the Power Within gallery, devoted to earthquakes and volcanoes. Step inside the 'quake simulator, which recreates the effects of the 1995 Kobe earthquake, and prepare to be all shook up in a mocked-up supermarket.

Not tired yet? Good, because there's plenty more to see – the gleaming new Darwin Centre for starters. Make sure you check out the programme of Nature Live talks, too; many are aimed at families, with topics ranging from carnivorous plants to bats or jungle beetles.

Super science

For an all-round top day out, it's hard to beat the **Science Museum** (*see p92*). We defy anyone to wander through the glorious free-for-all of the interactive Launchpad gallery without being tempted to pull a lever, build a bridge, refract a rainbow or blow a stupendous giant bubble. Bellowing down the 35-metre echo tube is another deeply satisying experience – and it's not often you get the chance to freeze your own shadow.

For proper explanations of why and how, children are advised to collar one of the museum's Explainers; walking, talking mines of information, clad in bright orange T-shirts. Though there's plenty to look at, under-eights may have trouble reaching and operating the exhibits in Launchpad; they can get hands-on in the Pattern Pod (suitable for over-fives). Smaller fry can explore the Garden play zone down in the basement, donning orange waterproofs to mess about with boats and floats and constructing wobbly edifices from huge building blocks.

A right royal collection

It might seem like a less than obvious place to take the children, but that's precisely the appeal of the august **Victoria & Albert Museum** (*see p67*). Free of the swarms of marauding children, it's less hectic than the Science and Natural History museums (if you avoid the busy temporary exhibitions and concentrate on the permanent collections, that is). The galleries are dotted with oddities that hold an unexpected appeal for children: Tippoo's Tiger, a bizarre, life-size 18th-century automaton depicting a man-eating tiger in the middle of his dinner, is always a hit. Then there are the impossibly tiny miniature portraits, towering platform shoes, impassive golden deities and swashbuckling samurai swords.

Though most of the priceless pieces are safely stowed behind glass, you can poke and prod certain exhibits: pick up a map and look for the hands-on symbols. Trying a Victorian corset on for size may be best undertaken before lunch or cakes in the excellent café; you can also weave Tudor tapestries and design your own coat of arms. If you're visiting at the weekend or during the school holidays, there are imaginative arty, crafty activities – a spot of mask-making, perhaps, or creating crazy fashion accessories.

Pirate ships & pedalos

After a morning in your museum of choice, an afternoon in **Hyde Park** and **Kensington Gardens** (see p123) is just the job. A ten-minute walk away, over 300 acres stretch before you. Horse-riders trot briskly along Rotten Row, in-line skaters speed past, and picnic-toting families hike across the grass in search of a scenic spot. Stroll up to the Serpentine, London's biggest boating lake, and take to the water in a pedalo; cheats can catch the eco-friendly solarshuttle across.

Head over to the southern side of the Serpentine for the Diana,

LUNCH BOX

Also in the area: Carluccio's Caffè, Gourmet Burger Kitchen, Paul.
Café Crêperie 2 Exhibition Road, SW7 2HF (7589 8947, www.kensington creperie.com). A bustling joint that serves up made-to-order sweet and savoury crêpes, in a convenient location for the museums.
Le Pain Quotidien 15-17 Exhibition Road, SW7 2HE (7486 6154, www.le painquotidien.co.uk). Pricey but tasty tartines, salads, sarnies and cakes, plus child-friendly sides of hummus, guacamole and various dips.
Lido Café On the Serpentine, Hyde Park, W2 2UH (7706 7098). Down-to-earth, delicious grub, served in a splendid location.
Orangery Kensington Palace, Kensington Gardens, W8 2UH (7376 0239, www.hrp.org.uk). Afternoon tea and light lunches served in stunning 18th-century surrounds; there's a childrens' menu and highchairs.

Princess of Wales memorial fountain; sit on the edge and cool your toes, but beware the slippery Cornish granite; proper dips are best taken in the park's lido and paddling pool (see p214).

North of here, in Kensington Gardens, is a tribute to the Princess that children will enjoy even more: the superb **Diana, Princess of Wales Memorial Playground** (see p121). Another draw is the famous statue of Peter Pan, on the west bank of the Long Water. It appeared on May Day morning, 1912, accompanied by a brief announcement in the Times: 'There is a surprise in store for the children who go to Kensington Gardens to feed the ducks in the Serpentine this morning.' Pay your respects to Peter, then head off to search for fairies in the flowerbeds.

Great Days Out

triumphs are marked with audio-visual displays, signed shirts, medals and other memorabilia. There are also sections on the Gunner's all-conquering women's team and on the club's FA Cup and European adventures. *Buggy access. Disabled access: lift, toilet. Nearest picnic place: Finsbury Park. Shop.*

Chelsea Museum

Stamford Bridge, Fulham Road, SW6 1HS (0871 984 1955/www.chelseafc.com). Fulham Broadway tube. **Open** 10.30am-4pm daily. *Tours* 11am, noon, 1pm, 2pm, 3pm daily. Closed match days & day before Champions League game. **Admission** £6; £4 under-16s. *Tour & museum* £15; £9 under-16s. **Credit** AmEx, MC, V. 7+

Chelsea are often mocked by larger clubs for having no history, but they've still managed to put together a cracking museum. Appropriately enough, it's located in the stand that occupies what was once the club's most notorious asset, the Shed, a crumbling terrace of matchless notoriety. These days, fans have more to shout about and the museum gives pride of place to recent acquisitions, such as José Mourinho's moody overcoat. There's also plenty on the club's history of glorious inconsistency, terrible away kits and affinity with celebrity – this is probably the only museum in the country that features a photograph of Raquel Welch (in a Chelsea kit and gun holster, no less). Kids will love the two huge scale models of the ground, and the chance to see the kits belonging to icons like Frank Lampard and Didier Drogba. They can also star in their own Chelsea-themed newspaper headline. Entry comes with an excellent tour, that takes in the dressing room and dug outs.
Buggy access. Café. Disabled access (call ahead): lift, toilets. Nappy-changing facilities. Nearest picnic place: Brompton Cemetery. Shop.

Lord's Cricket Ground & MCC Museum

St John's Wood Road, NW8 8QN (7616 8595/www.lords.org). St John's Wood tube/13, 46, 82, 113, 274 bus. **Open** Tour *Nov-Mar* noon, 2pm Mon-Fri; 10am, noon, 2pm Sat, Sun. *Apr-Oct* 10am, noon, 2pm daily. Closed some match & preparation days; phone for details. **Admission** £14; £8 5-15s, reductions; free under-5s; £37 family (2+2). **Credit** MC, V. 8+

Lord's Cricket Ground is home to the oldest sporting museum in the world. It is probably best enjoyed as part of one of the tours which take place twice daily Monday to Friday, and three times a day at weekends. Though relatively small in size, the museum is a treasure trove of artefacts, from early bats, balls, paintings and scorecards – some going back more than 200 years – to mementoes of modern times; there is also footage of some of the best moments in cricket's history.

The must-see exhibit, of course, is the original Ashes urn. This was first presented following what a *Sporting Times* newspaper reporter called the 'death of English cricket' after the victorious Australian tourists condemned the England side to their first ever defeat at the Oval in 1882. When England went 2-0 up in the four-match series in Australia, a group of Melbourne society women burned a bail from the top of some cricket stumps, placed the ashes inside the urn and presented them to the visiting captain.

The ground tour also offers visitors a look around the famous pavilion, its Long Room and committee rooms and, of course, the home and away dressing rooms and their balconies, as well as the media centre, grandstand and cricket centre. Tours do not take place on match days. *Buggy access. Disabled access: toilet, lift. Nappy-changing facilities. Nearest picnic place: St John's churchyard playground. Shop.*

Wimbledon Lawn Tennis Museum

All England Lawn Tennis Club, Church Road, SW19 5AE (8946 6131/www.wimbledon.org/museum). Southfields or South Wimbledon tube, then 493 bus. **Open** 10am-5pm daily. During championships, spectators only. *Tours* phone for details. **Admission** *Museum* £8.50; £7.50 reductions; £4.75 5-16s; free under-5s. *Museum & tour* £15.50; £13.75 reductions; £11 5-16s; free under-5s. **Credit** MC, V. 8+

This high-tech shrine to all things tennis is worth a visit for anyone with even so much as a passing interest in the game. In the cinema (with 200° screens), a film of a game between Maria Sharapova and Nuria Llagostera Vives allows visitors to see each move from five different camera angles, illustrating the body science of the game. Meanwhile, in a mock up of a 1980s changing room, three-time Wimbledon champ John McEnroe (well, in hologram form at least) is waiting to take you on a tour behind the scenes and share his reminiscences.

Visitors are guided through Wimbledon's history, decade by decade, as it developed into a British sporting institution. You can also try on tennis outfits from different ages (and feel the weight difference between court outfits for men and women from 1884), test your reflexes on interactive consoles such as 'reaction station' and

Sightseeing

'you are the umpire', and listen to broadcast snippets and interviews from significant final matches. Audio and visual guides are also available. Recommended.
Buggy access. Café. Disabled access: lift, toilet. Nappy-changing facilities. Nearest picnic place: venue grounds. Shop.

World Rugby Museum, Twickenham & Twickenham Stadium

Twickenham Stadium, Rugby Road, Twickenham, Middx TW1 1DZ (0870 405 2001/www.rfu.com/museum). Hounslow East tube, then 281 bus/Twickenham rail. **Open** *Museum* 10am-5pm Tue-Sat; 11am-5pm Sun. Last entry 4.30pm, ticket holders only match days. *Tours* 10.30am, noon, 1.30pm, 3pm Tue-Sat; 1pm, 3pm Sun (no tours match days). **Admission** *Combined ticket* £14; £8 under-16s, reductions; free under-5s; £40 family (2+3). Advance booking advisable. **Credit** AmEx, MC, V. 7+
This museum boasts the largest collection of rugby memorabilia in the world. With elegant presentation, it charts the history of the game

Churchill Museum & Cabinet War Rooms.

from – and indeed before – William Webb Ellis famously picked up the ball and ran with it during a football game at Rugby School in 1821. Learn how a proper set of rules were developed, the split with northern clubs that led to the emergence of rugby league, and the spread of the game throughout the country and overseas. Displays include strange-shaped early rugby balls, a jersey from the first-ever rugby international between Scotland and England in 1871, signed shirts from down the decades and a timeline of the history of the game, alongside major world developments. The upper floor has a library and temporary exhibition room. The museum is sometimes closed after match days; phone to check.
Buggy access. Disabled access: toilet. Nearest picnic place: benches around stadium. Shop.

WAR & THE ARMED FORCES

Churchill Museum & Cabinet War Rooms

Clive Steps, King Charles Street, SW1A 2AQ (7930 6961/www.iwm.org.uk). St James's Park or Westminster tube/3, 12, 24, 53, 159 bus. **Open** 9.30am-6pm daily (last entry 5pm). **Admission** £12.95; £6.50-£10.40 reductions; free under-16s (incl audio guide). **Credit** MC, V. **Map** p317 K9. 7+
A time capsule of world war sits beneath Whitehall, and is part of the impressive Imperial War Museum group. The nine cramped rooms of the Churchill Suite were where Britain's leaders conducted wartime business, while bombs exploded in the streets overhead. With its low ceilings and concrete bomb protection, it's an atmospheric (if slightly stifling) installation that brings the period vividly to life. The map room is particularly evocative. From August 2009, a new exhibition 'Undercover: Life in Churchill's Bunker' marks the 70th anniversary of the suite. This year's programme of family workshops in the school holidays will be themed around the exhibition.

Another, larger space in the warren of tunnels houses the multimedia Churchill Museum. Its centre-piece is a large timeline; an award-winning digital archive that chronicles every major incident of WSC's life, from the Boer War to his long twilight as an after-dinner speaker and recipient of awards. There's also a kind of virtual peepshow of Churchill's home in Chartwell, Kent. The great man's voice, face and words come at you from all sides, in every

Sightseeing

The jet set

You don't have to be a kid to know that fountains are fun, but time was when the closest anyone came to water-based frolics in London was a crafty paddle in Trafalgar Square. Now we are less po-faced, and the capital is covered in water features that invite everyone to jump right in. Many newly landscaped plazas feature jets that shoot straight out of the ground, often without warning and much to the delight of all those getting soaked. Several are in central locations – perfect to cool off overheated offspring, or as a bribe to round off a more educational day out.

Among the first – and biggest – of this new generation of very public fountains were those at **Somerset House** (*see p65*), where the courtyard accommodates 55 jets. On sunny days, families unpack beach towels and picnics, turning it into an urban seaside resort. Every half hour the fountains perform a choreographed dance, when the jets can reach up to six metres high; in the evenings, the water is illuminated with coloured lights.

Across the river, the rejuvenated **Southbank Centre** (*see p164*) has initiated a programme of temporary artist-designed water features, installed just outside the Royal Festival Hall on Riverside Terrace each summer (25 Apr-23 Oct 2009). This year sees the return for the third year of Jeppe Hein's popular 'Appearing Rooms'. Four chambers enclosed by walls of water fall away in turn, allowing visitors to step inside, then rise up to trap them there. All the amenities of the Southbank Centre are at hand, including cafés and an ice-cream stall, and at weekends and throughout the summer there is always something going on, be it free dance or street theatre.

Further along the South Bank, the spaces around **City Hall** (officially known as More London Riverside) have become a popular public playground. Alongside free performances in the Scoop amphitheatre, tranquil gardens and outdoor art exhibitions, the landscaped water features have already been appropriated by kids in swimsuits. The rising and falling jets are complemented by more sophisticated sculptural pieces: a narrow channel that scores a path across the site, and polished granite boxes that only reveal their aqueous surface when touched.

Further out east there are play fountains at the entrances to both the **02** and **Thames Barrier Park** (*see p119*); west there are smaller versions in **Duke of York Square** (King's Road) and **Lyric Square**, Hammersmith; and in central London at **Russell Square** (*see p63*).

Perhaps the capital's most famous, and most controversial, water feature is the **Diana, Princess of Wales Memorial Fountain** in Hyde Park (*see p123*), designed by landscape architect Kathryn Gustafson. A smooth ribbon of water follows the course of an oval, flowing in both directions from its highest point on the gentle slope to its lowest, passing through shallow cascades and whirlpools (presumably meant to echo the more turbulent times in Diana's short life) before terminating in a calm pool. Only months after it opened in July 2004, it was closed when it was discovered that children slipped on the wet granite surface. Since then it has been modified for safety, but these days visitors are only invited to 'sit on the edge of the fountain and refresh their feet'; full-scale frolicking is frowned upon, and should only be attempted when the on-duty supervisor's back is turned (though one feels Diana herself would have approved).

Note: Somerset House fountains run from 10am to 11pm daily but close when the courtyard is used for festivals or private events. Call 7845 4600 to check they are operating before you go.

Sightseeing

possible format. It's far from stiff and stuffy, and will appeal to most children – even if they end up simply playing around with all the technology. Staying here too long, though, would drive you mad: it's like being inside Winston's mind.

Buggy access. Café. Disabled access: lift, toilet. Nappy-changing facilities. Nearest picnic place: St James's Park. Shop.

Firepower Royal Artillery Museum

Royal Arsenal, SE18 6ST (8855 7755/www. firepower.org.uk). Woolwich Arsenal DLR/rail. **Open** 10.30am-5pm Wed-Sun & daily during school hols (last entry 4pm). **Admission** £5; £4.50 reductions; £2.50 5-16s; free under-5s; £12 family (2+2 or 1+3). **Credit** MC, V. 7+

Today, childhood rarely involves a celebration of guns and bangs, but lots of kids remain fascinated by warfare, artillery and soldiers. Occupying a series of converted Woolwich Arsenal buildings close to the river, the Gunners Museum is dedicated to the soldiers of the Royal Artillery (not the north London Premiership team). There is a footie connection though, which is remembered in the touching introductory film in the Breech Cinema: Arsenal FC started out as Woolwich Arsenal, when a group of armaments workers had a kickabout. After the film, brace yourselves for the Field of Fire audiovisual display, where four massive screens relay archive film footage of very loud warfare (dry ice included).

Even more appealing to youngsters is the new Camo Zone, where they can get their fingers on a trigger at the firing range, using sponge balls. There's also a bungee run and the chance to drive some radio-controlled tanks (activities cost £1.50 each and are supervised by friendly soldiers in fatigues). There are war game events recreating major battles with model soldiers on many weekends, so check the website for dates.

The on-site Pit Stop Café is a reasonably priced place for rations, although if the weather's good, bring a picnic and enjoy the Thameside vista. With the opening of Woolwich Arsenal DLR in January 2009, the site is now connected to the tube network.

Buggy access. Café. Disabled access: lift, toilet. Nappy-changing facilities. Nearest picnic place: riverside. Shop.

Guards Museum

Birdcage Walk, SW1E 6HQ (7414 3271/ www.theguardsmuseum.com). Victoria tube/ rail. **Open** 10am-4pm daily (last entry 3.30pm).

Admission £3; £2 reductions; £1 ex-military; free under-17s. **Credit** (shop) AmEx, MC, V. **Map** p316 J9. 7+

This small museum is dedicated to the history of Her Majesty's five foot regiments – the Scots, Irish, Welsh, Grenadier and Coldstream Guards. It houses military relics – flags, medals, uniforms, drums and weapons – covering every campaign in the regiments' histories. Children will probably get the most out of it as a follow-up to seeing the Changing of the Guard at nearby Buckingham Palace (*see p34*).

Highlights include the Grand Old Duke of York's bearskin (he commanded in peacetime, hence the nursery rhyme), plus assorted military medals, uniforms and personal effects. Worksheets for eight- to 14-year- olds add an extra dimension to a visit, and staff let kids try on bearskin hats and regimental tunics: they can have their photo taken for £5. The museum shop has an impressive collection of toy soldiers. *See also p36* **Great Days Out**.

Buggy access. Disabled access: lift. Nearest picnic place: St James's Park. Shop.

HMS Belfast

Morgan's Lane, Tooley Street, SE1 2JH (7940 6300/www.iwm.org.uk). Tower Hill tube/London Bridge tube/rail. **Open** Mar-Oct 10am-6pm daily. Nov-Feb 10am-5pm daily. Last entry 1hr before closing. **Admission** £10.70; £6.40-£8.60 reductions; free under-16s. **Credit** MC, V. **Map** p319 R8. 4+

HMS *Belfast* is the only surviving large light cruiser to have served in World War II. She went on to active service in Korea, before taking on peace-keeping duties in the 1950s and '60s. Now affiliated to the Imperial War Museum, *Belfast* has been preserved to reflect the different decades of her service and the various campaigns she served in.

With her nine decks, the ship is a vast playground of narrow ladders, stairs, cabins and walkways. There are guided tours, but it's just as much fun to scramble around the ship at random, from bridge to boiler room, galley, sick bay, dentist's, NAAFI canteen and mess deck; there's even an operating theatre. Models of sailors chatting, eating, cooking and having their teeth drilled add to the entertainment.

On the last weekend of every month, there are free drop-in family activities (held from 11am-1pm and 2-4pm), which might involve crafts, music or dance. The enjoyable, family-friendly 'Launch! Shipbuilding through the ages' exhibition runs until the end of 2010.

Buggy access. Café. Disabled access: toilet. Nearest picnic place: Potters Fields Park. Shop.

Sightseeing

Quick march to the **Guards Museum**, to try a bearskin hat for size. *See p101.*

Household Cavalry Museum

Horse Guards, Whitehall, SW1A 2AX (7930 3070/www.householdcavalrymuseum.org.uk). Embankment or Westminster tube/Charing Cross tube/rail. **Open** *Mar-Sept* 10am-6pm daily. *Oct-Feb* 10am-5pm daily. **Admission** £6; £4 5-16s, reductions; free under-5s; £15 family (2+3). **Credit** MC, V. 5+

The Household Cavalry comprises the oldest and most senior regiments in the British Army. Visitors can peer at medals and cuirasses (on special activity days, kids can even try one on) and watch video diaries of serving soldiers. The museum is separated from the stables by a glass wall, so you can sometimes see the magnificent horses being rubbed down after their official duties.

The Cavalry mounts the guard on Horse Guards Parade every day at 11am (10am on Sunday): this is a better place to see them in action than Buckingham Palace (*see p34*), since the crowds are thinner here, and you're not held far back from the action by railings. After the old and new guards have stared each other out in the centre of the parade ground for a quarter of an hour, if you nip through to the Whitehall side, you'll catch the departing guard's hilarious dismount choreography, which involves a synchronised, firm slap of approbation on each horse's neck before the gloved troopers all swing off. During school

holidays, children can settle down to listen to a story, follow detective trails or join craft workshops. *See also p36* **Great Days Out**. *Buggy access. Disabled access: toilet. Nearest picnic place: St James's Park. Shop.*

Imperial War Museum

Lambeth Road, SE1 6HZ (7416 5000/www. iwm.org.uk). Lambeth North tube/Elephant & Castle tube/rail. **Open** 10am-6pm daily. **Admission** free; charges may apply for special exhibitions. **Credit** MC, V. **Map** p406 N10. 5+

Housed in what was once the Bethlehem Royal Hospital (better known as Bedlam) on Lambeth Road, this fantastic museum really needs a whole day to explore. Luckily, the café is a good one and the grounds are perfect for a picnic, so pace yourselves.

There are guns, planes (some hanging from the ceiling), submarines, cannons, tanks and paintings of war in the main galleries, but there's far more to the museum than that. The collection covers conflicts, especially those involving Britain and the Commonwealth, from World War I to the present day. On the way to the lower floors and the galleries on World Wars I and II, any guilty hints of voyeurism are quickly scotched. A clock (which was set running at midnight on 1 January 2000, when the number of lives lost during the wars of the

20th century stood at 100 million) continues to count those dying in conflicts – calculated to be two per minute.

Family-friendly temporary exhibitions include The Children's War (until 1 Jan 2010), which looks at rationing, evacuation, air raids and blackouts from a child's perspective, and Horrible Histories: Terrible Trenches (until October 2010), based on Terry Deary's book about the privations of living in muddy squalor. The unflinching Holocaust Exhibition, which traces the history of anti-semitism and its shameful nadir in the death camps, is not recommended for under-14s. Upstairs, Crimes Against Humanity is a minimalist space in which a film exploring genocide and ethnic violence rolls relentlessly; it's unsuitable for under-16s. *Buggy access. Café. Disabled access: lift, toilet. Nappy-changing facilities. Nearest picnic place: museum grounds. Shop.*

National Army Museum

Royal Hospital Road, SW3 4HT (7730 0717/ recorded information 7881 2455/www.national-army-museum.ac.uk). Sloane Square tube/ 11, 137, 239 bus. **Open** 10am-5.30pm daily. **Admission** free. **Credit** (shop) AmEx, MC, V. **Map** p313 F12. 3+

There's plenty to satisfy a child's love of all things gruesome in this museum charting the history of the British Army (notices alert parents if there's anything unsuitable for younger children coming up). There are lots of galleries (including new temporary exhibition hall The White Space), so don't try and see them all in one go. Most appealing to children will be the English Civil War helmet that they can try on; the chainmail armour they can gasp at the weight of; the immense model of the Battle of Waterloo, starring 75,000 toy soldiers; and the skeleton of Napoleon's horse. The Redcoats Gallery shows how Brits conquered the world, while Nation in Arms covers both world wars, with a reconstruction of a World War I trench and a particularly good jungle area. We also liked the way we were exhorted to join the 1914 army by a virtual recruiting sergeant as soon as we stepped through the door.

Regular themed weekend events (Roundheads and Cavaliers on 5 & 6 Sept 2009, for example) and the Kids' Zone have gone a long way to broadening the museum's appeal. The latter is a free, interactive learning and play space for under-tens, with a castle and a cavalry charge of rocking horses, and opportunities to join in art activities, play board-games or read; it can be booked by the hour for birthday parties. There's also a soft play area for babies. *Buggy access. Café. Disabled access: lift, toilet. Nappy-changing facilities. Nearest picnic place: museum benches, Chelsea Hospital grounds. Shop.*

National Maritime Museum. See p104.

Sightseeing

National Maritime Museum

Romney Road, SE10 9NF (8858 4422/ information 8312 6565/www.nmm.ac.uk). Cutty Sark DLR/Greenwich DLR/rail. **Open** 10am-5pm daily. **Admission** free; donations appreciated. **Credit** MC, V. 4+

Britain's seafaring heritage takes centre stage at this vibrant, appealing museum, whose enormous collections are spread over three floors. Nine themed galleries address everything from the perils faced by early explorers to the slave trade. In the Ships of War gallery, doll's house owners will dream of getting their hands on the impossibly intricate model ships that were built for the Royal Navy in the 17th and 18th centuries; the *Royal George* is a beauty. In the All Hands gallery, kids can have a go at loading up a cargo ship or sending a semaphore signal, while the Bridge Gallery has a simulator where they can attempt to steer a ferry into port.

The Museum Highlights trail takes children through the different galleries in search of golden mermaids, the fatal bullet hole in Nelson's blood-stained jacket and, best of all, a real-life pirate's sword, while weekends and school holidays bring a good assortment of activities to get stuck into. Up the hill, the Royal Observatory and Planetarium (*see p28*) are also part of the NMM complex. *See also p126* **Great Days Out**.

Buggy access. Café. Disabled access; lift, toilet. Nappy-changing facilities. Nearest picnic place: Greenwich Park, museum grounds. Shop.

Royal Air Force Museum Hendon

Grahame Park Way, NW9 5LL (8205 2266/ www.rafmuseum.org). Colindale tube/Mill Hill Broadway rail/303 bus. **Open** 10am-6pm daily. *Tours daily; phone for details.* **Admission** free. *Tours* free. **Credit** MC, V. 3+

Hangers full of over 100 aircraft form the main attraction of this museum. Hendon Airfield has existed here since 1910, hence its claim to be the birthplace of aviation in Britain. Aircraft include a Camel, Tempest, Tiger Moth, Mosquito and Harrier – all parked at ground level or hung in dogfight poses from the rafters of the ultra-modern Milestones of Flight building. Excitingly, helicopters jut above your head as you sit in the café. Don't miss the miniature parachutists going up and down in a tube or dropping off a wire into the hands of kids eager to learn about the laws of gravity.

Plenty of other interactive games are available in the Aeronauts gallery, many in the guise of pilot aptitude tests. Only the flight simulator (over-eights only) carries an extra charge: everything else is gloriously free, so don't exhaust the kids with a full tour; you can come back as often as you like. More low-key than the Milestones of Flight gallery are the atmospheric and dimly lit Battle of Britain building and the restored Grahame-White Factory.

There is plenty of lethal hardware on display, from World War II doodlebugs to modern cluster bombs and cruise missiles, so be ready to field questions about man's inhumanity to man as you walk around the galleries. Special activity days take place throughout the year, particularly on military holidays; older kids can learn the principles of rocket science, while youngsters build their own cardboard flying machines. See the website for upcoming events.

Activities for children and adults take place all year, with a cluster in the summer holidays. The ever-popular workshops (book ahead) can include activities like hot-air balloon making, rocket science, and Search and Rescue role-play. Quizzes, Pulsar Battlezone interactive laser games, face-painting, aircraft displays and giant garden games might also be on the cards.

Buggy access. Café. Disabled access: lift, toilet. Nappy-changing facilities. Nearest picnic place: on-site picnic area. Restaurant. Shop.

Winston Churchill's Britain at War Experience

64-66 Tooley Street, SE1 2TF (7403 3171/ www.britainatwar.co.uk). London Bridge tube/ rail. **Open** *Apr-Oct* 10am-5pm daily. *Nov-Mar* 10am-4.30pm daily. **Admission** £11.45; £6.50 reductions; £5.50 5-15s; free under-5s; £29 family (2+2). **Credit** AmEx, MC, V. **Map** p319 Q8. 8+

The first excitement is the descent from the street into the museum, via an original London Underground lift. It's small and cramped down below, but that's part of the point. Visitors are delivered straight into a mocked-up Blitz-era Underground shelter, with sounds of an air raid rumbling overhead. The convincing set includes bunks, a temporary kitchen and library, original posters and newsreel clips from the time. Other displays explore the roles of women at war, the life of evacuated children and rationing. An ex-evacuee is on hand to show you his childhood photos, there's a BBC broadcasting room and a pub, and children will enjoy trying on tin helmets and gas masks in a dressing-up corner. The visit ends in a full-size street, where a bomb has just exploded – all chillingly staged to make you think the action occurred moments before. An hour or so probably suffices for the whole place.

Buggy access. Disabled access: toilet. Nearest picnic place: Southwark Cathedral gardens. Shop.

Parks & Gardens

Commune with the great outdoors.

Families are always leaving London to get a bit more outdoor space, then finding when they get to the countryside they have to get the car out for all but the most minor of excursions. It's true that most gardens in the capital don't extend very far, but London is famous for its green spaces; wherever you live, there's always a park nearby. What do kids love more than playing outside? Playing outside with other children, that's what. You don't usually find random playmates in the garden, but go to a park and suddenly it's an outdoor party, with play equipment that few parents could afford.

In this chapter we list the very best of London's celebrated green lungs. Some are huge and beautifully tended, with impressive botanic displays, while a fair few boast royal connections. Other spots we've chosen may seem slightly scruffy in comparison, but have their own particular attractions – be that play equipment, weird and wonderful natural inhabitants or community activities. Check parks' individual websites for details of school holiday events.

BOTANIC GARDENS

More botanic beauties can be found in **Chumleigh Gardens** (Burgess Park; *see p112*), the herb garden at the **Geffrye Museum** (*see p57*), **Ham House** (*see p48*), **Hampton Court Palace** (*see p39*) and **Syon House Gardens** (*see p50*).

Chelsea Physic Garden
66 Royal Hospital Road (entrance on Swan Walk), SW3 4HS (7352 5646/www.chelsea physicgarden.co.uk). Sloane Square tube/170 bus. **Open** *Apr-Oct* noon-5pm Wed-Fri; noon-6pm Sun, bank hol Mon. *Tours* times vary, phone to check. **Admission** £8; £5 5-15s, reductions; free under-5s. *Tours* free. **Credit** MC, V. **Map** p313 F12.
This lovely garden was planted in 1673 by the Worshipful Society of Apothecaries, and is still a working centre for botanical research. Come during the school holidays for seed-planting, pond-dipping, wildlife safaris and other earthy, outdoorsy pursuits; most are for seven to 11s. *Buggy access. Café. Disabled access: toilet. Nappy-changing facilities. Shop.*

Royal Botanic Gardens (Kew Gardens)
Richmond, Surrey TW9 3AB (8332 5655/ information 8940 1171/www.kew.org). Kew Gardens tube/rail/Kew Bridge rail/riverboat to Kew Pier. **Open** *Apr-Aug* 9.30am-6.30pm Mon-Fri; 9.30am-7.30pm Sat, Sun. *Sept-Oct* 9.30am-6pm daily. *Late Oct-early Feb* 9.30am-4.15pm daily. *Early Feb-late Mar* 9.30am-5.30pm daily. Last entry 30mins before closing. *Tours* 11am, 2pm daily. **Admission** £13; £11 reductions, late entry (after 4.45pm); free under-17s. **Credit** AmEx, MC, V.
Don't expect to get around these huge, world famous gardens in one day. The best way to have fun with children here is to let them lead the way. First stop for the little ones, then, is the Climbers & Creepers adventure playground. Here kids can clamber into a flower, through an illuminated blackberry tangle and dig for 'fossilised plants', while real insects buzz through see-through habitats. This is also the base where eight- to 11-year-olds and their guardians can come for a Midnight Rambler sleepover, which offers the chance to track local wildlife and earn prizes (£40 per person, April to October; book well in advance).

Second favourite, particularly on a freezing winter's day, is the lush, tropical Palm House, where children love climbing the spiral staircases to the upper walkways, and are delighted by the discovery of the Marine Display tanks in the basement. And don't forget the outdoor Treetop Walkway, 18m (59ft) up in the air. The rest of Kew's half a square mile is an extraordinary array of monuments, gardens and landscapes. The famous Pagoda has stunning views over London, once you've climbed its 253 steps, while the Alpine House, opened in spring 2006, is another must-see.

If you're exploring the gardens on foot, pick up a free map at the ticket office. Little ones might prefer to ride the Kew Explorer people-mover, which plies a circular route around the gardens (£3.50; £1 reductions). There are cafés and restaurants dotted here and there, but on a fine day you can't beat a picnic. Summer art shows, live music and a winter ice rink in front of the Temperate House (check website for dates) make Kew a year-round treat. Summer 2009 marks Kew's 250th anniversary; there's a new Global Garden to celebrate, and a special programme of walking tours of the gardens. *Buggy access. Cafés. Disabled access: toilet. Nappy-changing facilities. Restaurants. Shop.*

CEMETERIES

Abney Park Cemetery & Nature Reserve

Stoke Newington High Street, N16 0LN (7275 7557/www.abney-park.org.uk). Stoke Newington rail/73, 106, 149, 243, 276, 349 bus. **Open** *Cemetery* dawn-dusk daily. *Visitors' centre* 10am-4pm Mon-Fri. **Admission** free.

Most green spaces in London are freakishly free of undergrowth – all the better to spot potential muggers, perhaps. Not here though. Just as winsomely decayed as Highgate Cemetery but without the entry fee or Marx pilgrims, Abney Park Cemetery is a chaotic jumble of Victorian graves, trees, and blind corners. The slowly-decaying monuments – urns, angels, Celtic crosses, saints and shepherds – add romantic interest to this local nature reserve, where birds, butterflies and bats make their home.

There's an environmental classroom at the Stoke Newington High Street entrance, which hosts free workshops for children and adults: go on a mini beast hunt, examine beetles and bugs at close quarters, or take a tree tour and learn about the hundreds of different varieties on site. The visitors' centre doubles as a shop for guides to green London and other environmentally aware literature. From the Church Street entrance path, avoid turning left if you want to steer clear of men seeking men. *Buggy access. Disabled access: toilet (visitors' centre). Shop.*

Brompton Cemetery

Fulham Road, SW10 9UG (7352 1201/ www.royalparks.org.uk). West Brompton tube/rail. **Open** *Summer* 8am-8pm daily. *Winter* 8am-4pm daily. **Admission** free.

A formal layout and grand central avenue, leading to a chapel based on St Peter's Basilica in Rome, mark Brompton Cemetery out from its Victorian rivals. It has over 35,000 monuments to the dead, commemorating the famous and infamous, including suffragette Emmeline Pankhurst, shipping magnate Sir Samuel Cunard and boxer 'Gentleman' John Jackson, who taught Byron to box; his grave is marked by a lion. The peace and quiet is regularly disturbed by Chelsea FC's home games at neighbouring Stamford Bridge. Bond fans might also like to know that the cemetery was used as a set in *GoldenEye*. *Buggy access. Disabled access.*

Highgate Cemetery

Swain's Lane, N6 6PJ (8340 1834/www. highgate-cemetery.org). Highgate tube. **Open** *East cemetery* Apr-Oct 10am-5pm Mon-Fri; 11am-5pm Sat, Sun. Nov-Mar 10am-4pm Mon-Fri; 11am-4pm Sat, Sun. *West cemetery* by tour only; phone for details. **Admission** *East cemetery* £3. *West cemetery tours* £5; £1 8-16s. **No credit cards.**

As recently as 1981, this cemetery was thoroughly neglected, with a tangle of brambles, overgrown self-sown trees and crumbling exterior walls and buildings. Nowadays it's a Grade II-listed park with an entrance fee to boot. The cemetery is most famous for housing the grave of Karl Marx (East cemetery), and you'll often see pilgrims making their way to it through neighbouring Waterlow Park (*see p120*).

Children love the wild wood feel of the place; with its angels, shrouded urns and broken columns, this beautiful boneyard has a romantic atmosphere of ivy-covered neglect. Officially, youngsters are discouraged from visiting, unless they're coming to see the grave of a relative – but if you long to pay your respects to Marx, Mary Ann Evans (aka George Eliot), Christina Rossetti, scientist Michael Faraday, or any of the eminent figures who now repose in the East cemetery, you can bring children along, as long as they behave well. The atmospheric West cemetery, with its Lebanon Circle Vaults, Egyptian Avenue and Terrace Catacombs, is out of bounds to casual visitors; adults and children aged eight and over can take a guided tour. Both sites close for funerals, so phone before you visit. *Buggy & disabled access (East cemetery only).*

Kensal Green Cemetery

Harrow Road, W10 4RA (8969 0152/www. kensalgreen.co.uk). Kensal Green tube/rail/ 18, 23, 52, 70, 295, 316 bus. **Open** *Apr-Sept*

Blooming lovely: **Alexandra Park & Palace**. *See p110.*

9am-6pm Mon-Sat; 10am-6pm Sun. *Oct-Mar* 9am-5pm Mon-Sat; 10am-5pm Sun. *All year* 10am-1pm bank hols. *Tours* 2pm Sun. **Admission** free. *Tours* £5; £4 reductions. Behind an impressive neoclassical gate lies the beautiful garden cemetery of Kensal Green. Various 19th-century greats repose here, including Isambard Kingdom Brunel, William Thackeray, Anthony Trollope and Wilkie Collins, but the most impressive monuments are the ornate mausoleums of lesser names. There's also a Greek Revivalist chapel and mysterious catacombs, which you can visit on the two-hour guided cemetery tours that take place on Sunday afternoons (over-12s only). The annual Open Day is held in July (check the website for details), and has a village fête atmosphere with face painting, stalls, dressing-up and a motorcade of hearses.
Buggy access. Disabled access: toilet.

Nunhead Cemetery

Entrances on Limesford Road or Linden Grove, SE15 3LP (7732 9535/www.fonc. org.uk). Nunhead rail. **Open** *Summer* 8am-7pm daily. *Winter* 8am-4pm daily. *Tours* 2pm last Sun of mth. **Admission** free. *Tours* £2.
This tumbledown vision of gothic stonework and overgrown woodland is now part nature reserve, part cemetery. A 52-acre maze of Victorian commemoratory statuary with a restored chapel at its heart, it affords fine views over the city from its higher reaches. The Friends of Nunhead Cemetery run guided tours on the last Sunday of each month, while an annual open day takes place in May.
Buggy access.

CITY SPACES

Phoenix Garden

21 Stacey Street (entrance on St Giles Passage), WC2H 8DG (7379 3187/www. phoenixgarden.org). Tottenham Court Road tube. **Open** 8.30am-dusk daily. **Admission** free; donations appreciated. **Map** p315 K6.
The little-known Phoenix Garden lies on what was once part of an extensive leper hospital. These days, it's a favourite spot for workers in the West End to enjoy a peaceful sandwich, and an excellent picnic location for families out on a day trip. Its frog-filled pond, wildlife area, quiet crooked pathways, trellises and fragmented statues come as a green and pleasant surprise, tucked as they are between bustling Shaftesbury Avenue and Charing Cross Road; the entrance is next to the playground in the garden of St Giles-in-the-Fields. Check online for advance notice of child-friendly events such as the agricultural show, 'grow your own' workshops and afternoon Hallowe'en and Christmas parties.
Buggy access.

Sightseeing

Camden

Camden Town, especially the grubby and busy junction by the tube, may not seem like the most salubrious of destinations for a day out with the kids. Head off the main drag, though, and there's plenty to see and do for all ages.

Older children and teenagers, meanwhile, absolutely love the famous market, with its colourful, chaotic mix of street food vendors, stalls touting vintage clobber, cheap accessories and incense sticks, and wandering goths and punks.

On the waterfront

Children adore being by the water, even if they can't go in it. Join the Regent's Canal at **Camden Lock**, where the manually-operated twin lock is the first stopping point. It's particularly exciting if there happens to be a boat coming through. The canal was built in the early 19th century to connect the Grand Union Canal at Paddington with the Thames at Limehouse, but since the 1960s has been used mainly for leisure and pleasure.

The towpath in either direction leads to some great finds; note that although it is a designated cycle route, the path is too narrow for all but the most proficient of cyclists (scooters should be fine). To the east, a decent stroll away, are the bucolic delights of **Camley Street Natural Park** (*see p124*), a small but thriving nature reserve run by the London Wildlife Trust. A little further along, just past the tunnel under York Way, in the Battlebridge basin, lies the **London Canal Museum** (*see p83*), an old fashioned but homely shrine to life on Britain's canals; there's a children's corner and a real narrowboat to explore, along with the ice house used by enterprising ice-cream maker Carlo Gatti, who imported enormous blocks of ice from the frozen lakes of Norway.

From Camden Lock going west, families can stop off at the exclusive enclave of **Primrose Hill**, where kite flying and picnics in the park are popular pastimes. Carry on a little further, and you will begin to hear the strange grunts and squawks emanating from one of the capital's biggest attractions; **London Zoo** (*see p140*), a great day out in itself. The green expanse of **Regent's Park** (*see p123*) is just beyond, with a very good playground at the Gloucester Gate entrance.

Of course, you don't have to content yourself with merely walking alongside the water. The **London Waterbus Company** (www.londonwaterbus.co.uk) runs canal boat trips to Little Venice, where families could stop and see a performance at the lovely **Puppet Theatre Barge** (*see p185*). London Waterbus also runs day trips all the way to Limehouse on the Thames.

Market value

Camden Market is absolutely heaving at weekends, so try to come on a weekday if you don't want to lose sight of small children; most shops and stalls are open all week. Also be aware that Camden Town tube station is exit-only on Saturday and Sunday, which means a long walk up to Chalk Farm or down to Mornington Crescent for the tube if you don't want to catch the bus.

There are several different markets and hundreds of stalls to browse here, so pace yourself and be picky. Discerning shoppers tend to bypass the first market

---

you reach after turning north from the tube station – the one at Buck Street bearing the legend 'Camden Market' – unless their party has a teenager who is desperate for goth T-shirts and cheap tat.

North of the road bridge on Chalk Farm Road is the former Canal Market. Closed after a fire in February 2008, it re-opened in May 2009 with a new name, the **Canal Lock Village**, and an eclectic assortment of stalls. Alternatively, head straight for **Camden Lock Market**. Launched in 1975, this is where the whole thing began. There is a lovely open air square of stalls and shops selling crafts, jewellery, textiles, alternative fashion and accessories.

The extensive **Stables Market**, just north of Camden Lock, is still undergoing a redevelopment and expansion programme that has caused controversy locally. Here, there are plenty of jumbled displays of ethnic doo-dads, vintage clothes and furniture, and lots of child-friendly novelties and toy stalls. You'll also find all kinds of takeaway stands, offering foods from around the world.

Something for the grey matter

If all that shopping gets a little overwhelming, you could always incorporate a bit of culture into your Camden experience. On the road north, towards Chalk Farm is the iconic **Roundhouse**

(*see p178*), famed for its groundbreaking gigs in the 1960s and '70s (the Doors, Hendrix and Bowie all took to the stage here). Re-opened in 2006, it offers an avant-garde programme of music and theatre. The Roundhouse Studio also runs radio, film and music workshops for teenagers in the school holidays.

South of here, just off Parkway, is the Jewish Museum (*see p88*), due to reopen in winter 2009 after a major refurbishment project. The museum has expanded into the larger building at the back of the existing site, and will have five galleries with permanent exhibitions devoted to Jewish history in Britain.The first temporary exhibition will be 'Jews in the British Entertainment Industry'.

Sightseeing

Postman's Park

Between King Edward Street & Aldersgate Street, EC1R 4JR (7374 4127/www.cityof london.gov.uk/openspaces). St Paul's tube. **Open** 8am-dusk daily. **Admission** free. **Map** p318 O6.

Tranquil, fern-filled Postman's Park (named after its proximity to a large sorting office, long since demolished) is best known for the Watts Memorial to Heroic Sacrifice. It's a canopy-covered expanse of ceramic plaques, inscribed in florid Victorian style, that pay tribute to ordinary people who died trying to save others. 'Frederick Alfred Croft, Inspector, aged 31', begins one typical thumbnail drama. 'Saved a Lunatic Woman from Suicide at Woolwich Arsenal Station, But was Himself Run Over by the Train, Jan 11, 1878'. Many of the dead heroes were children, who tried to rescue drowning companions; their fates make gruesome lessons for their latter-day counterparts. *Buggy access.*

St Swithin's Garden

Oxford Court, off Cannon Street, EC4N 5AD (7374 4127/www.cityoflondon.gov.uk/ openspaces). Monument tube/Bank tube/DLR/ Cannon Street tube/rail. **Open** 8am-dusk Mon-Fri. **Admission** free. **Map** p319 Q7.

This carefully tended, walled garden is the burial place of Catrin Glendwr and two of her children. Catrin was the daughter of Owain Glendwr, the fiery Welsh hero whose uprising ended bloodily in 1413. There's a memorial sculpture dedicated not only to Catrin, but to the suffering of all women and children in war. *Buggy access.*

LOCAL PARKS

Alexandra Park & Palace

Alexandra Palace Way, N22 7AY (park 8444 7696/information 8365 2121/www.alexandra palace.com). Wood Green tube/Alexandra Palace rail/W3, 144 bus. **Open** *Park* 24hrs daily. *Palace* times vary, depending on exhibitions. **Admission** free.

Alexandra Palace isn't the prettiest building in north London, but it dominates the skyline around these parts. It was built as 'The People's Palace' in 1873, and was supposed to provide affordable entertainment for all. That's still true today, although the original building burned down just 16 days after its opening. (It was speedily rebuilt, and re-opened two years later). Inside, Ally Pally is mainly used for exhibitions, fairs and gigs, but there's also an ice-skating

rink. Outside, the children's playground behind the palace is a well-equipped and wholesome place in which to take the air, with a recently opened café next to the boating lake. The pitch-and-putt course is down the hill and popular with older children, while simply walking around the park affords breathtaking views of London. There's plenty of space for picnics, a farmers' market at the Hornsey Gate Entrance on Sundays (10am-3pm), and annual visits from the funfair and circus. Bonfire Night in November brings pyrotechnics that can be seen for miles around.

Buggy access. Café. Disabled access: lift, toilet. Nappy-changing facilities (ice rink).

Battersea Park

SW11 4NJ (8871 7530/adventure playground 8871 7539/www.wandsworth.gov.uk). Sloane Square tube, then 19, 137 bus/Battersea Park or Queenstown Road rail. **Open** 8am-dusk daily. **Map** p313 F13.

The land on which Battersea Park now sits was once a popular spot for duelling (the Duke of Wellington fought an abortive duel here in 1829, deliberately aiming wide of his opponent, the Earl of Winchilsea, who for his part shot his pistol into the air). The park was laid out in 1858, and was splendidly restored in 2004. Facilities range from fun water features (a boating lake, elegant fountains and a riverside promenade) to state-of-the-art sporting facilities and play areas, including a toddlers' playground and a challenging adventure playground for eight to 16s. Bikes can be hired out from London Recumbents (7498 6543; open at weekends, bank holidays and during school holidays), there are rowing boats and a land train in July and August, and open fishing is available from mid June to mid March; for permits, call 8871 7530. Battersea Park is also home to a rich array of wildlife, and the London Wildlife Trust has nature reserves here.

The Gondola al Parco café (7978 1655) serves Italian food, with tables overlooking the boating lake and live music on summer evenings. The prettiest landmark, though, is the lofty Peace Pagoda, donated in 1985 by Japanese monks and nuns to commemorate Hiroshima Day. It stands serenely opposite the Children's Zoo (*see* p140), on the park's northern edge.

Buggy access. Café. Disabled access: toilet. Nappy-changing facilities.

Brent Lodge Park

Church Road, W7 3BL (07940 021183/ www.ealing.gov.uk). Hanwell rail/E1, E2 bus. **Open** 7.30am-dusk daily. *Maze & animals* May-Aug 10.30am-6pm daily. Sept, Oct, Apr

Sightseeing

Off the rails

The **Parkland Walk** (www.parkland-walk. org.uk) runs the length of the disused Northern Heights railway line that links Finsbury Park with Highgate, and Highgate with Alexandra Palace, cutting through the terraced backs of Stroud Green, Crouch End and Muswell Hill on the way. The longest nature reserve in London is, of course, managed; the once notoriously muddy path was resurfaced in spring 2009 with shale and sand for efficient drainage. Nonetheless, it retains a hint of wilderness you won't find in most of London's parks (and offers great potential for snooping into other people's gardens).

The old tunnels into Highgate station are gated and closed to the public, so the walk is effectively cut in two. Highgate to Finsbury Park is the longer and more interesting stretch, and a gentle downhill stroll all the way; it's also a popular cycle route that's a safe ride for kids. From Highgate tube's Archway Road exit, walk south and turn left on to Holmesdale Road. About 100 yards on the left is the entrance to the Parkland Walk.

You begin in a wooded stretch that offers juicy blackberries in the autumn, and is good for hide and seek anytime. After the Stanhope Road exit, the bridges give way to tunnels as the track intersects the surrounding road network. The tunnels are favourites with graffiti artists (get the kids to pick their favourite artworks) and anyone who likes shouting for echoes.

The platforms of the old Crouch End Station remain on either side of the path; take a moment to imagine a steam engine pulling its load through this narrow track. The kids like to take the high road (the platforms) while parents take the low road (the path). Just after the station, look up as you walk past a series of recessed arches on your left. A spriggan (a creature from Cornish folklore) can be seen climbing out of one of them – a quietly disconcerting sculpture by Marilyn Collins, said to have inspired Stephen King to write his short story 'Crouch End'.

Around the corner on the right is an old adventure playground with brilliant rope swings, wooden walkways and long slides down the steep bank. It looks dishevelled but is loved by kids of all ages, probably because it isn't as sanitised as a playground. The path becomes more open from here, and you begin getting vistas of the city below. The route heads into Finsbury Park at the Oxford Road Gate; straight ahead, weary walkers can seek refreshment in the café by the boating lake. Finsbury Park's fantastic playground, built with a £5 million Heritage Lottery Fund, is also close by. If the kids are still hungry after all that exercise, stock up on cheap, delicious bagels at the Happening Bagel Bakery on Seven Sisters Road before heading for Finsbury Park tube. A good night's kip is guaranteed for all – dreams of the spriggan aside.

Sightseeing

10.30am-5pm daily. Nov-Mar 10.30am-4pm daily. *Indoor centre* 1.30-3pm Sat, Sun. Times may vary. **Admission** free. **No credit cards**.
Think of Hanwell and the Uxbridge Road springs to mind – but there is a villagey area near St Mary's Church, which includes this delightful local park. It's known locally as the Bunny Park, thanks to the rabbits that inhabit the Animal Centre, alongside sheep, goats, monkeys, mongooses, birds and reptiles. There's a café and a good playground, plus a maze with a look-out tower in its centre that was planted to mark the Millennium. The centre organises children's activity days in summer; phone for details.
Buggy access. Café. Disabled access: toilet. Nappy-changing facilities.

Brockwell Park

Dulwich Road, SE24 0PA (7926 0105/www. brockwellpark.com). Herne Hill rail. **Open** 7.30am-dusk daily. **Admission** free.
Brockwell Park is an essential green lung for the residents of Brixton and Herne Hill – though that hasn't stopped Lambeth Council from trying to shave a chunk off its south-eastern corner to make way for a new road junction. Tucked away behind the grassy slopes on the Tulse Hill side is one of south London's best playgrounds, with colour-coded sections for different age groups. There's an aerial slide and a massive sandpit; nearby are the duck ponds, with dense greenery screening out the council flats and signs with information on the coots, moorhens and tufted ducks.

Brockwell Park.

There's lots to do besides, with the community greenhouses offering digging pits and planting workshops, plus a long-established BMX track and all-weather tennis courts. The beautiful walled garden is also worth seeking out. On the Herne Hill side, the 1930s lido (*see p214*) has been restored to its former pomp and is open from May to September; it's absolutely packed on sunny days. Whippersnappers (7738 6633, www.whippersnappers.org) runs kids' music classes at the lido complex year-round.
It's a steep walk to the top of the hill, but well worth it for the view north over the city. Take a breather at the late-Georgian Brockwell Hall country house, now a café serving great wedges of lasagne and other pasta dishes, plus toothsome own-made cakes. The park also hosts a popular country show every July – albeit one with reggae soundtracking the vegetable competitions (*see p19*).
Buggy access. Café. Disabled access: toilet. Nappy-changing facilities.

Burgess Park

Albany Road, SE5 0RJ (7525 2000/www. southwark.gov.uk). Elephant & Castle tube/ rail, then 12, 42, 63, 68, 171, 343 bus. **Open** 24hrs daily. *Lake area* 8am-dusk daily. **Admission** free.
The land on which Burgess Park sits was once a canal with an industrial strip beside it. Since the 1940s the park has grown in stages, but never with an overall plan; luckily, in an area that sorely needs community spaces, it's about to get a £6 million overhaul. Locals have asked for cycle tracks, a café with outdoor seating, more benches along the old towpath and a complete renovation of the existing playground, indoor games room and kart track (7525 1101).
At present, most community activities are based in the Chumleigh Gardens section of the park, which is home to the Southwark Rangers Football team, a great little café with fry-ups, quiches, salads and jazz on sunny Sundays, and a thriving Peckham Sure Start scheme. Various garden styles are employed in the series of interconnecting plots; English country garden, fragrant Mediterranean, meditative Islamic and a splendid, flamboyant Caribbean garden. The Heart Garden is a fruit and vegetable patch planted, tended and harvested by people with long-term illnesses.
Buggy access. Café. Disabled access: toilet.

Clissold Park

Stoke Newington Church Street, N16 5HJ (park ranger 7923 3660/www.clissoldpark.com). Stoke Newington rail/73, 149, 329, 476 bus. **Open** 7.30am-dusk daily. **Admission** free.

On this flat expanse of grass it's hard to entirely escape traffic noise, but Clissold Park is still an appealing spot. Peek through the fences at the deer, rabbits, birds and goats in the small wildlife enclosure, or watch waterfowl gliding about on the ponds. The large playground has a good choice of activities for all ages, and is shaded by surrounding trees in summer. After complaints from locals, the cheap climbing frame installed in the sandpit last year has already been replaced by a more suitable structure. Younger children love scaring themselves on the wobbly bridge, while older kids favour the aerial four-way see-saw. Next to the playground, the tennis courts are home to the Hackney wing of the City Tennis Centre (7254 4235), offering family tennis evenings, coaching, junior clubs and tournaments.

The café, housed in Clissold Mansion, serves adequate refreshments and has a lovely terrace. The annual Stokefest is held here in June, and other events, like a visit from Carter's Steam Fair, take place in the summer. There's also a One O'Clock club, although it's in a rather desultory and unloved building and, at present, remains under-subscribed. Clissold House and Park are planning a major multi-million pound revamp, but details of exactly how the money will be spent are still being thrashed out.
Buggy access. Café. Disabled access (not café): toilet. Nappy-changing facilities (on request).

Coram's Fields
93 Guilford Street, WC1N 1DN (7837 6138/ www.coramsfields.org). Russell Square tube. **Open** *May-Aug* 9am-7pm daily. *Sept-Apr* 9am-dusk daily. **Admission** free. **Map** p317 L4.
Thomas Coram established the Foundling Hospital for abandoned children on this spot in 1747. The building was demolished in the 1920s, and a successful campaign to set out a children's park here finally bore fruit in 1936. *See also p62* **Great Days Out.**
Buggy access. Café. Disabled access: toilet. Nappy-changing facilities.

Crystal Palace Park
Thicket Road, SE20 8DT (park ranger 8778 9496/www.crystalpalacepark.org). Crystal Palace rail/2, 3, 63, 122, 157, 227 bus. **Open** 7.30am-dusk daily. **Admission** free.
Joseph Paxton's Crystal Palace, from which this park takes its name, is long gone. The glittering glass structure, originally created to house Hyde Park's Great Exhibition of 1851, was moved here after the exhibition; in 1936, it burned down in a devastating fire. The park, though, remains – and has just changed hands. The London Development Agency has taken over from the

local council, and has big plans for its future. It's an atmospheric place, enshrined in local folklore. A beautifully landscaped lake complex is home to Benjamin Waterhouse Hawkins' Victorian dinosaur sculptures, which caused outrage by backing up the theory of evolution, yet continue to give pleasure to kids – especially the T-Rex, who recently got a new arm (the tree he was gripping grew, and snapped off the old one). This was also the site where the Girl Guide movement was born, when a group of determined girls faced down Baden Powell at a Scout rally and demanded to join.

The LDA's plans include a review of all buildings and their current uses, so expect the museum, the National Sports Centre, café and community facilities to get a radical overhaul. Proposals also include a treetop walk and water features. The park's city farm reopened in 2008, and is still expanding its opening hours and programme of activities (*see p129*).
Buggy access. Café. Disabled access: toilet. Nappy-changing facilities.

Dulwich Park
College Road, SE21 7BQ (7525 2000/www. southwark.gov.uk). North Dulwich rail/12, 40, 176, 185, 312, P4 bus. **Open** 8am-dusk daily. **Admission** free.
This lovely local park sits on a cluster of meadows called five fields, and was formally landscaped in 1890. The locals adore it, especially since the 2006 revamp, but it's long been a favourite spot for appreciation of the greener things in life. Queen Mary was a regular visitor (one of the park's four gates is named after her), and was particularly fond of the spectacular American Garden, whose rhododendrons and azaleas bloom in May. Today's visitors can also enjoy the exceptionally child-friendly Pavilion Café (*see p231*), a super playground, novelty bike hire (8299 6636, www.londonrecumbents.com) and a Barbara Hepworth sculpture, *Divided Circle Two Forms.*
The playground is one of the best in the area, with web-like climbing facilities, swings, slides and the new Ability Whirl, a safe, robust roundabout that can be used by able-bodied and disabled children. A community officer runs a programme of children's activities from the Francis Peek Centre (phone for details).
Buggy access. Café. Disabled access: toilet. Nappy-changing facilities (café).

Hampstead Heath
NW5 1QR (8348 9908/www.cityoflondon. gov.uk/openspaces). Kentish Town tube/Gospel Oak or Hampstead Heath rail/214, C2, C11 bus. **Open** dawn-dusk daily. **Admission** free.

Great Days Out
Hampstead Heath

The best climbing tree in London is on Hampstead Heath (*see p113*). No, we're not going to tell you where – you have to find it for yourself. And no, we're not going to give you a clue. You've already had one. It's on Hampstead Heath.

That means you have less than 800 acres to search – of which only 500 or thereabouts are coated with trees. So the probability of finding the Tree is rather better than that of winning the Lottery or, indeed, finding the proverbial needle in a haystack. Besides, there's plenty more to do while you look.

A little bit of this, a little bit of that

The Heath, as it is simply known to locals, is London's greatest lung. Perhaps that's why it is lung shaped. It sits there on its sandy ridge north of the West End and puffs out great gusts of freedom, fun and good health.

It is so big it can enclose within its borders 18 ponds, a lido (**Parliament Hill Lido**, *see p213*), a duelling ground, a large stately home with its own estate, a good number of other mansions, a hamlet (entitled, suitably enough, the Vale of Health), a zoo (in **Golders Hill Park**, on the tip of the West Heath), several sports fields and tennis courts, a concert site, a couple of bandstands, a pergola that is as long as Canary Wharf is tall, a Rembrandt, a hill offering the best view of the London skyline (the view is protected by law, you know), two fairground sites, several gardens and nurseries, fantastic wild flora, some fauna, its own police force and three very decent caffs.

It is a remarkable space, and the part of the metropolis that offers children the very best chance to have a breather and be, well, themselves.

Green peace

How do you get there? Easily. Hampstead and Kentish Town stations are both on the Northern Line, as is Golders Green – though the latter would leave you with a longer uphill walk to the less obviously attractive (to kids) part of the Heath. The nearest rail stations are Gospel Oak and Hampstead Heath on the transverse Overground line (formerly the North London Link). But buses are probably best. There are loads of them skirting the Heath from most points of the compass. Whichever direction you approach from, you will quickly find yourself absorbed: absorbed into the environment and its unique ambiance; absorbed in your own mind with the strange miracle that has somehow permitted an authentic slab of wilderness to materialise so confidently slap-bang in the middle of the greatest city in the world.

Part of that authenticity and confidence derives from the fact that the Heath is so obviously old. It seems unlikely that Boudicca, charioteering queen of the Iceni, is buried in the 'tumulus' that surmounts one of the several crests of Parliament Hill Fields, but it's a nice local myth. It is also a fabulous place to sit and watch dusk fall over London on summer evenings, away from the populous top of Parliament Hill itself. The children can slink about in the long grass; you can assume your proper status as king or queen of the tribe, as you chomp on a prosciutto sandwich and listen to the movement among the branches behind you on the barrow.

The fact is, Hampstead Heath is in the historical records going all the way back to Ethelred the Unready, one of the last Saxon kings. Some details have changed over the years, for which we ought to be grateful. The remains of highwaymen no longer swing in metal cages at Gibbet Elms. And there's an argument that says the perennial removal of undergrowth among the trees is for the best (the more densely wooded parts of the West Heath are perhaps not the best place for children to wander, accompanied or otherwise).

But certain, more child-friendly, traditions stick like burrs. You can swim and fish in the various **Ponds** (*see p213*) It is almost obligatory to fly kites on Parliament Hill. And there is surely no better spot to spend fireworks night than on the Heath – the display is free and it encompasses the whole of London, in every direction.

Make like an Old Master

Freedom is the joy of the place. You really can let children go pretty much wild in the country here. And even if the price of ice-cream at **Kenwood House** (*see p58*) is steep, you can at least offset the cost by gazing in solemn wonder at the Rembrandt self-portrait inside, and then sit like a Reynolds family on the elegant sward in front of the house running down to Sham Bridge and

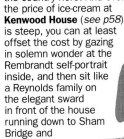

LUNCH BOX

Also in the area: Pizza Express, Strada, Carluccios Caffé, Zizzi.
Al Parco *2 Highgate West Hill, N6 6JS (8340 5900)*. Great thin crust pizzas and pasta dishes.
Brew House *Kenwood, Hampstead Lane, NW3 7JR (8341 5384/www. companyofcooks.com)*. Good, self-service food eaten inside or out on the beautiful terrace. *See p223*.
Golders Hill Park Refreshment House *North End Way, NW3 7HD (8455 8010)*. Family favourites in a beautiful setting. *See p230*.
Kalendar *15A Swains Lane, N6 6QX (8348 8300)*. Friendly service, good food and lots of outdoor tables. Be prepared to queue…
Parliament Hill Café *Parliament Hill, Hampstead Heath, NW5 1QR (7485 6606)*. Surprisingly great Italian food at low prices, dispensed from an unprepossessing 1960s park hut.

---

the concert platform. If you're here during the summer, you might even get to hear a concert. And from there it is but a ten-minute walk to the Best Climbing Tree in London. You want to go south, but not as far as South Meadow. And you need to stay alert on the Duelling Ground. Musket balls can leave unsightly holes in even the sturdiest of modern fabrics.

The 800-acre heath is as far from the manicured flowerbeds of the Royal Parks as you could hope to find, and the only place in London to have a day out in the countryside. Down on Parliament Hill to the south, facilities include an imaginative playground and paddling pool, still looking spanking new after its award-winning refurb, and packed with state-of-the-art equipment designed to challenge children rather than keep them boringly safe. There's a superb One O'Clock Club, a running track and a lido down here too, though families might want to try a more adventurous swimming experience in the famous open-air swimming ponds.

Fishing is available in six of the ponds (though you need a rod licence and a free Heath fishing permit). There are also tennis courses, bat walks, nature trails, a 'secret garden' and a wildlife pond. Clowns, magicians, storytellers and puppeteers perform in various locations in the holidays. Check the website and local press for news of the Hampstead Heath consultation and management plan, and for details of family events. An alternative focal point is over to the north west: the listed Pergola, built in the 1920s by Lord Leverhulme to join together two parts of his estate, is free to enter and fun to explore. At Golders Hill you'll find a free zoo (small, but well kept) and a butterfly house in a converted greenhouse. The Kenwood Estate, though officially part of the Heath, is run by English Heritage. *See also p114* **Great Days Out**. *Buggy access. Cafés. Disabled access: toilet. Nappy-changing facilities.*

Highbury Fields

Highbury Crescent, N5 1RR (7527 4953/www. islington.gov.uk). Highbury & Islington tube/ rail/19, 30, 43, 271 bus. **Open** *Park* 24hrs. *Playground* dawn-dusk daily. **Admission** free.
This 29-acre park is Islington's largest green space, much needed in this densely-packed urban area. Get the children to imagine the scene when, in 1666, 200,000 Londoners fled here to escape the Great Fire. Hidden behind Highbury Pool and a series of high bushes is an unusual playground that combines old-fashioned thrills (such as a circular train requiring *Flintstones*-style propulsion, and an excitingly long, steep slide) with more recent additions, like the flying fox and giant, web-like climbing frames. The outdoor tennis courts have been refurbished, and are used by the excellent Islington Tennis Centre. A stroll across Highbury Fields takes you from busy Upper Street past imposing period terraces to Highbury Barn, a trendy enclave with several excellent food shops, restaurants and child-friendly cafés.
Buggy access. Café.

Holland Park

Ilchester Place, W8 6LU (7471 9813/Ecology Centre 7471 9809/www.rbkc.gov.uk). Holland Park tube/9, 27, 28, 49 bus. **Open** 8am-dusk daily. **Admission** free. **Map** p314 A9.
Holland Park is not just any old local park; there are so many intriguing nooks and crannies to explore that it's worth a day trip in its own right. Children over five will want to start with the many and varied excitements on offer at the adventure playground (there's an alternative playground for under-fives too). The paths take you past formal gardens and fountains, imperious peacocks and plenty of squirrels and rabbits. Look out, too, for the open-air theatre, the peaceful Japanese Garden with a pond full of colourful koi carp, and an Ecology Centre which provides information, site maps and nets for pond-dipping. Whippersnappers (7738 6633, www.whippersnappers.org) puts on weekly musical and puppet workshops in the Youth Hostel, and the Friends of Holland Park organise holiday activities for five- to ten-year-olds. Also in the park are tennis courts, sports fields and two art spaces, the Ice House and the Orangery. Take public transport unless it's a Sunday, as parking is expensive.
Come lunchtime, there's Marco Pierre White's smart but surprisingly child-friendly Belvedere (*see p239*) for special occasions, or a smart Italian café and ice-cream kiosk for everyday treats. On sunny days though, well-to-do families from the chichi surrounding neighbourhoods lay out their rugs and hampers for all-day picnics.
Buggy access. Café. Disabled access: toilet. Nappy-changing facilities. Restaurant.

Manor House Gardens

Old Road, SE13 5SY (8318 1358/www. lewisham.gov.uk). Hither Green rail. **Open** *Café & park* 7.30am-dusk daily. *House & library* 9am-7pm Mon-Fri; 9am-6pm Sat; 10am-4pm Sun. **Admission** free.
Manor House itself is now a thriving public library, while its gardens have become a lovely public park. The central lake has a fountain in the middle and flocks of wildfowl living in its waters, while the handsome playground is made of natural materials and incorporates rocks, wooden see-saws, balance bars, climbing frames and swings. There are also tennis courts and an area for ball games. On one side of it is a wildlife garden; on the other is the friendly park café, with a menu of simple, own-made hot meals, ice-creams, drinks and snacks. A compact farmers' market takes place here on the first Saturday of the month.
Buggy access. Café. Disabled access: toilet.

Holland Park.

Mile End Park

*Locksley Street, E14 7EJ (7364 4147/children's
park 7093 2253/www.towerhamlets.gov.uk).
Mile End tube.* **Open** *24hrs daily. Children's
park 10am-dusk daily.* **Admission** *free.*
The idea for Mile End Park was first mooted in
the 1940s, but it was 50 years in the making. It
comprises 90 acres of reclaimed industrial land,
which runs south of Victoria Park in a long strip
alongside Regent's Canal. For many Londoners
it is the quintessential modern urban park,
divided into dramatically different sections. The
south end of the park has a great playground,
with a rope slide, scrambling wall, complicated
climbing frame, swings and a see-saw, as well
as a dedicated area for under-fives that includes
a vast sandpit. New apparatus installed in the
playground is designed to appeal to children
with disabilities as well as to their able-bodied
playmates, with a huge, bird-nest-style swing
and a ramped bridge.

There's also the Ecology Park, with its large
climbing wall; the site-specific works and
pavilion of the Arts Park; the Terraced Garden;
the Sports Park (including Mile End Stadium);
the canalside Kirk's Place, which is good for
picnics; and an electric go-kart track. During the
school holidays there are structured events for
children. In the middle of the park, the café and
Palm Tree Pub provide refreshments.
*Buggy access. Café. Disabled access: toilet.
Nappy-changing facilities.*

Morden Hall Park

*Morden Hall Road, Morden, Surrey SM4
5JD (8545 6850/www.nationaltrust.org.uk).
Morden tube.* **Open** *8am-6pm daily.*
Admission *free.*

Morden Hall Park sits on the floodplain of the
River Wandle, creating marshy wetlands that
shelter a whole host of birds (look out for leggy
herons and the bright blue flash of a kingfisher).
There are also rolling meadows and woodlands
in this 125-acre swathe of uncommonly
beautiful National Trust parkland. Morden Hall
itself is run as a private restaurant, but there's
the wonderful watermill to enjoy and the Snuff
Mill Environmental Centre, which runs
children's activities on the first and third
Sundays of the month. Craftspeople, furniture
restorers and artists occupy many of the old
estate buildings, and the Riverside Café is a
relaxing place to sit back and take stock of the
lovely surrounds.
*Buggy access. Café. Disabled access: toilet.
Nappy-changing facilities. Shop.*

Myatt's Fields

*Cormont Road, SE5 9RA (7926 9000/www.
lambeth.gov.uk). Oval tube/Loughborough
Junction rail/P5, 36, 185, 436 bus.* **Open**
7.30am-dusk daily. **Admission** *free.*
This Victorian garden, with its bandstand,
tranquil gardens and colourful seasonal
bedding displays, is fighting fit after a £2.6
million makeover. There are now tennis courts,
a brand-new playground with a splashy wet
zone and a One O'Clock Club. *See p118* **Field
of dreams**.
Buggy access.

Queen's Park

*Kingswood Avenue, NW6 6SG (8969 5661/
www.cityoflondon.gov.uk/openspaces). Queen's
Park tube/rail.* **Open** *7.30am-dusk daily.*
Admission *free.*

Sightseeing

Set in a densely populated area, this park is well used by locals. It has a great playground with a giant sandpit, a paddling pool, a small animal enclosure and patrolling wardens. At the northern end is a wild, overgrown area, where a nature trail displays pictures of the small beasts you might encounter. The café serves own-made cakes and local Disotto's ice-cream. There's also a lovely ornamental garden, a pitch-and-putt area, a pétanque pitch and six all-weather tennis courts. Children's entertainment takes place at the bandstand during the summer holidays. Each September, the annual Queen's Park Day brings fancy dress competitions, face-painting, a dog show and puppetry.
Buggy access. Café. Disabled access: toilet. Nappy-changing facilities.

Ravenscourt Park
Ravenscourt Road, W6 0UL (www.lbhf.gov.uk). Ravenscourt Park tube. **Open** 7.30am-dusk daily. **Admission** free.

Field of dreams

Myatt's Fields (*see p117*) isn't just a park with a fabulous new playground – it's proof that community spirit is thriving in the depths of urban London. Hidden between Camberwell and Brixton, these gardens are flanked by grand townhouses and claustrophobic estates. The area is notorious for guns, drugs and teen pregnancy – yet every summer, locals from both sides of the park have got together to hold the kind of fêtes that would make a country parish proud.

Realising that their enthusiasm for the area wasn't matched by the rusting playground and its crumbling structures, locals launched a campaign to get the dream park they felt they deserved. Eight long years of fundraising followed. Local children were taken to the best playgrounds in London, bringing their roller-blades to test the terrain, and asked to submit ideas. The campaign finally secured a cool £2.6 million from the Heritage Lottery Fund and Lambeth Council, and one of the finest local playgrounds in London was born.

The beauty of this place is that it caters for everyone from tots to teens. There are four kinds of swings, slides, rockers and roundabouts, plus climbing frames, climbing walls and mounds. The spaces under the play frames are set up as kitchens and shop counters; games of battleships and number puzzles are set into the walls. A sensory trail leads to a set of giant wooden chimes, and the centrepiece is a spongy map of the world which will become a quirky play fountain each summer.

Justly proud of their park, the locals hold regular events here; sign up to the newsletter at www.myattsfieldspark.info and become part of the park's brilliantly close-knit community.

Sightseeing

Ravenscourt is less a traditional park, more a secret garden; though larger than your average private acreage, it has a sweetly local feel and is suitably off the beaten track. Nestling between the messy bustle of Hammersmith and the quiet splendour of Chiswick, it's a hidden oasis of bucolic tranquility. The first mention of Ravenscourt Park was in the 13th century; documents record the existence of a manor house, surrounded by a moat that was fed by Stamford Brook. Disaster struck during World War II, when the house was devastated by an incendiary bomb. Only the stable block survived, and is now home to the park café. It's conveniently close to the seriously fun adventure playground (intrepid adults are often spotted commandeering the rope slide).

There's also a paddling pool, a nature trail, passable tennis courts, a bowling lawn and a pitch-and-putt course. Bonfire night is the biggest date in the diary, as enormous crowds gather to 'ooh' and 'ahh' over spectacular rockets that bathe the park in an ethereal glow. In April, the ever-popular Carter's Steam Fair rolls into the park.
Buggy access. Café. Disabled access. Nappy-changing facilities.

Southwark Park
Gomm Road, SE16 2UA (art gallery 7237 1230/www.southwark.gov.uk). Canada Water tube. **Open** *Park* 7.30am-1hr before dusk daily. *Gallery (during exhibitions)* Summer noon-6pm Wed-Sun. Winter 11am-4pm Wed-Sun. **Admission** free.
This prime, 63-acre slab of parkland does good service to the surrounding community. In 1998, a pretty new bandstand was erected, along with a decent children's play area; over a decade later, the whole place is still looking shipshape, thanks to the efforts of the energetic Friends of Southwark Park commitee and the vandal-busting wardens.

There is plenty to encourage older children to take up sports, with an athletics track (often used by Millwall Football Club, along with the astroturf pitches) and free tennis courts. The park also has a thriving arty scene, the hub of which is the Café Gallery Project. It holds frequent exhibitions and workshops on Saturdays and during the summer holidays, called the DIY Family Art Club; check online at www.cafegalleryprojects.com for details of the club, and the summer Children's Exhibition and winter Open Exhibition. Parkside Café & Bar, just across from the gallery, serves hot meals and sandwiches.
Buggy access. Café. Disabled access: toilet. Nappy-changing facilities (in gallery).

Thames Barrier Park
North Woolwich Road, E16 2HP (7476 3741/ www.thamesbarrierpark.org.uk). Pontoon Dock DLR. **Open** 7am-dusk daily. **Admission** free.
This is not a park that visitors forget in a hurry, with its distinctive topiary and views over the shiny curves of the Thames Barrier. When it opened in 2001, it was London's first new park in half a century.

The Barrier's visitors' centre is on the south side; the tea pavilion serves excellent coffee. A concrete and granite channel the width of a small motorway, called the Green Dock, is filled with fragrant honeysuckle and wavy yew hedges: it has superb hide-and-seek potential, with the two pedestrian bridges overhead adding an extra dimension to the game. The kids will also want to go wild at the fountain plaza, where 32 vertical jets beg to be played with. On the riverfront is the Pavilion of Remembrance, erected to remember local victims of the Blitz. The manicured, flat lawns are perfect for picnics and games; there's also a playground packed with apparatus, plus a basketball hoop and five-a-side court.

The park is fantastic for waterfowl watching too: ducks, geese, swans and oyster catchers pick around on the gleaming mudflats, herons feed along the shore at low tide, and large numbers of teal, shelduck and cormorants enjoy the river's bounty.
Buggy access. Café. Disabled access: toilet. Nappy-changing facilities.

Victoria Park
Old Ford Road, E3 5DS (8985 1957/ www.towerhamlets.gov.uk). Mile End tube/ Cambridge Heath or Hackney Wick rail/8, 26, 30, 55, 253, 277, S2 bus. **Open** 8am-dusk daily. **Admission** free.
Victoria Park was laid out by Sir James Pennethorne – a pupil of John Nash, who designed Regent's Park. You can see the influence of the grand master in the landscaping of this gracious park, which is the pride and joy of Hackney's residents.

With its imposing, wide carriageways, ornate lampposts and wrought-iron gates, Victoria Park is the only place out east where you can pretend you're in the countryside. It did go through a shabby period, but has now smartened up its act. There are fish in the Western Lake (you can help deplete the stock by applying for a free fishing licence); Britain's oldest model boat club convenes around the other lake, near Crown Gate East, every second Sunday. The Pools Playground, with its landscaped paddling pools, is a real favourite with all ages, and there's a fallow deer enclosure

Sightseeing

on the east side, tennis courts and a bowling green, plus football, hockey and cricket pitches. The jolly Lakeside Pavilion Café is packed to the rafters by families enjoying great organic food, sausages from Marylebone's famous Ginger Pig butchers and memorable coffee. *Buggy access. Café. Disabled access: toilet. Nappy-changing facilities.*

Wanstead Park

Entrance via Warren Road or Northumberland Avenue, E11 2LT (8508 0028/www.cityof london.gov.uk/openspaces). Wanstead tube. **Open** dawn-dusk daily. **Admission** free.
Managed alongside Epping Forest (*see p128*) by the City of London, Wanstead Park is a heavily wooded green space with several beautiful water features. Fishing is free here, and you can catch bream, carp, perch, tench and roach on a spot by the Ornamental Water. At the fenced-off end is a ruined grotto, built in the early 1760s, with a boathouse that's now in a photogenic state of disrepair. The other important ruin in the park is the Temple, once a fancy summerhouse; it's open one week a month in the summer (phone for dates, and for details of summer outdoor theatre, community operas and guided walks). Children will also appreciate the ball-throwing and kite-flying possibilities on the extensive grassy area between the Temple and the tea stall. The park's Wildlife Group (www.wren-group.net) is a good point of contact for animal-lovers; look out, too, for the horses being ridden around the park by members of a nearby riding school.
Buggy access. Café.

Waterlow Park

Highgate Hill, N6 5HG (Lauderdale House 8348 8716/café 8341 4807/www.waterlow park.co.uk). Archway tube/143, 210, 271, W5 bus. **Open** 7.30am-dusk. **Admission** free.
Once the hillside garden of pretty, 16th-century Lauderdale House, Waterlow Park was donated to the public by low-cost housing pioneer Sydney Waterlow as a 'garden for the gardenless'. With its majestic vistas, mature trees, formal gardens, tennis courts and beautiful seasonal planting, it's a delightful spot all year round.
Lauderdale House has a café on its west-facing terrace, and runs a year-round programme of kids' activities that includes music, dance and drama classes, and lively children's theatre events every Saturday morning. Until recently, a small toddlers' area was the only formal playground, but a new adventure playground, built from natural materials, was opened in April 2009. Aimed at six- to 13-year-olds, it can

be found to the west of the lowest pond. In the old depot building, Waterlow Park Centre houses exhibitions and has an activities room available for hire.
Buggy access. Café. Disabled access: toilet.

West Ham Park

Upton Lane, E7 9PU (8472 3584/www.cityof london.gov.uk/openspaces). Stratford tube/rail/ 104, 238 bus. **Open** 7.30am-30mins before dusk daily. **Admission** free.
This lovely, 77-acre park is run by the City of London, which has been in charge since locals persuaded the corporation to buy what was then a private botanic garden for the public in 1874. Its ornamental gardens and established trees are glorious; as one of the few London parks to have its own plant nursery, it also has spectacular border planting. Full time park attendants make it feel safe, while the playground has plenty of colourful climbing apparatus. Highlights include a wooden prairie locomotive to clamber on, a Wendy house corner and the pre-war paddling pool, open from late May to August.
More unusually, 2009 sees the establishment of community vegetable plots here. There are 12 tennis courts (lucky locals have access to the annual tennis clinic, which is held in June), three cricket nets (Essex CCC runs free training for under-16s in July), two match-quality cricket tables, two football pitches (one all-weather), a running track and a rounders area. From late July to August, free children's events are held at the bandstand on Monday and Friday afternoons (3-4pm); a very popular bouncy castle (also free) appears on Wednesdays (noon to 5pm); and there are occasional Sunday concerts. The only thing missing is a café, though an ice-cream van takes up position near the playground from Easter to October.
Buggy access. Disabled access: toilet. Nappy-changing facilities.

Wimbledon Common

Windmill Road, SW19 5NR (8788 7655/www. wpcc.org.uk). Putney rail, then 93 bus/85 bus. **Open** 24hrs daily. **Admission** free.
North Londoners bang on about Hampstead Heath being a slice of the countryside in the city; south Londoners scoff and retort that Wimbledon Common is twice the size. With more than 1,000 acres of woodland, scrubland and heathland, the Common is a haven for joggers, walkers and anyone who loves the outdoors. There are cricket, football and rugby pitches, a golf course, a bog, nine ponds, and around 16 miles (over 25km) of bridleways. There's also a windmill, which is now a museum

Sightseeing

Thames Barrier Park. *See p119.*

(*see p85*). The common is patrolled by rangers, on horseback and on foot, who are a mine of information about the common and nearby Putney Heath, both of which are designated SSSIs (Sites of Special Scientific Interest). They're based in the Information Centre, which also provides leaflets on the plant and animal life on the common, as well as the history of the area; it's open seven days a week. Best of all is a video microscope showing insects and other flora and fauna in minute detail; specimens are changed regularly, and you can insert your own for display. Every Saturday at 9am, there's a free park run organised by volunteers; the Wildlife Watch Club for eight- to 14-year-olds takes place on the first Sunday of the month from 10am to noon (£2).
Buggy access. Café. Disabled access: toilet. Nappy-changing facilities (café).

PLAYGROUNDS

Diana, Princess of Wales' Memorial Playground
Near Black Lion Gate, Broad Walk, Kensington Gardens, W8 2UH (7298 2117/recorded information 7298 2141/www.royalparks.org.uk). Bayswater tube/70, 94, 148, 390 bus. **Open** *Summer* 10am-7.45pm daily. *Winter* 10am-4pm daily. Times vary, phone or check website for details. **Admission** free. Adults & over-12s must be accompanied by a child. **Map** p310 C7.

Not to be confused with the Princess Diana Memorial in Hyde Park, with its tempting water sculpture, this commemorative play area is easily the best bit of Kensington Gardens for a child. A huge pirate ship on its own beach takes centre stage (bring buckets and spades). Beyond this lies the tepee camp: a trio of wigwams, each large enough to hold a sizeable tribe, and a tree-house encampment with walkways, ladders, slides and 'tree phones'.

The area's connection with *Peter Pan* creator JM Barrie is remembered in scenes from the story, etched into the glass in the Home Under the Ground. Many of the playground's attractions appeal to the senses (scented shrubs, whispering willows and bamboo are planted throughout), and much of the equipment has been designed for use by children with special needs, including those in wheelchairs. There's plenty of seating for parents; unaccompanied adults aren't allowed in. A programme of free entertainment includes visits by clowns and storytelling sessions; check the website for details. The café has a good children's menu. *See also p96* **Great Days Out**.
Buggy access. Café. Disabled access: toilet. Nappy-changing facilities.

Glamis Adventure Playground
Glamis Road, E1W 3DQ (7702 8301/www. glamisadventure.org.uk). Shadwell DLR. **Open** *Term-time* 3.15-7pm Tue (girls only); 3.15-7pm Wed-Fri; 10am-4pm Sat. *School holidays* 10am-5.30pm Mon-Fri. Times may vary, phone for details. **Admission** free.

The idea behind this community project was to create a space where children can take controlled risks while they are playing – and it must be one of the few playgrounds in the country where children are actively encouraged to build and light a bonfire. There's an amazing climbing structure, as well as swings and slides, and a vegetable garden to get grubby in. Indoor activities include arts, crafts and cooking. The playground won Adventure Playground of the Year 2007.
Buggy access. Disabled access: toilet.

Kimber Adventure Playground
King George's Park, Kimber Road, SW18 4NN (8870 2168). Earlsfield rail, then 44 or 270 bus. **Open** *Term-time* 2.30-7pm Wed-Fri; 11am-6pm Sat, Sun. *School holidays* 11am-6pm daily. **Admission** free.

Kids can swing around on monkey bars, climbing frames, big swings, tyres and ropes at this newly-refurbished adventure playground; there's also a brilliant BMX track to zoom round. (If you don't have your own BMX, you can

Sightseeing

A playtime pow-wow at the **Diana, Princess of Wales' Memorial Playground.** *See p121.*

usually hire one at the playground.) There's also a five-ramp skateboard park for those that favour four-wheeled stunts.

Buggy access. Disabled access: toilet. Shop.

Lady Allen Adventure Playground

Chivalry Road, Wandsworth Common, SW11 1HT (7228 0278/www.kids.org.uk). Clapham Junction rail. **Open** *Term-time* 10.30am-5pm Tue (under-8s only); 3-5pm Wed-Fri; 10am-noon Sat. *School holidays* 10am-noon Mon, Wed-Fri; 10am-3pm Tue. **Admission** free, donations appreciated. **No credit cards.**

The northerly tip of Wandsworth Common is home to this purpose-built playground for local children with special needs. Tuesday is for the under-eights and their carers; the rest of the time, it's open to all under-15s (able-bodied children are welcome). Kids can dig, make dens and climb in the wild wood, or play on traditional playground equipment. Indoors there is a room for soft play, a video games room and a corner for arts and crafts. The operation is staffed by volunteers; call ahead before visiting.

Buggy access. Disabled access: toilet. Nappy-changing facilities.

Somerford Grove Adventure Playground

Park Lane Close, Northumberland Park, N17 OHL (8808 2644/www.haringey-play.org.uk). Tottenham Hale tube/rail/Northumberland Park or White Hart Lane rail. **Open** *Term-time* 3.15-6.30pm Wed-Fri; 1-6pm Sat. *School holidays* 1-6pm Mon-Fri. **Admission** free.

The winner of Adventure Playground of the Year 2008, Somerford Grove's features include imaginative climbing structures, den building opportunities, a stream and a pond, plus traditional play equipment. Indoor activities include arts, crafts and cooking.

Buggy access. Disabled access: toilet. Nappy-changing facilities.

ROYAL PARKS

Bushy Park

Hampton Court Road, Hampton Court, Surrey TW12 2EJ (8979 1586/www.royalparks.org.uk). Hampton Wick, Hampton Court or Teddington Rail/111, 216, 265, 411, R68 bus. **Open** *Pedestrians* Jan-Aug, Oct, Dec 24hrs daily. Sept, Nov 8am-10.30pm daily. *Vehicle access* 6.30am-dusk daily. **Admission** free.

This is the second largest of the Royal Parks, but perhaps one of the least familiar to Londoners. It sits right next to its more famous neighbour, Hampton Court Park; its central attraction, the majestic, mile-long Chestnut Avenue, was designed by Christopher Wren as a grand driveway to Hampton Court Palace. During World War I and II, much of the park's open land was dug up to grow vegetables, and

Eisenhower (who didn't fancy being in the centre of town), made his base here – hence the memorial near the Warren Plantation. The last few years have seen the park improved in myriad small ways, thanks to an injection of lottery cash. There are new paths and trees, better access to the woodland areas to the west and an agreeable visitors' centre and café. *Buggy access. Café. Disabled access: toilet.*

Greenwich Park

Blackheath Gate, Charlton Way, SE10 8QY (8858 2608/www.royalparks.org.uk). Cutty Sark DLR/Greenwich DLR/rail/Maze Hill rail/1, 53, 177, 180, 188, 286 bus/riverboat to Greenwich Pier. **Open** 6am-dusk daily. **Admission** free.

Part of the Greenwich World Heritage Site, this lovely, hilly stretch of green affords wonderful views over the Thames, to Canary Wharf and Docklands and the City of London. *See also p126* **Great Days Out.**
Buggy access. Cafés. Disabled access: toilet. Nappy-changing facilities.

Hyde Park & Kensington Gardens

W2 2UH (7298 2100/www.royalparks.org.uk). Hyde Park Corner, Knightsbridge, Lancaster Gate or Marble Arch tube/2, 8, 10, 12, 23, 73, 94 bus. **Open** *Hyde Park* 5am-midnight daily. *Kensington Gardens* 6am-dusk daily. **Admission** free. **Map** p311 E7.

It's easy to forget you're slap bang in the middle of the centre of London in this grand patch of turf, which makes for a brilliant family excursion. Along with tennis courts, cafés, fountains, a lido and a boating lake, it's also home to a superb playground (*see p121*). Check online for up-and-coming events, which include some brilliant guided walks: bats, autumn leaves and tree identification are among the themes. *See also p96* **Great Days Out.**
Buggy access. Cafés. Disabled access: toilet. Nappy-changing facilities. Restaurant.

Regent's Park

NW1 4NR (7486 7905/boating lake 7724 4069/www.royalparks.org.uk). Baker Street, Camden Town, Great Portland Street or Regent's Park tube. **Open** 5am-dusk daily. **Admission** free. **Map** p314 G3.

This grand circular park was designed by John Nash as the Prince Regent's garden for a summer house that was never built. With its sports fields, boating lake, rose garden and the star attractions of London Zoo and the Open Air Theatre within its boundaries, this is a park with something for everyone. *See also p138* **Great Days Out.**
Buggy access. Cafés. Disabled access: toilet. Nappy-changing facilities. Restaurant.

Richmond Park

Richmond, Surrey TW10 5HS (8948 3209/www.royalparks.org.uk). Richmond tube/rail/Norbiton rail. **Open** *Summer* 7am-dusk. *Winter* 7.30am-dusk. **Admission** free.

This park has had royal connections since the 13th century, and is the biggest city park in Europe. Herds of red and fallow deer roam freely, a source of endless fascination for children (but don't let them get too close). The park is also home to all sorts of birds and insects – including 1,000 species of beetle. Children who don't get out of town much should be taken straight to the Isabella Plantation, a beautiful, tranquil woodland garden that's dotted with streams, ponds and bridges. Planted with camellias, azaleas, magnolias and rhododendrons, it's best seen in all its glory in early summer or late September.

There are plenty of benches and grassy glades where you can picnic, and the park's Petersham Gate has a playground. From the top of nearby King Henry VIII's mound (the hot-tempered king had a hunting lodge here), you get a spectacular view right across London. Alternatively, you could stroll along Terrace Walk, a Victorian promenade that runs from philosopher Bertrand Russell's childhood home, Pembroke Lodge (now a licensed café, and a

Regent's Park.

Sightseeing

good lunch spot), and beyond the park to Richmond Hill. A well-kept cycle path follows the perimeter; hire kids' bikes and adult bikes with tag-alongs or children's seats from Roehampton Gate (7581 1188). Like all the Royal Parks, Richmond hosts a summer events programme for families. For details, consult the notice at the gate lodge or check the website. *Buggy access. Disabled access: toilet. Café. Restaurant.*

St James's Park

SW1A 2JB (7930 1793/www.royalparks.org.uk). St James's Park tube/3, 11, 12, 24, 53, 211 bus. **Open** 5am-midnight daily. **Admission** free. **Map** p317 K8.

St James's is surrounded by three palaces; Westminster (now the Houses of Parliament), Buckingham and St James's. It's the park that keeps closest to its royal connections, with the Changing of the Guard and the Trooping of the Colour taking place on Horse Guards Parade. There's also a rich array of wildlife to spot, from pelicans and black swans to incredibly tame grey squirrels. The latter will eat from your hand – though watch out, as they can be vicious little critters. *See also p36* **Great Days Out.** *Buggy access. Café. Disabled access: toilet. Nappy-changing facilities. Restaurant.*

WILDLIFE SANCTUARIES

Camley Street Natural Park

12 Camley Street, NW1 0PW (7833 2311/ www.wildlondon.org.uk). King's Cross tube/ rail. **Open** 10am-5pm daily. **Admission** free. **Map** p315 L2.

A visit to Camley Street is a reminder that beautiful things come in small packages. It's amazing (and cheering) that this small oasis of wildlife has been left to flourish within the multi-million-pound King's Cross development. It sits on the site of a former coal yard on the banks of Regent's Canal, and is run by the London Wildlife Trust.

Enter the wrought iron gates and explore the winding nature trails, ponds and lovingly-tended gardens. The wood-cabin visitors' centre has nature displays and resident rabbits, plus a large, bulrushed pond full of frogs, newts and other slimy creatures that kids adore. From 10am to 3pm on Saturdays and Sundays, children can come pond-dipping and insect-hunting, assisted by park volunteers; special events for kids also run throughout the year. *Buggy access. Disabled access: toilet. Nappy-changing facilities.*

East Ham Nature Reserve

Norman Road, E6 4HN (8470 4525). East Ham tube/Beckton DLR. **Open** 10am-5pm Tue-Fri. **Admission** free.

Managed as a nature reserve since 1977, this green spot occupies the site of the largest churchyard in London, and has three beguilingly shaggy nature trails to follow. The funny little museum comprises a small room dotted with stuffed birds and mammals (all looking a little on the weary side), plus cases of beetles and butterflies. *Buggy access. Disabled access: toilet.*

East Sheen Common Nature Trail

East Sheen Common, Fife Road, SW14 7EW (Borough Ecology Officer 8831 6125/www. richmond.gov.uk). Hammersmith tube, then 33 bus/Mortlake rail, then 15min walk. **Open** dawn-dusk daily. **Admission** free.

The National Trust runs this nature trail, which wends its way through 13 areas of woodlands, ponds and streams, marked with orange posts. A wildlife-watching leaflet tells you all about the animals and insects that live here; you'll be lucky to see the badgers, but visit in spring and you should hear frogs croaking and woodpeckers tapping. Summer brings butterflies to the meadow flowers and woodland floor, while autumn provides berries for the birds. Contact the ranger for details of children's activities and guided walks.

Greenwich Peninsula Ecology Park

Thames Path, John Harrison Way, SE10 0QZ (8293 1904/www.urbanecology.org.uk). North Greenwich tube/108, 161, 422, 472, 486 bus. **Open** 10am-5pm Wed-Sun. **Admission** free.

In the middle of a resolutely urban, industrial peninsular overlooking the Thames, the Ecology Park is a pond-dipping, bird-watching paradise. The park is reserved for school visits on Mondays and Tuesdays; the rest of the week, you'll have this wetland area, with its woodland, marsh, meadowland, lakes and streams, all to yourself. *Buggy access. Disabled access: toilet. Nappy-changing facilities.*

Gunnersbury Triangle Nature Reserve

Bollo Lane, W4 5LW (8747 3881/www.wild london.org.uk). Chiswick Park tube. **Open** *Reserve* 24hrs daily. *Information Cabin* June-Sept 10am-4.30pm Tue-Sat. Oct-May 10am-4.30pm Tue, Sun. **Admission** free.

Camley Street Natural Park.

Sightseeing

With its birch and willow woodland, marsh and meadowland, this nature reserve is the scene of much ecological activity. It is run by the London Wildlife Trust and offers conservation workshops and free drop-in activities for kids. When the small information cabin is open you can pick up trail leaflets, find out about tours and hire a net for pond-dipping purposes. *Buggy access.*

Highgate Wood & Queen's Wood
Muswell Hill Road, N10 3JN (8444 6129/ www.cityoflondon.gov.uk/openspaces). Highgate tube/43, 134, 263 bus. **Open** 7.30am-dusk daily. **Admission** free.
Queen's Wood is the quieter section of this sprawling woodland park – originally part of the ancient Forest of Middlesex – perhaps because it offers some very steep climbs. Even in winter, its dense oaks and hornbeams drown out traffic noise, giving the impression that you're rambling through a wild wood miles from the city. Listen out for the woodpeckers, whose pecking reverberates around the sun-dappled glades. There's also a deeply thrilling rope swing, if you can find it.
More popular than Queen's Wood is the flatter Highgate Woods on the other side of Muswell Hill Road, where the wide paths suit buggies and budding cyclists. Head into the less well-trodden areas for a proper adventure. The centrepiece of Highgate Woods is its large, well-equipped playground, complete with sandpits, climbing equipment of various levels of difficulty and a flying fox ride that gets very busy at peak times. Great thought has gone into providing fun and challenges for the various age

groups, and there's a separate area for the under-fives to call their own. The playground is pleasantly shady in summer – cooler for all concerned, as well as making hats and sun cream less of a repetitive chore. Highgate's other great asset is its café, reached by crossing the cricket pitch. The food is the usual park fare – soups, pasta dishes and cake predominate – but the quality is a cut above what you'll find elsewhere. Throughout the year, an imaginative set of activities is offered in the woods, from outdoor storytelling sessions to evening bat watches, beetle safaris and treasure hunts. Consult the website before setting out, as some events require pre-booking.
Buggy access. Café. Disabled access: toilet. Nappy-changing facilities.

Islington Ecology Centre
Gillespie Park Nature Reserve, 191 Drayton Park, N5 1PH (7527 4374/www.islington. gov.uk). Arsenal tube. **Open** *Park* 8am-dusk daily. Closed Arsenal FC weekend home matches. *Centre* 9am-4pm Mon-Fri; Sun noon-4pm; Sat varies, phone for details. **Admission** free.
Staff at Islington's largest nature reserve are endlessly enthusiastic and helpful on the subject of all things ecological. Fashioned from derelict railway land in the 1980s, the site has woods, meadows, wetland and ponds, with the Ecology Centre forming its educational heart. The events programme includes plenty of family-orientated events, from moth evenings to craft sessions. Nature-themed workshops run in the holidays; ring for details.
Buggy access.

Great Days Out
Greenwich

Half the fun of a day out in Greenwich is getting here: we always enjoy boarding a Thames Clipper from central London and disembarking at the pier. It's a fitting way to arrive at a place that's famed for its maritime links, where the *Cutty Sark* is berthed in a less-than-restful retirement and the National Maritime Museum showcases all sorts of nautical booty.

Back from the riverfront, the green swathes of Greenwich Park sweep up to the domed Royal Observatory, perched on its lofty hilltop; at the foot of the park stand the National Maritime Museum and dignified Old Naval College. (Close by, a small boating lake satisfies small visitors with nautical ambitions of their own.)

So heady a mix of fresh air, beautiful architecture and educationally-improving sights is irresistible to families, who flock here for action-packed days out.

A life on the ocean wave

If you've arrived by boat, you'll reach dry land by the **Cutty Sark**. This plucky little tea clipper embarked on her maiden voyage in 1869, and sailed all over the world; in 1954 she retired to Greenwich's dry docks. She's currently in the midst of a huge renovation project (which faced a severe setback when a fire broke out in May 2007), and is due to re-open in late 2010. In the meantime, you can pay your respects and check the progress from a viewing platform, though there's not always an awful lot to see.

A short stroll upriver, the **Old Royal Naval College** (*see p84*) is an imposing affair, set in splendid gardens. It's free to peek at the chapel and magnificent Painted Hall – though the latter's lofty depictions of allegorical scenes may not appeal to children. Weekend and school-holiday 'Tactile Tales' sessions bring the stories to life, though, with the help of a special storytelling rug. Costume-clad historical figures also pop by at weekends, so you might meet a loquacious Samuel Pepys or a 19th-century Greenwich pensioner.

Just across Romney Road, the **National Maritime Museum** (*see p104*) is a tribute to the nation's rich seafaring history, with vast collections of maritime art, maps, instruments and naval attire. Loading cargo, firing cannons and steering a ferry safely into port in the All Hands and Bridge galleries sorts out the salty sea dogs from the cack-handed landlubbers (check opening hours before you turn up). After a quick foray to see the highlights of the collection (the blood-stained jacket in which Nelson met his end, for instance, or Prince Frederick's gorgeously gilded State Barge), it's time to press on.

Toe the line

Muster your energies, then tackle the steep ascent across the park to the **Royal Observatory & Planetarium** (*see p28*). It's topped by an onion-shaped dome that houses the world's seventh largest telescope, and the mysterious-looking Time Ball – a red bobble, on top of a pole – that was first erected in 1833. Every day it rises to the top of its mast then falls at precisely 1pm; in the days before clocks and watches were common, the ships that plied the river relied on it.

After admiring the view, head for the courtyard. The Meridian Line that marks the place where the eastern and western hemispheres meet is set in the flagstones; posing for a picture with one foot on each side is *de rigeur*. At night, a dramatic green laser beam is projected into the sky to mark the line.

Inside, the star turns are the Weller Astronomy interactive galleries (where you can touch a four-and-a-half-million-year-old meteorite or guide a space mission) and the spectacular Planetarium. Be engulfed in dust storms on Mars or swoop over earth's polar ice caps before re-emerging, blinking, into the daylight.

The green, green grass of Greenwich

Sprawling over 183 acres, **Greenwich Park** (*see p123*) is the area's crowning glory. It's big enough to accommodate all sorts, from entwined lovers and peacefully dozing sun-worshippers to frisbee- and ball-chasing kids and families.

The boating lake is at the Greenwich end of the Park, to the left from Park Row and there's also a decent playground by the Maze Hill entrance, with storytelling sessions, puppeteers, dance and crafts in the summer holidays. Summer Sundays also bring trumpet trios and brass bands to the bandstand, which is set towards the Blackheath end of the park: spread a picnic rug nearby and enjoy the music drifting across the grass.

The park's teeming with wildlife, too – not least the herd of red and fallow deer that roams the enclosed Wilderness area, which has hides for nosy humans dotted around its perimeter (it's in the south-eastern corner of the park). You can also take a gander at the Secret Garden Wildlife Centre, which runs wildlife-related activities and tours of the nature trail on

its once-monthly drop-in days. Butterflies flit across the grassland area, and if you're lucky (and very quiet) you might hear a woodpecker at work in the trees.

For those who've forgotton their picnics, there's the lovely, hexagon-shaped **Pavilion Tea House** (*see p233*). Set amid the chestnut trees, the café's outdoor tables are a heavenly spot for lunch.

Sightseeing

London Wildlife Trust Centre for Wildlife Gardening

28 Marsden Road, SE15 4EE (7252 9186/ www.wildlondon.org.uk). East Dulwich rail. **Open** 10.30am-4.30pm Tue-Thur, Sun. **Admission** free.

This leafy site was once an unlovely council bus depot, until the London Wildlife Trust took it on in the late 1980s. It's now a firm favourite with green-fingered Peckham families, who head off on nature forays amid the woodland and marshland. There's a herb garden, a pond area and a nursery for plants and trees; here, locals can pick up plants for their own gardens, giving a donation to the LWT. For children, there's a play area, sandpit and parent-and-toddler group, and the visitors' centre has tanks of fish and stick insects to peep at.

Buggy access. Disabled access: toilet. Nappy-changing facilities. Shop.

WIDE OPEN SPACES

Epping Forest

Information Centre, High Beech, Loughton, Essex IG10 4AF (8508 0028/www.cityof london.gov.uk/openspaces). Loughton or Theydon Bois tube/Chingford rail. **Open** *Information Centre* Summer 11am-6pm daily. Winter 10am-3pm daily. *Forest* 24hrs daily. **Admission** free.

Epping Forest is 12 miles (19km) long and 22 miles (35km) across, and was saved from development by the Corporation of London in 1878. Commoners still have grazing rights and, each summer, English Longhorn cattle can be seen chewing the cud. For most visitors, it's the walking, horse riding or cycling opportunities that are the biggest draw. The forest contains Iron Age earthworks and two listed buildings – the Temple in Wanstead Park and the fully restored, 16th-century Queen Elizabeth's Hunting Lodge (Rangers Road, E4 7QH, 8529 6681; under-16s must be accompanied by an adult). The latter has a quiz trail, weekend craft activities and Tudor-themed dressing up; in the kitchen area, you can smell food made from 400-year-old recipes.

If you're coming to Epping Forest by public transport, be prepared for some exercise. Chingford railway station gives access to the Hunting Lodge and some lovely strolls at the south end. Loughton and Theydon Bois (Central line) are the forest's nearest tube stops, though it's a two-mile uphill walk from both. The best advice is to get a map and plan your route in advance – or take the car. At High Beech car park there's a small tea hut, as well as the Epping Forest Field Centre. For a real back-to-nature feeling, between May and September you can pitch your tent at the Debden House campsite (Debden Green, Loughton, Essex IG10 2NZ, 8508 3008; £7/night, £3.50/night under-16s, free under-threes) and listen to the owls hoot. The Heritage Lottery Fund has granted £4.7 million to the forest; improvement works begin in Autumn 2009.

Buggy access. Disabled access: toilet. Nappy-changing facilities. Shop.

Lee Valley Park

NE London (Hackney, Walthamstow, Waltham Abbey, Cheshunt, Broxbourne, Hoddesdon) E10-EN11 (01992 717711/www.leevalley park.org.uk). **Open** 24hrs daily. **Admission** varies; phone or check website for details. **Credit** MC, V.

This linear swathe of parkland is 26 miles (35km) long, running on both sides of the River Lee from just east of Hackney all the way through Essex and into Hertfordshire. It has a network of lakes, waterways, parks and countryside areas, and there's plenty to do. A gentle guided walk is a good way to start; the well-signposted park is ideal for picnics, walking or fishing. It's also a nature lover's paradise. Some 32 species of mammals are said to make their home in the park, along with 21 species of dragonfly. Waymarked walks, some providing easy buggy access, take you to see orchids, grasshoppers and waterlilies. The birdwatching is excellent: winter brings 10,000 migrant waterbirds from chillier climes, and summer is the time to enjoy the kingfishers.

Other attractions include the Lee Valley Riding Centre (*see p207*) and Lee Valley Ice Centre (*see p211*), which offers family sessions at the weekends and during school holidays. The erstwhile Lee Valley Cycle Circuit has been handed over to the Olympic builders to become a velopark in time for 2012. Lee Valley Boat Centre (Old Nazeing Road, Broxbourne, Herts EN10 6LX, 01992 462085, www.leevalleyboats. co.uk) hires boats by the hour and organises narrowboat holidays.

The fascinating town of Waltham Abbey, which borders the park, has plenty of cafés and shops and an Augustinian abbey, founded in 1060 by King Harold. The exciting Royal Gunpowder Mills (Beaulieu Drive, Waltham Abbey, Essex EN9 1JY, 01992 707370, www.royalgunpowdermills.com) and Epping Forest (*see above*) are also just a ten-minute drive from the town.

Buggy access. Disabled access: toilet. Kiosk. Nappy-changing facilities.

Meet the Animals

Where to find fur, feathers and fins in the city.

London may not have a jungle, an ocean or rolling open fields, but there's a surprising variety of species to be found if you know where to look. And we're not talking about foxes, pigeons and squirrels. Below we list the aquariums, zoos, city farms and wetland reserves that form part of this great city. Want to come nose to nose with a shark, feed a giraffe, help milk a cow, spot a white-faced whistling duck or simply learn the means of food production? It's all possible in one corner of London or another. Some of London's parks also have animal enclosures, so it's worth taking a look at the **Parks & Gardens** chapter too (*see pp105-128*).

AQUARIUMS

Horniman Museum

100 London Road, SE23 3PQ (8699 1872/ www.horniman.ac.uk). Forest Hill rail/176, 185, 197, 356, P4 bus. **Open** 10.30am-5.30pm daily. **Admission** free; donations appreciated. **Credit** MC, V.

This curiosity of a museum (*see p73*) holds an amazing aquarium, which houses hundreds of species of aquatic animals and plants across seven distinct zones. New in the last year is a very large lobster, some young seahorses and a clutch of anableps, whose more common name is the four-eyed fish (they only have two eyes but can see above and below the water simultaneously). Visitors working their way around explore the diverse nature of ecosystems from across the globe and read about the threats such fragile environments face. Ecosystems covered include British pond life, Devonshire rockpools, Fijian coral reefs, mangrove swamps and South American rainforests. The tank-viewing dens and interactive displays are always a favourite with children. The aquarium is currently conducting a specialised study of newts (which can be found in the Horniman garden's nature trail) and how their capacity for limb regeneration might be of use to human medicine. Check the website for details of events and activities.

Buggy access. Café. Disabled access: lift, toilet. Nappy-changing facilities. Nearest picnic place: museum gardens. Shop.

Sea Life London Aquarium

County Hall (riverfront entrance), Riverside Building, SE1 7PB (7967 8000/tours 7967 8002/www.londonaquarium.co.uk). Westminster tube/Waterloo tube/rail. **Open** 10am-6pm Mon-Fri (last entry 5pm); 10am-7pm Sat, Sun (last entry 6pm). *Tours* (groups of 10 or more) phone for details. **Admission** £15.25; £9.75-£13.25 reductions; £11.75 3-14s; free under-3s; £50 family (2+2). **Credit** MC, V. **Map** p317 M9.

The London Aquarium has been rebranded, and reopened on April 7 2009. Of course, all this is an excuse to charge even more (prices have leapt up since last year) and you may baulk at all the inducements to sample (lesser) attractions that share its County Hall premises. However, it's hard to be churlish once inside the aquarium itself. In addition to the hundreds of varieties of fish and sea life from all over the world, including stingrays, seven different varieties of shark, piranhas and sea scorpions, the big new attraction is the Shark Walk, which allows visitors to traverse a floating glass platform with sharks swimming just below their feet. Californian cownose rays which swim in synchronised formation are another new feature, as is a tunnel constructed from a 25-metre-long whale skeleton, beneath which visitors can view a tropical ocean of fish, coral and green turtles.

To get the best value, time your visit to coincide with feeding times (check the website for the day's schedule); the sharks are usually fed at 2.30pm. If you're pushing a buggy, enter and leave from the London Eye side; you'll avoid McDonald's and the tricky steps up to Westminster Bridge. *Buggy access. Disabled access: lift, toilet. Nappy-changing facilities. Nearest picnic place: Jubilee Gardens. Shop.*

FARMS

Crystal Palace Park Farm

The Croft, Ledrington Road, SE19 2BS (8778 5572/www.crystalpalaceparkfarm.co.uk). Crystal Palace rail. **Open** 10.30am-noon;

Sightseeing

Kentish Town City Farm. *See p132.*

2.30-4pm Mon, Tue, Thur & Fri; noon-4pm Sat, Sun & Bank Hol Mon. **Admission** free. **No credit cards**.

This farm was shut for many years, with only the animal paintings on the old stable doors left to remind park visitors of its former use. However, Crystal Palace Park Farm reopened in April 2008, much to the delight of local residents. Set within the park, it's a city farm with a small yard and paddocks with the added bonus of lovely views.

There are kune pigs, alpacas, goats, Shetland ponies and a reptile room. Children will like climbing the steep ramp to see the smaller mammals. The facility is very well used by local schools, who get guided tours with an education officer. In the afternoons, casual visitors can often handle the smaller animals, if there's a free member of staff handy. The neighbouring Capel Manor College (8778 5572, www.capel.ac.uk) runs full time animal care courses for 16- to 18-year-olds. There's no café on site, but the surrounding park is perfect for leisurely family picnics.

Buggy access. Disabled access: ramp, toilet. Nappy-changing facilities. Nearest picnic place: Crystal Palace Park.

Deen City Farm & Community Garden

39 Windsor Avenue, SW19 2RR (8543 5300/ www.deencityfarm.co.uk). Colliers Wood tube, then 200 bus. **Open** 10am-4.30pm Tue-Sun, bank hol Mon. **Admission** free; donations appreciated. **No credit cards**.

This farm is a member of the Rare Breeds Survival Trust and has a wide range of unusual species. Set on beautiful National Trust land within the Morden Hall Park Estate, it is noticeably different from London's other city farms. The strutting white peacocks parade their spectacular feathers, often accompanied by a competitively exhibitionist turkey. Meanwhile the other animals quietly compete for visitors' attention. New breeds to the farm this year include some hardy Shetland sheep, and the farm is currently awaiting the arrival of a consignment of new pigs. There are also ducks, chickens and geese, alpacas, and a huddle of rabbits and guinea pigs that you can handle at certain times (check when you arrive). There's a generous area for pony rides – £1 per ride for the under-eights on Wednesdays (noon), weekends (3pm) and school holidays – and sandwiches and cakes in the cheerful café are refreshingly cheap.

Buggy access. Café. Disabled access: toilet. Nappy-changing facilities. Nearest picnic place: Morden Hall Park. Shop.

Freightliners City Farm

Paradise Park, Sheringham Road, off Liverpool Road, N7 8PF (7609 0467/ www.freightlinersfarm.org.uk). Caledonian Road or Holloway Road tube/Highbury & Islington tube/rail. **Open** *Summer* 10am-4.45pm Tue-Sun, bank hol Mon. *Winter* 10am-4pm Tue-Sun. **Admission** free; donations appreciated. **No credit cards**.

It's hard to believe that busy Holloway Road has a farm just behind it, but here it is. The half-hectare site is as much community centre as working farm, with cookery lessons for teenagers running in the café, volunteer bee-keeping activities and a Dad's Club planned for Saturday mornings. There's a weekly gardening club on Wednesdays, an 'Adopt an Animal' scheme and various events throughout the summer holidays. You can even hold a party on the farm.

Freightliners is home to amiable cows, sheep, goats and two pigs called Tina and Tamara, as well as all kinds of poultry. The collection of animals, many of them rare breeds, is impressive. Giant Flemish rabbits are the biggest you'll see anywhere, while exotic cockerels with feathered feet squawk in your path. You can buy hen and duck eggs of all hues, plus seasonal, own-grown fruit, vegetables and plants.

Buggy access. Café. Disabled access: toilet. Nappy-changing facilities. Nearest picnic place: farm picnic area. Shop.

Hackney City Farm

1A Goldsmiths Row, E2 8QA (7729 6381/ www.hackneycityfarm.co.uk). Cambridge Heath Road rail, then 26, 48, 55 bus. **Open** 10am-4.30pm Tue-Sun, bank hol Mon. **Admission** free; donations appreciated. **Credit** MC, V.

Rural it ain't, but this tiny, bucolic idyll is much appreciated by residents in one of the least leafy corners of London. Around the small courtyard, outbuildings house some very pretty Golden Guernsey goats, sheep, pigs, Larry the donkey, chickens, geese, ducks and some smaller fluffier animals, including rabbits and guinea pigs. The larger animals get to frolic in a small field out back during the day. The farm does a healthy trade in eggs, and in November 2008 brought in some Tamworth pigs from Mudchute City Farm to begin pork production.

The inviting farm garden has raised beds full of seasonal vegetables, a plant nursery and a play area with a sandpit, wigwams and trails. Award-winning onsite café Frizzante sources ingredients locally where possible and offers rustic food inspired by regional Italian cooking. It's worth checking out the noticeboard

Sightseeing

for activities aimed at children and parents; popular pottery sessions cost £5 for two hours. *Buggy access. Café. Disabled access: toilet. Nappy-changing facilities. Nearest picnic place: gardens. Shop.*

Hounslow Urban Farm
A312 at Faggs Road, Feltham, Middx TW14 0LZ (8831 9658/www.hounslow.info). Hatton Cross tube, then 15min walk or 90, 285, 490 bus. **Open** *Summer* 10am-5pm daily (last entry 4pm). *Winter* 11am-4pm Sat, Sun (last entry 3pm). Times & days may vary, phone or check website for details. **Admission** £4.25-£5; £3.50-£4.25 reductions; £2.75-£3.50 2-16s; free under-2s; £12-£15 family (2+2). **No credit cards.**
London's largest community farm rears rare, endangered and historic breeds as part of a conservation programme, and offers plenty of opportunities for petting and feeding. Bags of feed are on sale at the new shop, which also sells cuddly toys, peacock feathers and all manner of animal themed souvenirs, and gives shelter to the farm's parrot and its lounge of lizards. Within its 29 acres, the farm houses British saddleback pigs, goats, ducks, Shetland ponies, alpacas, chipmunks and a recently-arrived donkey. Turn up at the right time of year and you could be lucky enough to feed the orphan lambs and peek at the piglets. You can even buy a small animal – such as a rabbit or a guinea pig – and get some helpful care advice. Activities are held daily and throughout the school holidays: animal handling, scarecrow-making and pig racing might feature, with a children's entertainer on bank holiday Mondays and every Tuesday during the holidays. There is a picnic area and a café for coffees and snacks, and a brace of new pedal tractors in the playground.
Buggy access. Café. Shop. Disabled access: toilet. Nappy-changing facilities. Nearest picnic place: farm picnic area.

Kentish Town City Farm
1 Cressfield Close, off Grafton Road, NW5 4BN (7916 5421/www.ktcityfarm.org.uk). Chalk Farm tube/Kentish Town tube/rail/Gospel Oak rail. **Open** 9am-5pm daily. **Admission** free; donations appreciated. **No credit cards.**
Just a short walk from Parliament Hill Fields is London's oldest city farm. The name may have changed since 1972, when it was known as Fun Art Farm, but the ethos remains the same. This was the model for London's other community led city farms, and provides much more than a chance to gawp at some livestock. The site is far

larger than first appearances suggest, stretching along the back of the railway, way beyond the farmyard into fields and well-tended vegetable gardens. There's also a frog-filled pond with a dipping platform to investigate.
Livestock includes farmyard ducks, goats, pigs, horses, cows, chickens and sheep, including some rare breeds. As well as petting the animals, children can get involved with their care by mucking out (arrive by 9am) and feeding them (with supervision), and taking care of the site. During the holidays, a host of activities are held in the farm centre and children's parties can be held here at weekends (these include use of the kitchen). There are after-school clubs too: practical city farming, pottery and cookery classes. There's a two year waiting list to join the Camden Pony Club, which is based here, but the Riding School offers weekend pony rides from March to September, weather permitting (1.30pm, Sat & Sun, £1). The farm welcomes school visits from all boroughs, and holds May Day celebrations, a summer Horse Show, an Easter egg hunt, Apple Day activities and a Christmas fair.
Buggy access. Disabled access: toilet. Nappy-changing facilities. Nearest picnic place: farm grounds.

Lee Valley Park Farms
Stubbins Hall Lane, Crooked Mile, Waltham Abbey, Essex EN9 2EG (01992 892781/ www.leevalleypark.org.uk). Broxbourne or Cheshunt rail. **Open** Mar-Oct 10am-5pm daily. Closed Nov-Feb. **Admission** £6.80; £5.40 reductions, 2-16s; free under-2s; £26.80 family (2+3). **Credit** MC, V.
There are actually two farms here. Hayes Hill is a traditional farm and rare-breeds centre, while Holyfield Hall is its commercial neighbour. At Hayes Hill, try persuading the children that the animals are more exciting than the pedal tractors or the new soft play feature, Bundle Barn. They can also meet Tallulah the Tamworth and Barbara the Berkshire pig, as well as some Essex pigs (a seriously endangered species). There are also goats, sheep, llamas, water buffalo and chickens. In the spring, visitors are encouraged to bottle-feed the new lambs. Stroking Rex the 'therapy' rabbit is another draw – but watch out for Newton the bearded dragon.
If all this is a bit cosy, visitors can watch the cows being milked (from 2.30pm daily) over at Holyfield Hall and learn about large scale dairy production. There are guided tours for school parties, tractor-trailer rides and pig races at various times of the year (weather permitting).
Buggy access. Café. Disabled access: toilet. Nappy-changing facilities. Nearest picnic place: farm picnic areas. Shop.

Sightseeing

Animals that won't bite

It's all very well petting real animals, but what about the iconic London animals that don't move? Small children will love the statue of Paddington Bear, standing on the main concourse of the station he was named after on his arrival from darkest Peru. For older children, the bronze lions of Trafalgar Square are legendary for those who relish a difficult climb. Young children should admire these four majestic beasts from the ground, but teenagers will like the challenge and the genuine danger associated with scaling the stone plinth and attempting to climb on to their shiny bronze backs.

In Park Lane, just east of Hyde Park's Speakers' Corner, stand a horse, two mules and a dog cast from bronze. They form part of David Backhouse's sculpture *Animals In War*, a tribute to the millions of animals that lost their lives in World War I. And don't forget the camel in Embankment Gardens that commemorates the noble work of the Camel Corps.

Another little memorial to look out for, this time while walking on the Thames Path at Greenwich, stands in the small riverside garden on Ballast Quay, just past the Cutty Sark Tavern. It's a little goat kid, made from material salvaged from the river, rearing up as if to nibble some leaves from a tree. A plaque beside it reads: 'In memory of the millions of animals who died not from foot and mouth but from the cure for foot and mouth.'

A gorilla stands in Crystal Palace Park (*see p113*), on the north side of the boating lake; David Wynne's sculpture of London Zoo's primate resident Guy, who was quite a celebrity in the 1960s and '70s. (While you're here, don't miss the gigantic dinosaur sculptures in the lake complex; unveiled in 1854, they're wildly inaccurate, as young palaeontologists will note.) Wynne also created the dolphin swimming through the air with a young boy catching a ride on his fin on the corner of Cheyne Walk and Albert Bridge.

While Dr Johnson was writing his dictionary, his cat Hodge was his faithful companion. Boswell's account of the writer's life even remembers Johnson procuring oysters for his furry friend. A statue of Hodge sits by Dr Johnson's House (*see p76*) in Gough Square.

For a peculiar adventure, seek out Jamrach's Tiger, a statue that lies in the Tobacco Dock shopping centre, which stopped trading in 1990 but remains mysteriously and eerily open to the public. The tiger escaped from pet shop Jamrach's Emporium in Wapping, and mauled a passing youth.

Sightseeing

Mudchute City Farm

Mudchute City Farm

*Pier Street, Isle of Dogs, E14 3HP (7515
5901/www.mudchute.org). Crossharbour,
Mudchute or Island Gardens DLR.* **Open**
9am-5pm daily. **Admission** free; donations
appreciated. **No credit cards.**
Sensitive landscaping blocks out the urban
sprawl on this 27-acre plot, but the looming towers
of Canary Wharf leave visitors in no doubt they
are still in the city. Once the kids have seen the
animals, there are lots of paths through well-
established woods and hedgerows to explore;
wherever you roam on site, you can still hear the
donkeys. Early risers can join the duck walk at
9am, and kids can handle the smaller animals
(including ferrets and guinea pigs) in Pets'
Corner from 9.30am-4pm. Visitors can also help
to feed the larger animals – rare breed cows,
Tamworth pigs, goats, llamas and horses – which
adds to the excitement. Volunteers have done
quite a bit to smarten up Mudchute in the past
year. There's now a bread oven in the café, and
the facilities are available for hire for private
parties. There's an after school club for five- to
12-year-olds and plenty of seasonal events to
enjoy. The site lends itself to picnics, but the café
is too good to ignore (*see p231*).
*Buggy access. Café. Disabled access: toilet.
Nappy-changing facilities. Nearest picnic place:
farm grounds. Shop.*

Newham City Farm

*Stansfeld Road, E6 5LT (7474 4960).
Royal Albert DLR/262, 300, 376 bus.*
Open *Summer* 10am-5pm Tue-Sun,
bank hol Mon. *Winter* 10am-4pm Tue-Sun.
Admission free; donations appreciated.
No credit cards.
Newham was established in the first wave of
the City Farm movement in London, and has
been going strong now for over 30 years.
Alongside the usual farmyard poultry, sheep,
pigs and goats, the largest animal on the farm
is Blaze, a shire horse, who pulls a dray cart
that visitors can ride in. There are also some
smaller, furrier chaps (rabbits, guinea pigs
and two ferrets), and a twittering house of
finches and a kookaburra. The visitors'
centre runs plenty of holiday activities,
such as the ever-popular 'Be a Farmer for a
Day' sessions (you will need to book these in
advance) and various other drop-in activities.
Fun Days offer the likes of sheep-shearing
demonstrations and felt-making and visitors
can also taste the honey produced by bees
from the farm's own hives. As well as some
picnic space, there's a café serving teas, coffees
and light snacks.
*Buggy access. Café. Disabled access: toilet.
Nappy-changing facilities. Nearest picnic place:
farm picnic area. Shop.*

Spitalfields City Farm

*Buxton Street, off Brick Lane, E1 5AR
(7247 8762/www.spitalfieldscityfarm.org).
Whitechapel tube.* **Open** *Summer* 10am-
4.30pm Tue-Sun. *Winter* 10am-4pm Tue-Sun.
Admission free; donations appreciated.
No credit cards.
Just around the corner from the gleaming towers
of the City is this compact community farm.
There's a daily goat-milking demo, mice and
rabbits for stroking, and a full complement of
cows, pigs and sheep. Children can take part in
workshops on dairy farming, healthy eating,
sustainability and animal welfare. Outside the
farmyard, there is much to see. The Ideas Garden
is a mini gardening museum, while another
small patch is being planted up as a forest.

In spring, the Wildlife Garden is gorgeous, as
bluebells, snowdrops and foxgloves nod in the
pungent breeze, scented by wild garlic. Keen
eight- to 13-year-olds can join the Young Farmers'
Club, which runs a play scheme on Saturdays
from 10.30am-3.30pm; there's also a parent and
toddler group for under-fives (Tue, Sun). Veg,
fruit and plants are on sale, and the new raised
picnic area has a fire pit for outdoor cooking.
Young visitors can enjoy donkey rides on
Wednesdays (noon-1pm, £1), and special annual
events include the Sheep and Wool Fayre in May,
October's Apple Day and the Christmas Fair.
*Buggy access. Disabled access: toilet. Nappy-
changing facilities. Nearest picnic place: Allen
Gardens. Shop.*

Surrey Docks Farm

*South Wharf, Rotherhithe Street, SE16 5ET
(7231 1010/www.surreydocksfarm.org.uk).
Canada Water tube, then 381, C10 bus.*
Open 10am-5pm Tue-Sun. **Admission** free;
donations appreciated. **No credit cards.**
The city around this Rotherhithe institution
has changed dramatically since the farm
was dreamt up in 1975, and it's now hemmed
in by the gated developments and luxury flats
of Surrey Quays. Sheep, goats and chickens
mooch around a central farmyard, while out
in the pens there are organically-reared cows,
pigs, donkeys and horses, fenced in by
delightful wrought metal railings – just one
example of resident blacksmith Kevin Boys'
handiwork. (This is the only City Farm in
London to have a working forge, which offers
classes to local schoolchildren.) Kids can also
learn a lot about food production from the dairy,
milking barn, bee room, orchard, herb garden
and vegetable plots. The farm café has moved

Stroke a fluffy rabbit or pet a horse at **Spitalfields City Farm**.

Sightseeing

London Zoo. *See p140.*

from Mediterranean-style grub to Modern British recently, but continues to use as much fresh produce from the farm as possible; there's also a farm shop. If the kids seem inspired, they can always return on the third Saturday of every month for the Young Farmers' Club (eight to 13s) and learn more.
Buggy access. Café. Disabled access: toilet. Nearest picnic place: riverside. Shop.

Vauxhall City Farm

165 Tyers Street, SE11 5HS (7582 4204/ www.vauxhallcityfarm.info). Vauxhall tube/rail/ 2, 36, 44, 77 bus. **Open** 10.30am-4pm Wed-Sun. **Admission** free; donations appreciated. **No credit cards.**
This tiny sliver of mud and muck is Vauxhall's answer to the countryside. Many of the animals – Poppy and Pepper, a pair of Anglo Nubian goats, plus their black Wensleydale sheep friends – inhabit a specially constructed straw-bale animal house, built by Barbara Jones in 2001, with sedums on the roof to attract bees. Start here and then wander through to the duck pond and community garden. There's no café, but you can picnic near the rabbit and chicken enclosures. The farm runs pony-riding sessions in nearby Spring Gardens for children and riders with disabilities, hosts the Ruby Rhymes

under-fives singing group on Fridays, and holds classes in art, spinning, dyeing and weaving (plants for natural dyes are grown in a special garden). Facilities are fairly basic – and the chatter of the radio can spoil the bucolic feel – but, together with the slippery pathways, cloying mud and occasional dollop of horse muck, this gives a passable representation of a working farm.
Buggy access. Disabled access: toilet. Nappy-changing facilities. Nearest picnic place: Spring Gardens.

Woodlands Farm

331 Shooters Hill, Welling, Kent DA16 3RP (8319 8900/www.thewoodlandsfarmtrust.org). Falconwood rail/89, 486 bus. **Open** 9.30am-4.30pm daily. **Admission** free; donations appreciated. **No credit cards.**
Woodlands Farm and the ancient Oxleas Wood were almost flattened by the Department of Transport, to make way for a motorway. Happily, public support saved the site and in 1997 it became one of Greater London's newest city farms. The farm's ideology is based on sustainable and organic methods of producing food. As well as its livestock, it has an award-winning cottage garden, a sensory garden and a wildlife garden, not to mention orchards and

meadows. The residents include noisy geese, hens, guinea pigs, a flock of sheep, Daisy the British white cow and two Vietnamese pot-bellied pigs called Doris and Iris. The farm hosts educational group visits, giving lessons on conservation, composting, farm animal care and the history of farming. Keep an eye on the events diary to see what's in the offing. The farm also sells logs, manure, eggs and hay at good prices. Children who sign up as volunteers can help feed and muck out the animals on Saturday mornings, but must be accompanied by a carer or parent; call the farm for details.
Buggy access. Café (weekends, summer only). Nearest picnic place: farm grounds. Shop.

WETLAND RESERVES

Greenwich Peninsula Ecology Park
Thames Path, John Harrison Way, SE10 0QZ (8293 1904/www.urbanecology.org.uk). North Greenwich tube/108, 161, 422, 472, 486 bus. **Open** 10am-5pm Wed-Sun. **Admission** free.
The construction of the Blackwall Tunnel destroyed much of the area's natural marshland, but it began to creep back after the gasworks were decommissioned late last century. This patch underwent a huge regeneration project in 1997 to become a freshwater habitat for frogs, toads, newts and many species of birds. There are themed quiz trails and word searches, and kids can collect the materials to make paintings, collages or sketches. Take to the hides to watch the birds without disturbing them, or borrow the necessary equipment to get up close and personal with the wildlife (the visitors centre provides pond dipping nets, trays, magnifiers, bug jars and binoculars).
Buggy access. Disabled access: toilet. Nappy-changing facilities. Nearest picnic place: southern park.

WWT Wetland Centre
Queen Elizabeth's Walk, SW13 9WT (8409 4400/www.wwt.org.uk/london). Hammersmith tube, then 33, 72, 209 (alight at Red Lion pub) or 283 bus (Duck Bus direct to Centre). **Open** *Summer* 9.30am-6pm daily. *Winter* 9.30am-5pm daily (last entry 1hr before closing). *Tours* 11am, 2pm daily. *Feeding tours* 3pm daily. **Admission** £9.50; £7.10 reductions; £5.25 4-16s; free under-4s; £26.55 family (2+2). *Tours* free. **Credit** MC, V.
On the banks of the Thames at Barnes lies this enormous wildlife reserve. Set over 104 acres, the

Great Days Out
Marylebone

Bounded by brash, busy Oxford Street to the south and stately Regent's Park to the north, Marylebone is an affable (and affluent) little enclave. Its leafy squares, terraces of Georgian townhouses and boutique-lined high street are perfect for a leisurely stroll – particularly on Sundays, when one of London's largest farmer's markets sets up shop here.

Once the children's tolerance for shopping has worn off, Regent's Park is a hop, skip and a jump away, while for rainy days, the Wallace Collection is a little-known treasure. Kids may be unmoved by the promise of Old Masters and 18th-century porcelain, but the magnificent armoury is another matter entirely. And there's always Madame Tussaud's…

Up in arms

Entrance to the **Wallace Collection** (*see p69*), a grand, 18th-century townhouse-turned-museum, is absolutely free; inside, all sorts of treasures await. Anyone with a penchant for chivalry, derring-do and gory battles will be enraptured by the array of armour, ranging from gold-inlaid scimitars and creepy, beak-fronted helmets to the mighty cannons and gleaming suits.

Elsewhere, you can gawp at Frans Hals' *Laughing Cavalier* (sporting a magnificent moustache), marvel at Louis XV's commode and admire Catherine the Great's lovely Sèvres porcelain ice-cream cooler.

Kids can try the weighty suits of armour on for size in the

Conservation Gallery, or pick up a free Warrior Kings trail at the information desk, which takes you round all manner of jewel-encrusted weaponry. Visiting on the first Sunday of the month? Then prepare to get sketching at one of the Little Draw drop-in workshops. There's also armour-handling, hat-designing and watercolour painting sessions on the busy events calendar; most cost a mere £4.

Wax lyrical

If all that sounds terribly serious and you've got cash to burn, you could head down to the gaudy attractions of **Madame Tussaud's** (*see p64*). Where else could you have your picture taken next to Amy Winehouse, Johnny Depp and the Queen in one afternoon? Yes, ultimately, you're paying to see a collection of waxwork models, but Madame Tussaud's isn't world famous by accident; there's a lot of effort put in to contextualising the figures and providing interactive excitement. The Spirit of London ride is our personal favourite.

Head upmarket

Marylebone is a mecca for foodies, thanks to fine food emporiums such as La Fromagerie and the Ginger Pig (both on Moxon Street), and a host of swish restaurants. More exciting to children is the vibrant **Marylebone Farmer's Market** (www.lfm.org.uk), where grown-ups can sample slivers of whiffy cheese and compare olive oils while kids eye up the slabs of home-made cake. It's held on Sunday mornings in the Cramer Street car park, which is just off the high street. If you're around on Saturday, head for the chichi **Cabbages & Frocks** (www.cabbagesandfrocks.co.uk) market, in the grounds of St Mary's Parish Church. Friendly stallholders sell jewellery and clothes alongside salamis, artisan breads and all sorts of on-the-spot little somethings to keep you going until lunch. Topped with pastel swirls of icing and covered with pretty handmade sugar flowers, Peggy's Cupcakes are irresistible.

Coming up roses

To work off your foodie excesses in the fresh air, head north for **Regent's Park** (*see p123*). In early summer, the breeze is particularly fragrant, as the Inner Circle's magnificent rose gardens come into bloom. There's plenty of resident wildlife, too, particularly around the lakes. The ducks will relish a bit of birdseed or a crust from your sarnies (wholemeal only though, as white bread doesn't do them a power of good); according to park authorities, the swans are particularly partial to a leaf of lettuce or two.

At the top of the park, more animals await at the famous **London Zoo** (*see p140*). Though its entrance charges are substantial, the zoo does offer an inimitable day out. There are far too many attractions to list – though we've got a particularly soft spot for the walk-through Butterfly Paradise, where enormous tropical butterflies swoop by in the hot, humid air. Tons of special events run throughout the day, too, from storytelling sessions in the brilliant, brand-new Animal Adventure children's zoo and play area to meet-the-spider events, and the classic penguins' feeding time. Incidentally, our favourite way to keep an eye on the time is by consulting the extraordinary clock outside the Blackburn Pavilion; be there on the half hour as it whirrs and clanks into action, and prepare to be amazed.

LUNCH BOX

Also in the area: Ask, Carluccio's Caffè, Paul, Ping Pong, Pizza Express, Tootsies Grill, Wagamama.

Boathouse Café *The Boating Lake, Hanover Gate, Regent's Park NW1 4NU (7724 4069).* Survey the boating lake from the ample terrace at this family-friendly joint, which serves pizza, pasta and snacks.

Fishworks *89 Marylebone High Street, W1U 4QW (7935 9796/ www.fishworks.co.uk).* The £5 kids' menu includes fishfingers, fishcakes and mussels, with ice-cream to follow; for refuseniks, there's spaghetti in tomato sauce.

Golden Hind *73 Marylebone Lane, W1U 2PN (7486 3644).* Proper fish and chips, kids' portions and a warm welcome for families.

Honest Sausage *Inner Circle, off Chester Road, Regent's Park NW1 4NU (7224 3872/www.honest sausage.com).* Bacon butties or free-range bangers, served in a bread bun or atop a heap of mash.

Great Days Out

centre is home to rare international breeds such as New Zealand's beautiful black swans and white-faced whistling ducks, while every season brings new migratory visitors, including lapwings, hobbies and ospreys. There's a bat house under construction, plus six existing observation hides; the largest is the three-storey Peacock Tower, which even has a lift.

You can take free guided tours with well-informed, friendly bird-watchers, or simply enjoy romping around the paths past the main lake, reed beds, ponds and wetland meadows. The Discovery Centre is a game attempt at recreating wetland habitats, such as mangrove swamps, indoors (fibreglass crocodiles and all), and there are various water-based games for the kids to try. Kids aged three to 11 will happily ignore the birds and play for hours in the adventure playground, shooting through the water-vole tunnels, tackling the climbing walls and flying through the air on zip wires. There's a self-service restaurant with lovely views over the main lake, which offers a tempting array of edibles. *Buggy access. Café. Disabled access: lift, toilet. Nappy-changing facilities. Nearest picnic place: centre picnic areas. Shop.*

ZOOS

Battersea Park Children's Zoo
Queenstown Road, Battersea Park, SW11 4NJ (7924 5826/www.batterseazoo.co.uk). Sloane Square tube, then 19, 137 bus/Battersea Park or Queenstown Road rail/156, 345 bus. **Open** *Summer* 10am-5.30pm daily (last entry 5pm). *Winter* 10am-dusk daily. **Admission** £6.50; £4.95 2-15s; free under-2s; £20.50 family (2+2). **Credit** MC, V. **Map** p313 F13.

Those that find London Zoo overwhelming in terms of visitor numbers, choice of exhibits and sheer square footage may find this small riverside zoo a less daunting prospect. Kids can chatter with the squirrel monkeys and brown capuchins, watch mice running around in their own doll's house and crawl down a pair of tunnels, popping up in a bubble in the meerkats' den. New Zealand kune pigs provide vocal entertainment with top-volume snorting to amuse the toddlers, and the mynah birds might have a word with you, if you're lucky. At weekends, visitors can watch feeding times (meerkats and otters 11am & 2.30pm; monkeys 11am & 3pm) and get friendly with the farm animals at Barley Mo Farm at noon and 3.30pm. The Lemon Tree café provides basic lunch fare, and there's a pretty good playground for all ages. One warning: you have to enter and leave via the gift shop, so get your excuses in early.

Buggy access. Café. Disabled access: toilet. Nappy-changing facilities. Nearest picnic place: zoo picnic area. Shop.

London Zoo
Outer Circle, Regent's Park, NW1 4RY (7722 3333/www.zsl.org). Baker Street or Camden Town tube, then 274 or C2 bus. **Open** *Mar-June, Sept, Oct* 10am-5.30pm daily. *July, Aug* 10am-6pm daily. *Nov-Feb* 10am-4pm daily. Last entry 1hr before closing. **Admission** (including £1.70 voluntary contribution) £18.50; £17 reductions; £15 3-15s; free under-3s; £60.50 family (2+2 or 1+3). **Credit** AmEx, MC, V. **Map** p314 G2.

The zoo offers a sneak preview of its attractions from the north side of Regent's Park and the banks of Regent's canal, where strange bird calls echo and flashes of brightly coloured fur can be glimpsed through the netting. London Zoo has revamped itself significantly over the last ten years, with animals rehoused in imaginative enclosures that follow the 'natural habitat' philosophy of zookeeping. The most exciting addition in recent years is Gorilla Kingdom, where visitors can get within a foot of three adult gorillas – albeit separated by a sheet of reinforced glass. The nearby colobus monkeys are also great fun to watch, expecially if you catch them careering through their aerial net tunnel.

There's so much to do and see here that the best way to enjoy it is with an annual pass. Staying for a couple of hours is then guilt free and allows children to get the most out of one or two exhibits without museum legs setting in. Otherwise it's a dash around Into Africa, the indoor Clore Rainforest Lookout, the Meet The Monkeys walkthrough and insect extravaganza B.U.G.S., then Butterfly Paradise tunnel and the Aquarium. Between them lurk lions, tigers, hippos, camels and flamingos: all impossible to walk past quickly. Daily events include the 'Animals In Action' display at noon, which has the audience ducking as hawks, vultures, owls and parrots soar millimetres above their heads for strategically placed titbits while a keeper relays amusing anecdotes. Better than a science lesson any day.

The new Children's Zoo, unveiled in Easter 2009, was designed for children by children. Here, kids can groom goats and sheep, meet the llamas, climb with coatis, explore the tunnels in the Roots Zone or listen to a story in the tipi. The Splash Zone will have parents cursing, unless they've been organised enough to bring spare clothes and shoes; you have been warned. *See also p138* **Great Days Out.**

Buggy access. Café. Disabled access: toilet. Nappy-changing facilities. Nearest picnic place: zoo picnic areas. Restaurant. Shop.

Activities

Parties

Fight for your right…

It seems there's nothing you can't hire for a children's party. You can arrive by pony-drawn carriage, spend your day with snakes, then leave by fire engine. Then again, you may decide the best sort of knees-up needs nothing more than pass-the-parcel, balloons and bunting, with a candle-topped cake at the end.

Whatever sort of party you're planning, and whatever your budget, there are places that can help – and party planners who'll organise the whole thing (at a price). Specialists also abound, from eco-friendly tableware and party bag companies to a gluten-free bakers.

If you're reluctant to sacrifice your living room, there are plenty of reasonably priced halls; that extra £50 could be worth it to save your carpet. Most play centres (*see p179-181*) also offer special party deals, though it's often cheaper to ignore the package and just turn up; check if their insurance allows cakes with candles.

We focused on birthdays, but the teen-friendly companies are all great for bah and bat mitzvahs, and many entertainers also specialise in keeping tiny wedding guests amused.

ACTIVITY PARTIES

Arts & crafts

For more artistic options, *see p194*. Clapham's **Papered Parlour** (*see p195*) also offers adorable arts and crafts parties, on two sweetly old-fashioned themes.

Arty Party
8675 7055/www.artyparty.co.uk.
A team of professional artists arrive with all the materials to make jewelled mirrors, jaunty wooden boats, towering giraffes and other crafty items in their two- to three-hour party packages. Staff are pretty undaunted by rowdy kids, having held workshops for crowds of 400 at park fun days. They charge £230 for up to 20 kids aged over four.

Jewel Party
07590 077460/www.jewelparty.co.uk.
Children as young as three return home from a Jewel Party bedecked in necklaces, rings and bracelets of their own making. Parties are themed according to the materials used, with beads and sweetie jewellery being the big favourites. Boys enjoy the Fimo clay workshops, bashing out Gothic signet rings and pirate-style necklets. The company has cannily introduced a recession-busting package of a 40-minute bracelet workshop at £75 for up to ten kids. Otherwise, standard packages start at £150 for one-and-a-half hours, with invites included.

Pottery Café
735 Fulham Road, SW6 5UL (7736 2157/ www.pottery-cafe.com). Parsons Green tube/ 14, 414 bus. **Open** 11am-6pm Mon; 10am-6pm Tue, Wed, Fri, Sat; 10am-10pm Thur; 11am-5pm Sun. **Credit** MC, V.
This café and paint-your-own studio offers children's parties for £19.95 a head. In a separate party room, kids aged seven and over can make a joyful mess painting their very own piece of pottery. It's not just mugs and plates; most popular with the kids are the beautiful money-boxes, shaped like dragons and fire-engines. The package includes invites, balloons, a party leader, sandwiches and a drink – as well as the glazed and fired results of the children's artistic endeavours. (You return a week later to collect the pieces.) You're welcome to bring your own food and cake.
Buggy access. Café. Disabled access. Nappy-changing facilities.
Branch 322 Richmond Road, Twickenham, Middx TW1 2DU (8744 3000).

Soap & Bubble Company
8402 7565/www.soapandbubble.com.

Soap & Bubble Company. *See p143.*

Soap & Bubble arrive equipped with all the ingredients to make soaps, chocolate lip balm, body glitter, bubble bath and even floating ducks. All they ask you to provide is a bit of space and a large table. The team will even tidy up afterwards, leaving you with not only a spotless party room, but a child eager to jump in the bath to test their home-made concoctions. Two-hour parties start at £175 for up to eight kids aged eight and above.

Cookery

For cookery lessons and workshops, *see also p197* **Kids' Cookery School** and **Munchkins**.

Cookie Crumbles
0845 601 4173/www.cookiecrumbles.net.
Kids from four to 15 prepare their own three-course meals during these absorbing parties. Even non-foodie children enjoy bashing out dough and getting covered in flour while preparing such goodies as pizza snakes and ricotta ravioli. Two-hour parties start at £165 for six kids, with CC providing all ingredients and equipment; you won't even have to lift a spoon. The company also produces birthday gift boxes, containing everything small chefs need to bake various sweet treats. Over the years, Cookie Crumbles' workshop programmes have taught over 10,000 children how to cook, so you can rest assured they really know their onions… and sausages, and tiramisu.

Gill's Cookery Workshop
7 North Square, NW11 7AA (8458 2608/ www.gillscookeryworkshop.co.uk). Golders Green tube.
Fancy a party without piles of sausage rolls cluttering your freezer? Gill Roberts invites your guests to her kitchen, where for three hours they cater their own party. Popular themes include the American party (burgers and brownies) or Italian pizzas and ice-cream. Kids also bake a mini birthday cake to take home. Parties start at £250, and are suitable for four to 16s.

Firemen

Hot Hire
07947 028899/www.hot-hire.co.uk.
Imagine the thrill as a real fire engine turns up at your party, complete with qualified fireman. Kids get to ride in the engine and try out the hose, followed by an optional disco and games (you can sound the siren if your party is on private land). Hold your party on a school night and the fire engine can meet your guests at the school gate and drive them to your venue. Packages for three- to 16-year-olds start at £99, with a free fireman's helmet for each child. And yes, mothers do get a ride if there's time at the end.

Pamper parties

Mini Makeovers
8398 0107/www.minimakeovers.com.
Girlies aged five to 15 are treated to a makeover and manicure, before rounding things off with a celebratory disco. The little ones adore being prettied up as fairies and princesses, while teens favour Hannah Montana and *High School Musical* parties. The basic package costs £160 for eight kids, with dance classes, photoshoots and limousine hire as optional extras.

Performance

For more clubs and companies that run term-time music and drama courses, as well as staging parties, *see chapter* **Arts & Entertainment**.

Blueberry Playsongs Parties
8677 6871/www.blueberry.clara.co.uk.
These fun, guitar-led musical parties for one- to six-year-olds involve dancing, bubbles, party games and puppets. Packages start from £85, including 20 balloons and a gift for the birthday child. *See also p176.*

Drama Parties
0151 336 4302/www.dramaparties.com.
Parties run by the Little Actors Theatre Company give four to 14s the chance to experience a full drama workshop with a party atmosphere. Themes include *Winnie The Pooh*, *Mamma Mia* and the ever popular *Grease*; if the birthday boy or girl has a particular passion, you can suggest your own theme. Prices start at £130 for an hour, with invites and thank-you cards thrown in.

Funky Chicks
8302 6992/www.funky-chicks.co.uk.
Day-glo lycra-clad dancers host these disco parties, aimed at five- to 12-year-olds. Competitions, dressing up and innovative party games accompany a dance class, with the birthday child taking a starring role in a final performance. You'll probably need to hire a hall to accommodate the team's acrobatic moves and body popping, and book well in advance as they are becoming very popular. Spectacular parties start at £500 for two hours.

Activities

Ask the organiser

Julia Banfield, Arty Party
See p145.
What's your most popular party package?
Clay self-portraits.
Which package do you enjoy presenting the most?
Papier-maché birds.
How do you adapt to suit different ages?
The children just work to their own ability, but older kids make more intricate things.
Best experience?
Children's delight with what they've made.
And your worst?
Mums who can't bear not being in control!
Why are you in the business?
My husband and I both studied art at uni, and we enjoy working with children.

Jim Sennett, Campaign Paintball
See p151.
What's your most popular party package?
Dodge City, a replica Wild West town with saloon and bar.
Which package do you enjoy presenting the most?
I love the Dark Tower, a *Lord of the Rings*-inspired zone set among the oak trees.
How do you adapt to suit different ages?
We group players according to age.
Best experience?
When Chelsea Football Club came down.

And your worst?
When we had to stop because of torrential rain; everyone was wet and miserable.
Why are you in the business?
I love the outdoors, and I'm my own boss!

Lindsey Parker, Animal Magic
See p148.
What's your most popular party package?
The children meet ten animals from our selection of 30 different species.
Which package do you enjoy presenting the most?
I enjoy working with the disabled groups.
How do you adapt to suit different ages?
No need – animals work with anyone!
Best experience?
I'll never forget when a young girl from a disabled home who hadn't talked for three years after a stroke saw one of our dogs and spoke out. Everyone was in tears.
And your worst?
I was almost late for a party when I got stuck on the M25 for six hours.
Why are you in the business?
I love working with animals and children.

Carola Weymouth, Cookie Crumbles
See p145.
What's your most popular party package?
Four to sevens adore the menu with

Campaign Paintball

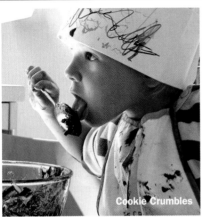

Cookie Crumbles

Pottery Café

Activities

chocolate rings, pizza snakes and pancake pillows. Older children enjoy the Disco Divas menu.

Which package do you enjoy presenting the most?
I love working with younger kids; often it's their first experience of cooking.

How do you adapt to suit different ages?
We tailor menus to different age groups.

Best experience?
After a private cooking session with the royal family in Saudi Arabia, the children said, 'That was the best thing we've ever done?' It touched me to think that with all the money they have, this was something they really enjoyed.

And your worst?
I went to the house of a Japanese client, who didn't have a kitchen: he thought we'd bring it with us! Luckily we borrowed the neighbours' kitchens.

Why are you in the business?
Schools that teach food technology often put children off; I believe it should be fun.

Alex Mannion, Pottery Café
See p143.

What's your most popular party package?
We only offer one package, which includes a piece of pottery to paint for each guest, plus sandwiches, crisps, a drink, invitations and balloons.

Which package do you enjoy presenting the most?
All groups are good fun!

How do you adapt to suit different ages?
Our staff are trained to deal with children or adults; we're very family oriented.

Best experience?
When we opened our party room and had our first party there. It's so pink and girly!

And your worst?
We had a room full of boys under seven who started throwing sandwiches. We don't have parties for that age group now!

Why are you in the business?
Like all the staff here, I enjoy being in a creative and sociable environment.

James Walker, Movie Parties
See p148.

What's your most popular party package?
James Bond by a slim margin; Murder Mystery is our second most popular.

Which package do you enjoy presenting the most?
All of them!

How do you adapt to suit different ages?
Children develop storylines themselves.

Best experience?
It's great when the whole family comes to see the première at the end.

And your worst?
Sometimes when they see how much fun it is, the adults want to get involved too!

Why are you in the business?
My vision is that in ten years' time, someone will be accepting an Oscar or a BAFTA and saying 'I wouldn't be here if it hadn't have been for my Movie Party!'

Acting Up

For children, drama is usually confined to the school nativity and the odd extra-curricular club. But for little ones with more intense thespian yearnings, or parents looking for a less run-of-the-mill party experience, you can now invite the theatre into your home.

Instead of sending clowns, magicians or quirky characters to keep the children entertained, **Little Actors Theatre Company** (*see p145* Drama Parties) provides actors. The emphasis is on encouraging the children to use their imagination, taking themes such as fairies, pirates, wizards and witches as the starting point, then devising weird and wonderful plots.

With 20 years of experience treading the boards, the last 15 of those working with children, Equity member Samantha Giblin is the ringleader of fun – though the kids also direct proceedings. 'The children are encouraged to project their voices and we instruct them in stagecraft, but we don't prescribe what happens on the day,' she explains. 'The rest is down to their imagination.' (Most recently, 'artistic differences' between two equally stubborn birthday girls resulted in a play that was a mixture of *The Wizard of Oz* and zoo animals.)

Less outgoing children have nothing to fear from the experience. 'We would never shove a shy child into centre stage,' Samantha says. 'We want to encourage, not intimidate. Children can be our helpers for the day if they'd prefer, or part of a crowd scene.'

For the most part it's beneficial to the entire 'creative process' if parents are wallflowers for the afternoon, rather than distracting their offspring – though as Samantha points out, the villain's roles are always popular for dads.

This experience isn't about being the loudest, most confident participant, or reeling off Shakespeare's soliloquies. Instead, it's about having fun and, (whisper it), learning a few new skills. 'We offer a completely interactive experience,' explains Samantha. 'It's creative, instructive and imaginative – and every single child is involved, so they're less likely to get bored.' Curtain up!

Jigsaw
8447 4530/www.jigsaw-arts.co.uk.
This long-running stage school has recently branched out into imaginative performance parties. The teachers that coach the weekend classes take three- to 12-year-old partygoers through wizard school, cheerleading camp or a mini *It's a Knockout*, among other themed packages; parties cost from £120 for one hour.

Kate Gielgud Acting Parties
8964 5490/www.tiddleywinks.co.uk.
Custom-written dramas centring on the birthday child are Kate's speciality. Born with an infectious passion for drama (she's Sir John's great-niece), her parties are absorbing affairs with themes such as James/Jane Bond and classy murder mysteries. Prices start at £300 for two hours, and she arrives with scripts and costumes. Plays can be adapted for four- to 13-year-olds.

Movie Parties
7387 4341/www.movie-parties.co.uk.
Movie-mad eight to 16s get eight hours to plan, rehearse, shoot, edit and screen their own film with a team of professionals. Each child gets a DVD of the finished result to take home. Themes include *Charlie's Angels*, *Harry Potter* and *Pirates of the Caribbean*, using your house and local parks as the backdrop to all sorts of scenes of derring-do; finally the kids can leap over your garden fence brandishing a sword with total impunity. It costs £1,300 for a maximum of 12 guests.

Science & nature

Animal Magic
01323 482211/www.animal-magic.co.uk.
Lindsey Parker and her team bring a host of furry (and scaly) friends to parties for one- to 16-year-olds. Little ones get to hold and stroke rabbits and guinea pigs, while teens are fascinated by the geckos and snakes. Particularly popular is 'Mouse Town', a wooden construction put together by the kids for a colony of mice to explore. Parties, starting from £95 for one hour, can be themed – Harry Potter, for example, might involve meeting a crew of owls, snakes and a bearded dragon. The team bring their own disinfectant to wipe up any little animal accidents.

Science Boffins
0800 019 2636/www.scienceboffins.com.
Kids' excitement levels reach a peak as mini volcanos erupt, balloons self-inflate, light goes

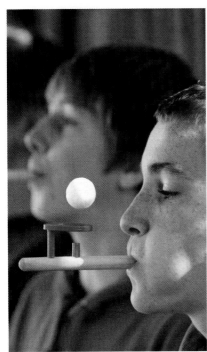

Activities

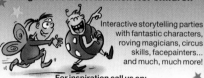

round corners and bottles become rockets. For parents, it's pretty exciting that all experiments are guaranteed safe and mess free. Parties start at £195 for one hour, which buys you a qualified boffin who'll hold five- to 11-year-olds enthralled with competitions and experiments of an educational bent.

Sport

Campaign Paintball
Old Lane, Cobham, Surrey KT11 1NH (01932 865999/www.campaignpaintball.com). Effingham Junction rail.
A short jaunt southwest of London, Campaign's site is divided into action-packed play zones. The eerily authentic Dodge City is a big hit, along with the Jungle zone and spooky Dark Tower. Packages for ten to 15s cost £24.95 per child including 300 paintballs, seven games, tuition and a barbecue lunch. The day ends with a trophy presentation.

League One Sports Academy
8446 0891/www.leagueone.co.uk.
Children's football parties (three to 12s) with a bit of basketball and cricket thrown in for good measure. The coaches keep up the party atmosphere, taking into account any varying skill levels, with the birthday child receiving a trophy to take home. Parties start at £190 for 90 minutes, with all equipment provided. The company's headquarters are in north London, but staff will consider coming to you if you have a large enough space.

CAKES

Cake Store
111 Sydenham Road, SE26 5EZ (8778 4705/ www.thecakestore.co.uk). Sydenham rail. **Open** 8am-5.30pm Mon-Sat. **Credit** MC, V.
Having recently launched a mega new website, Cake Store can now deliver its creations to the whole of London. Colourful cakes include pirate ships (£89), ivy clad fairy castles (£65) and a yellow brick road (£95) – there's nothing this bakery cannot construct from a humble vanilla sponge, it seems.
Buggy access. Delivery service. Disabled access.

Chorak
122 High Road, N2 9ED (8365 3330). East Finchley tube/263 bus. **Open** 8am-6pm daily.
No credit cards.
Novelty handmade birthday cakes start at £68 for a 25-35-portion job, going up to £105 for a

65-portion extravaganza. Cartoon favourites are a speciality, whether it's a picture iced onto a cake or a 3D creation leaping out at your guests. Eggless cakes are available.
Branch 229-231 Muswell Hill Broadway, N10 1DE (8815 5998).

Crumbs and Doilies
www.crumbsanddoilies.co.uk.
De rigueur on the kids' party circuit are cupcakes. Gone are the squabbles over slice sizes and wilting paper plates; instead, each child can clutch their very own cake in a sticky fist. C&D are a leader in this revolution, offering six flavours and over 200 different decorations. Organic eggs, flour and carrots are used along with Valrhona chocolate. A dozen cupcakes will set you back £22; pastel stands on which to display them (from £10) are an optional extra. Tasting can be done at the Saturday stall at the King's Road farmer's market.

Dunn's
6 The Broadway, N8 9SN (8340 1614/www. dunns-bakery.co.uk). Finsbury Park tube/rail, then W7 bus/Crouch Hill rail/41, 91 bus. **Open** 7am-6pm Mon-Sat; 11am-5pm Sun. **Credit** MC, V.
Fruit or sponge based party cakes are adorned with stars like Upsy Daisy and Ben 10, or the birthday child's photograph, with prices starting at £46. Older kids may enjoy the glamour of seeing themselves on the magazine cover cake (£75). A standard sponge (that's 14 servings) costs £28.
Buggy access. Delivery service. Disabled access..

Euphorium Bakery
202 Upper Street, N1 1RQ (7704 6905/ www.euphoriumbakery.com). Highbury & Islington tube/rail. **Open** 7am-10.30pm Mon-Fri; 8am-10.30pm Sat, Sun. **Credit** MC, V.
Starting from £13 for an eight-inch cake, even the basic numbers here are banana or apple flavoured, filled with berries or covered in crisp chocolate. Prices include your choice of message, which can be iced on to the cake or inscribed on a choccie plaque. A gluten-free Chocolate Lover's cake is available (£30/ten servings).
Buggy access.
Branches 26A Chapel Market, N1 9EN (7837 7010); 211 Haverstock Hill, NW3 4QN (7431 8944); 45 South End Road, NW3 2QB (7794 2344).

Konditor & Cook
22 Cornwall Road, SE1 8TW (7261 0456/ www.konditorandcook.com). Waterloo tube/rail.

Primrose Bakery

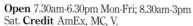

Open 7.30am-6.30pm Mon-Fri; 8.30am-3pm Sat. **Credit** AmEx, MC, V.

Chocolate curly whirly, lemon chiffon and frosted carrot cakes are the specialities of this famed London bakery. Dinky 'magic cakes' are perfect for parties; mini lemon fondant fancies iced with pictures or letters that can be lined up to spell out a name or birthday message. An eight-inch cake starts at £20.40, while Magic Cakes cost £37 per dozen.

Buggy access. Delivery service. Disabled access. **Branches** 10 Stoney Street, SE1 9AD (7407 5100); 46 Gray's Inn Road, WC1X 8LR (7404 6300); Curzon Soho, 99 Shaftesbury Avenue, W1D 5DY (7292 1684); 30 St Mary Axe, EC3A 8BF (0845 262 3030).

Lola's Kitchen
Unit 2, Primrose Hill Workshops, Oppidans Road, NW3 3AG (7483 3394/www.lolas-kitchen.co.uk). Chalk Farm tube. **Open** for collection only, phone for details. **Credit** MC, V.
Lola's lovely cupcakes come in a dizzying array of flavours (chocolate, coconut, peanut butter, rocky road and red velvet, to name but a few), with a seemingly endless array of decorations. The online ordering system is easy to use; purchases can be delivered or picked up from the bakery. Traditionalists who like one big cake

to slice can go for proper birthday cakes, adorned with mini cupcakes, or the 'showgirl' – a giant cupcake that feeds 15 (£45). Mini cupcakes start at £1 apiece, with a minimum order of 24. If you want to taste before you buy, Lola's wares are stocked in Harrods, Selfridges and various high-end delis.
Delivery service.

Margaret's Cakes of Distinction
224 Camberwell Road, SE5 0ED (7701 1940). Elephant & Castle tube/rail, then 12, 45, 68, 176 bus. **Open** 9am-5pm Mon-Sat. **No credit cards**.
Margaret takes care over her pretty sponge- or madeira-based cakes, all of which can be personalised with marzipan figures. A basic birthday number starts at £25.
Buggy access. Disabled access.

Marnie Searchwell
7735 1444/www.marniesearchwell.co.uk. **No credit cards**.
Gluten-free cakes in various enticing flavours are Marnie's speciality, and they really are delectable. She uses organic ingredients as much as possible, from the eggs to the buttercream, and can alter recipes for those sensitive to dairy, eggs and corn. A simple, iced seven-inch cake starts at £45, with more

elaborate creations starting at £70. Each cake is carefully handbaked and delivered by Marnie and her son, so do give her at least two weeks' notice. She also offers a near-impossible to resist cake of the month club. *Delivery service.*

No Weird Stuff
01334 310037/www.noweirdstuff.co.uk.
Credit MC, V.
Is it possible to have a sugar-free kids' party? This mail order company can help the miracle come to pass, with their range of no added sugar, gluten-free cakes, which are also free from artificial flavourings and preservatives. The sweetness is achieved using xylitol, a natural sweetener derived from birch trees, while the gluten-free flour is milled on the premises to ensure there's no contamination. Cakes arrive undecorated, leaving you to add your own toppings, with prices starting at £5.99 for an eight-portion cake. *Mail order.*

Primrose Bakery
69 Gloucester Avenue, NW1 8LD (7483 4222/ www.primrosebakery.org.uk). Chalk Farm tube. **Open** 8.30am-6pm Mon-Sat; 10am-5.30pm Sun. **Credit** MC, V.
Gorgeous cupcakes and swirly layer cakes come in a flurry of unusual flavours, such as lime and coconut or rose (decorated with petals), as well as classic vanilla and chocolate offerings (made using 70% cocoa). Mini alphabet cupcakes forming the birthday child's name are particularly popular. Cupcakes start at £1.15 each, and standard cakes at around £30. *Buggy access. Delivery service.* **Branch** 42 Tavistock Street, WC2E 7PB (7836 3638).

COSTUMES

If you're looking for inexpensive TV character or classic costumes (princesses, pirates and the like), it's worth checking out Asda, Mothercare, Argos and TK Maxx. For more toyshops and boutiques with dressing-up gear, *see p279.*

Online

J&M Toys
01274 599314/www.jandmtoys.co.uk.
Over 150 costumes are stocked by this children's fancy dress specialist, for ages three to ten: soldiers, brides, snowmen, firemen, pilots,

astronauts and more. Most striking is the medieval regalia; decorated wooden swords and shields cost £9.50, with dramatic silver helms (helmets to you and me) at £1.50. Dreamy satin princess dresses are £7.95, with a coned hat at £3.75. Also in stock is a range of Roman, courtier and Victorian wear to tie in with Key Stage 2 workshops.

Natural Nursery
01392 207243/www.naturalnursery.co.uk.
Natural Nursery sells a dinky range of eco-friendly dressing-up outfits for toddlers (18 months to three years old). The pretty bumble bee, ladybird, ballerina and fairy dresses (£14.99-£19.99) are all fair trade; an adorable cotton doggy oufit is a recent addition to the line.

Shops

Angels
119 Shaftesbury Avenue, WC2H 8AE (7836 5678/www.fancydress.com). Leicester Square or Tottenham Court Road tube. **Open** 9.30am-5.30pm Mon, Tue, Thur, Fri; 10.30am-7pm Wed. **Credit** AmEx, MC, V.
This Oscar-winning costumiers stocks some 10,000 outfits in myriad themes, catering for kids, adults and even dogs. Anakin Skywalker, Jack Sparrow and various football team-supporting fairies are among the new outfits for this year. Order online or pop to the shop to try before you buy. Prices start around £20. *Buggy access. Disabled access. Mail order (0845 054 8854).*

Escapade
45-46 Chalk Farm Road NW1 8AJ (7485 7384/www.escapade.co.uk). Camden Town tube. **Open** 10am-7pm Mon-Fri; 10am-6pm Sat; noon-5pm Sun. **Credit** AmEx, MC, V.
A host of TV hero dress-ups include Ben 10, the *High School Musical* cast, Lewis Hamilton, Spongebob and the Teletubbies. The full range is available online, with a selection in Camden to try on for size. Fairies, cowboys and authentic looking astronauts are also stocked, along with nativity costumes; prices start at £8.49. Giant cardboard characters (from £26.99) can be bought to enhance your party theme, Winnie The Pooh, Daleks and a talking C-3PO among them. *Buggy access. Delivery service. Disabled access. Mail order.*

Harlequin
254 Lee High Road, SE13 5PR (8852 0193). Hither Green or Lewisham rail/DLR/21, 261 bus. **Open** 10.30am-5.30pm Mon; 10am-

Activities

5.30pm Tue, Thur-Sat; 10am-1pm Wed.
Credit MC, V.
Ever popular princess, knight and bandit outfits start at £9.95, with Spider-Man, Scooby Doo and Batgirl from £29.95. Harlequin also specialises in accessories, so the shop's lined with hats, boas, wigs and pompoms.
Buggy access.

Party Superstores
268 Lavender Hill, SW11 1LJ (7924 3210/ www.partysuperstores.co.uk). Clapham Junction rail/39, 77, 345 bus. **Open** 9am-6pm Mon-Sat; 10.30am-4.30pm Sun. **Credit** AmEx, MC, V.
All manner of fancy dress kits are supplemented by shelf after shelf of accessories, wigs and crazy hats (from £1.99). Superheroes are big with the boys, with full Batman regalia costing from £24.99; girls like to browse the drawers of glittery wands, tiaras and fairy wings. Over 50 different sorts of themed tableware are also stocked, while the full balloon service includes inflation and delivery.
Buggy access. Delivery service. Disabled access. Mail order.

Preposterous Presents
262 Upper Street, N1 2UQ (7226 4166/ www.preposterouspresents.co.uk). Highbury & Islington tube/rail. **Open** 10am-6pm Mon-Sat; 12.30-4.30pm Sun. **Credit** MC, V.
PP specialise in putting an outfit together from scratch; tell them who you want to be transformed into, and they will flit round gathering accessories and wigs until you look the part. Ready-assembled costumes sets are also available, including knights, fairies and various animals (from £15); accessory kits start at £4.99. Whoopee cushions, itching powder and fake blood abound.
Buggy access. Disabled access.

ENTERTAINERS

Action Station
0870 770 2705/www.theactionstation.co.uk.
Entertainers of all shapes and specialities are represented by this agency, from storytelling spacemen and spies to mermaids, cheerleaders, drama teachers, make-up artists and DJs. Children of all ages are catered for, while prices start at £150 for an hour.

Ali Do Lali
01494 774300/www.alidolali.com.
Do Lali arrives on a magic carpet, then proceeds to thrill the assembled youngsters with fire eating, sword swallowing and magic. Toddlers particularly like his puppets and special drawing board – an illustration of the birthday child which magically comes alive. A one-hour show starts at £160. If you've booked him before, Do Lali pledges to deliver a different act whenever he returns.

Amanda
8578 0234/07946 707695/www.amandas actionkids.co.uk.
Bringing new meaning to the words 'high energy', Amanda whirls one- to six-year-olds through two giddy hours of dancing, music and parachute games, like a sugar-coated Su Pollard. Prices start at £140 for a party led by one of her team, but it's worth shelling out an extra £30 for Amanda herself.

Christopher Howell
7993 4544/www.christopherhowell.net/ kids.htm.
A respected close-up magician, Howell puts on absorbing shows for children. An hour-long party (from £175) features magic, storytelling, balloon modelling and the chance for kids to perform various illusions. Shows are suitable for children aged four to six.

Jenty the Gentle Clown
07957 121764/www.jentythegentleclown.com.
Specialising in parties for under-threes, Jenty can also hype it up with a disco and limbo dancing for kids up to 11. Traditional games, face-painting, magic and singalongs with the banjo are all part of the fun. Jenty charges £145 for one hour, £195 for two.

Juggling John
0845 644 6659/www.jugglingjohn.com.
John has four party packages to suit different age ranges from babies to ten-year-olds, with ball juggling to amuse the tinies and fire juggling for those with older kids (and high ceilings). Magic, clowning and escapology also feature. Prices start at £125 for an hour.

Little Blisters
8392 9093/www.childrensentertainment-surrey.co.uk.
These beautiful parties (from £100 per hour) feature fairies, mermaids and Kitty Willow the Magical Cat. Ava de Souza has a funny yet gentle style, and aims her performances at three-to seven-year-olds.

Magic Mikey
0808 100 2140/www.magicmikey.co.uk.

Westway – for sport, for fun, for everyone

From Perfect Parties to Training for Excellence plus open after-school and weekend sessions for all!

Book Online Now

Climbing age 5 up | Handball – learn Eton Fives – age 8 up
Football age 5 up | Tennis age 3 up (lessons, coaching, open sessions)
Term-time and holiday programmes in all sports

Westway Sports Centre:

England's largest indoor climbing centre, 12 tennis courts, 6 football pitches, 4 Eton fives handball courts, basketball, netball, gym and more.

Westway is an LTA High Performance Tennis Centre with London's leading junior development programme

020 8969 0992
www.westwaysportscentre.org.uk

Book Online Now at:
www.westwaysportscentre.org.uk

**Sport for health, fitness and wellbeing
Run as a social enterprise
by Westway Development Trust
Registered charity no. 1123127**

To find out more about participation, sponsorship or supporting young sportspeople from under-privileged backgrounds call **020 8962 5735**

Natural Nursery. *See p153*.

A one-man powerhouse who thrills four to 12s with a mixture of puppetry, games, magic and above all humour, Mikey also comes with a belting disco. One of his two-hour shows costs around £275.

Mel's Magic
01992 552026/www.mels-magic.co.uk.
Used to intimate gatherings as well as large crowds, Mel is adept at mingling and performing close-up tricks as well as presenting her full show (ages three to ten), complete with a magically appearing live rabbit.You can also book her circus skills workshop, where kids of six and above can learn to unicycle, juggle and stilt-walk. Her fees start at £165 for one hour.

Merlin Entertainments
8866 6327/01494 479027/
www.merlinents.co.uk.
Merlin is sure to represent a party host of your liking: clowns, magicians, puppeteers and DJs can be hired here, and circus skills workshops, craft parties, musical workshops and even an animal encounter show can all be arranged. Staff are adept at mixing and matching performers for larger events: you could have an animal show with a break for magic in the middle, for instance. Prices start at £130 for an hour-long performance.

Mr Happy Magic
01245 426016/www.mrhappymagic.com.
Parties are packed with magic, games, puppets and an optional disco. Happy (his real name since he changed it by deed poll) is ably assisted by Charlie the Dog – beloved by his audience of three- to seven-year-olds. Two hours of silliness start at £170.

Oranges and Lemons
07900 447218/www.orangesandlemons
parties.co.uk.
Juliet keeps crowds of children entranced with the sheer force of her personality, along with a lively mix of traditional games, crafts and storytelling. A two hour party costs from £180.

Pekko's Puppets
8575 2311/www.pekkospuppets.co.uk.
Stephen Novy's handsomely constructed puppet plays can appear at your party courtesy of his mobile booths. Stories, with singing, encompass folk tales from China, Scotland, Europe and Africa. Pekko is a friendly bird who presents the shows for younger kids, while for older kids there is even some Shakespeare. Novy can also perform his shows in French. Prices start at £150 for one hour.

Silly Millie the Clown
7823 8329/07939 239397/www.sillymillie
theclown.co.uk.
Happy, giggly parties with Silly Millie's cheeky take on party games, karaoke, plate spinning and magic. Three- to nine-year-olds adore her shows, with the older kids taught a card trick or two. Millie charges from £85 per hour.

HALLS FOR HIRE

Other inspired venues can be found on *p161*.

Dragon Hall
17 Stukeley Street, WC2B 5LT (7404 7274/
www.dragonhall.org.uk). Holborn tube. **Open**
9am-11.30pm daily. **No credit cards**.
This central community centre has three rooms, with kitchen facilities, for hire. The smallest is £30/hr, while the 200-seater main hall is £55/hr with a PA system as an optional extra. The main hall comes with tables and chairs and has a dance floor.

East Dulwich Community Centre
46 Darrell Road, SE22 9NL (8693 4411).
East Dulwich rail. **Open** 9am-11pm Sat;
11am-9pm Sun. **No credit cards**.

A sturdy hall with a kitchen, with room for 120 kids, costs from £35 an hour. There's a stage, toilets and a large playground.

Highbury Fields One & Two O'Clock Club

Bandstand, Highbury Fields, Baalbec Road, N5 1UP (7704 9337/www.islington.gov.uk). Highbury & Islington tube/rail. **Open** Summer noon-6pm Sat, Sun. Winter 10am-4pm Sat, Sun. **No credit cards.**
At weekends, you can hire this children's centre – complete with all the play equipment, kitchen and private outdoor space – from £90 in the winter, and £100 in the summer.

Old Cholmeley Boy's Club

68 Boleyn Road, N16 8JG (07963 778636). Dalston Kingsland rail. **Open** 9am-6pm daily. **No credit cards.**
A quirky venue with a large main room, scattered with sofas, where 150 kids can party (£50-£70 for an afternoon). Kitchen and music facilities are available, as is a terrace.

EQUIPMENT HIRE

Play equipment

Cool Parties

0844 450 0045/www.cool-parties.co.uk.

After ten minutes on this website, you could fill your garden with bouncy castles, slides, trampolines, inflatable sumo wrestlers, a rodeo bull and a quad bike circuit. A package of soft play equipment, perfect for toddlers, starts at £95 per day, while a full inflatable obstacle course costs £140. Cool can also provide you with more sensible gear such as marquees, staff, child-sized tables and hall hire in north and west London. Entertainment packages, including electric car parties and teddy bear making sessions start at around £15 per child.

PK Entertainments

07771 546 676/www.fairandfete.co.uk.
An entire old-fashioned funfair can be hired through PK, with swingboats, hoopla, roundabouts and chair-o-planes. If money's no object you can hire everything, or pick a favourite stall or two. Prices start at £100 for the coconut shy (complete with 50 nuts), with slippery poles going for £120 and swingboats for £160. The company can also provide Punch & Judy, stilt-walkers and assorted entertainers.

Marquee hire

Sunset Marquees

Unit 5, Glenville Mews, Kimber Road, SW18 4NJ (8874 4897/www.sunsetmarquees.com). Southfields tube. **Open** 8am-6pm daily. **No credit cards.**
Sunset offer marquees in all sizes, with no pegs or hammering required (some models simply

Amanda. *See p154.*

Pro-Active 4 Parties & Entertainment

pop up). That means you can erect your marquee on hard surfaces as well as grass, and it's blissfully fuss-free. A small marquee for 15 children starts at £190 for a weekend's hire. Chairs, lighting and stages can also be provided. *Delivery & set-up service.*

Sound equipment

Capital Hire
3 Stean Street, E8 4ED (7249 6000/www. capitalhire.com). London Fields rail. **Open** 9am-6pm Mon-Sat. **Credit** MC, V.
Rob and his friendly team can loan you a two-speaker sound system with iPod mixer from £140 for a three day hire. Units with whizzy LED lighting are £40 and, if the church hall is a bit scuffed, they even hire out dancefloors from 50p per sq/ft. A twinkling star cloth backdrop (from £40) will transform even the dowdiest of venues into the best disco in town.
Delivery & set-up service.

Young's Disco Centre
2 Malden Road, NW5 3HR (7485 1115/ www.justadisco.co.uk). Chalk Farm tube. **Open** by appointment 9am-7pm Mon-Sat. **Credit** MC, V.
The special children's party package (sound system and disco lights) costs from £95 for 24 hours' hire. On top of that, Young's can provide DJs, bubbles, dancefloors and candyfloss machines, and prides itself on its set-up service, delivery and collection.
Delivery & set-up service.

ORGANISERS

See also p281 **Mystical Fairies**.

Adam Ants
8959 1045/www.adamantsparties.com.
Ants can sort out all kinds of party-related tasks, from providing paper plates to arranging the entertainment for the big day. Girls can arrive in style in a Cinderella coach drawn by two white shetland ponies, while boys might just want to give the bouncy castles a good bashing. Traditional sports days can also be organised. Call for prices.

Birthday Dreams
7700 2525/www.birthdaydreams.co.uk.
Kinloch Castle in Islington, Birthday Dreams' spectacular venue, can be transformed into a jungle, princess palace or knight's fort for your child's party. Captivating entertainers include Safari Pete from the *Paul O'Grady Show*, with

his animal encounters party. Castle packages start at £450, which includes a cake and full catering; there are even canapés for the parents. Party bags and waiting staff are also provided, so the entertainers can stay in character while the serious business of sandwich serving is going on. BD can also organise parties in your home, with a clean up service as extra.

Boo! Productions
7287 9090/07768 311068/
www.booparties.com.
Breathtaking bespoke parties. Boo! can transform your venue, with every inch decorated to create a magical underwater world, a pirate ship, or even the set of the *Wizard of Oz*. The cast of actors restage your favourite tales, with themed arts and crafts, games and audience participation; check out the video on the website. For those with less room (and cash), there are 'Entertainer in a Suitcase' packages from £170. Full venue transformation starts at £2,000, but staff can also snazz up a lounge with a backdrop and props.

Nellie Shepherd Events
0114 263 0998/07710 479852/
www.nellieshepherdevents.com.
The expert Shepherd and her team organise themed parties, transforming your chosen venue into a winter wonderland, fairy glade or circus then adding entertainment, face-painting and catering. Packages start at £500. You can also hire each element separately: a decorations box, say, or a themed crafts party.

Pro-Active 4 Parties & Entertainment
0845 257 5005/www.proactive4parties.co.uk.
These high-octane parties focus on sports, circus skills and discos. A long list of themes includes *Gladiators*, Boot Camp, *X Factor*, Mini Olympics, *High School Musical* and the ever popular Active Mayhem, which features an array of team sports. Staff are happy to come to your home, but most of the activities require plenty of space, and walls impervious to footballs. Parties are for children aged four and above, and prices start at £200.

Twizzle Parties
8392 0860/www.twizzle.co.uk.
Put your party into Twizzle's hands and you won't have to arrange a thing. From decorations, entertainment and play equipment to catering, sound equipment and venue hire, Twizzle offers a bespoke party service for one to 16s (from £165). Pick and mix from its recommendations;

a toddler party could feature a nursery rhyme sing-along, supervised soft play and face painting, while teens might opt to drive a real tank and be trained by SAS professionals.

PARTYWARE & PARAPHERNALIA

Baker Ross
0844 576 8922/www.bakerross.co.uk.
This online store has hundreds of ideas for craft parties and gifts, be they beady, sparkly or foamy. It also offers no end of party bag toys and DIY decorations.

Balloonland
12 Hale Lane, NW7 3NX (8906 3302/www. the-party-shop.co.uk). Edgware tube/Mill Hill Broadway rail/221, 240 bus. **Open** 9am-5.30pm Mon-Fri; 9.30am-5.30pm Sat. **Credit** AmEx, MC, V.
Balloons come any way you want them at Ballonland. Flat or inflated, plain or shaped, latex or foil… they can even arrive singing or as part of a bouquet. Balloonland also stocks general party goods, including party bags, paper plates and tablecloths covering every TV and film theme imaginable. Balloons are available online, but you need to call the shop if you want them pre-inflated or delivered.
Buggy access. Delivery service. Disabled access. Mail order.

Circus Circus
176 Wandsworth Bridge Road, SW6 2UQ (7731 4128/www.circuscircus.co.uk). Fulham Broadway tube. **Open** 10am-6pm daily. **Credit** MC, V.
Friendly staff are happy to talk you through the enormous range of partyware, and can even help you to find caterers, venues and bouncy castles for hire. Plates and decorations abound, adorned with Barbie, Peppa Pig and other heroes of the small screen. The likes of balloon arches, party games, fancy dress and pinatas complete the stock.
Buggy access. Delivery service. Disabled access. Mail order.

CYP
0870 034 0010/www.cyp.co.uk.
A dizzying array of CDs, downloads and musical games. Kids can sing along with the *High School Musical* soundtrack or groove with the party DVDs. Many of the CDs come with free activity sheets. Prices start at £5.

Activities

Happy Green Earth
0845 388 0931/www.happygreenearth.com.
This online independent specialises in eco-friendly party bags in sweet designs, ranging from pirates to polka dots. Alternatively invest in the blank cotton bags (which come with fabric crayons) for the kids to decorate. Prices start at 10p for pink or blue candy-striped paper bags. Fillers include organic chocolate lollies and appealing wooden trinkets. Beeswax candles, biodegradable tableware and cotton bunting also feature.

Kidzcraft
01793 327022/www.kidzcraft.co.uk.
Click on the theme of your choice and Kidzcraft will present you with a range of crafty ideas for your very own art party. All manner of craft kits are available here including pottery to paint and treasure chests to adorn (from £2.50). T-shirt decorating kits are another hot seller. Proud hosts can submit photos of the kids' efforts to the online gallery.

Little Cherry
01784 470570/www.littlecherry.co.uk.
Want to avoid the post-party guilt of sending bags full of plastic to the landfill? Little Cherry stocks biodegradable, compostable and recycled partyware. The recycled paper plates come in vivid colours – or your guests can eat off sialli- or palm-leaf plates. Their cotton and recycled paper party bags can be bought ready-filled or empty.

Great places to party

Colour House Children's Theatre
Front seats for the delightful show, ending with the cast singing *Happy Birthday* to the guest of honour. Then the empty theatre is yours. From £145, with catering, entertainment and a mini disco all available on top. *See p187.*

Lauderdale House
This beautiful manor house in the middle of Waterlow Park near Highgate offers a bright and airy room for children's parties at £65 per hour (plus £47 cleaning fee). Most people bring their own food, although the Lauderdale Restaurant (8455 4445) can cater. The playgrounds and terraces outside provide a chance to run off steam. *See p189.*

Discover
A Story Builder takes the children on an hour's journey on the magical Story Trail, followed by a craft workshop in the private party room. Prices start at £6.50 per child, with great party bags and books as extras. Bring your own food. *See p172.*

Gambado
Play centres are terrific for parties. From £10 per child, the stylish Gambado offers unlimited drinks, balloons, your own host and a hot buffet. The guest of honour even gets to sit on a throne when resting from 80 minutes of play, dodgems and carousel rides. *See p181.*

Kentish Town City Farm
KT now has a nice big room to hire, at £50 for two hours (they allow you setting up and cleaning time). It comes complete with a kitchen and tables – and entrance to the farm is free, for all sorts of animal encounters. *See p132.*

London Zoo
Bring over ten kids and get 20% off your entrance fees; one adult is admitted free with every ten children. It's a marvellous day out, and one of the few zoos that can be enjoyed year round; most enclosures have indoor as well as outdoor viewing areas. *See p140.*

Rainforest Café
The party package is £14.50 per child for a two course meal and jam-packed activity bag. That's the same price as the usual deluxe kids meal, but with every six guests you get a free birthday cake. Insist on sitting in the upper dining room to party among the amazing animatronics. *See chapter* **Eating**.

WWT Wetland Centre
An hour and a half's entertainment comes courtesy of your own 'explainer'; small guests are also treated to goodie bags and a picnic in the Mongolian yurt. Packages cost from £250 per party, with entrance fees to the enchanting park and wonderful playground included. *See p137.*

Activities

Mexicolore

7622 9577/www.mexicolore.co.uk.
Mexicolore make and import authentic Mexican pinatas (made of papier-maché, not cardboard). Prices start at £20, and staff will make up custom designs to order. Fill 'em up (the traditional stuffing is sweeties) and let the kids expend all that extra energy bashing it to bits.

Non-Stop Party Shop

214-216 Kensington High Street, W8 7RG (7937 7200/www.nonstopparty.co.uk). High Street Kensington tube/10, 27, 391 bus. **Open** 9.30am-6pm Mon-Sat; 11am-5pm Sun. **Credit** MC, V.
A great shop to browse, whether you're after cards, fancy dress and wigs or tableware and decorations. Non-Stop specialises in bespoke balloon decorations to personalise your venue; for those that just want some balloons to kick about, you can buy a pump or hire a helium cylinder. This is also one of the few London shops where you can buy fireworks year round. *Buggy access. Delivery service. Mail order.*

Party Ark

01572 748609/www.partyark.co.uk.
This user-friendly website sells partyware in TV, classic and age-specific themes. The one-click party packs have everything you need in your chosen theme in one order, so you don't have to browse. Another nice touch is ideas panels for bewildered parents – a description of who each TV character is and what your child will expect from, say, an *Angelina Ballerina* or *Lazy Town* party (the latter involves Daddy donning a purple catsuit). First birthdays are a speciality (celebratory sippy cups, £2.90).

Party Directory

01252 851601/www.partydirectory4kids.co.uk.
Very reasonably priced tableware, party bags and novelties. Balloon kits come complete with a helium cylinder, 40 balloons and a sizing guide to prevent overfilling. All the popular themes are here, from *Little Mermaid* to *In the Night Garden*; we particularly like the quirky food trays and boxes, shaped like cadillacs or pirate galleons. Party planner advice will ensure you don't forget a thing for the big day.

Party Party

3 & 11 Southampton Road, NW5 4JS (7267 9084/www.partypartyuk.com). Chalk Farm tube/Gospel Oak rail/24 bus. **Open** 9.30am-5.30pm Mon-Sat. **Credit** MC, V.
No.3 stocks decorations and a large range of bargain balloons, while No.11 is the shop to go

to for tableware and costumes. If you'd rather not leave the sofa, you can browse the entire stock online. Knowledgeable staff can talk you through the numerous balloon options; you can even bring in last year's foil numbers to be re-inflated. A lovely range of pinatas are also stocked. If you don't fancy excitable children wielding a big stick in your house, go for a 'pull' pinata, which showers the kids with sweeties once they locate the lucky ribbon. *Buggy access. Delivery service. Disabled access. Mail order.*

Party Party

9-13 Ridley Road, E8 2NP (7254 5168/www.ppshop.co.uk). Dalston Kingsland rail/30, 38, 56, 67, 76, 149, 236, 242, 243, 277 bus. **Open** 9am-5.30pm Mon-Thur; 9am-6.30pm Fri, Sat. **Credit** AmEx, MC, V.
A stalwart of the east London party scene, Party Party has recently opened a branch in Kilburn, stocking the same dizzying array of banners, fancy dress, pinatas and partyware. A massive selection of cake decorations and novelty bakeware takes centre stage, from ready-made icing (£4.29) for nervous chefs to 3D train-shaped cake pans (£14.49) for the more ambitious. Even the candles are special, with footballs, jungle characters and dinosaurs ready to grant your birthday wishes. *Buggy access. Mail order.*
Branch 206 Kilburn High Road, NW6 4JH (7624 4295).

Party Pieces

01635 201844/www.partypieces.co.uk.
Lovely tableware, party bags, decorations and CDs galore. Of particular note are the cake kits (with everything you need to create a 3D masterpiece in your kitchen) and the 'scene setters'; giant backdrops that turn your walls into Dora's jungle or a princess's ballroom. Other stock includes party game kits, candy floss and popcorn machines and some splendid invitations and thank-you cards. Filled party bags start at £1.25, and there are loads of brilliant bits and bobs for under a pound if you'd rather assemble your own.

Planet Party

8340 1228/www.planetparty.co.uk.
Beautiful partyware in classic or unusual themes, including spaceman, ballerina, bowling or sleepovers. Personalised plates, party bags and food boxes are a speciality (from 50p), with a range for twins and joint birthdays. Planet Party can also arrange your entire shin-dig in their Finchley venue or your home.

Activities

Arts & Entertainment

Family-friendly cultural offerings take centre stage.

London's packed cultural calendar isn't just for grown-ups – in fact, all the theatre shows, arty workshops, dance and drama lessons, cookery classes and film clubs are enough to make an adult green with envy. Rather than presenting a watered-down version of their usual fare, the best companies and venues aim to inspire kids' creativity, infusing their family offerings with boundless imagination and energy.

Even the most august of cultural establishments throw their dignity to the winds for special family days, concerts, meet-the-orchestra sessions and drop-in kids' activities. If you'd assumed that places like the **Royal Opera House** (*see p172*) and **Wigmore Hall** (*see p179*) and would be too grand to welcome sticky-fingered small fry, think again. London's galleries and museums (*see pp56-104*) and attractions (*see pp28-55*) also run all manner of action-packed workshops and family-friendly events, particularly at weekends and during the school holidays.

Whether your kids are into drama, music, cookery, art or film-making, drop-in classes, after-school clubs and longer courses abound; kids can try circus skills one day, sculpture the next. You might uncover a hidden talent for stilt-walking or a penchant for percussion – or you might just have lots of fun.

ARTS CENTRES

Barbican Centre
Silk Street, EC2Y 8DS (box office 7638 8891/ cinema 7382 7000/www.barbican.org.uk). Barbican tube/Moorgate tube/rail. **Open** *Box office* (by phone) 9am-8pm Mon-Sat; 11am-8pm Sun (in person) 9am-9pm Mon-Sat; noon-9pm Sun. **Admission** *Library* free. *Exhibitions, films, shows, workshops* phone for details. **Membership** £20-£25/yr. **Credit** AmEx, MC, V. **Map** p318 P5.
This angular, concrete art complex may look slightly forboding, but venture inside and you'll be pleasantly surprised. Maps and painted yellow lines lead confused visitors through the residential blocks that surround the centre – an intricate maze of walkways, stairs, identikit towers and split level ramps. There are some pockets of unexpected calm for everyone to enjoy: the fountains in the inner courtyard, the Waterside Café and the library, with its extensive children's section. Best of all is the conservatory, open to the public on Sunday afternoons (unless hired for a private event), where exotic palms, ferns and flowers soar towards the sky and stately koi carp patrol the ponds.

The Barbican's busy programme of cultural offerings also has plenty to appeal to small fry. For starters, there's the Saturday-morning Family Film Club, with a lively mix of movies, themed activities and monthly workshops. Screenings (£3.50-£5.50) are aimed at kids aged five to 11 and their parents; book ahead. One-off mini-seasons and special events for families also dot the Barbican's calendar, including the Animate The World! animation-fest in May and the London Children's Film Festival in November. The complex is also home to the London Symphony Orchestra, whose family concerts (*see p178* **Meet the musicians**) combine music and storytelling to great effect. *Buggy access. Cafés. Disabled access: lift, toilet. Nappy-changing facilities. Restaurants. Shops.*

Rich Mix
35-47 Bethnal Green Road, E1 6LA (7613 7498/www.richmix.org.uk). Bethnal Green or Liverpool Street tube/rail. **Open** *Box office* 9.30am-9.30pm daily. **Admission** prices vary; phone for details. **Credit** MC, V.
This vast former textiles factory now houses a cross-cultural arts and media centre – with an edgy, East End flavour all of its own. There are monthly storytelling and performance poetry sessions, plus inexpensive film-making workshops for five to 12s on selected Sundays and school holiday dates, with a maximum of ten kids per session. Meanwhile, Saturday and Sunday mornings bring Kids' Cine Time, with

tickets at a mere £1.50 per child; major Hollywood releases and animations dominate the programme. Family tickets, available before 5pm on weekdays and all day on Saturdays and Sundays are also brilliant value, while friendly parent and baby screenings take place on Monday evenings. Check online for details of the youth programme, which could encompass anything from graffiti projects to krumping and Bollywood dance classes.

Buggy access. Cafés. Disabled access: lift, toilet. Nappy-changing facilities.

Southbank Centre

Belvedere Road, SE1 8XX (0871 663 2500/ www.southbankcentre.co.uk). Embankment tube/Waterloo tube/rail. **Open** *Box office & foyer* 10am-8pm daily. *Hayward Gallery* 10am-6pm Mon-Thur, Sat, Sun; 10am-10pm Fri. **Admission** prices vary; phone for details. **Credit** AmEx, MC, V. **Map** p317 M8.

Set by the Thames, with the London Eye looming overhead, the Southbank Centre is a cultural behemoth of many parts – namely the Royal Festival Hall, the Queen Elizabeth Hall, the Hayward Gallery and the Saison Poetry Library. It offers a heady blend of theatre, puppet shows, contemporary and classical music, dance and art, including plenty of free events; the website has a comprehensive rundown of upcoming child-friendly offerings, including concerts by the Philharmonia and London Philharmonic orchestras (*see p178* **Meet the musicians**).

Simply wandering about can be richly rewarding though – you might stumble across a weird sound sculpture, find dancers waltzing across the terrace or catch a gospel choir in full throttle. It's always worth checking out what's going on in the Clore Ballroom – the venue for regular school holiday events and family activities, with treasure trails, performances, storytelling and large-scale drawing escapades, usually all free. The Royal Festival Hall's music learning space, Spirit Level, also includes a technology area where young people can experiment with composition and sound-making (book workshops in advance). *See also p30* **Great Days Out**.

Buggy access. Cafés. Disabled access: lift, toilet. Nappy-changing facilities. Restaurants.

Tricycle Theatre & Cinema

269 Kilburn High Road, NW6 7JR (box office 7328 1000/www.tricycle.co.uk). Kilburn tube/Brondesbury rail. **Open** *Box office* 10am-9pm Mon-Sat; 2-8pm Sun. *Children's shows* 11.30am, 2pm Sat. *Children's films* 1pm Sat.

Southbank Centre.

Vision of loveliness. Kids wear 3D glasses to watch films at the **BFI IMAX**.

Tickets *Theatre* (Sat) £5; £4 reductions.
Films (Sat) £4.50; £3.50 reductions, under-16s.
Credit MC, V.
An art gallery, cinema and theatre in one, with
its own buzzy café and bar, the Tricycle has deep
local roots and a real community feel. There's a
brilliant line-up of children's theatre, events and
groups, from preschooler activity sessions and
performances of *Goldilocks and the Three Bears*
(teddies are welcome too) to drama workshops
and youth theatre groups for older children and
teens. Half-term and holiday workshops focus on
magic, theatre, circus skills and even fuzzy felt,
while term-time after-school classes currently
focus on guitar and street dance. Kids' cinema
matinée screenings are at 1pm on Saturdays.
*Buggy access. Disabled access: lift, toilet.
Nappy-changing facilities. Restaurant.*

CINEMAS

The capital is superb for cinema, catering
to film buffs of all ages. As well as a wealth
of kids' cinema clubs and weekend matinée
screenings to choose from, children even
have their own festival. The **London
Children's Film Festival**, now in its fifth

year, generally takes place in November;
its headquarters are the **Barbican** (*see
p163*), but independent cinemas city-wide
also get involved in the fun.
  If you don't mind blowing the budget
on the latest blockbuster screening and a
bucket of absurdly-priced popcorn, go to
Leicester Square. It's home to the glitzy,
glossy flagships of **Vue** (0871 224 0240,
www.myvue.com), the **Odeon** (0871 224
4007, www.odeon.co.uk) and the **Empire**
(0871 4714 714, www.empirecinemas.co.uk).
Some of the big chains also do their own
version of Watch with Baby screenings, as
pioneered at the **Clapham Picturehouse**
(*see p166*) and now a regular feature in all
Picturehouses. In addition to the cinemas
below, don't forget the **Tricycle** (*see left*).

BFI IMAX
*1 Charlie Chaplin Walk, SE1 8XR (0870 787
2525/www.bfi.org.uk/imax). Waterloo tube/rail.*
Open *Box office* (by phone) 10.30am-7.30pm
daily; (in person) from 30mins before screening.
Admission £13.50; £9.75 reductions; £8.75
4-14s; free under-4s. IMAX short films £9;
£6.25 reductions; £5.75 4-14s; free under-4s.
Credit AmEx, MC, V.

Set in a sunken traffic island by Waterloo station, a distinctive circular building houses the UK's biggest cinema screen – over 20m (65ft) high and 26m (85ft) wide. Children love donning 3D glasses to watch special effects-heavy films such as *Monsters Vs Aliens 3D* and *Under the Sea*; it's an intense, larger-than-life experience, so avoid anything too alarming for younger children. Non-IMAX mainstream films are also shown. *See also p30* **Great Days Out**. *Bar. Buggy access. Café. Disabled access: lift, toilet. Nappy-changing facilities.*

BFI Southbank

Belvedere Road, SE1 8XT (box office 7928 3232/www.bfi.org.uk). Embankment tube/ Waterloo tube/rail. **Open** *Box office* (by phone) 11.30am-8.30pm daily; (in person) 11am-8.30pm daily **Tickets** £5-£9 non-members; £6.40-£7.60 members; phone for children's prices. **Membership** £35/yr; £20/yr reductions. **Credit** AmEx, MC, V. **Map** p317 M8.
Following its 2007 revamp, the four-screen British Film Institute (better known as the BFI) has gone from strength to strength. Check the schedule for parent and toddler showings and kids' screenings, both of which combine classic and current hits. At the monthly Fundays, meanwhile, activities accompany the film and the Benugo café-bar serves a special menu. Another brilliant feature is being able to watch film and television clips in the Mediatheque. *See also p30* **Great Days Out**. *Buggy access. Café. Disabled access: lift, toilet. Nappy-changing facilities. Restaurant.*

Clapham Picturehouse

76 Venn Street, SW4 0AT (0871 704 2055/ www.picturehouses.co.uk). Clapham Common tube/35, 37 bus. **Open** *Box office* (by phone) 9.30am-8.30pm daily; (in person) noon-8.30pm daily. *Kids' club activities* 11.15am, *screening* 11.45am Sat. **Tickets** £6.50-£10.50; £5-£7 reductions; £5 3-15s. *Kids' club* £3. **Membership** *Kids' club* £4/yr. **Credit** AmEx, MC, V.
This much-loved local cinema was the first in London to offer parent-and-baby screenings. Big Scream! sessions for parents and babies still run every Thursday at 10.30am, and innovative autism-friendly screenings have also been introduced. There are Kids' Club Saturday matinées for three- to ten-year-olds, with craft workshops before the film; young members can go into the projection room and start the film as a birthday treat. *Buggy access. Café. Disabled access: toilet. Nappy-changing facilities.*

Electric Cinema

191 Portobello Road, W11 2ED (7908 9696/ www.the-electric.co.uk). Ladbroke Grove or Notting Hill Gate tube/52 bus. **Open** *Box office* 9am-8.30pm Mon-Sat; 10am-8.30pm Sun. **Tickets** *Kids' club* £5 over-3s. *Workshops* (1st Sat of month) £3. **Credit** AmEx, MC, V. **Map** p310 A7.
A far cry from your average multiplex, Notting Hill's Electric Cinema brings a touch of glamour to a trip to the flicks. Plush leather seating, footstools and tables make for a truly luxurious cinematic experience, with superior snacks to munch on; adults can quaff a glass of chilled pinot grigio or even a cocktail. There's a Saturday morning Kids' Club (10.30am), while friendly Electric Scream! shows for parents and under-ones are held at 3pm on Mondays (except bank holidays). *Buggy access. Disabled access: lift, toilet.*

Greenwich Picturehouse

180 Greenwich High Road, SE10 8NN (0871 704 2059/www.picturehouses.co.uk). Cutty Sark DLR/Greenwich rail/DLR. **Open** *Box office* (by phone) 9.30am-8.30pm daily; (in person) 11am-10pm daily. *Kids' Club* 11am Sat. **Tickets** £6-£10; £5.50-6.50 under-14s, reductions. *Kids' club* £4.50. **Membership** *Kids' club* £4.50/yr. **Credit** AmEx, MC, V.
Opened in 2005, the four-screen Greenwich outpost of the acclaimed Picturehouse chain has its own tapas bar. There's a children's film club on Saturday mornings, suitable for fives to 15s, plus Big Scream! events at 11.30am on Wednesday and Friday. *Buggy access. Café. Disabled access: lift, toilet. Nappy-changing facilities. Restaurant.*

Phoenix

52 High Road, N2 9PJ (8444 6789/www. phoenixcinema.co.uk). East Finchley tube. **Open** *Box office* 15mins before first screening. *Kids' club* noon Sat. **Tickets** £6-£9; £6 under-16s, reductions. **Credit** AmEx, MC, V.
East Finchley's single-screen art deco treasure offers Bringing Up Baby screenings and Saturday-afternoon Kids' Club movies, kicking off with a hands-on activity workshop, games or a quiz, aimed at five- to eight-year-olds. The cinema can also be hired out for birthday parties; call for details. *Buggy access. Disabled access: lift, toilet.*

Rio Cinema

103-107 Kingsland High Street, E8 2PB (7241 9410/www.riocinema.co.uk). Dalston Kingsland rail/Liverpool Street tube/rail, then 67, 77, 149 bus. **Open** *Box office* (by phone)

'*WICKED* WILL ENTRANCE EVERY GENERATION IN WONDER, WIT AND SUSPENSE.'

Time Out

WICKED

ticketmaster 0844 826 8000

See 0871 230 1561

Discover more at WickedTheMusical.co.uk

APOLLO VICTORIA THEATRE • LONDON

© WLPL

The reel thing. **BFI Southbank**. *See p166.*

2-8pm daily; (in person) from 30 mins before screening. *Children's screening* 4pm Tue; 11am Sat. **Tickets** £6-£8; £5 2-16s; *Children's screening* £2.50; £1.50 under-16s. **Credit** AmEx, MC, V.

Expect an engaging, unusual mix of films at this Dalston favourite, which isn't afraid to eschew predictable Hollywood fodder in favour of more interesting smaller films and cinematic classics. Youthful members of the Saturday Morning Picture Club are given a special card to be stamped, with a free visit after ten stamps and a poster after 25 – a generous offer, considering how inexpensive tickets are. A parent-and-baby club operates on selected Tuesday and Thursday lunchtimes, with a secure place to park pushchairs, and the school holidays bring daily matinées for five- to 15-year-olds.
Buggy access. Café. Disabled access: toilet.

Ritzy Picturehouse

Brixton Oval, Coldharbour Lane, SW2 1JG (0870 755 0062/www.picturehouses.co.uk). Brixton tube/rail. **Open** *Box office* (by phone) 9.30am-8.30pm daily. *Kids' club* 10.30am Sat. **Tickets** £6.50-£8.50; £4.50-£5 under-14s. *Kids' club* £3; £2 3-15s. **Membership** *Kids' club* £3/yr. **Credit** AmEx, MC, V.

Opened in 1911, this local landmark has survived numerous owners and name changes, not to mention near-demolition and dastardly redevelopment plans. Now part of the Picturehouse family, it hosts Big Scream! sessions on Fridays at 11am, which are open to parents with under-ones. Children as young as three can join the inexpensive Saturday Kids' Club, and there are regular autism-friendly screenings; call the box office or check online for details. There's also a laid-back café bar, which offers a kids' menu.
Buggy access. Café. Disabled access: lift, toilet. Nappy-changing facilities.

Stratford East Picturehouse

Theatre Square, Salway Road, E15 1BX (0870 755 0064/www.picturehouses.co.uk). Stratford tube/rail/DLR. **Open** *Box office* (by phone) 9.30am-8.30pm daily. *Kids' club* 10.50am Sat. **Tickets** £6-£7; £4.40 under-14s. *Kids' club* £6; £3 3-10s. **Membership** *Kids' club* £4/yr. **Credit** MC, V.

Attractions for families and children at this Picturehouse branch include a children's film club where creative activities, fun and games take place before a screening. The club is suitable for three- to ten-year-olds, and membership entitles you to attend the first film for free.
Bar. Buggy access. Disabled access: lift, toilet. Nappy-changing facilities.

Activities

COMEDY

Comedy Club 4 Kids
*Soho Theatre, 21 Dean Street, London W1D
3NE (box office 7478 0100/www.sohotheatre.
com). Tottenham Court Road, Leicester Square
or Oxford Circus tube.* **Open** *Box office* 10am-
7pm Mon-Sat. **Credit** MC, V. **Map** p315 K6.
Stand-up comedy sets for over-sixes; *see right*
Funny Business.
*Bar. Buggy access. Café. Disabled access: lift,
toilets. Restaurant.*

DANCE

Discos & clubs

Toddlers generally embrace disco dancing
with gusto – and now there are clubs where
tinies can show their elders a move or two.
Cynics might say it's a sign that children
are growing up too fast while their parents
can't bear to grow up at all – but a spirited
burst of *We are Family* soon drowns the
naysayers out.

The following events take place at
various venues across town; check online
to find out where the next disco will be.

Babygroove
www.babygroove.co.uk.
Launched in 2007, Babygroove plays house and
disco sounds to party-loving families.

Baby Loves Disco
www.babylovesdisco.co.uk.
An import from the US, BLD is thriving on these
shores. Sunday-afternoon discos take place in a
handful of venues, accompanied by choice 1970s
and '80s tunes.

Planet Angel
www.planetangel.net.
Planet Angel's Sunday-afternoon 'Chilled'
gatherings have been running in north London
since 2001. It aims to create a positive, safe, social
environment for children of all ages.

Whirl-Y-Gig
www.whirl-y-gig.org.uk.
This long-established collective welcomes
families to its events – a joyous mix of carnival
and alternative clubbing, with some eclectic
tunes. A favourite venue is Jacks (7-9 Crucifix
Lane, SE1 3JW). Under-18s must be accompanied
by a parent, and you have to call ahead.

Tuition

For all things dance-related in the capital,
including children's classes for all abilities,
visit www.londondance.com.

Chisenhale Dance Space
*64-84 Chisenhale Road, E3 5QZ (8981 6617/
www.chisenhaledancespace.co.uk). Mile End
tube.* **Fees** £36/£24 2-8s, reductions; £5 11-17s
youth group. **Credit** MC, V.

Funny business

The Soho Theatre's monthly **Comedy Club 4 Kids** (*see left*) is a winning combination of top-flight adult comedic talent and gags, without the rude bits. Well, not *all* the rude bits. This is aimed at children, after all, so there is a fair amount of scatologically inclined material, but nothing that would make parents blanch (a recent set included a ditty on words rhyming with 'kangaroo' and 'sea'). It's staged along the same lines as a late-night comedy club, with the compère whipping the audience into a heckle-inducing frenzy, before the first (often palpably nervous) comedian takes to the stage.

As with all comedy nights, it has to cater to the audience – and on past occasions, a few performers have been felled by their underestimation of children's sophistication. On the whole, though, the pitch is spot-on, and hilarity generally ensues. Parents can also take pride in the fact that their children are learning essential tools to survive in the playground, arming themselves with quips and yarns aplenty to win approval and ward off jibes.

For the more ardent comedy fan, the theatre also offers classes where kids can hone their stand-up skills; star performers get the chance to make a special appearance at the monthly show. Past events have yielded some agonisingly true-to-life observational sets from the junior acts, while accomplished adult comics have included Radio 4 veterans and presenters from children's TV.

Check www.comedy4kids.co.uk for dates and details of forthcoming acts, but be sure to book ahead; the events have a sizeable following.

This Bow-based dance studio offers creative dance courses for two to eights, plus a Saturday youth group where 11 to 17s are taught a blend of street, contemporary, jazz and creative dance. Guest choreographers from other disciplines, from ballet to Bollywood, have been known to drop in to share their wisdom. *Buggy access.*

Dance Attic
368 North End Road, SW6 1LY (7610 2055/ www.danceattic.com). Fulham Broadway tube. **Fees** *£2/day; £40/6mths; £70/yr; £15/6 mths, £25/yr 13-16s; free under-13s.* **Classes** *£4-£6. Children's ballet £50-£62/11wk term.* **Credit** MC, V.
Ballet classes for over-threes go up to Intermediate level, with RAD exams at each grade. There's also a shop stocking leotards, ballet shoes and other dance essentials. *Shop.*

Danceworks
16 Balderton Street, W1K 6TN (7629 6183/ www.danceworks.net). Bond Street or Marble Arch tube. **Classes** times vary; phone for details. **Fees** *Membership £2-£5/day; £123/year. Classes £4-£11/class.* **Credit** AmEx, MC, V.
Six studios occupy Danceworks' stately Victorian premises, offering a vast array of adults' classes. For kids, there's ballet, jazz and tap, plus drop-in street dance for 11 to 16s. *Buggy access. Nappy-changing facilities.*

Diddi Dance
07973 982790/www.diddidance.com.
These energetic, exuberant dance and movement classes for two to fours are great fun. Free taster sessions are offered, so you can see if your little darling likes it before committing to a four or eight-week block. Dance-themed birthday parties can also be arranged.

East London Dance
Various venues around east London (8279 1050/www.eastlondondance.org). **Classes** times vary; phone for details. **Fees** *free-£1.* **No credit cards.**
Brazilian samba, street dance and creative, contemporary styles are favoured by this creative community.

Greenwich Dance Agency
Borough Hall, Royal Hill, SE10 8RE (8293 9741/www.greenwichdance.org.uk). Greenwich rail. **Classes** times vary; phone for details **Fees** *Drop-in £4 0-12s. Courses £18-£24/term 6-12s.* **Credit** MC, V.

A packed programme has something for children of all ages, starting with relaxed drop-in classes for zero to twos. At the other end of the spectrum, 13 to 20s can work with professional choreographers, fusing multiple styles and techniques. In all age groups, the focus is on creativity and having fun. *Buggy access. Disabled access: toilet. Nappy-changing facilities.*

Laban
Creekside, SE8 3DZ (8691 8600/www.laban. org). Cutty Sark DLR/Deptford rail. **Classes & fees** times & prices vary; phone for details. **Credit** MC, V.
Deptford is the slightly unlikely home to this stunning contemporary dance conservatoire, housed in an iconic, semi-translucent building designed by Herzog & de Meuron. Children's movement, contemporary dance and classical ballet lessons run throughout the week, though many have a sizeable waiting list. Once your child is in a class, however, the experience is fantastic; the annual Children's Show, presenting work by students aged from four to 14, showcases the kids' talents – and is invariably packed with proud parents. *Buggy access. Disabled access: toilet. Café. Nappy-changing facilities.*

Pineapple Performing Arts School
7 Langley Street, WC2H 9JA (8351 8839/ www.pineapplearts.com). Covent Garden tube. **Classes** *Drop-in 1-2pm (under-13s), 2-3pm (12-16s) Sat; 1-2pm (12-16s), 2-3pm (under-13s) Sun. Term classes 11am-noon (3-4s), 11am-2pm (5-12s), 2-5pm (13-17s) Sun.* **Fees** *£90/12wk term 3-4s; £295/12wk term over-4s; £6 drop-in session; £195 holiday course. Trial class £25. Registration fee £30-£35.* **Credit** MC, V. **Map** p315 L6.
Drop-in musical, theatre, dance, ballet and street dance classes are held at these legendary Covent Garden studios every weekend; just turn up, hand over your £6 and dance. Those prepared to commit to 12-week terms can sign up for the lively Sunday School, comprising 'Pineapple Chunks' sessions for tinies, junior classes for kids and early teens, and senior classes for 13- to 17-year-olds. Intensive musical theatre and street dance courses are offered during the Easter and summer holidays. *Café.*

The Place
17 Duke's Road, WC1H 9PY (box office 7121 1100/classes 7121 1090/www.theplace.org.uk). Euston tube/rail. **Classes** times vary; phone for details. **Fees** *from £75-£95/11wk term;*

Pineapple Performing Arts School.

£5 discount for 2nd or subsequent class taken by same student or a sibling. **Credit** MC, V. **Map** p315 K3.

The ethos at this contemporary dance hub is that anyone can learn to dance; the centre is accessible to all ages, as well as to the disabled. There is, however, a waiting list. A steady stream of parents and kids head here on Saturdays, when classes for five- to 18-year-olds range from playful, free-form First Moves sessions to contemporary dance. More unusually, there are choreography classes for children, and all-boys 'Energiser' sessions. Shift, a company for talented 13- to 19-year-old dancers, meets twice weekly during term time to perform work by a range of choreographers; hotly-contested auditions are held every September.
Bar. Buggy access. Café. Disabled access: toilet.

Royal Academy of Dance
36 Battersea Square, SW11 3RA (7326 8000/ www.rad.org.uk). Clapham Junction rail/170 bus. **Classes** times vary; phone for details. **Fees** £6-£12.50/class; £60-£154/term. **Credit** AmEx, MC, V.
The Academy's studios are a hotbed for all sorts of dance styles. Popular classes include West End jazz, tap and contemporary, with various offerings for different age groups and abilities. The ballet department accepts pupils of two-and-a-half and above, and there are all-boys' ballet lessons for six to nines and eight to 11s. Summer schools and workshops keep dance-mad children on their toes during school hols.
Buggy access.

Venues

See also **Chisenhale Dance Space** (*see p169*), **Laban** and **The Place** (for both, *see p170*).

Royal Opera House
Bow Street, WC2E 9DD (box office 7304 4000/ www.royaloperahouse.org). Covent Garden tube. **Open** *Box office* 10am-8pm Mon-Sat. *Tours* daily (times vary, book in advance). **Tours** £9; £8 reductions; £7 9-16s. **Credit** AmEx, MC, V. **Map** p317 L6.
Despite its status as one of the world's great opera houses (and home to the Royal Ballet to boot), the ROH doesn't rest on its laurels. Inside it's bright and airy, with sumptuous costumes on display and splendid views over Covent Garden's crowds and street entertainers from the upstairs café. Families are warmly welcomed with all sorts of special events, from puppet-making in the light-flooded Paul Hamlyn Hall to musical, magical afternoons with players from

the orchestra, choreographers and composers, where everyone gets involved. Look out for child-friendly Christmas spectaculars such as the *Nutcracker. See also p46* **Great Days Out**. *Buggy access. Café. Disabled access: lift, toilet. Nappy-changing facilities. Restaurant. Shop.*

Sadler's Wells
Rosebery Avenue, EC1R 4TN (0844 412 4300/ www.sadlerswells.com). Angel tube. **Open** *Box office* 9am-8.30pm Mon-Sat. **Credit** AmEx, MC, V.
As the epicentre of dance in London, Sadler's Wells attracts all sorts of dance superstars – including some child-friendly companies, like the London Children's Ballet. Elsewhere in the programme, there's lots to interest older children and teens, including Breakin' Convention – a high-octane annual hip hop jamboree. In the adjacent Lilian Bayliss Theatre, the two-week Connect Festival is another good bet for families, mixing lively workshops with performances from dancers of all ages. The Peacock Theatre (Portugal Street, WC2A 2HT, 0844 412 4322) is a satellite venue for Sadler's Wells, with family shows every Christmas.
Bar. Buggy access. Cafés. Disabled access: lift, toilet. Nappy-changing facilities. Restaurant.

LITERATURE

Libraries

British Library
96 Euston Road, NW1 2DB (7412 7676/ Learning/7412 7797/www.bl.uk). Euston or King's Cross tube/rail. **Open** 9.30am-6pm Mon, Wed-Fri; 9.30am-8pm Tue; 9.30am-5pm Sat; 11am-5pm Sun, bank hols. **Credit** MC, V. **Map** p317 K3.
Kids can't fail to be impressed by the sheer scale of the British Library – a red brick behemoth that's home to over 150 million pieces of writing. What's more, its collection is growing at a fearsome rate: every year, the library receives a copy of everything published in the UK and Ireland, including books, newspapers, maps, magazines, prints and drawings. Its most prized treasures are on display in the dimly-lit Sir John Ritblat Gallery, including the Magna Carta, Lewis Carroll's *Alice's Adventure Under Ground* and some scribbled Beatles lyrics. Temporary exhibitions in the PACCAR Gallery are often accompanied by walkthrough workshops and special events. A smaller gallery in the entrance hall contains interactive displays on music and culture linked to the National Sound Archives.

The education department arranges regular storytelling sessions and hands-on workshops for families during the school holidays – see www.bl.uk/learning for details. Finally, the café is now a Peyton and Byrne establishment, which means delectable treacle tarts, extravagant cupcakes and a nice line in quiches, proper sausage rolls and hot meals – at a price, mind. *Buggy access. Café. Disabled access: lift, toilet. Nappy-changing facilities. Restaurant. Shop.*

Charlton House

Charlton Road, SE7 8RE (8856 3951/ www.greenwich.gov.uk). Charlton rail/53, 54, 380, 422 bus. **Open** *Library* 2-7pm Mon, Thur; 9.30am-12.30pm, 1.30-5.30pm Tue, Fri; 9.30am-12.30pm, 1.30-5pm Sat. *Toy Library* (term-time only) 9.30am-12.30pm Tue, Fri (2-5s); 9.30am-12.30pm Thur (under-2s). **Admission** free. **No credit cards.**
This handsome, early 17th-century red brick mansion now houses a community centre and library. Traces of its past grandeur remain – not least the creaky oak staircase, marble fireplaces and ornate plaster ceilings. The library has a good children's section, and runs preschooler play and story sessions. Charlton Toy Library (8319 0055, www.charltontoylibrary.co.uk) is also based here, and has music and story sessions on Thursday mornings. The mulberry tree outside, dating from 1608, still bears fruit that sometimes finds its way into the crumbles, cakes and chutneys sold in the Mulberry Café. Visit at 1pm on a Friday and you'll be treated to a free concert by musicians from the Trinity College of Music, who also put on a soaring Christmas concert. *Buggy access. Café. Disabled access: lift, toilet. Nappy-changing facilities.*

Idea Store

321 Whitechapel Road, E1 1BU (7364 4332/ www.ideastore.co.uk). Whitechapel tube. **Open** 9am-9pm Mon-Thur; 9am-6pm Fri; 9am-5pm Sat; 11am-5pm Sun. **Credit** MC, V.

Rock-a-bye baby

The last time we saw Neal Whitmore, he was called Neal X, had a foot-high white quiff and was playing guitar with '80s cyberpunks Sigue Sigue Sputnik. Two decades on, the quiff is a little tamer and Whitmore spends his days playing guitar to under-eights in the Hampstead area. His Songsters sessions have become essential gigs for the hip offspring of NW3; even Gwyneth Paltrow's brood have been known to bop along.

Whitmore is a leading light of the 'kindie scene' – quality music for children made by real musicians. Belle & Sebastian and Dan Zanes of the Del Fuegos have both recorded children's songs, while American alt-country pioneer Jason Ringenberg has reinvented himself as 'Farmer Jason'. Whitmore got into it when he became a dad, and 'found that most of the music available was just really awful.' The prospect of hearing cheesy versions of *Wheels on the Bus* 500 times a day drove him to despair.

Happily, he met business partner Caroline Chan, whose children's shows mixed the likes of Old MacDonald with jazz classics and songs by the Beatles, and was inspired. Together, the pair have released three themed CDs – farm, jungle and seaside – which combine original compositions with classic sing-along songs, and are surprisingly enjoyable for adults and children alike. 'A friend said to me he was really worried, because his kids went off to bed and he let the CD play on!' jokes the affable 48-year-old.

The weekly Songsters shows are a way for Whitmore to flex his musical muscles between grown-up work. (He is off on tour with Marc Almond later this year, and recently produced an album by Spanish electro-glam outfit Fangoria.) What Whitmore enjoys is the way that Songsters balances his life: 'Making pop music is really tragic unless you're 20. This is a way of staying grounded.'

Having performed in front of adults and preschoolers, however, he has noticed some similarities. 'If you keep the tempo up, children can really go wild – just like drunken teenagers.' He certainly works hard for his preschool fans, building up a sweat as he breaks into a punky sing-along version of *Here Comes the Sun*. The kids are, he says, his toughest critics. 'The thing about children is that they're not polite. If they don't like you, they'll just walk away.'
Songsters is on Wednesdays (9.30am & 11am) at Fleet Community Centre, NW3. For more information phone 7813 3320 or visit www.greenmeansgo.co.uk.

Activities

Music House for Children. *See p176.*

Built by Adjaye Associates, Whitechapel's glass-fronted Idea Store is a 21st-century take on the library. In addition to its book collections, it offers state-of-the-art learning and information services and an airy fourth-floor café. All sorts of groups meet here, from toddler and parent get-togethers to drop-in homework clubs – there's even a gathering for comic book and manga fans (nine to 16s), along with Wii and Playstation 2-playing sessions. For 16 and overs, the borough's network of Idea Stores offer over 900 courses. A handful of courses are aimed at families – among them, creative dance, art and design and cookery classes for parents and children. Call or check online for dates, prices and age restrictions. *Buggy access. Café. Crèche. Disabled access: lift, toilet. Nappy-changing facilities.* **Branches** 1 Gladstone Place, Roman Road, E3 5ES (7364 4332); 1 Vesey Path, East India Dock Road, E14 6BT (7364 4332); Churchill Place, E14 5RB (7364 4332).

Peckham Library
122 Peckham Hill Street, SE15 5JR (7525 2000/www.southwark.gov.uk). Peckham Rye or Queen's Road rail/12, 36, 63, 171 bus. **Open** 9am-8pm Mon, Tue, Thur, Fri; 10am-8pm Wed; 10am-5pm Sat; noon-4pm Sun. **No credit cards.**

Will Alsop's unusual-looking library plays host to a rich array of children's activities, including creative baby and toddler sessions and Sure Start and family reading groups. Mondays and Fridays bring in the Homework Club (4-7pm), while the teenage reading group's activities range far beyond reading: open mic nights, creative writing workshops, debates and manga nights were on the schedule last time we dropped by. An extended programme of holiday workshops is also run. The square outside hosts a friendly farmers' market on Sunday mornings. *Buggy access. Disabled access: lift, toilet. Nappy-changing facilities.*

Storytelling

Discover
1 Bridge Terrace, E15 4BG (8536 5555/www. discover.org). Stratford tube/rail/DLR. **Open** *Term-time* 10am-5pm Tue-Fri; 11am-5pm Sat, Sun. *Holidays* 10am-5pm Mon-Fri; 11am-5pm Sat, Sun. **Admission** *Garden* free. *Story trail* £4; £3.50 reductions; free under-2s; £14 family (2+2). **Credit** MC, V.

A fantastic centre for creative learning with an imaginative story garden. Kids can stand in 'Hootah' cones and have their stories recorded for a visiting space monster, or just enjoy themselves on the themed playground equipment. Indoors, the story den features interactive exhibitions about tales from around the world, and children can go on a trail across an indoor river via a wooden footbridge that talks. New interactive exhibition Pirates Ahoy! involves a large wooden boat with sails and rigging, maps, telescopes and dressing-up. Children can explore a secret cave, land on a magical island and find the hidden treasure. It's a great place to hold a birthday party; call for details of party packages. *Buggy access. Café. Disabled access: lift, toilet. Nappy-changing facilities.*

MUSIC

Tuition

Blackheath Conservatoire
19-21 Lee Road, SE3 9RQ (8852 0234/ www.conservatoire.org.uk). Blackheath rail. **Classes** times vary; phone or check website for details. **Fees** from £77/term. **Credit** MC, V.
Musical children can enrol in all sorts of classes and courses here, covering everything from percussion-playing to jazz singing. If one-on-one

Camden
arts centre

Spiral Festival 09
29-30 August 2009, 12-5.30pm

Admission Free

Artist led activities for families

Contemporary Art Exhibitions

Café / Bookshop / Garden

Recycle found objects into new artworks, navigate oddly
familiar environments and become involved with ceramics for
an experience quite unlike any other both inside and out!

 Finchley Road / Hampstead

T: 020 7472 5500

www.camdenartscentre.org

 ARTS COUNCIL ENGLAND

Camden
Funded by Camden Council

clore duffield foundation

tuition is too expensive, kids can learn different instruments in small groups, divided into three different age ranges. There are various choirs and instrumental ensembles, meeting mainly on Saturdays, plus vibrant music, drama and art courses all year round.
Buggy access.

Blueberry

Various venues (8677 6871/www.blueberry.clara.co.uk). **Fees** from £60/10wk term. **No credit cards.**
Operating in south-west and west London, these lovely little groups are aimed at parents and tinies (nine months to threes). Sessions involve a good sing-song, with grown-ups guiding their offspring through the accompanying actions, and cheery group games. Two to fours, meanwhile, can attend Big Kids Blueberry without their elders in tow. For Blueberry birthday parties, *see p145*.

Centre for Young Musicians

Morley College, 61 Westminster Bridge Road, SE1 7HT (7928 3844/www.cym.org.uk). Lambeth North tube. **Classes** 9am-5pm Sat term-time only. **Fees** vary. **No credit cards.**
Children must audition for a place on the Saturday classes that run at the Centre for Young Musicians and its two satellite annexes – Notre Dame High School and Johanna Primary School. Auditions are held for all levels and staff have a keen eye for musical potential, although absolute beginners shouldn't apply. Open access courses for six to 18s run in the school holidays, alongside GCSE revision sessions; check online for further details.
Buggy access. Café. Disabled access: toilet. Nappy-changing facilities.

Guildhall School of Music & Drama

Silk Street, EC2Y 8DT (7382 7160/www.gsmd.ac.uk). Barbican tube/Moorgate tube/rail. **Classes** 8am-6pm Sat. **Fees** basic course from £2,310/term. **Credit** MC, V.
Only the most talented young musicians are singled out to attend this world-class conservatoire's Junior Guildhall instrumental training, held on Saturday mornings. Entry is by audition, and standards are extremely high. The school also runs a String Training Programme for beginners aged four to 11, which includes instrumental training and music appreciation. Talented musicians who can't afford the fee can apply for local authority grants or Guildhall scholarship funding. The Guildhall's Drama Course (13- to 18-year-olds) involves a more informal audition process.

London Suzuki Group

7471 5549/www.londonsuzukigroup.co.uk. **Fees** from £34/hr. **No credit cards.**
Dr Shinichi Suzuki's belief that musical ability is inherent in all newborn children inspired a ground-breaking school of music in Japan. This led to the foundation of the London Suzuki Group in 1972; its teachers (covering violin, viola, cello and piano) apply Dr Suzuki's methods to teach over-threes to mid teens. The key is learning through listening, and then playing for pleasure. Classes are held after school and at weekends, and are for members only, while Day Bonanzas for kids include group lessons and musical games. To find a teacher in your area, check the website.

Musical Express

Southfields Methodist Church, 423 Durnsford Road, SW19 8EE; Wimbledon Rugby Club, Barham Road, Copse Hill, SW20 0ET (8946 6043/www.musicalexpress.co.uk). **Classes** times vary; phone for details. **Fees** 1st session free, then from £6-£7/class. **No credit cards.**
Set up by a music therapist, Musical Express groups are for babies and under-sixes, giving young children the means to express themselves and develop core social skills with instruments and 'action songs'. Parents and carers must accompany under-threes, though older children attend alone. Hour-long sessions for over-threes include some time spent mastering Jolly Phonics, in which children learn each letter's sound with the help of an accompanying action.

Music House for Children

Bush Hall, 310 Uxbridge Road, W12 7LJ (8932 2652/www.musichouseforchildren.co.uk). Shepherd's Bush Market tube. **Classes** times vary; phone for details. **Fees** £7-£13/drop-in class. **Credit** MC, V.
Headquartered in Bush Hall, a beautifully restored former dance hall, this well-established operation provides tuition for all ages. Puppets and bubbles keep tinies spellbound at baby music sessions, while toddlers are inspired to throw all sorts of weird and wonderful shapes at the story-led creative dance classes.
Older children can learn keyboard, percussion and drums, guitar and violin, with a maximum of five pupils per class; two-to-one lessons offer a wider choice of instruments, and cost £15 per child for a half-hour class (nine to 15s). There's home tuition for fives and over, too, starting at £20 for half an hour, plus various holiday shows and workshops.
Buggy access. Café. Disabled access: toilet. Nappy-changing facilities. Shop.

Trinity College of Music.
See p178.

Meet the musicians

Keen to hear the boom of a bassoon or catch some oboes in action? Going to watch an orchestra perform needn't be a staid and stuffy affair. The **Philharmonic Orchestra** (7840 4200, www.lpo.co.uk) offers a brilliant introduction to the orchestra for children aged five to 11, with three yearly Funharmonics days at London's Southbank Centre (*see p164*). The interactive events begin with free music, face-painting and circus skills workshops to get everyone warmed up before an action-packed, hour-long narrated concert begins.

Musical events aimed at seven to 12s are also available at the Barbican Centre (*see p163*) with the **London Symphony Orchestra** (7588 1116, www.lso.co.uk). The orchestra offers Discovery Family Concerts, which start at 2.30pm and last around an hour; tickets for under-16s are only £4 and it's £7 for adults. Another option if you live in Hackney, Islington or the City (or if your children go to school in one of these boroughs), is the **LSO St**

Luke's Youth Choir. No previous musical experience is required, just an enthusiasm for singing, and there's no charge either. It's run by singer and conductor Gareth Malone, and is open to young people aged eight and upwards. New members are welcome, if spaces are available, in the first two weeks of each half term.

The vibrant, youthful **Southbank Sinfonia** (7921 0370, www.southbanksinfonia. co.uk), set up to give promising graduates a showcase for their talents, is also keen to encourage kids. Saturday Spectaculars (£6 per ticket) at the Cadogan Hall kick off with activities in the specially-decorated foyer, led by costumed staff: making *Peter and the Wolf* puppets, say, or going on a pirate's treasure hunt. Players come down to demonstrate their instruments: if you're lucky, you might even get a go. Then it's time for the concert – under an hour, so kids don't get too wriggly. Themes are suitably loud and lively (Circuses, the Mad Hatter's Musical Tea Party) and a narrator explains the action.

Royal College of Music
Prince Consort Road, SW7 2BS (7589 3643/ www.rcm.ac.uk). South Kensington tube/9, 10, 52, 452 bus. **Classes** 9am-5pm Sat. **Fees** £879/term. **Credit** MC, V. **Map** p313 D9.
Children (eight to 18s) who pass the stringent auditions can attend individually-tailored lessons at the RCM. Lessons run from 9am to 5pm on Saturdays, in conjunction with the school term, and focus almost exclusively on classical instruments. As you'd expect, it's heavily oversubscribed. For inspiration, check online for details of (usually free) performances staged by pupils throughout the year.
Buggy access. Disabled access: lift, toilets.

Trinity College of Music
King Charles Court, Old Royal Naval College, SE10 9JF (8305 4444/www.tcm.ac.uk). Cutty Sark DLR. **Classes** 9am-6pm Sat. **Fees** £715/term. **No credit cards**.
This august conservatoire was the first in the UK to open its doors to schoolchildren on Saturdays, back in 1906. 'Intensive but fun' all-day sessions at Junior Trinity (three to 19s) nurture musical creativity with improvisation and composition work; students are also encouraged to play in ensembles. String Time, a

special programme for young players aged from three to 11, also takes place on Saturday mornings. Auditions are held in March and May, and you can hear the current students in action at the college's regular Open Days.
Buggy access. Café. Disabled access: lift, toilets.

Venues

English National Opera
The Coliseum, St Martin's Lane, WC2N 4ES (education 7632 8484/box office 7632 8300/ www.eno.org). Leicester Square tube. **Open** Box office 10am-8pm Mon-Sat. **Tickets** £10-£83. **Credit** AmEx, MC, V. **Map** p315 L7.
Family Days at the ENO involve hands-on activities and theatre tours, linked to the current production; join the mailing list for updates on forthcoming events. Run in collaboration with St Marylebone School (7935 9501), 'takepart!' is a buzzing music theatre Saturday school for four to 18s, with auditions in spring and autumn.
Bar. Buggy access. Disabled access: lift, toilet. Restaurant.

Roundhouse
Chalk Farm Road, NW1 8EH (7424 9991/box office 0870 389 1846/www.roundhouse.org.uk).

Activities

LSO St. Luke's Youth Choir.

Chalk Farm or Camden Town tube. **Open**
Box office 11am-6pm Mon-Sat. **Tickets**
£10-£25. **Credit** MC, V.
The iconic former railway engine shed is
Camden's pride and joy, hosting arty gigs, theatre
and visually stunning multimedia events, plus
quirky contemporary circus and performance
acts. While not all the shows are suitable for
families, creative opportunities for young people
lie at the heart of the Roundhouse Studios, tucked
below the circular hall. The eclectic workshops
often focus on multimedia skills: filming as part
of a camera crew, producing a radio show and
costume design have all featured in the past, at a
mere £2 a day. *See also p108* **Great Days Out**.
*Bars. Buggy access. Café. Disabled access: toilet.
Nappy-changing facilities.*

Royal Albert Hall
*Kensington Gore, SW7 2AP (7589 8212/
www.royalalberthall.com). South Kensington or
Knightsbridge tube.* **Open** *Box office* 9am-9pm
daily. **Tickets** £5-£150. **Credit** AmEx, MC, V.
Map p313 D9.
The 5,200-capacity rotunda dubbed 'the nation's
village hall' is best known for hosting the annual
BBC Proms from July to September. Under-16s
are eligible for half-price tickets to every concert
(bar the famed Last Night), and there are free

family events before selected performances at
the nearby Royal College of Music. You're given
a bit of background on the stories behind that
evening's music, and kids are encouraged to
bring their instruments along. In the daytime,
guided tours let you peep at the auditorium
(where, if you're lucky, rehearsals may be
underway for that evening's performance); two
children can go free with every paying adult (£8).
*Bars. Buggy access. Café. Disabled access: lift,
toilet. Nappy-changing facilities. Restaurants.
Shop.*

Wigmore Hall
*36 Wigmore Street, W1U 2BP (7935 2141/
education 7258 8227/www.wigmore-hall.
org.uk). Bond Street or Oxford Circus tube.*
Open *Box office* 10am-5pm daily (8.30pm
on performance nights). **Tickets** £10-£25.
Credit AmEx, DC, MC, V. **Map** p314 H5.
With its acres of marble, wooden panelling and
plush red seating, this art deco recital hall oozes
grandeur. Happily, small fry are made very
welcome, thanks to a programme of family,
community and outreach projects. The star
attraction is Chamber Tots: immensely popular
music and movement classes for two- to five-
year-olds. Once-monthly family concerts,
generally of specially-commissioned works, are
also great fun, and suitable for five-and-overs.
Regular Family Days bring more opportunities
to try a spot of composing, do some painting or
meet the musicians and their instruments.
*Bar. Buggy access. Disabled access: toilet.
Nappy-changing facilities. Restaurant.*

PLAYTIME

Indoor play centres

Bramley's Big Adventure
*136 Bramley Road, W10 6TJ (8960 1515/
www.bramleysbig.co.uk). Latimer Road tube.*
Open *Term-time* 10am-6pm Mon-Fri; 10am-
6.30pm Sat, Sun. *Holidays* 10am-6.30pm daily.
Membership £20/yr. **Admission** *Members*
£2.50 under-2s; £4 2-5s; £5 over-5s; free
adults. *Non-members* £3.50 under-2s; £5
2-5s; £5.50 over-5s; 50p adults. **Credit**
AmEx, MC, V.
Organised chaos reigns at Bramley's, tucked
beneath the Westway flyover. The centrepiece is
a giant three-level play frame, incorporating
slides, ball pools, swings and dens, with separate
areas for less rambunctious under-fives and
babies. There's no time limit on play sessions, so
children can play all day; free Wi-Fi lets parents

Activities

Eddie Catz.

catch up on work while their offspring tear about. The café offers organic and fair trade grub; ask about children's parties, which include meals and party bags.
Buggy access. Café. Disabled access: toilet. Nappy-changing facilities.

Discovery Planet
1st floor, Surrey Quays Shopping Centre, Redriff Road, SE16 7LL (7237 2388/www. discovery-planet.co.uk). Canada Water tube. **Open** 10am-6pm Mon-Sat; 11am-5pm Sun. **Admission** £3.49-£4.49 under-2s; £3.99-£4.99 2-10s; free adults & babies. **Credit** (over £10) MC, V.
Filled with brightly coloured tubes, tunnels, ball ponds and slides, this huge indoor area gives under-tens the chance to climb, slide and throw themselves about for two action-packed hours.
Buggy access. Disabled access: lift, toilet. Nappy-changing facilities.

Eddie Catz
68-70 High Street, SW15 1SF (0845 201 1268/www.eddiecatz.com). Putney Bridge tube. **Open** 9.30am-6.30pm Mon-Sat; 10am-5pm Sun. **Admission** £4.50 under 90cm; £5.50 90cm-1.55m; £1 over 1.55m; free babies under 8mths. **Credit** MC, V.
For younger children, Eddie Catz offers a soft play area, a modestly sized adventure play frame and movement and music classes (for which an extra charge applies). Five to tens can play video games, air hockey and mini-basketball.
Buggy access. Café. Disabled access: lift, toilet. Nappy-changing facilities. Shop.
Branch 42 Station Road, SW19 2LP (8288 8178).

Gambado
7 Station Court, Townmead Road, SW6 2PY (7384 1635/www.gambado.com). Fulham Broadway tube/391 bus. **Open** 9.30am-6.30pm daily. **Admission** £7.45 1-2s; £9.45 3-10s; £2.50 adults; free under-1s. **Credit** MC, V.
Cheery staff and masses of things to do mean Gambado's is eternally popular, despite the hefty entry fee. Kids soon vanish into the depths of the thrilling multi-level climbing frame, which incorporates ball ponds, slides (enclosed twirly tunnels plus bumpy ones large enough for parents to join in), trampolines, assault courses and mini dodgems. Tinies get a soft-play section with big Lego bricks and face-painting. You can refuel on healthy fare at the café, and there's free internet access for the adults. At weekends, it's usually full of birthday parties.
Buggy access. Café. Disabled access: toilet. Nappy-changing facilities.

It's a Kid's Thing
279 Magdalen Road, SW18 3NZ (8739 0909/ www.itsakidsthing.co.uk). Earlsfield rail. **Open** 9am-6pm daily. **Admission** £5 over-2s; £4 under-2s; £2 siblings. Prices of activities vary; check website for details. **Credit** MC, V.
If you find the decibel levels and commotion of bigger play centres unbearable, this sociable, small-scale outfit is a welcome alternative. Children swarm over the two-tier playzone and soft-play area while their parents look on from the café; there's a decent kids' menu, with the option to swap chips for mash or half a jacket potato. Grown-ups fill up on pastas and panini as their offspring play; come the weekend, it's all about relaxing over an all-day fry-up and the papers. The activities schedule includes Socatots, baby massage and messy art; check the timetable for details of free singing and dance sessions for toddlers.
Buggy access. Café. Disabled access: toilet. Nappy-changing facilities.

Kidspace
Colonnades, 619 Purley Way, Croydon, Surrey CR0 4RQ (8686 0040/www.kidspace adventures.com). Waddon rail/119, 289 bus. **Open** *Term-time* 9.30am-7pm Mon-Thur; 9.30am-8pm Fri; 9am-8pm Sat; 9am-7pm Sun. *Holidays* 9am-7pm Mon-Thur, Sun; 9am-8pm Fri, Sat. **Admission** *Weekdays* £5.50; £2.50 adults; free under-1s. *Weekends & holidays* £5.50 under-3s; £8.50 over-3s; £5.50 adults. **Credit** AmEx, MC, V.
London's biggest indoor play centre is a cut above the competition, thanks to its towering wooden climbing frame, the Orb. Unusually, parents are allowed to explore alongside their children, zooming down the 'black hole' slide, getting lost in the labyrinth or dodging cannon fire in Thunderball City. Crazy golf, a climbing wall and cavern maze, mini go-karts and a multi-sensory play area for toddlers round off a very full family day out.
Buggy access. Café. Disabled access: lift, toilet. Nappy-changing facilities. Shop.

Kidzmania
28 Powell Road, E5 8DJ (8533 5556). Clapton rail. **Open** 10am-6pm daily. **Admission** £4.50 4-12s; £3.50 under-4s; free adults. **No credit cards.**
This indoor adventure play centre doubles up as a popular children's party venue, with its own café and full on-site catering (special party menus can be prepared). There are ball pools, climbing frames, slides and bouncy castles to entertain the troops.
Buggy access. Café. Nappy-changing facilities.

Activities

Pirate's Playhouse

The Castle Climbing Centre, 271 Green Lanes, N4 2HA (8800 1771). Manor House tube, then 141, 341 bus. **Open** 10am-6pm Mon-Thur; 10am-7pm Fri-Sun. **Admission** £3.90 walkers; £2.50 crawlers; free adults and babes in arms. **No credit cards.**

Just off Clissold Park, this playframe is filled with thrilling slides and obstacle courses. It seems small until you look up – its height providing true challenge to clambering pre-teens, while there is a large separate toddler area with a spotless ball pool and soft-play puzzles. Parents can sit in comfort around the frame or in a cosy sofa-and-magazine bedecked side room if they trust junior out of sight. Very friendly staff serve good coffee and sandwiches.

Buggy access. Café. Nappy-changing facilities.

THEATRE

Tuition

Allsorts

Office: 34 Pember Road, NW10 5LS (8969 3249/www.allsortsdrama.com). **Classes** phone for details. **Fees** £100-£180/10wk term; from £80 4-day workshop; 20% sibling discount. **Credit** MC, V.

Alumni from Allsorts have won starring roles in some big-budget flicks: Anna Popplewell (Susan in the *Chronicles of Narnia*) enrolled here at the age of six. Children (four to 16) don't need any previous experience to sign up for the Saturday school and holiday workshops; working in small groups, they are encouraged to take a creative approach, with lots of role-playing and improvisation. Teachers can also arrange bespoke at-home acting tuition and drama parties.

Dramarama

8446 0891/www.dramarama.co.uk. Holiday courses: South Hampstead High School, Maresfield Gardens, NW3 5SS. Term-time classes: South Hampstead Junior School, Netherhall Gardens, NW3 5RN. Finchley Road & Frognal rail. **Fees** phone for details. **No credit cards.**

Kids of all ages and abilities can get involved in acting with Dramarama's after-school clubs, Saturday workshops and half-term and holiday courses. Three- to four-year-old thespians can become Dramatots, while older children work towards Trinity Guildhall Performance Art exams; these are recognised qualifications in drama, the more advanced grades of which can be converted into university-entrance UCAS points. There's also a birthday-party service for six to 14s, with themes ranging from mermaids to murder mysteries.

Helen O'Grady's Children's Drama Academy

Office: Northside Vale, Guernsey, GY3 5TX (01481 200250/www.helenogrady.co.uk). **Classes** times vary; phone for details. **Fees** £98/14wk term. **No credit cards.**

The academy's weekly one-hour workshops aim to build kids' self-esteem, confidence and social skills. The lower and upper primary groups (five to eights and nine to 11s, respectively) learn clear speech and fluent delivery, while the Youth Theatre (13-17s) develops more advanced dramatic techniques. A production is held at the end of the summer term. Check the website to find your nearest group.

Hoxton Hall

130 Hoxton Street, N1 6SH (7684 0060/ www.hoxtonhall.co.uk). Old Street tube/rail. **Classes** times vary; phone for details. **Fees** £20/8wk term. **No credit cards.**

Activities

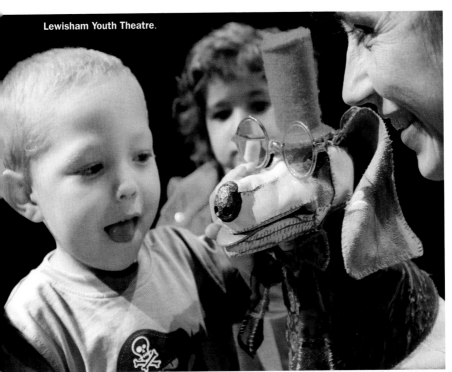
Lewisham Youth Theatre.

This refurbished Victorian music hall runs a vibrant Youth Arts club for seven to 19s, incorporating dance, drama and music. Children's abilities and ideas are taken seriously here, and they're given plenty of access to the hall's extensive facilities: seven- to ten-year-old Music Stars can compose and record their own songs in the recording studio, while the street dance group (11-17s) devises performances for the main stage with the help of professional choreographers and dancers.
Buggy access. Café.

Lewisham Youth Theatre

Broadway Theatre, Catford Broadway, SE6 4RU (8690 3428/box office 8690 0002/ www.lewishamyouththeatre.com). Catford or Catford Bridge rail/75, 181, 185, 202, 660 bus. **Classes** *Junior Youth Theatre (8-11s, 12-14s) 90 mins Wed. Senior Youth Theatre (15-21s) 6-8pm Mon. ROAR! Children's Theatre (2-11s & families) Oct-Dec 11.30am Sat.* **Tickets** £4.50 (ROAR!). **Credit** (Box office) MC, V.
Founded in 1987, Lewisham Youth Theatre has forged itself a reputation for innovation, variety and high standards. It's also stuck to its aim of making theatre accessible to everyone: there are no auditions, and classes and workshops are free to attend. Most recruitment takes place through schools, but some places are allocated on a first come, first served basis. The Junior Youth Theatre is divided into two age groups, but there's some crossover with the Senior Youth Theatre; all classes work towards full productions. For details of children's theatre performances at Broadway Theatre, *see p187. Buggy access. Café. Disabled access: toilets.*

London Bubble Theatre Company

5 Elephant Lane, SE16 4JD (7237 4434/ www.londonbubble.org.uk). Bermondsey, Canada Water or Rotherhithe tube. **Open** *Box office* July-Sept 10am-6pm Mon-Fri. **Classes** phone for details. **Fees** £45/11wk term. **Credit** MC, V.
The Bubble's exemplary arts programme includes term-time theatre groups for six to eights, nine to 12s and 13-17s. There are no nail-biting auditions; all you need to take part are enthusiasm and commitment (though there may be a waiting list, as places are much in demand). Check online for details of the summer Open Performance Theatre Project, open to all ages.

Little Angel Theatre.

Activities

Millfield Theatre School

Silver Street, N18 1PJ (box office 8807 6680/ www.millfieldtheatre.co.uk). Silver Street rail/34, 102, 144, 217, 231, W6 bus. **Open** *Box office* 10am-6pm Mon-Fri. **Classes** (4-5s) 10.30am-noon, (6-7s) 12.30-2pm, (8-14s) 11am-2pm Sun; (14-25s) varies. **Fees** (4-5s, 6-7s, 14-25s) £100/10wk term; (8-14s) £185/10wk term. **Credit** MC, V.

Sundays at Millfield are devoted to children's theatre, with four- to 14-year-olds split into four age groups (over-14s meet on Wednesdays). If acting doesn't appeal, kids can enrol in all sorts of alternative classes, including ballet, tap, creative clay and chess; the set design course, which allows young artists to design a working set for the youth theatre's summer production, is an inspired new addition to the programme. The theatre itself presents a regular calendar of musicals, comedies and drama, as well as some perky touring shows and the time-honoured Christmas panto.

Buggy access. Disabled access: toilets.

National Youth Music Theatre

Head office: 2-4 Great Eastern Street, EC2A 3NW (7422 8290/www.nymt.org.uk). Old Street tube/rail. **Classes** phone for details. **Fees** prices vary; phone for details. **Credit** MC, V.

The NYMT has had a hand in the making of many a glittering career, with the likes of Jamie Bell, Matt Lucas and Jude Law among its alumni. The company continues to audition young hopefuls for its amazing shows; check online for details of auditions and regional workshops. Stage-management opportunities appeal to those keen to work behind the scenes, while young musicians can audition for orchestral roles.

Perform

Office: 49 Chalton Street, NW1 1LT (0845 400 4000/www.perform.org.uk). **Classes** phone for details. **Fees** £135/10wk term (weekday); £190/10wk term (weekends); free trials. **Credit** MC, V.

The four Cs (confidence, communication, concentration and co-ordination) are the focus at Perform – and you're never too young to start learning the basics. Story- and song-packed Mini Ps classes are aimed at three-month to three-year-olds, while sessions for four to eights and eight to 12s blend acting, singing and dancing. See the website for details of venues, and information on the party service.

Stagecoach Theatre Arts

Head office: Courthouse, Elm Grove, Walton-on-Thames, Surrey KT12 1LZ (01932 254333/

www.stagecoach.co.uk). **Fees** £315/12-13wk term (6-16s); £157.50/12-13wk term (4-7s). **Credit** MC, V.

From humble beginnings in Surrey, this performing arts school has become a global concern, with an attendant performers' agency for young people that's the largest in the UK. The school itself has 60 branches in London alone, offering its starry-eyed pupils a solid grounding in dance, drama and singing. Four to sixes start with half an hour's tuition in each discipline per week, which climbs to an hour for older children. Some students work towards exams in their second or subsequent year, while third-year pupils can audition for the Stagecoach National Showcase Production in London. Holiday workshops are also organised.

Sylvia Young Theatre School
Rossmore Road, NW1 6NJ (7402 0673/ www.sylviayoungtheatreschool.co.uk). Baker Street tube/Marylebone tube/rail. **Classes** phone for details. **Fees** *Classes* £74-£95/12wk term. *Summer school* (10-18s) £285-£300/wk. **Credit** MC, V.

Thanks to the surfeit of soap stalwarts and pop stars who have honed their talents here over the years (Billie Piper, Amy Winehouse, Leona Lewis and Keeley Hawes among them), Sylvia Young's has become a household name. The full-time stage school (with around 160 pupils aged from ten to 16) and Saturday school (fours to 18s) are famously oversubscribed; there are also evening classes on Thursdays. The Easter and summer holidays bring assorted theatre and musical theatre workshops for fame-hungry eights and overs.

Puppet theatres

Little Angel Theatre
14 Dagmar Passage, off Cross Street, N1 2DN (7226 1787/www.littleangeltheatre.com). Angel tube/Highbury & Islington tube/rail, then 4, 19, 30, 43 bus. **Open** *Box office* 10am-6pm Mon-Fri; 9am-4pm Sat, Sun. **Tickets** £6-£8. **Credit** MC, V.

Themes, styles and stories are drawn from an eclectic array of cultural traditions at this acclaimed puppet theatre, which was established in 1961. Productions are often aimed at fives and above, with occasional shows for the very young and special Baby Friendly performances. The Saturday Puppet Club offers weekly sessions for various age groups; for a one-off puppet-making workshop, book a place on a family fun day.
Buggy access. Disabled access: toilet. Nappy-changing facilities. Shop.

Puppet Theatre Barge
Opposite 35 Blomfield Road, W9 2PF (7249 6876/www.puppetbarge.com). Warwick Avenue tube. **Open** *Box office* 10am-8pm daily. **Tickets** £10; £8.50 under-16s, reductions. **Credit** MC, V.

The fact that this diminutive theatre is afloat enchants younger visitors almost as much as the prospect of a performance. The 50-seater barge is moored on the towpath in Little Venice between November and mid July, with marionette shows at 3pm on Saturdays and Sundays and more frequent performances in the holidays. Come July, the barge floats merrily off down the Thames to perform at Richmond, with a show every day but Sunday during August, and weekend perfomances through September until early October. Pay attention to age recommendations, as longer shows can be tiring for little ones, and book ahead to secure seats near the front, which help children stay focused. *See also p108* **Great Days Out***. Buggy Access.*

Touring companies

Kazzum
7539 3500/www.kazzum.org
The Kazzum children's theatre collective has toured schools, theatres, libraries, parks and festivals with its productions, which range from playful interactive pieces to specially commissioned plays that tackle hard-hitting contemporary issues. Celebrating difference and diversity lies at the heart of its body of work.

Oily Cart
8672 6329/www.oilycart.org.uk.
Oily Cart's performances are aimed at two groups who might otherwise miss out on the magic of theatre: very young children and children with special needs. At its brilliant, multi-sensory productions, children in the audience become part of the performance, invited to explore the set and interact with the delightfully quirky performers. In the last show, *How Long is a Piece of String?*, toddlers tugged on ropes to start the music and lights, and pedalled away to set a Heath-Robinson-esque machine whirring into motion. Out popped a succession of string babies, which the children were asked to look after while they searched for the babies' missing parents. Shows tour the country, but most start in London with a three-to six-week run: audience sizes are tiny, so tickets are soon snapped up by those in the know. The next big show is planned for Spring 2010, but in the meantime there's the Christmas performance to look forward to.

Quicksilver Theatre

7241 2942/www.quicksilvertheatre.org.
Led by its dynamic joint artistic directors, Guy
Holland and Carey English, this Hackney-based
collective tours the UK with its innovative
productions. The company has a firm grasp of
what preschoolers enjoy ('small shows for small
people in small places'), but are equally adept
when it comes to producing visually striking,
thought-provoking plays for older children.
Creative collaborations with other companies
reap rich rewards: look out for *La Di Dada*, a
shadow and light show created with Indefinite
Articles that's scheduled to go on tour in 2010.

Theatre Centre

7729 3066/www.theatre-centre.co.uk.
Founded in 1953 by the late Brian Way
(a pioneering director, educator and writer),
Theatre Centre takes its productions to schools,
theatres and festivals across the country. The
company has a reputation for excellence and
technical invention, and also champions up-and-
coming new writers.

Theatre-Rites

7953 7102/www.theatre-rites.co.uk.
In the capable hands of Sue Buckmaster,
Theatre-Rites is flourishing. It made its name
with daring, site-specific works, starting with
1996's astounding *Houseworks*, which took over
an entire house in Brixton. Staging shows in the
unlikeliest of venues (a hospital ward, say, or a
disused salts factory) is still a major strand of
its work, but the company isn't afraid to branch
out. Its shows might involve puppets,
percussionists, trapeze artists and jugglers;
whatever the theme, the visuals are invariably
stunning. *Mischief*, an award-winning, endlessly
inventive collaboration with choreographer
Arthur Pita, adds dance to the mix – along with
giant, bendy foam shapes and an onstage
keyboard- and guitar-playing beatboxer. There
are two to three touring productions a year,
which always stop by London for a night or two.

Venues

Albany

*Douglas Way, SE8 4AG (8692 4446/www.the
albany.org.uk). Deptford rail/21, 36, 47, 136,
171, 177, 188, 225, 453 bus.* **Open** *Box office*
9am-9pm Mon-Fri; 10am-5pm Sat; 2hrs before
performance Sun. **Tickets** *Family Sunday* £5.
Credit MC, V.
Deptford's sparky multimedia and performing
arts centre retains a lively neighbourhood focus.
Family Sunday events (Sept-Apr) range from

specially written pieces and musical stories with
sing-along songs to the jumping Baby Grooves
disco; tickets cost a fiver. There's a programme
of free activities for 13-19s too; check the website
or sign up to the Facebook group. The venue can
also be hired out for parties.
*Buggy access. Café. Disabled access: lift, toilet.
Nappy-changing facilities.*

artsdepot

*5 Nether Street, N12 0GA (8369 5454/www.
artsdepot.co.uk). West Finchley or Woodside
Park tube.* **Open** *Box office* 9am-5.30pm
Mon-Fri; 10am-5.30pm Sat; noon-5.30pm
Sun (later during performances). **Tickets**
free-£18. **Credit** MC, V.
Opened in 2004, this dynamic arts centre throws
open its doors to children and families, offering
a richly varied line-up of performances, classes
and courses. Children's theatre shows take place
in the 150-seat studio on Saturdays and Sundays,
with a different company in residence each week.
For those that would rather take to the stage,
Bright Sparks Theatre Company (eight to 12s)
meets on Friday, and there are Saturday drama
and story making sessions for younger children;
meanwhile, artsdepot members aged from 13 to
19 can attend free playwriting and drama
groups. Other offerings on the busy learning
programme run the gamut from terrific messy
play mornings to street dance and art classes.
Innovative, week-long summer holiday courses
might involve anything from turning recycled
materials into artistic masterpieces to learning
fast-paced dance routines to accompany the
latest chart hits.
*Buggy access. Café. Disabled access: lift, toilet.
Nappy-changing facilities.*

BAC (Battersea Arts Centre)

*Lavender Hill, SW11 5TN (7223 2223/www.
bac.org.uk). Clapham Common tube, then 345
bus/Clapham Junction rail/77, 77A, 156 bus.*
Open *Box office* 10am-6pm Mon-Fri; 3-6pm
Sat. **Tickets** free-£15. **Credit** MC, V.
Its Victorian premises may look eminently
traditional, but inside, the BAC is a hotbed of
ground-breaking theatre. In the past, shows have
tended to be for adults, but ambitious plans are
afoot to produce more work that's both for and
by young people. In the meantime, 12 to 25s can
join the in-house young people's theatre group,
YPT. Its members often get the chance to work
with the BAC's prestigious guest companies and
artists (the likes of Punchdrunk and Forced
Entertainment), which has resulted in some
brilliantly experimental pieces.
*Bar. Buggy access. Café. Disabled access:
lift, toilet. Nappy-changing facilities.*

Puppet Theatre Barge. *See p185.*

Broadway Theatre

Catford Broadway, SE6 4RU (8690 0002/ www.broadwaytheatre.org.uk). Catford or Catford Bridge rail/75, 181, 185, 202, 660 bus. **Open** *Box office* 10am-6pm Mon-Sat. **Tickets** £3.50-£22. **Credit** MC, V.

On Saturday mornings, local families flock to this listed art deco theatre for ROAR! matinées, presented by leading children's theatre companies. Aimed at three- to eight-year-olds, shows usually take place in the intimate 100-seater studio – although the main auditorium is sometimes used to accommodate the rollicking Christmas pantomime and other large-scale shows. Note that there are no performances from the end of July to the beginning of September, as the entire theatre shuts down for the summer. The acclaimed Lewisham Youth Theatre (*see p183*) is also based at the theatre, with drama groups for various ages.

Buggy access. Café. Disabled access: lift, toilet. Nappy-changing facilities.

Chickenshed

Chase Side, N14 4PE (8292 9222/www. chickenshed.org.uk). Cockfosters or Oakwood tube. **Open** *Box office* 10am-6pm Mon-Fri; 10am-5pm Sat. **Tickets** *Shows* £4-£18. *Workshops* phone for details. **Credit** MC, V.

Since its inception in 1974, Chickenshed has firmly upheld its ethos that 'everyone is welcome, and everyone is valued'. Over-fives can join the Children's Theatre group, while the Youth Theatre is open to over-13s: the waiting list is enormous, but we're assured that everyone eventually gets in. On Friday and Saturdays, colourful Tales from the Shed performances bring all sorts of stories to life for under-sevens.

Bar. Buggy access. Café. Disabled access: lift, toilet. Nappy-changing facilities. Shop.

Colour House Children's Theatre

Merton Abbey Mills, Watermill Way, SW19 2RD (8542 5511/www.colourhousetheatre. co.uk). Colliers Wood tube. **Open** *Box office*

Jackson's Lane.

10am-5pm daily; 1hr before show. **Shows** 2pm, 4pm Sat, Sun. **Tickets** £7. **Credit** MC, V. Witty, often musical renditions of classics such as *Sleeping Beauty*, *Snow White* and *Robinson Crusoe* are the forte at this sweet little riverside venue. After-show birthday parties with a mini disco can be arranged, with front row seats for the guests and a tuneful rendition of *Happy Birthday* from the cast at the end of the performance. For details of children's theatre workshops and groups, call 8623 9600. *Buggy access. Disabled access: toilet. Nappy-changing facilities (in Merton Abbey Mills). Shop.*

Hackney Empire
291 Mare Street, E8 1EJ (box office 8985 2424/www.hackneyempire.co.uk). Hackney Central rail/38, 106, 253, 277, D6 bus. **Open** *Box office* 10am-9pm Mon-Sat; noon-6pm Sun. *Tours* phone for times. **Tickets** prices vary; phone for details. **Tours** £10; £7 reductions. **Credit** MC, V.
Variety is the spice of life at this East End institution, which was lovingly revamped in 2004. Amid the cracking line-up, there's plenty for families, from touring stage shows of hit children's TV shows (*LazyTown, Scooby Doo* and the like) to adaptations of much-loved poems and storybooks. The education department also runs an Artist Development Programme for 13- to 19-year-olds; check the website for details. *Buggy access. Disabled access: toilet. Nappy-changing facilities.*

Half Moon Young People's Theatre
43 White Horse Road, E1 0ND (7709 8900/ www.halfmoon.org.uk). Limehouse DLR/rail. **Open** *Box office* Apr-Sept 10am-6pm Mon-Fri. Oct-Mar 10am-6pm Mon-Fri; 9.30am-4.30pm Sat. **Tickets** £5. **Credit** MC, V.
As well as staging children's theatre shows from September to April, this place also nurtures creative talent. Seven youth theatre groups give kids aged between five and 17 the chance to express themselves: there are no auditions to get in, and young people are encouraged to join in regardless of race, sex, ability or financial situation. In the holidays, there are various hands-on workshops and courses, often culminating with a performance for friends and families on the final day. *Buggy access. Disabled access: lift, toilet. Nappy-changing facilities.*

Jackson's Lane
269A Archway Road, N6 5AA (8341 4421/ www.jacksonslane.org.uk). Highgate tube. **Open** *Box office* 10am-10pm Tue-Sat; 10am-5pm Sun. **Tickets** £5.95-£12.50. **Credit** MC, V.

A handsome red brick gothic church conversion, Jackson's Lane is home to a 170-capacity theatre, a wonderfully atmospheric dance studio and four additional rehearsal and workshop spaces. On Sundays at 2pm, touring children's theatre companies take to the stage, with free jazz in the café after the performance. A splendid programme of children's courses includes unusual offerings such as film-making or fencing, along with tap, drama and dance for tinies with energy to burn. *Bar. Buggy access. Café. Disabled access: toilet. Nappy-changing facilities.*

Lauderdale House
Highgate Hill, Waterlow Park, N6 5HG (8348 8716/www.lauderdalehouse.co.uk). Archway tube, then 143, 210, 271, W5 bus. **Open** *Box office* 30mins before performance. **Tickets** £4.50; £3 reductions. **No credit cards.**
Set amid ornamental gardens on the edge of peaceful Waterlow Park (*see p120*), this grand, 16th-century mansion was once home to Nell Gwynne, the mistress of Charles II. Art and photography exhibitions now occupy its stately lobby (occasionally expanding into the upper and lower galleries), but the big lure for parents is the jam-packed kids' activities programme. In term-time, most of the action takes place at weekends: Saturdays bring energetic panto-style children's shows and sing-along sessions at 10am and 11.30am, while Sunday mornings are set aside for family-friendly classical music concerts (recommended from five or six years and up). Weekday drop-in classes for preschoolers focus on music, art and movement; the programme expands in the school holidays to incorporate workshops in arts, dance and drama for kids of all ages. *Buggy access. Café. Disabled access: toilet.*

Lyric Hammersmith Theatre
Lyric Square, King Street, W6 0QL (0871 221 1722/www.lyric.co.uk). Hammersmith tube. **Open** *Box office* 9.30am-7pm Mon-Sat (until 8pm on performance days). **Tickets** £9-£27; £10 under-16s, reductions, students (restrictions apply). **Credit** MC, V.
The Lyric remains one of London's most future-focused theatres for children's programming, largely thanks to its pioneering Creative Learning schedule. It gives 11- to 19-year-old west Londoners access to high-quality arts facilities and teaching, with an after-school club, courses and workshops. Fourteen- to 19s can also join the Lyric Young Company (£5), which yields rich returns in the shape of weekly drama classes, one-off masterclasses and the chance to audition for the company's shows.

Activities

The studio is the venue for most kids' events: top-notch Saturday morning theatricals, school holiday workshops and preschooler specials in the week. Look out for rambunctious Messy Play workshops, held after selected Saturday shows; there are only 25 places on each, so book as early as you can. The Summer Party – a free, one-day theatre festival for all the family – takes place in early July; the 2009 event, on 11 July, will have a floral theme.
Buggy access. Café. Disabled access: lift, toilet. Nappy-changing facilities.

National Theatre

South Bank, SE1 9PX (box office 7452 3000/ information 7452 3400/www.nationaltheatre. org.uk). Waterloo tube/rail. **Open** *Box office* 9.30am-8pm Mon-Sat. **Credit** AmEx, MC, V. **Map** p317 M8.

While most plays at the National's trio of world-class theatres (the Olivier, the Lyttleton and the Cottesloe) are aimed at grown-ups, the odd family-friendly production does tread the boards. But you don't need to shell out for a ticket to have fun here. For a start, there are the free early-evening concerts held in the foyer from Monday to Saturday (and on Saturday lunchtimes), which could include anything from swirling, foot-stamping flamenco to boogie woogie piano. Another spot with plenty going on is the outdoor Theatre Square – home to the terrific Watch This Space season, which generally runs from July to mid September. Wacky street theatre performers, art installations, intrepid tightrope-walkers and puppeteers run riot on the astroturf lawn; the Thrills and Spills day is always a highlight. For a full run-down of what's going on, check online.

Nurturing new talent is also part of the agenda. The New Connections programme commissions renowned playwrights and authors (William Boyd, David Mamet and Anthony Horowitz were among those who took part in 2009) to write a new play for young performers, which schools and youth theatres nationwide can then produce. One production of each script is chosen for performance in a week-long summer festival at the National. Young actors can also join the National Theatre Young Company, made up of 13- to 19-year-old performers.

If you'd rather peek behind the scenes than take centre stage, backstage tours (£7, £5 under-18s; £13 family; not suitable for under-sevens) lead visitors into the rehearsal rooms, costume and prop workshops, dressing rooms and stages. *See also p30* **Great Days Out**.
Bars. Buggy access. Café. Disabled access: lift, toilet. Nappy-changing facilities. Restaurants. Shop.

Nettlefold Theatre

West Norwood Library, 1 Norwood High Street, SE27 9JX (7926 8070/www.lambeth. gov.uk). West Norwood rail/2, 68, 196, 468 bus. **Open** *Box office* 9am-10pm Mon-Sat; 9.30am-6pm Sun. **Tickets** £5. **Credit** MC, V.

This 200-seat theatre is built into West Norwood Library and runs one child-oriented show a month (usually on a Saturday at 2pm). Another draw is the Bigfoot Theatre Company (0870 011 4307, www. bigfoot-theatre.co.uk), which runs drama, singing, dance and movement classes for sixes and over between 10am and noon every Saturday during term time.
Buggy access. Disabled access: lift, toilet. Nappy-changing facilities.

New Wimbledon Theatre

The Broadway, SW19 1QG (0870 060 6646/ www.theambassadors.com/newwimbledon). Wimbledon tube/rail. **Open** *Box office* 10am-6pm Mon-Sat. **Tickets** phone for details. **Credit** MC, V.

A steady stream of touring hits swap the bright lights of the West End for the suburban surrounds of Wimbledon to visit this popular theatre. Early 2009 brought David Woods' charming adaptation of *The Tiger Who Came to Tea*; in the autumn, *High School Musical 2* is set to be a sure-fire hit. The end-of-year panto is always a spectacular, no-expense-spared affair.
Bar. Buggy access. Disabled access: lift, toilet. Shop.

Open Air Theatre

Inner Circle, Regent's Park, NW1 4NU (box office 0844 826 4242/www.openairtheatre.org). Baker Street tube. **Open** *Box office* Feb-Sept 9am-9pm daily. **Tickets** £10-£45. **Credit** AmEx, MC, V. **Map** p314 G3.

However old you are, there's something magical about seeing Shakespeare performed amid a leafy, rustling semi-circle of trees – particularly if the weather's kind. The season always includes a musical and a children's play; for 2009 it was *The Tempest*, 're-imagined for everyone aged six and over' (all tickets £12). If rainy weather stops play, tickets will be exchanged for a later performance – subject to availability – but umbrellas, thick jumpers and blankets are always advisable.
Buggy access. Café. Disabled access: toilet.

Polka Theatre

240 Broadway, SW19 1SB (8543 4888/ www.polkatheatre.com). South Wimbledon tube/Wimbledon tube/rail, then 57, 93, 219, 493 bus. **Open** *Box office* (by phone)

9.30am-4.30pm Mon; 9am-6pm Tue-Fri; 10am-4.30pm Sat; (in person) 9.30am-4.30pm Tue-Fri; 10am-4.30pm Sat. **Tickets** £6.50-£11.50. **Credit** MC, V. This children's theatre pioneer has been up and running since 1979. Daily shows are staged by touring companies in the main auditorium, while shorter works for babies and toddlers take over the Adventure Theatre once a week. There are also in-house productions, workshops and storytelling sessions for families and schools. Dramatic offerings aside, there's an appealing little playground and Wendy house, a reading corner and a cheerful café – a top place for lunch. The Polka Youth Theatre (£80 per term, subsidised places available) runs once-a-week sessions for under-13s, while day-long workshops are a treat for children in the school holidays. There are after-school groups for three to 13s, with end-of-term performances for friends and family. *Buggy access. Café. Disabled access: lift, toilet. Nappy-changing facilities.*

Shakespeare's Globe

21 New Globe Walk, SE1 9DT (7401 9919/tours 7902 1500/www.shakespeares-globe.org). Southwark or Mansion House tube/London Bridge tube/rail. **Open** *Box office* 10am-6pm daily. *Tours* May-Sept 9am-12.30pm daily. Oct-Apr 10am-5pm daily. **Tickets** £5-£33. *Tours* £10; £8.50 reductions; £6.50 5-15s; free under-5s; £25 family (2+3). **Credit** AmEx, MC, V. **Map** p318 O7. Fidgety younger kids won't be inclined to sit – or stand – through the shows at this meticulously-reconstructed Elizabethan theatre, but older children will appreciate the atmospheric setting. Eight to 11s can also attend Childplay sessions on selected Saturdays, watching part of the play as groundlings, and taking part in themed workshops. A huge range of talks, tours and activities – many conducted by staff wearing full period costume – takes place with schools during term time, while holiday workshops and excellent seasonal events open the floor to families. *See also p30* **Great Days Out**. *Café. Disabled access: lift, toilet. Nappy-changing facilities. Restaurant. Shop.*

Unicorn Theatre for Children

147 Tooley Street, SE1 2HZ (box office 7645 0560/www.unicorntheatre.com). London Bridge tube/rail. **Open** *Box office* 9.30am-6pm Mon-Fri; 10am-6pm Sat; noon-5pm Sun. **Tickets** £9.50-£14.50. **Credit** MC, V. **Map** p319 R9. Set on the Southbank, this airy, modern theatre was designed in collaboration with local schoolchildren. A giant sculpture of a white unicorn rears above theatre-goers in the foyer, while performance spaces include the 300-seater Weston Theatre and more intimate Clore Theatre. Expect a few surprises: in summer 2009, the stage set for a production of *Twelfth Night* was a living, growing garden, which happily sprouted away during the month-long run. In-house productions are accompanied by special Family Days, where everyone's encouraged to muck in with the activities and workshops; prices include tickets to the show, and the chance to meet the actors afterwards. Visiting theatre companies also drop in for shorter runs, presenting all sorts of brilliant plays and puppet shows for nought to 19s. *Buggy access. Café. Disabled access: lift, toilet.*

Warehouse Theatre

62 Dingwall Road, Croydon CR0 2NF (8680 4060/www.warehousetheatre.co.uk). East Croydon rail. **Open** *Box office* 10am-5pm Mon; 10am-8.30pm Tue; 10am-10pm Wed-Sat; 3-7pm Sun. **Tickets** £8-£15; £5 2-16s. **Credit** AmEx, MC, V. Housed in a converted Victorian cement warehouse, hidden away behind East Croydon station, the Warehouse is an unassuming gem. Theatre4Kidz shows take place every Saturday, while a variety of touring shows entertain those as young as two. Croydon Young People's Theatre (CRYPT) offers a creative base for 13- to 16-year-olds; it meets 2-5pm every Saturday during term time, and puts on an annual summer show. The fee per term is a mere £12, and application forms are available online. *Bar. Buggy access. Café. Disabled access: toilet.*

West End shows

As well as calling the box office to find out what ages shows are suitable for, it's a good idea to check the running length. With many musicals clocking in at two hours, the evening can turn into a frenzy of wriggling and needing-the-loo requests. If you've got young children in your party, it's probably best to avoid the West End altogether and go to a more intimate, child-specific venue in another part of town, where the plays are shorter, the house lights brighter and the bangs less likely to scare.

For two weeks in August, families can take advantage of **Kids Week** (www.kidsweek.co.uk). Run by the **Society of London Theatres** (SOLT, 7557 6700, www.officiallondontheatre.co.uk), it offers five to 16s free admission to West End shows, provided they are accompanied by a paying adult; up to two additional children can get in at half-price. Children can also go backstage, meet the stars and take part in workshops. For more on Kids Week, and information on the capital's best family-friendly shows, subscribe to the free family bulletin on the SOLT website.

Billy Elliot the Musical

Victoria Palace Theatre, Victoria Street, SW1E 5EA (0870 895 5577/www.billyelliot themusical.com). Victoria tube/rail. **Times** 7.30pm Mon-Sat. *Matinée* 2.30pm Thur, Sat. **Tickets** £17.50-£62.50. **Credit** AmEx, MC, V. **Map** p316 H10.

It would take a pretty cynical heart not to be warmed by this tale of a motherless miner's son with a passion for ballet, set to music by none other than Sir Elton John. The production (adapted from the film) contains strong language, and isn't suitable for under-eights. *Bars. Disabled access: toilet.*

Grease

Piccadilly Theatre, 16 Denman Street, W1D 7DY (0844 412 6666/www.greasethemusical. co.uk). Piccadilly Circus tube. **Times** 7.30pm Mon-Thur, Sat; 8.30pm Fri. *Matinée* 3pm Sat; 5pm Fri. **Tickets** £15-£53.50. **Credit** AmEx, MC, V. **Map** p316 J6.

Grease is still the word – who can resist Danny's quiff, or show-stopping tunes like *You're the One that I Want* and *Greased Lightnin'*? Die-hard fans certainly can't get enough of it – though the younger generation might think *High School Musical* has the edge. Philistines! *Bars. Disabled access: toilet.*

Hairspray

Shaftesbury Theatre, 210 Shaftesbury Avenue, WC2H 8DP (7379 5399/www.hairspraythe musical.co.uk). Holborn or Tottenham Court Road tube. **Times** 7.30pm Mon-Sat. *Matinée* 3pm Thur, Sat. **Tickets** £22.50-£62.50. **Credit** AmEx, MC, V. **Map** p315 K6.

Beehive-haired, chubby-cheeked heroine Tracy Turnblad shimmies her way to success – and makes a stand against '60s racial prejudice on the way. Cheesy, preposterous and insanely uplifting stuff for older kids. *Bars. Disabled access: toilet.*

Legally Blonde

Savoy Theatre, Strand, WC2R 0ET (0870 164 8787/www.legallyblondethemusical.co.uk). Charing Cross tube/rail. **Times** 7.30pm Mon-Sat. *Matineé* 2.30pm Tue, Sat. **Tickets** £20-£60. **Credit** AmEx, MC, V. **Map** p317 L7.

Polka Theatre. *See p190.*

Opening in December 2009, this hotly-awaited Broadway transfer follows the exploits of its indomitably girly, pink-loving heroine (played by Sheridan Smith) and her equally chic chihuahua, Bruiser, as the pair hit Harvard Law School. *Bars. Disabled access: toilet.*

Les Misérables

Queen's Theatre, Shaftesbury Avenue, W1D 6BA (0844 847 1607/www.lesmis.com). Leicester Square or Piccadilly Circus tube. **Times** 7.30pm Mon-Sat. *Matinée* 2.30pm Wed, Sat. **Tickets** £17.50-£60. **Credit** AmEx, MC, V. **Map** p315 K6.

Victor Hugo's tale of revolution in 19th-century France has been running for over 20 years – longer than the young visitors to its Kids' Club have been alive. The two-and-a-half hour experience gives eights to 15s the chance to tour backstage, meet a cast member and re-enact a scene from the show. *Bars. Disabled access: toilet.*

Lion King

Lyceum Theatre, Wellington Street, WC2E 7RQ (0844 844 0005/www.disney.co.uk/ musicaltheatre). Covent Garden tube/Charing

Cross tube/rail. **Times** 7.30pm Tue-Sat.
Matinée 2pm Wed, Sat; 3pm Sun. **Tickets** £20-
£59.50. **Credit** AmEx, MC, V. **Map** p317 L7.
Most kids are familiar with Simba thanks to
Disney's classic film; the stage production ups
the ante with stunning sets, a combination of
puppetry and live actors and a heady cocktail of
West End choruses and African rhythms.
Bars. Disabled access: toilet.

Mamma Mia!

*Prince of Wales Theatre, Coventry Street,
W1V 8AS (0844 482 5115/www.mamma-
mia.com). Piccadilly Circus tube.* **Times**
7.30pm Mon-Thur, Sat; 8.30pm Fri. *Matinée*
5pm Fri; 3pm Sat. **Tickets** £20-£59. **Credit**
AmEx, MC, V. **Map** p317 K7.
Despite a somewhat sketchy plot, *Mamma Mia!*
is awash with feel-good, singalong Abba hits.
Bars. Disabled access: toilet.

Oliver!

*Theatre Royal, Catherine Street, WC2B 5JF
(0844 482 5138/www.oliverthemusical.com).
Covent Garden tube.* **Times** 7.30pm Mon-Sat.
Matinée 2.30pm Wed, Sat. **Tickets** £17.50-
£60. **Credit** AmEx, MC, V. **Map** p317 L/M6.

Give the kids a taste for Dickens with the
famous tale of the boy who asked for more;
irresistibly catchy numbers like *Food, Glorious
Food, Consider Yourself* and *Oom Pah Pah*
ensure that the evening goes with a swing.
Bars. Disabled access: toilet.

Sister Act

*London Palladium, Argyll Street, W1F 7TF
(0871 297 0748/www.sisteractthemusical.com).
Oxford Circus tube.* **Times** 7.30pm Mon-Sat.
Matinée 3pm Wed, Sat. **Tickets** £17.50-£85.
Credit AmEx, MC, V. **Map** p314 J6.
The hot ticket at the Palladium is *Sister Act* – a
spirited adaptation of the hit 1992 film. Lounge
singer Deloris Von Cartier is on the run from the
mob and decides to go undercover as a nun,
causing mayhem but improving the choir no end.
Bars. Disabled access: toilet.

Stomp

*Ambassadors Theatre, West Street, WC2H
9ND (0844 811 2334/www.stomp.co.uk).
Leicester Square tube.* **Times** 8pm Mon, Thur-
Sat; 6pm Sun. *Matinée* 3pm Thur, Sat; 3pm
Sun. **Tickets** £25-£47.50. **Credit** AmEx,
MC, V. **Map** p315 K6.

An international smash hit, Stomp finds music in all kinds of everyday objects – including the kitchen sink. The show's a blast, and the lack of dialogue makes it accessible to everyone. *Bars.*

Wicked

Apollo Victoria, Wilton Road, SW1V 1LG (0844 826 8000/www.wickedthemusical.co.uk). Victoria tube/rail. **Times** 7.30pm Mon-Sat. *Matinée* 2.30pm Wed, Sat. **Tickets** £15-£60. **Credit** AmEx, MC, V. **Map** p316 H10.
The much-maligned Wicked Witch of the West wasn't really wicked at all, according to this smart, pacy rejoinder to the *Wizard of Oz*. For eights and above.
Bars. Disabled access: toilet.

WORKSHOPS & ACTIVITIES

Brilliant Kids

7 Station Terrace, NW10 5RT (8964 4120/ www.brilliantkids.co.uk). Kensal Green tube/ Kensal Rise rail. **Open** 8am-6pm Mon-Fri; 9am-5pm Sat; 10am-4pm Sun. **Fees** £5-£7/ class. **Credit** MC, V.
Attached to an awesome little café (*see p224*), this sociable, Ofsted-registered art and activities club runs junk modelling and collage sessions, cookery clubs and gardening for children aged from six months. Supervised play sessions for one-and-aboves give parents the chance to take a breather and sip their coffee in peace.
Buggy access. Café. Disabled access: toilet.

Maggie & Rose

58 Pembroke Road, W8 6NX (7371 2200/ www.maggieandrose.co.uk). Earl's Court or West Kensington tube. **Classes** times vary; phone for details. **Fees** £500/yr membership; £180/12wk course. **Credit** MC, V.
This 'private members' club' for families is aimed squarely at upwardly mobile mummies and daddies. Membership brings discounts on its imaginative range of activities, but prices are still steep – half an hour's Baby Bunnies Music during Easter half term costs £12.50 for members and £17.50 for non-members. Most activities run on a termly basis; birthday parties can also be arranged.
Buggy access.

That Place on the Corner

1-3 Green Lanes, N16 9BS (7704 0079/ www.thatplaceonthecorner.co.uk). Highbury & Islington tube/rail/Canonbury rail/21, 73, 141, *276, 341, 476 bus.* **Open** 9.30am-6pm Mon-Thur; 9.30am-8pm Fri; 10am-3pm Sat; 10am-3.30pm Sun. **Fees** £4-£5. **Credit** MC, V.
Alongside its splendid, family-friendly café (*see p234*), That Place offers a whole host of activities. Preschoolers can get stuck into Rucksack Music, Drama Tots and Tip Toes Dance, to name but a few of the classes, while kids of all ages are welcome at the face-painting and pizza-baking sessions.
Buggy access. Café. Disabled access: toilet. Nappy-changing facilities.

Archaeology

Young Archaeologists Club @ UCL

Institute of Archaeology, 31-34 Gordon Square, WC1H 0PY (7679 7495/www.ucl.ac.uk/ archaeology).
The Institute of Archaeology supports a children's club for eight- to 16-year-olds which meets on the third Saturday of each month, from 11am till 1pm; call first before going.

Museum of London Archaeology Service

7410 2228/www.museumoflondon archaeology.org.uk.
Keen beans can sign up for The Museum of London's Young Archaeologists Club (YAC), aimed at eight to 16s. It has two branches in central London, with once-monthly meet-ups in Hackney and Rotherhithe. Activities include walking the Thames' foreshore to collect objects washed up at low tide, identifying animal bones and making mosaics, Roman-style.

Art & crafts

All Fired Up

34 East Dulwich Road, SE22 9AX (7732 6688/www.allfiredupceramics.co.uk). East Dulwich or Peckham Rye rail. **Open** 9.30am-6pm Mon, Tue, Sat; 9.30am-10pm Wed-Fri; 10.30am-4.30pm Sun. **Fees** *Studio* £3/day. *Workshops & courses* phone for details. **Credit** MC, V.
The shelves of plain white ceramics (from cartoon characters to sensible crockery) are crying out for colour – which kids happily apply, with varying levels of accuracy. Tables are equipped with palettes, sponges, water and brushes, while friendly staff offer tactful advice. Painted objects are glazed, fired, gift-wrapped and ready for collection in ten days. Birthday parties are run for groups of eight or more children, aged five to 15 (from £10 per head).
Buggy access.

Art 4 Fun

172 West End Lane, NW6 1SD (7794 0800/ www.art4fun.com). West Hampstead tube/rail. **Open** 10am-6pm Mon, Wed-Sun; 10am-8pm Tue. **Fees** *Studio* £5.95/day. *Workshops & courses* phone for details. **Credit** MC, V.
Children can give full rein to their artistic talents, daubing designs on to ceramics, T-shirts, tiles and flower pots. Tie-dye, mosaic-making, pottery and glass-painting are among the other options. Arty parties are a speciality, with no minimum numbers required, and there are half- and full-day school-holiday workshops for six to tens. *Buggy access. Café.*

Art Yard

318 Upper Richmond Road West, SW14 7JN (8878 1336/www.artyard.co.uk). Mortlake rail/33 bus. **Classes** *Term-time* 4-5.30pm Mon, Tue, Thur. *School hols* 10am-3pm Mon-Fri. **Fees** £145/term. **Credit** MC, V.
This appealingly chaotic, colourful studio hosts after-school art clubs and school holiday courses and workshops. They might involve creating paintings, prints, collages and papier-mâché masterpieces – or even a spot of cookery.

London Brass Rubbing Centre

St Martin-in-the-Fields, Trafalgar Square, WC2N 4JJ (7766 1122/www2.stmartin-in-the-fields.org). Leicester Square tube/Charing Cross tube/rail. **Open** 10am-7pm Mon-Wed; 10am-9pm Thur-Sat; 11.30am-6pm Sun. **Fees** from £4.50. **Credit** MC, V. **Map** p317 L7.
See p67 **Bold as brass.**

Papered Parlour

7 Prescott Place, SW4 6BS (7627 8703/www.thepaperedparlour.co.uk). Clapham Common or Clapham North tube. **Classes** *Term-time* 4.30-6pm Thur; 10am-noon Sat. *Holidays* 10am-4pm Thur; 10am-noon Sat. **Fees** *Term-time* £72/6wk. *Holidays* £35/day; £12 Sat. **No credit cards.**
Kitted out like a 1940s parlour, this lovely little place runs a Fidgeting Fingers After School club (five to 11s), with lashings of sculpture, sewing and painting. Holiday workshops might involve making a 1930s dollshouse or designing quirky T-shirts, while birthday parties eschew the usual clichéd themes in favour of Mad Hatter's Tea Party- or Willy Wonka-inspired arty challenges.

Shirley Stewart's Pottery Courses

Lewisham Arthouse, 140 Lewisham Way, SE14 6PD (8694 9011/www.shirley-stewart.co.uk). Deptford Bridge DLR/New Cross rail. **Fees** £10. **Credit** phone for details.

Lewisham Arthouse is a co-operative based in a Grade II-listed building. Artists rent studio space here, and Shirley Stewart is among them. Her throwing and studio pottery workshops for five and overs are held during term time, though extra sessions can be arranged for the holidays. Parties are available for £12 per child, which includes materials and firings. *Buggy access. Disabled access (ground floor): toilet.*

Smarty Paints

85 Nightingale Lane, SW12 8NX (8772 8702/ www.smartypaints.co.uk). Clapham South tube/ Wandsworth Common rail. **Open** 10am-6pm Mon-Sat; 11am-6pm Sun. **Fees** *Studio* £6. **Credit** MC, V.
Everyone can get involved at this bright ceramic painting studio, next to Munchkin Lane children's café: printing small children's paint-covered hands and feet is a popular option, though there are all manner of stencils and brushes for more complex designs. Children's classes include T-shirt painting. *Buggy access.*

Stitchclub

www.stitchclub.co.uk.
Stitchclub runs sewing classes for children aged from eight and up at 11 London venues; birthday party packages are available too, for a maximum of eight guests. If you can't get to the lessons, the online store sells dinky sewing and knitting kits, plus kids' sewing machines and craft books.

Circus skills

Albert & Friends Instant Circus

8237 1170/www.albertandfriendsinstant circus.co.uk.
Held at two west London venues, Albert's circus workshops teach three to 16s skills such as juggling, diabolo and stilt-walking. Over-eights can attend the aerial sessions and learn corde lisse, static trapeze and other daredevil feats. For more, *see p196* **Clowning around.**

Circus Space

Coronet Street, N1 6HD (7729 9522/www.thecircusspace.co.uk). Old Street tube/rail.
Accompanied by their intrepid parents, under-eights can enrol for a term of Tiny Tops circus skills and games. The Sunday morning 'Little Top' course introduces eight- to 12-year-olds to acrobatics, juggling, static trapeze and more; once tutors think kids are ready, they can join the Big Tops. Gifted over-11s who are serious about circus can try out for the London Youth Circus.

Activities

Clowning around

'A physical activity that requires you to think' is how the eponymous Albert of **Albert & Friends Instant Circus** (*see p195*) sums up the somewhat nebulous discipline of circus skills. 'Circus allows young people to challenge themselves physically and mentally, in ways children just aren't often asked to these days,' says Albert (real name Ian Scott Owens). 'What we try to do is show young people what they are capable of, and give them some goals.' He also believes circus helps children concentrate better at school, and is currently making a case for circus skills to become part of the National Curriculum.

A registered charity, Albert & Friends operates out of Hammersmith's Riverside Studios, running holiday and after school workshops in the borough, and touring schools and disability care centres across the capital. Started in 1983 by Albert/Scott Owens (a classically trained musician turned clown from Australia) in west London parks, the organisation has grown over a quarter of a century to become the biggest youth circus in the UK. With links around the world, it has performed at a stellar line-up of festivals and events, from the Macy's Thanksgiving Day parade in New York to the Edinburgh Festival.

'We never tell anyone they can't do something,' says Albert. 'Their physical make-up doesn't matter – it's up to them to set their own goals. We currently have a girl in a wheelchair who is determined to walk on stilts.'

At a holiday workshop we drop into, the atmosphere is open and relaxed – a far cry from the disciplinarian approach of sports such as gymnastics. Children take the lead, helping themselves from a box of tricks that includes diabolos, hoops, stilts, ropes, balls to balance on, unicycles and a low tightrope. Staff, all ex-Albert's pupils themselves, give the kids room to experiment while being on hand to assist, demonstrate equipment, oversee safety and encourage kids to push a newly-mastered skill a step further. Many of the children have been coming for several years and work together in their own groups, helping and encouraging each other, and sharing new skills. There is very little down time or queuing for a turn; in other words, no time to get bored.

'We tend to push them quite quickly into stilt walking to give them a sense of achievement,' says Albert. 'Unicycling takes a bit longer. Ground skills [diabolos, rings, balancing] are the easiest, but young people do take to the air quite quickly. The skills you need to perform things like trapeze do require a certain level of physical aptitude, though.

'We try to broaden the subject out by teaching things like street dance alongside the circus skills. We have one girl who is a champion Irish dancer and great at double dutching [skipping with two ropes, turned in opposite directions], so she's learning to do both on stilts.' A couple of boys in the group, meanwhile, are trying to master the art of skipping... on unicycles.

After just one day, a complete circus skills novice can have learnt to walk on stilts while simultaneously spinning a plate; performed a human pyramid; and fallen off a unicycle. They will feel incredibly pleased with themselves.

'We had to use our brains as well as our bodies,' she says. 'On stilts you can't just stand still or you'll fall over. You have to keep moving. The best part was getting to try things you don't usually get to do.'
Albert & Friends will be at the 2009 Edinburgh Festival, and hosting the next London International Youth Circus in 2010.

Cooking

Billingsgate Seafood Training School

Office 30, Billingsgate Market, Trafalgar Way, E14 5ST (7517 3548/www.seafood training.org). Canary Wharf tube. **Open** phone or check website. **Fees** check website. **No credit cards.**
Parent and child courses at Billingsgate's superb seafood school teach eight to 14s some seriously useful skills: cleaning squid, skinning fish, preparing sardines and gutting mackerel. Participants consume one of the three fishy dishes they've made for lunch, taking the other two home to impress the rest of the family – along with all sorts of gory stories with which to impress squeamish younger siblings.

La Cucina Caldesi

118 Marylebone Lane, W1U 2QF (7487 0750/ www.caldesi.com). Baker Street/Regent's Park tube. **Open** 10.30am-12.30pm Sat. **Fees** £40. **Credit** AmEx, MC, V.
School holidays and half terms, plus the odd weekend, bring brilliant kids' classes to this smart Italian cookery school. Sunday-morning Family Lunch sessions start with a trip to Marylebone Farmer's Market; afterwards, you'll be shown how to transform your purchases into tasty seasonal pasta dishes, salads and desserts.

Kids' Cookery School

107 Gunnersbury Lane, W3 8HQ (8992 8882/ www.thekidscookeryschool.co.uk). Acton Town tube. **Open** *Office* 9am-5.30pm Mon-Fri. **Fees** *School hols* £15/75mins; £30/2.5hrs; £50/5hrs. **No credit cards.**
A registered charity company with its own space in west London, the Kids' Cookery School is dedicated to bringing cooking into young people's lives. On-site classes and workshops run throughout the week and during the school holidays, while parties for children aged five and over are held on Saturdays (£30 per child); don't forget to bring your own birthday cake.
Buggy access. Disabled access.

Munchkins

8269 1331/www.munchkinskidscooking.co.uk.
Set up by a friendly former primary school teacher, Munchkins runs children's cooking courses and private classes in term time and during the holidays. Its hands-on, jolly sessions work wonders with fussy eaters. The team can also arrange baking or make-your-own-meal parties, with optional extras such as games and face-painting; prices start from £110 for six kids.

Film & new media

For a cinema-mad child's dream birthday treat, check out Movie Parties (*see p148*).

Film Club

www.filmclub.org
Film Club aims to put movies on the (extra) curriculum by loaning films to participating after-school film clubs, free of charge, and running specially devised film seasons. The website also gives a useful list of films, categorised by age group.

Film London

www.filmlondon.org.uk.
London's film and media agency supports projects across the capital.

Filmsteps

0870 024 2522/www.filmsteps.com.
Fast-paced five-day summer holiday film schools (£275) teach seven- to 16-year-olds the essentials of making a feature film, from planning the storyboards to operating the cameras. Thrillingly, their handiwork is premièred in the autumn, at a local cinema. Meanwhile, term-time Film Schools meet in Maida Vale, Belsize Park and Teddington once a week, producing everything from pop videos to film trailers; it costs £235 per term, but there are sibling discounts and scholarships.

First Light

www.firstlightmovies.com.
Funded by the UK Film Council, First Light funds film projects for five- to 18-year-olds, offering courses across the country via schools and educational groups. Its subsidiary website, www.filmstreet.co.uk, provides a bright and breezy starting point for under-12s exploring filmmaking, while www.media-box.co.uk offers funding for projects involving 13- to 19-year-olds.

Mouth That Roars

23 Charlotte Road, EC2A 3PB (7729 2323/ www.mouththatroars.com). Old Street tube/rail. **Open** 5-8pm Wed, Thur; noon-5pm Sun.
This east London charity offers training in video production. Thirteens to 19s who live in Hackney can make a film in a day at its studio and editing suite (sessions are free and run on a drop-in basis), which also hosts weekly film screenings.

Young Film Academy

20 Fitzroy Square, W1T 6EJ (7387 4341/ www.youngfilmacademy.co.uk). Notting Hill Gate tube. **Fees** from £95/day; £390/4 day course. **No credit cards.**

Activities

'Passion starts early' is the YFA's guiding principle – and its ever-expanding programme of courses, workshops, schools events and parties aims to give young film-makers a helping hand. So far, it has enabled over 5,000 seven- to 18-year-olds to make their first film. Check online for details of its fast-paced, fun courses, and look out for its one-day workshops at big film festivals (sessions at the London Children's Film Festival were a sell-out success) and during the summer hols.

Modern languages

Club Petit Pierrot
7385 5565/www.clubpetitpierrot.uk.com. **Classes** phone for details. **Fees** from £99/term. **No credit cards.**
Pupils at Club Petit Pierrot (ranging from eight months to nine years old) are taught in small groups, by native teachers, with an emphasis on learning through play. The lessons are entirely in French – though plenty of songs, rhymes, dancing, storytelling, arts and crafts and puppets mean it's not half as scary as it sounds. Younger children attend with their parents at the *ateliers des petites*, while over-threes can be dropped off for longer sessions. Saturday and holiday clubs come highly recommended, and home tuition is also available.

Easy Mandarin
Pont Street, SW1X 0AA (7828 2998/www.easy mandarinuk.com). Victoria tube/rail. **Classes** *3-5s, 6-8s* 9.30-10.30am, 10.30-11.30am Sat; *9-14s, 15-18s* 11.30am-1pm Sat. **Fees** vary; phone for details. **No credit cards.**
Ambitious parents are racing to sign their offspring up for these classes. It's just as well that Miss Jin, Miss Fei and their colleagues run such fun-filled Knightsbridge- and Victoria-based Saturday morning Chinese classes for ages three to 18.

French & Spanish à la Carte
97 Revelstoke Road, SW18 5NL (8946 4777/www.frenchandspanishalacarte.co.uk). Wimbledon Park tube/Earlsfield rail. **Classes** phone for details. **Fees** from £115/term. **No credit cards.**
This language school gives south London's two- to five-year-olds a head start with its weekly playgroups (Tuesday and Thursday, or Wednesday and Friday mornings), involving an hour of activity and an hour of free play, while a teacher chats to them in French or Spanish. After-school clubs and holiday courses are offered for older children.

Le Club Tricolore
7924 4649/www.leclubtricolore.co.uk. **Classes** phone for details. **Fees** from £160/term; £30/yr membership. **No credit cards.**
Teresa Scibor and her team of native French speakers hold mother and toddler groups in the Northcote Road area where children absorb the language by means of role-playing or sing-alongs. In the holidays, the team run fun activity days (£35 for five-and-overs; £25 half days for under-fives).

WILDLIFE
For details of London's aquariums, city farms, wetland reserves and zoos, *see pp129-140.*

Oasis Children's Nature Garden
Larkhall Lane & Studley Road, SW4 2SP (7498 2329/www.oasisplay.org.uk). Stockwell tube. **Open** *After-school Club* 3.30-5.30pm Wed-Fri. *Term-time* 11am-2pm Sat. *School hols* 10am-noon, 2-4pm Tue-Sat. **Admission** 50p.
Once an unloved and unlovely wasteland, the Nature Garden is now a flourishing green getaway from the inner city, with its own wildflower meadow, ponds and woodland. Activities at its Saturday Nature Club, after-school Play Project and summer holiday sessions include pond-dipping and gardening, as well as arts and crafts and cookery. Sessions are aimed at five-and-overs, although younger children are welcome if accompanied by an adult; there are also Friday morning meet-ups specifically for under-fives and their carers. The garden is one of three projects run by the Oasis Children's Venture (the others are cycling and karting centres); see the website for details.

Roots & Shoots
Walnut Tree Walk, SE11 6DN (7587 1131/ www.roots-and-shoots.org.uk). Lambeth North tube. **Open** 10am-4pm Mon-Fri; phone before visiting. **Admission** free; donations welcomed.
There's a wealth of plants and wildlife crammed into this peaceful, half-acre garden – tended by a charity that has offered vocational training for young people for 25 years. Everyone's welcome, from the beetles that live in the log pile to the local schoolchildren who come here to discover the garden's insects, animals and wild flowers. The centre is also home to the London Beekeepers' Association; the honey – fantastically flavoured because of the diversity of plants available from a million city gardens – is sold here, but sells out in a trice. Note the restricted opening hours, and call before visiting.

Sport & Leisure

Burn off excess energy with a whole host of sporting pursuits.

London is increasingly operating under the shadow of the 2012 Olympic Games. In particular, and quite understandably, when it comes to sport. Last year, the government pledged to spend £32 million on making 'coaching and competition' available to all children by 2012, and has set a curriculum target of five hours of sport and recreation a week.

Even if all schools reached this target (and campaigners say this is unlikely), children need to exercise for longer than that to burn off the calories they consume. Obesity in children is a growing concern. Luckily, in London there's a wider choice of sports facilities than elsewhere in the country, and despite London's much-publicised swimming pool crisis (there aren't enough to go round, let alone train our Olympic competitors), new sports and leisure centres are still being built. Oh, and don't forget all those gorgeous free green spaces listed in **Parks & Gardens** (*see pp105-128*).

There are plenty of professionals to help make exercise fun. Organisations running activity clubs for toddlers include **Tumbletots** (www.tumbletots.com) and **Crechendo** (www.crechendo.com), while local councils run affordable (often free) sports camps in the school holidays. Many independent schools host a variety of private youth sports organisations that put on intensive rugby, football, tennis and cricket coaching when term ends. These courses may be more expensive than their council counterparts, but they're worth the money for children who show a genuine talent for a particular sport. To find a specific course or club near you, try your council website, or contact the individual sport's governing bodies (*see p208*).

CLIMBING

Castle Climbing Centre
Green Lanes, N4 2HA (8211 7000/ www.castle-climbing.co.uk). Manor House tube.
This Stoke Newington climbing centre is housed in an old water tower. Children's classes for nine-to 14-year-olds are held on Monday and Tuesday, and during the holidays. For private tuition, the Gecko Club (www.geckos.co.uk) is based here (£40/hr plus £10 admission). Call for details of the party service.

Mile End Climbing Wall
Haverfield Road, E3 5BE (8980 0289/ www.mileendwall.org.uk). Mile End tube.
Popular east London wall. Eight- to 16-year-olds can attend beginner sessions (£6) on Friday evenings and Saturday mornings. Birthday parties can be held here, and there's a busy summer holiday programme.

CRICKET

Brit Oval
Kennington, SE11 5SS (7582 7764/ www.surreycricket.com). Oval tube.
Admission *Surrey matches* £12-£20; £6-£10 under-16s. **Credit** MC, V.
Surrey's homely – but still Test-class – cricket ground here in Kennington offers an admirable youth programme.

Lord's Cricket Ground
St John's Wood Road, NW8 8QN (Middlesex 7289 1300/www.middlesexccc.com; MCC 7432 1000/www.lords.org). St John's Wood tube/13, 46, 82, 113, 274 bus. **Admission** Middlesex matches £14-£20; £5-£7 under-16s, reductions. **Credit** MC, V.
Even the youngest of fans will have heard of Lord's, the home ground of Middlesex and main ground for England. Tours allow visitors a look behind the scenes, including access to the Long

Room, which boasts an art gallery depicting the great and good of the sport. Fans can also have a look at the players' dressing rooms and the MCC Museum, where the Ashes urn is stored. For more details, *see p98*.

Playing cricket

Cricket is still associated with toffs – not helped by a sharp decline in cricket-playing in state schools. Various initiatives have been launched to raise the profile of the national summer sport among children and teens. Back in 1990, a group of volunteers formed Capital Kids Cricket (www.capitalkidscricket.co.uk) to promote cricket for children in the inner city. The clubs listed below have also stepped in to promote coaching for 16-and-unders. Try the following indoor centres:

Ken Barrington Cricket Centre
Brit Oval, Kennington, SE11 5SS (7820 5739). Oval tube.

MCC Indoor School
Lord's Cricket Ground, St John's Wood Road, NW8 8QN (7616 8612/www.lords.org/kids). St John's Wood tube/13, 46, 82, 113, 274 bus.

Middlesex County Cricket Club
East End Road, N3 2TA (8346 8020/ www.middlesexccc.com). Finchley Central tube.

CYCLING

Despite the increasing popularity of cycling, British children still fall well behind their continental peers when it comes to taking the bike to school. In Britain, 90 per cent own bikes but less than three per cent cycle to school. Safety is the issue – a UK cyclist is 12 times more likely to be killed or injured than a Danish one.

In 2008, the government pledged £55 million to train pupils to ride safely. Safe Routes to Schools supports projects that encourage cycling and walking to school, by improving street design, calming traffic and linking with the 12,000 mile (19,000 kilometre) National Cycle Network. Most local authorities include Safe Routes to Schools schemes in their local transport plans. Sustrans (www.sustrans.org.uk) is the pressure group that is working to create a safer environment for cycling. The following organisations offer more

information: Bike to School Week (www.bikeforall.net); the London Cycling Campaign (www.lcc.org.uk); Go-Ride (www.go-ride.org.uk).

Bikeability
www.bikeability.org.uk.
A scheme designed to give young cyclists the skills and confidence to ride their bikes on the roads. Kids are encouraged to achieve three levels of cycling proficiency.

Capital Sport – Gentle Cycling
01296 631 671/www.capital-sport.co.uk
Gentle cycling holidays and bike tours through London and along the River Thames. The Thames and Royalty Tour and day tours from London Bridge are ideal for families and take in palaces, royal parks and riverside cycling.

Cycle Training UK
7231 6005/www.cycletraining.co.uk.
Instructors offer individual tuition and accompanied journeys to school anywhere in Greater London. Of its participants, 81% have said they cycle more often and more confidently. The website has details of which London boroughs offer free or subsidised training.

Cycling Instructor
www.cyclinginstructor.com.
Cycling lessons in schools for adults and children. The training organisation delivers Bikeability qualifications (*see above*) too.

Herne Hill Velodrome
Burbage Road, SE24 9HE (www.vcl.org.uk). Herne Hill rail.
Many south London children begin their cycling careers here at the venerable home of track cycling, founded in 1892. The VC Londres club was set up to encourage children on to bikes, and holds weekly Friday evening sessions.

London Recumbents
Battersea Park 7498 6543/ Dulwich Park 8299 6636/www.londonrecumbents.co.uk.
London Recumbents offers an enormous range of bikes for hire and for sale at Dulwich and Battersea Parks. There are various trailer attachments and tandems to accommodate children, plus high-quality kids' bikes (including the head-turning recumbents).

London School of Cycling
7249 3779/www.londonschoolofcycling.co.uk.
Private tuition for all ages and abilities, as well as cycle-maintenance workshops.

Castle Climbing Centre. *See p199.*

Activities

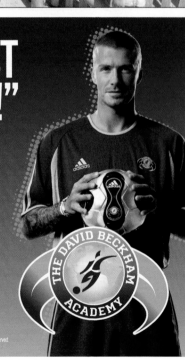

FOOTBALL

Playing football

Boys and girls over six can learn football skills on coaching courses, fun days and skills clinics at all of London's professional clubs, staffed by FA-qualified coaches. Check the club websites listed on pp204-205 (details are usually listed on the 'Community' pages) for venues and dates. The FA have created a resource, 'Girls United', which includes a club finder facility: visit www.thefa.com/girlsunited.

David Beckham Academy
East Parkside, Greenwich Peninsula, SE10 0JF (8269 4620/www.thedavidbeckham academy.com). North Greenwich tube.
It's not just the Becks memorabilia that grabs children's interest – there are also two full-size indoor pitches and highly qualified coaches. The football camps run Monday to Friday in school holidays and follow the same lines as the schools education programme, plus coaching and skills sessions. Courses are non-residential and cost £190 (three days) or £270 (five days). That might seem pricey, but all children receive a package of Adidas kit, including footwear, as well as healthy lunches and refreshments. There are also one and two day (£85/£140) courses and after-school sessions (£6); call or check the website for details.

Elms Football School
8954 8787/www.theelms.co.uk.
The Elms in Stanmore offers Saturday and Sunday coaching, holiday courses and a school of excellence.

European Football Academy
www.footballcamps.co.uk.
Week-long residential and day camps in England, Ireland, Scotland, Germany and Luxembourg, as well as Safari camps in Zambia and Malawi. They take place in school holidays for girls, boys and teams aged eight to 18.

Football Academy
Langston Road, Loughton, Essex IG10 3TQ (0870 084 2111/www.footballacademyuk.com). Debden tube.
This centre has ten all-weather, floodlit, five-a-side pitches for hire. Holiday and weekend sessions are led by FA-qualified coaches under the guidance of former West Ham star John Moncur and other ex-professionals, and children's parties can be arranged.

Goals Soccer Centres
www.goalsfootball.co.uk.
There are 12 of these centres in London. Each has all-weather, floodlit pitches with junior leagues, birthday parties and coaching at weekends and school holidays.

Lambeth Dribblers
8835 9570.
Part-funded by Chelsea, this project provides free coaching for young children on the astroturf at Brixton Recreation Centre, while enabling enthusiastic dads (it's specifically aimed at fathers, not mothers) to have a kickaround with their kids.

Little Kickers
01235 859250/www.littlekickers.co.uk.
Hugely popular classes developed by a group of FA-qualified coaches and nursery-school teachers for pre-schoolers (18 months and up) as a gentle introduction to football. The programme operates all over London.

London Football Academy
8882 9100/www.londonfootballacademy.co.uk.
Holiday courses, skill schools, birthday parties and inexpensive Saturday morning soccer school sessions in Alexandra Park.

North London Girls League
07912 050374/email natalie.huntley@londonfa.com.
A dynamic organisation for female footie fans just near the Westway, catering for players under 15.

Peter Hucker Soccer
8536 4141/www.peterhucker-soccer.com.
Former Queens Park Rangers goalkeeper Peter Hucker runs this highly rated scheme. Based in Barking and Wanstead, this organisation offers weekly pay-and-play coaching sessions, and matchplay. It can also arrange footballing parties for fives to 16s. Hucker was also responsible for founding the East London & Essex Small-Sided Soccer League (07961 867501, 01375 650833, www.eleleague.com).

Powerleague
www.powerleague.co.uk.
There are 13 Power League centres dotted around the capital, each providing all-weather, floodlit pitches. Most centres offer coaching, mini matches at weekends and during the school holidays, as well as junior leagues. If there's a birthday coming up, you can also book a pitch for a party.

Activities

Sharpshooters Football
07873 583366/www.sharpshooters
football.co.uk.
Tooting Bec Common and other venues in south-west London play host to Sunday pay-and-play sessions for four- to 11-year-olds, plus holiday courses and footie-themed birthday parties. Talented youngsters can progress to 'Sharp Shooter Select' sessions.

South East London & Kent Youth Football League
www.selkent.org.uk.
Leagues for young players, from mini-soccer for under-sevens to 11-a-sides for under-16s. The website includes a very useful 'players wanted' page, including a section on girls' football teams.

South London Special League
8319 8111/www.sl-sl.co.uk.
This league helps players with special needs to participate in football. The London FA website (www.londonfa.com) has an extensive section devoted to opportunities for children with physical and learning disabilities, and many of the community programmes run by London's professional clubs cater for special needs.

Watching football
The football season runs from August to May, and club websites include regularly updated ticket information. Ticket prices

Little Kickers. *See p203.*

and membership packages are far too numerous to list for each club; as a rule, Premier League match seats are £30-£60 for an adult, but are reduced by up to half for kids and members (if discounts are offered) for some cup fixtures. Coca-Cola Championship and Coca-Cola League prices are around £15-£40, with reductions for children and club members.

Wembley Stadium
Wembley, HA9 0WS (0844 980 8801/
www.wembleystadium.com). Wembley Park tube/Wembley Central tube/rail/Wembley Stadium rail.
The new Wembley Stadium received a considerable amount of schtick for the time it took for building works to be completed and the terrible state of its pitch once it was opened (being relaid at the time of writing). But now it's a cracking ground that's built on an epic scale; the top tier is up in the clouds and the overhead arch is a suitably iconic replacement for the famous twin towers. It's not even particularly difficult to get to, especially if you avoid the tube and take the overground from Marylebone – you'll be there in ten minutes; ideal for shielding the kids from the inevitable crush on the tube. You can also take excellent tours of the stadium that explore everything from the press box to the tunnel. The tours end in the royal box, where fans young and old get to brandish a very battered FA Cup to the piped cheers of the crowd and dream of glory.

Wembley may be grand, but it can be surprisingly easy to procure a ticket for some of the less distinguished fixtures (play-off finals or non-league cup finals), or even for England games, especially friendly matches.

Barclays Premier League

Arsenal
Emirates Stadium, Ashburton Grove, N7 7AF (7619 5000/www.arsenal.com). Arsenal tube.
For the club's museum, *see p98.*

Chelsea
Stamford Bridge, Fulham Road, SW6 1HS (0871 984 1955/www.chelseafc.com). Fulham Broadway tube.
For the club's museum, *see p98.*

Fulham
Craven Cottage, Stevenage Road, SW6 6HH (0870 442 1222/www.fulhamfc.com). Putney Bridge tube.
Stadium tours are available.

Tottenham Hotspur

White Hart Lane, Bill Nicholson Way, 748 High Road, N17 0AP (0844 499 5000/www. spurs.co.uk). White Hart Lane rail. **Tours** 11am, 1pm non-match Sats. **Admission** *Tours* £14.25; £7.60 under-16s, reductions. **Credit** MC, V.

Book in advance for tours of pitch-side, tunnel, changing rooms, boardroom and press room. Don't turn up on spec, as they don't always run.

West Ham United

Boleyn Ground, Green Street, E13 9AZ (0870 112 2700/www.whufc.com). Upton Park tube. Tours run on selected Wednesdays for which you must book in advance.

Coca-Cola Championship

Crystal Palace

Selhurst Park, Whitehorse Lane, SE25 6PU (8768 6000/www.cpfc.co.uk). Selhurst rail.

Queens Park Rangers

Loftus Road, South Africa Road, W12 7PA (8743 0262/www.qpr.co.uk). White City tube.

Watford

Vicarage Road, Watford, Herts WD18 0ER (0845 442 1881/www.watfordfc.com). Watford High Street rail.

Coca-Cola League

Barnet

Underhill Stadium, Barnet Lane, Herts, EN5 2DN (8441 6932/www.barnetfc.com). High Barnet tube.

Brentford

Griffin Park, Braemar Road, Brentford, Middx TW8 0NT (0845 345 6442/www.brentfordfc. premiumtv.co.uk). Brentford rail.

Charlton Athletic

The Valley, Floyd Road, SE7 8BL (0871 226 1905/www.charlton-athletic.co.uk). Charlton rail.

Leyton Orient

Matchroom Stadium, Brisbane Road, E10 5NE (0871 310 1881/www.leytonorient.com). Leyton tube.

Millwall

The Den, Zampa Road, SE16 3LN (7232 1222/www.millwallfc.co.uk). South Bermondsey rail/Surrey Quays tube from 2010.

GOLF

Golf isn't the easiest sport for kids to pick up, so the English Golf Union (*see p208*) has developed Tri-Golf for six- to 12-year-olds, and is introducing the game in primary schools. Introduce a child to the basics at one of London's driving ranges; course professionals may offer lessons to develop good habits. The TopGolf system (www.topgolf.co.uk) is a point-scoring game using balls with a microchip inside. TopGolf is played at its centres in Addlestone (01932 858551), Chigwell (8500 2644) and Watford (01923 222045).

Beckenham Place Park

The Mansion, Beckenham Place Park, Beckenham, Kent BR3 5BP (8650 2292/ www.glendalegolf.com). Beckenham Hill rail. Kids can practice at this course at a reduced rate all day during the week and after 1pm on the weekends. Lessons are on Saturdays at 10am (£3). It costs £10 for juniors to play a round at weekends, £6.50 on weekdays.

Central London Junior Golf Academy

Burntwood Lane, SW17 0AT (8871 2468/ www.clgc.co.uk). Tooting Bec tube/Earlsfield rail/G1 bus.

Junior membership of the academy (£35 annual fee) gets children priority booking and a discount on after school sessions (£75 with discount for an eight-week course) and Easter and Summer camps (£150 per week with discount for six- to eight-year-olds; £200 per week with discount for nine to 16s). Individual lessons are £20/30min and £40/hr.

KARTING & MOTOR SPORTS

Karts exceed speeds of 30mph (50kmph) and are suitable for over eights: there are two pedals (stop and go) and no gearbox to confuse the issue. These venues welcome children and can be booked for parties.

Brands Hatch

Fawkham, Longfield, Kent DA3 8NG (01474 872331/www.motorsportvision.co.uk). Swanley rail, then taxi.

The biggest motor-racing venue in the area, Brands Hatch has loads of things to do on two and four wheels, including YoungDrive!, which puts over-13s in control of a Renault Clio.

Activities

Playscape Pro Racing
390 Streatham High Road, SW16 6HX (8677 8677/www.playscape.co.uk). Streatham rail.
Bookable for children's parties (over-eights only) or half-hour taster sessions. Enthusiasts can join the Kids' Racing Academy, on the first Saturday of each month (8.30am-1pm, £35).

MARTIAL ARTS

Training in martial arts imparts self-confidence, body awareness, assertiveness and resilience. Most local sports centres will be home to at least one martial arts club; many more are based in church halls and community centres. Try to find a club with a lively but disciplined atmosphere, with well-organised and age-appropriate teaching. Ask instructors about their qualifications: the grading systems in judo and karate, for example, help ensure teachers are of a suitable standard. Note, however, that a black belt is not a teaching qualification. Ask for proof of insurance cover: martial arts usually involve physical contact, and accidents can happen. The following venues offer classes.

Bob Breen Academy
16 Hoxton Square, N1 6NT (7729 5789/ www.bobbreen.co.uk). Old Street tube/rail.
Kick-boxing skills and effective self-defence techniques for children aged seven to 16 at this well known and highly respected academy.

Hwarang Academy
Swiss Cottage Community Centre, 19 Winchester Road, NW3 3NR (07941 081 009/www.taekwondo-london-2012.com). Swiss Cottage tube.
Tae kwon do, a Korean martial art, is now an Olympic sport. These classes are for four-year-olds and upwards.

London School of Capoeira
Units 1 & 2, Leeds Place, Tollington Park, N4 3RF (7281 2020/www.londonschoolofcapoeira. co.uk). Finsbury Park tube/rail.
Capoeira is a Brazilian martial art, combining acrobatics and dance, in which creative play is a strong element. These classes are for six- to 16-year-olds.

Moving East
St Matthias Church Hall, Wordsworth Road, N16 8DD (7503 3101/www.movingeast.co.uk). Dalston Kingsland rail.

Judo and aikido (as well as dance and capoeira) classes for children are held at this friendly centre devoted to Japanese martial arts. Ages range from four to six for dance, five to ten for aikido and seven to 15 for judo.

Shaolin Temple UK
207A Junction Road, N19 5QA (7687 8333/ www.shaolintempleuk.org). Tufnell Park tube.
Shi Yanzi, a 34th generation fighting monk, and other Shaolin masters teach traditional kung fu, Chinese kick-boxing, meditation and t'ai chi at this temple. Weekly classes for children (fives and above) are also offered.

RIDING

Riding is one of the most rewarding sports going (as well as one of the most expensive), and riders who learn as children often develop a lifetime passion. Greater London is full of riding stables, some in unexpected places – the Isle of Dogs and Catford both boast their very own riding schools. The back of a horse is a great vantage point on which to view London's stunning greenery, from **Richmond Park** *(see p123)* to **Epping Forest** *(see p128)*. If you ring in advance, some establishments will happily let you watch a lesson; ask the stables if they run taster sessions for newcomers.

Riders must wear a BSI-approved hard hat (establishments usually lend or rent) and boots with a small heel rather than trainers or wellies. Lessons must be booked in advance. **Decathlon** *(see p278)* is a great place for buying inexpensive equipment and clothes. Some centres run 'own a pony' days and weeks, and offer birthday party packages. Many stables can cater easily for riders with disabilities, though not all have equipment to winch riders on to horses or ponies. All the establishments listed below are British Horse Society-approved (www.bhs.org.uk); it is not advisable to ride at non-BHS approved centres.

Deen City Farm & Riding School
39 Windsor Avenue, SW19 2RR (8543 5858/ www.deencityfarm.co.uk). Colliers Wood tube, then 20min walk/Phipps Bridge tramlink/200 bus. **Lessons** *Group* £20/45min. *Individual* £21/30min.
Lessons for children aged eight and over in flatwork and jumping (there's no hacking), from

beginners to advanced. Over-12s can volunteer at the yard at weekends and in school holidays. 'Own a pony' days for eight- to 12-year-olds cost a reasonable £20 per day (without ride) or £30 (with ride), and competitions are held throughout the year. The school is a Pony Club Centre, and is approved by the Riding for the Disabled Association.

Ealing Riding School

17-19 Gunnersbury Avenue, W5 3XD (8992 3808/www.ealingridingschool.biz). Ealing Common tube. **Lessons** *Group £25/hr. Individual £32/hr.*

Under fives can learn beginners or improvers skills in flatwork or jumping; lessons are held in an outdoor manège. Pony days (£55), in school holidays, include two hours of lessons and four hours learning stable management and skills such as mucking out and grooming.

Hyde Park & Kensington Stables

63 Bathurst Mews, W2 2SB (7723 2813/ www.hydeparkstables.com). Lancaster Gate tube. **Lessons** *Group £55-£59/hr. Individual £79-£95/hr.*

Hour-long lessons for children aged five and up with patient, streetwise ponies; prices reflect the glamorous location. The stables is a Pony Club Centre (£22 annual fee) with a membership of around 50 children.

Kingston Riding Centre

38 Crescent Road, Kingston-upon-Thames, Surrey KT2 7RG (8546 6361/www.kingston ridingcentre.com). Richmond tube/rail, then 371 bus/Norbiton rail then 10min walk. **Lessons** *Group £36-£38/hr. Individual £54-£72/hr.*

There are 25 horses at this well-equipped yard, which caters to all levels of riders. Richmond Park *(see p123)* is used for hacks, and the owners organise regular events, competitions and popular courses for children (£165 for four days). Facilities include a floodlit indoor school, an outdoor arena and, in summer months, a cross-country course. Closed Mondays.

Lee Valley Riding Centre

71 Lea Bridge Road, E10 7QL (8546 6361/ www.leevalleypark.org.uk). Clapton rail/48, 55, 56 bus. **Lessons** *Group £36-£38/hr. Individual £30-£36/30min, £54-£72/hr. Taster session £10-£12.60/30min.*

The friendly Lee Valley Riding Centre offers placid ponies on which to enjoy the open spaces of Walthamstow Marshes. The superb facilities include one indoor and two outdoor arenas; experienced riders can use the cross-country

London School of Capoeira.

course. Children aged from three-and-a-half can have private lessons, while five-and-overs can participate in group lessons. Over-tens with some riding and pony-handling experience can become stable helpers, and there are also 'Own a Pony' sessions.

London Equestrian Centre

Lullington Garth, N12 7BP (8349 1345/www. londonridingschool.com). Mill Hill East tube. **Lessons** *Group £27/30min. Individual £25-£31/30min.*

There are 30 horses and ponies at this yard, which caters for riders of all abilities; there's even a Tiny Tots session for three-year-olds. The centre is affiliated to the Pony Club, and runs pony days and weeks in school holidays. Birthday parties are held here, and young people aged from 13 can help out at the yard in return for free rides.

Mount Mascal Stables

Vicarage Road, Bexley, Kent DA5 2AW (8300 3947/www.mountmascalstables.com). Bexley rail. **Lessons** *Group £18/hr. Individual £26/hr.*

Down in south London, this busy centre is home to 40 horses and ponies, and gives lessons to over-fives. Children's fun days (£30; for riders six years and above with some experience) allow

Governing bodies

Amateur Boxing Association of England
www.abae.co.uk

Amateur Rowing Association
82376700/www.ara-rowing.org

Amateur Swimming Association
01509 618 700/
www.britishswimming.co.uk

Badminton England
01908 268 400/
www.badmintonengland.co.uk

BaseballSoftballUK
7453 7055/www.baseballsoftballuk.com

British Canoe Union
0845 370 9500/www.bcu.org.uk

British Dragon Boat Racing Association
www.dragonboat.org.uk

British Fencing Association
8742 3032/www.britishfencing.com

British Gymnastics
0845 129 7129/
www.british-gymnastics.org

British Mountaineering Council
0161 445 6111/www.thebmc.co.uk

British Orienteering Federation
01629 734042/
www.britishorienteering.org.uk

British Tenpin Bowling Association
8478 1745/www.btba.org.uk

British Waterski
www.britishwaterski.org.uk

England Squash & Racketball
01612 314 499/
www.englandsquash.com

England & Wales Cricket Board
www.ecb.co.uk

England Basketball
0114 284 1060/
www.englandbasketball.co.uk

English Golf Union
01526 354500/
www.englishgolfunion.org

English Table Tennis Association
01424 722525/
www.englishtabletennis.org.uk

Football Association
7745 4545/www.thefa.com

Lawn Tennis Association
8487 7000/www.lta.org.uk

LondonBaseball
www.londonsports.com/baseball

London Sports Forum for Disabled People
7717 1699/
www.londonsportsforum.org.uk

London Windsurf Association
01895 846707/
www.lwawindsurfing.co.uk

National Ice Skating Association
0115 988 8060/www.iceskating.org.uk

Royal Yachting Association
0845 345 0400/www.rya.org.uk

Rugby Football Union
8892 2000/www.rfu.com

Ski Club of Great Britain
0845 458 0780/www.skiclub.co.uk

Wheelpower
01296 395995/www.wheelpower.org.uk
The umbrella body for 17 wheelchair sports, from archery to rugby.

Activities

kids to practise riding, experience stable management and play a variety of games. The centre has two indoor schools, two outdoor grass arenas and two outdoor all-weather manèges. More experienced riders can hack out in the stunning Joyden's Wood. Birthday parties for six to 12 kids can be arranged for weekends or in school holidays.

Mudchute Equestrian Centre
Mudchute Park & Farm, Pier Street, E14 3HP (7515 5901 /www.mudchute.org). Mudchute, Crossharbour or Island Gardens DLR/D3, D6, D7, D8 bus. **Lessons** *Group* £16-£19/hr. *Individual* £30-£40/45min.
This hugely popular riding school at the Mudchute City Farm *(see p134)* on the Isle of Dogs is friendly, down-to-earth and very welcoming to new riders. Lessons are some of the most reasonably priced in London, and are open to children over seven. It's a Pony Club Centre, enabling local kids who don't own a pony to study for badges and certificates.

Ross Nye's Riding Stables
8 Bathurst Mews, W2 2SB (7262 3791/ www.rossnyestables.co.uk). Lancaster Gate tube. **Lessons** *Group* £50/hr. *Individual* £60/hr.
At the posher end of the spectrum, this stables forms the Hyde Park branch of the Pony Club; membership gives reduced prices for lessons which take place in the park. Clients aged from six can learn to ride here.

Stag Lodge Stables
Robin Hood Gate, Richmond Park, SW15 3RS (8974 6066/www.ridinginlondon.com). East Putney tube/Putney rail, then 85 bus/Kingston rail then 85 bus. **Lessons** *Group* £30-£35/hr. *Individual* £30/30min, £45-£60/hr.
There are 40 or so horses and ponies (ranging from Shetlands to Irish hunters) at this stables in historic Richmond Park *(see p123)*. Threes to sevens can enjoy half-hour lead-rein rides through the park (£30); jumping or flatwork lessons for all abilities take place in one of two outdoor manèges. There are pony weeks for the over-sixes in school holidays and half term (£275 for four days) – book well ahead.

Trent Park Equestrian Centre
Bramley Road, N14 4XS (8363 8630/www. trentpark.com). Oakwood tube. **Lessons** *Group* £23-£30/hr. *Individual* £38-£42/hr.
A caring attitude towards young riders (fours and over) and this equestrian centre's location make this a popular place to ride. Hacking is £28 per hour, Pony days are £60 and four-day riding weeks (£220) are held in the school holidays.

Willowtree Riding Establishment
The Stables, Ronver Road, SE12 0NL (8857 6438/www.willowtreeridinglondon.co.uk). Grove Park or Lee rail. **Lessons** *Group* from £9/30min, £17.50/hr. *Individual* from £18/30min.
The Welsh ponies are particularly popular at this friendly yard, where children over four can learn to ride. Young and nervous riders are welcome. Lessons (flatwork only) take place in a covered, full-size indoor arena. Most teaching is at weekends and in the holidays.

Wimbledon Village Stables
24A-B High Street, SW19 5DX (8946 8579/www.wvstables.com). Wimbledon tube/rail. **Lessons** *Group* £55/hr. *Individual* £28/30min.
Although it largely caters for adult riders, children are welcome at this centre, which has a small selection of quiet, safe ponies and a popular holiday scheme for five- to ten-year-olds (£160 for three afternoons). Riding takes place on leafy Wimbledon Common *(see p120)*, where the centre has use of two outdoor arenas for flatwork and jumping lessons. Riders must become members to ride regularly.

RUGBY UNION
A bargain compared to football. All London clubs feature top international players and there's never any problem getting tickets. The season runs from September to May.

Guinness Premiership

Harlequins
Twickenham Stoop Stadium, Langhorn Drive, Twickenham, Middx TW2 7SX (8410 6000/www.quins.co.uk). Twickenham rail. **Admission** £17-£40; £8-£10 2-16s.

Saracens
Vicarage Road, Watford, Herts WD18 0EP (01727 792800/www.saracens.com). Watford High Street rail. **Admission** £15-£50; £5-£10 2-16s.

National League

London Welsh
Old Deer Park, Kew Road, Richmond, Surrey TW9 2AZ (8940 2368/www.london-welsh.co.uk). Richmond tube/rail. **Admission** £12-£17; £6-£8.50 reductions; free under-16s.

Activities

One giant leap

You'll probably have seen some of London's parkour enthusiasts going loco on the South Bank. Also known as free-running, the sport of parkour is best seen as a sort of urban ballet in which practitioners use the furniture of the street – bollards, rooftops, railings and steps – to get themselves from place to place, as gracefully and athletically as possible. It's a spectacle that fascinates children – and one company, Parkour Generations, is taking advantage of this with special weekly classes aimed at anyone under 19.

London schools have also cottoned on to parkour's potential. The Westminster Sports Unit has recently started funding trainers to teach parkour at 14 schools in the borough. Not only is it an excellent way to improve health and fitness, it's also seen as having enough street credibility to attract some of the borough's more disaffected pupils. The Parkour for Schools programme is being viewed with interest by other London boroughs: three schools in Sutton have already started their own weekly classes with Parkour Generations.

With its combination of gymnastics and running, parkour has obvious health benefits. That said, the fact it encourages kids to leap from high objects does raise some concerns – a 14-year-old died after attempting a parkour leap between buildings in 2005. However, teachers stress that students have to agree not to perform parkour moves on school premises without supervision. And look at it this way: at least after a few lessons your kids will have learned how to fall correctly – something that every parent knows will come in very handy, given the amount of time children spend nursing cuts, bruises and scrapes.
For more information check www.parkour generations.com.

SKATEBOARDING & BMX

Just as popular now as in the 1970s, skateboarding and BMX means getting fit and making friends. For details of festivals and special events look at the Skateboarders Association website (www.ukskate.org.uk). BMX became an olympic sport in 2003 – check the website of the governing body of British cycling (www.britishcycling.org.uk) for news.

BaySixty6 Skate Park
Bay 65-66, Acklam Road, W10 5YU (8969 4669/www.baysixty6.com). Ladbroke Grove tube. **Membership** free. **Prices** £6/5hrs Mon-Fri, 4hrs Sat, Sun; £3 beginners 10am-noon Sat, Sun.
This famous park sprawls beneath the Westway and includes a medium half-pipe, a mini ramp and funboxes, grind boxes, ledges and rails aplenty. Some skaters complain about the £6 entry fee, but the high quality of the ramps goes some way to making up for it.

Cantelowes Skatepark
Cantelowes Gardens, Camden Road, NW1 (www.cantelowesskatepark.co.uk). Kentish Town tube/rail/Camden Road rail. **Open** 11am-9pm daily.
After a £1.5m makeover, this free skatepark reopened in 2007 and draws a devoted crowd of regulars. It has hosted qualifying rounds for Quiksilver's Bowlriders championship for the last two years.

Harrow Skatepark
Christchurch Avenue, Wealdstone, Middx HA3 5BD (www.harrowskatepark.co.uk). Harrow & Wealdstone tube/rail.
This has a clover-leaf, kidney bowls and a challenging concrete half-pipe.

Meanwhile
Meanwhile Gardens, off Great Western Road, W10 (www.mgca.f2s.com). Westbourne Park tube.
Close to the Grand Union, this community garden's skatepark features three concrete bowls of varying steepness and size, but no flatland – so it's not for wobbly beginners.

SKATING

On ice
Temporary rinks pop up all over town in winter time inside museums, galleries, parks and shopping centres.

This small ice rink near the Holloway Road runs popular after-school sessions and six-week courses for children. Anyone over four is welcome; they can have ice-skating birthday parties here too, with all the necessary equipment provided. The leisure centre also offers ice hockey sessions for the over-sixes.

Queens
17 Queensway, W2 4QP (7229 0172/ www.queensiceandbowl.co.uk). Bayswater or Queensway tube.
Beginners and families are nicely looked after at this well-known ice rink, which holds legendary disco nights on Fridays and Saturdays. Children's lessons cost £65 for a six-week course. Hot Belgian waffles in the café are also a big hit with kids. There's also a 12 lane Tenpin Bowling centre here *(see p216)*.

Somerset House
Strand, WC2R 1LA (7845 4600/ www.somersethouse.org.uk). Holborn or Temple tube.
The magnificent courtyard at Somerset House is probably London's most iconic temporary rink when it is iced over from late November until late January. Enjoy a skating session before embarking on an improving interlude in the art galleries *(see p65)*.

Streatham Ice Arena
386 Streatham High Road, SW16 6HT (8769 7771/www.streathamicearena.co.uk). Streatham rail.
Hugely popular south London venue which offers the combined attractions of an ice rink and karting track (Playscape, *see p206*). Locals have campaigned for improvements, with particular concern for the future of the rink (Streatham has had one since 1931); see Streatham Ice Skating Action Group's website at www.sisag.org.uk. The rink offers reasonably-priced six-week courses for all ages, including classes for toddlers.

On tarmac
Citiskate (www.citiskate.co.uk) teaches hundreds of Londoners of all ages how to skate in parks, leisure centres and schools. The instructors all hold qualifications from UKISA (United Kingdom Inline Skating Association); lessons are available daily. Citiskate's weekly Sunday Rollerstroll (www.rollerstroll.com) and Battersea Park's Easy Peasy skate on Saturday (www.easypeasyskate.com) are popular, family-friendly group skates.

Session times at London's permanent ice rinks vary, so call ahead before you visit; venues are generally open 10am-10pm.

Alexandra Palace Ice Rink
Alexandra Palace Way, N22 7AY (8365 2121/ www.alexandrapalace.com). Wood Green tube/ Alexandra Palace rail/W3 bus.
This lofty arena runs courses for children aged five to 15 on Saturday mornings and early on weekday evenings.

Broadgate Ice Arena
Broadgate Circle, Eldon Street, EC2A 2BQ (Summer 7505 4000/Winter 7505 4068/www. broadgateice.co.uk). Liverpool Street tube/rail.
Compact, City-based rink that's open from mid-November to March and is very child-friendly. Often less crowded than the other outdoor rinks.

Lee Valley Ice Centre
Lea Bridge Road, E10 7QL (8533 3154/ www.leevalleypark.org.uk). Clapton rail.
Disco nights are a big hit at this modern, well-maintained and comparatively warm rink. It's never too busy, and the ice rink is a good size. Lessons are also offered.

Michael Sobell Leisure Centre
Hornsey Road, N7 7NY (7609 2166/www. aquaterra.org). Finsbury Park tube/rail.

Activities

SKIING & SNOWBOARDING

There are a number of dry ski slopes in the London area. Bear in mind that the minimum requirement is to be able to perform a controlled snowplough turn and use the ski lift.

Bromley Ski Centre

Sandy Lane, St Paul's Cray, Orpington, Kent BR5 3HY (01689 876812/www.c-v-s.co.uk/ bromleyski). St Mary Cray rail/321 bus.
There are two lifts to serve the 120m (394ft) main slope, and there's also a mogul field and nursery slope. Skiing and snowboarding taster sessions cost £17. Booking is essential.

Sandown Sports Club

More Lane, Esher, Surrey KT10 8AN (01372 467132/www.sandownsports.co.uk). Esher rail.
A big but friendly ski centre with four nursery slopes and a curving, 120-metre main slope. The open practice sessions are strictly for competent skiers and snowboarders; otherwise, there are lessons for under-sevens (£24/30mins) and seven-and-overs (£43/hr). Call for details of parties, during which kids can speed down the slopes on sledges and circular 'ringos'.

Snow Centre

St Albans Hill, Hemel Hempstead, Herts, HP3 9NH (01442 241321/www.thesnowcentre.com) Hemel Hempstead rail then taxi.
This new snow centre in Hemel Hempstead opened in May 2009 and claims to be the best and biggest in the UK. The main slope is 160m and has two lifts, and there's also a 100m lesson slope equipped with rope tows. There's also a snow play area for children aged two to six, lessons for six-and-overs and snow school in half-term and school holidays.

Snozone

Xscape, 602 Marlborough Gate, Milton Keynes, Bucks MK9 3XS (0871 222 5670/www.snozoneuk.com). Milton Keynes Central rail.
One of the UK's largest indoor snow domes, with three slopes (in reality they're joined, so they resemble one wide slope): two of 170m (558ft) and one of 135m (443ft), with button lifts running all the way to the top. The place can feel a bit like a big fridge as it is below freezing on the slopes, but it's a good (if pricey) place to find your ski legs. Three-and-overs can also try a spot of tobogganing (under-sevens must be accompanied by a grown-up).

SWIMMING

As part of the drive towards increasing fitness for 2012, many London boroughs now provide free swimming at designated times for 16-and-unders (18 in Hackney) under the Swim4Life scheme. Children must pre-register; see www.gll.org for a list of participating authorities.

Most local authority pools run lessons for children, plus parent-and-baby sessions to develop water confidence in those as young as three months. These are very popular, so may have long waiting lists; ask at your local pool for details. Most of the pools recommended below are open daily; phone for times.

Barnet Copthall Pools

Champions Way, NW4 1PX (8457 9900/ www.gll.org). Mill Hill East tube.
Three pools and a diving area, with coaching and clubs to join if you fancy taking the plunge.

Brentford Fountain Leisure Centre

658 Chiswick High Road, Brentford, Middx TW8 0HJ (0845 456 6675/www.hounslow. gov.uk). Gunnersbury tube/Kew Bridge rail.
A very pleasant leisure facility which has a warm, shallow teaching pool, an exciting 40m (130ft) aquaslide, underwater lighting and a wave machine.

Crystal Palace National Sports Centre

Ledrington Road, SE19 2BB (8778 0131/ www.gll.org). Crystal Palace rail.
The National Sports Centre in the middle of Crystal Palace Park houses one of the capital's two 50m (160ft) Olympic-size pools; this venerable pool also has fine diving facilities (rare across the country).

Goresbrook Leisure Centre

Ripple Road, Dagenham, Essex RM9 6XW (8227 3976/www.barking-dagenham.gov.uk). Becontree tube.
The fun pool in this Dagenham centre has child-friendly fountains, as well as cascades and a 60m (195ft) flume. There's also a small area for proper length swimming.

Ironmonger Row Baths

1-11 Ironmonger Row, EC1V 3QF (7253 4011/www.aquaterra.org). Old Street tube/rail.
One of only three remaining Turkish baths in London. Various toys and floats come out for

Activities

Saturday's family fun time, while eight to 15s can attend Super Swim sessions – a heady mix of water polo, lifesaving skills and snorkelling.

Kingfisher Leisure Centre
Fairfield Road, Kingston, Surrey, KT1 2PY (8541 4576/www.kingfisherleisurecentre.co.uk). Kingston rail.
This friendly family centre has a teaching pool, and a main pool with a beach area and wave machine. In other words, there is a little something for everyone.

Latchmere Leisure Centre
Burns Road, SW11 5AD (7207 8004/www. latchmereleisurecentre.co.uk). Clapham Junction rail.
The Latchmere Leisure Centre has a decent swimming pool for those who want to swim lanes. There's also a teaching pool and a beach area, with a wave machine and slide which will appeal to children.

Leyton Leisure Lagoon
763 High Road, E10 5AB (8558 8858/ www.gll.org). Leyton tube/69, 97 bus.
This east London pool has flume, slides, fountains, rapids and cascades to liven up swimming sessions.

Pavilion Leisure Centre
Kentish Way, Bromley, Kent BR1 3EF (8313 9911/www.bromleymytime.org.uk). Bromley South rail.
Large leisure pool with shallows, flumes and a wave machine, lane swimming and a separate toddlers' pool.

Queen Mother Sports Centre
223 Vauxhall Bridge Road, SW1V 1EL (7630 5522/www.courtneys.co.uk). Victoria tube/rail.
The three terrific pools in this refurbished centre mean it's always popular with schoolkids.

Spa at Beckenham
24 Beckenham Road, Beckenham, Kent BR3 4PF (8650 0233/www.bromleymytime.org.uk). Clock House rail.
An award-winning leisure centre with loads of sports facilities, two swimming pools, the Space Zone soft-play area for children and a crèche.

Tottenham Green Leisure Centre
1 Philip Lane, N15 4JA (8489 5322/ www.haringey.gov.uk). Seven Sisters tube/rail.
This perennially popular leisure centre has lane swimming and diving in the main pool, and waves and slides in the 'beach pool'.

Waterfront Leisure Centre
Woolwich High Street, SE18 6DL (8317 5000/www.gll.org). Woolwich Arsenal rail/ 96, 177 bus.
Greenwich borough's flagship centre. Four pools, six slides, waves, rapids and a water 'volcano' keep the crowds happy.

Open-air swimming

London's outdoor pools (lidos) are in a mixed state. Some are in terminal decline, while others have been reopened after expensive refurbs. For full details of London's outdoor pools (and to join the campaign to reopen those that have closed), visit www.lidos.org.uk.

Brockwell Lido
Brockwell Park, Dulwich Road, SE24 0PA (7274 3088/www.brockwell-lido.co.uk). Herne Hill rail. **Open** May-Sept, check website for times. **Admission** check website for details.
Rescued from the dead, this wonderful 1930s lido has been transformed by a Heritage Lottery Fund grant. Whippersnappers runs a brilliant range of classes at the pool, from babies' and toddlers' drop-in sessions to kathak dance classes for five to sevens and circus skills, acrobatics and street dance for older kids.

Finchley Lido
Great North Leisure Park, Chaplin Square, High Road, North Finchley, N12 0GL (8343 9830/www.gll.org). East Finchley tube. **Open** check website. **Admission** check website.
There are two indoor pools here, but it's the outdoor pool and sun terrace that make it such a popular draw for locals in the summer.

Hampstead Heath Swimming Ponds & Parliament Hill Lido
7485 4491/www.cityoflondon.gov.uk. Lido: Parliament Hill Fields, Gordon House Road, NW5 1LP. Gospel Oak rail. Men & women's ponds: Millfield Lane, N6. Gospel Oak rail. Mixed pond: East Heath Road, NW3. Hampstead Heath rail. **Open** check website for times. **Admission** Lido £4.30; £2.70 reductions; £12.80 family (2+2). Ponds £2; £1 reductions. Season tickets and early/late entry discounts available.
Hampstead's wonderfully atmospheric pools are reserved for children of eight and above; under-15s must be supervised. The unheated, Grade II-listed lido is thronged with families on sunny afternoons, and also has a paddling pool.

Activities

On your marks...

The mini-marathon for kids has been a part of the London Marathon since 1986. Run over the last 2.65 miles of the course – generally starting from Old Billingsgate Market on the North Bank at Southwark Bridge to the main finishing point on the Mall – the event was at first restricted to representatives of London's boroughs, but has since been expanded to involve runners from counties all over the UK.

It's a prestigious event – the results appear in national newspapers and the race is seen as the biggest road-running event for children in the UK – so competition is fierce. Most boroughs organise their own trials in March to help select the half-dozen or so runners who will represent them in the April race. Some boroughs also provide training meetings ahead of the trials – Hackney, for instance, organises free sessions every Sunday for any child who has attended school in the borough from January, with weekly practice races in the three age groups: under-13s, under-15s and under-17s. If your child is interested in competing, take a look at your local borough's website for details of training and trials.

Hampton Heated Open Air Pool
High Street, Hampton, Middx TW12 2ST (8255 1116/www.hamptonpool.co.uk). *Hampton rail.* **Open** times vary according to season so check the website **Admission** weekends £6.50; weekdays £4.50; reductions £3.50; children (4-15) £2.50; family (2 +3) £15. The water is heated to 28° at this pool, and when the sun's shining it's hard to beat. There's a shallow learner pool for babies and toddlers, along with various group and private swimming lessons. The complex is open all year round.

London Fields Lido
London Fields Westside, E8 3EU (7254 9038/ www.gll.org). London Fields rail/26, 48, 55, 106, 236 bus. **Open** call for details. **Admission** £4; £2.40 under-16s.
Another recently resurrected lido, Hackney Council reopened this 50m (164ft) pool in autumn 2006. The water's heated to 25°, and there are two on-site cafés.

Oasis Sports Centre
32 Endell Street, WC2H 9AG (7831 1804/ www.gll.org). Tottenham Court Road tube. **Open** 7.30am-9pm Mon-Fri; 9.30am-5.30pm Sat, Sun. **Admission** £3.60; £1.40 5-16s; free under-5s; £6.75 family (2+2).
This excellent 28m (90ft) outdoor pool is open all year round, and is particularly appealing on winter days, when steam rises from the surface (if you can persuade the kids to brave the chilly dash from the changing rooms). Families should beware visiting at lunchtimes or after work, when stressed media types descend in force.

Pools on the Park
Old Deer Park, Twickenham Road, Richmond, Surrey TW9 2SF (8940 0561/www.spring health.net). Richmond rail. **Open** 6.30am-7.45pm Mon; 6.30am-10pm Tue; 6.30am-9pm Wed; 6.30am-9pm Thur; 6.30am-8.30pm Fri; 8am-5.45pm Sat; 7am-5.45pm Sun. **Admission** £3.80; £1.55-£3.05 reductions; free under-5s. Prices may vary during peak season.
This well-maintained sports complex inside the picturesque Old Deer Park features a 33m (110ft) heated outdoor pool, and one the same size and temperature inside.

Serpentine Lido
Hyde Park, W2 2UH (7706 3422/ www.serpentinelido.com). Knightsbridge or South Kensington tube. **Open** *Mid June-mid Sept* 10am-6pm daily. **Admission** £4; £1-£3 reductions.

Right in the centre of town, this picturesque freshwater pool and its paddling pool are a London institution, exerting a siren song to hot, stressed-out parents and kids on sticky summer's days.

Tooting Bec Lido

Tooting Bec Road, SW16 1RU (8871 7198/ www.slsc.org.uk/www.tootingbeclido.co.uk). Streatham rail. **Open** *Late May-Aug* 6am-8pm daily. *Sept* 6am-5pm daily. *Oct-May* 7am-2pm daily (club members only). **Admission** £4.50; £3 reductions and under-16s; free under-5s; £12 family (2+2).

At 94m (308ft) by 25m (82ft), this art deco beauty is the second-largest open-air pool in Europe. Understandably, it's immensely popular with locals, and has a paddling pool for splash-happy toddlers.

TENNIS

Tennis is working hard to break out of its white middle-class straitjacket. Tennis for Free (TFF) is a campaign to give access *gratuit* to Britain's 33,000 public courts to increase participation in tennis nationwide. It's aimed to help all ages, regardless of ability, background, race and financial circumstance. To learn more about the scheme, visit www.tennisforfree.com, type in your borough and check availability.

Holiday tennis courses at Easter and in the summer can be found in most London boroughs, but need booking well ahead: keep an eye on council websites and contact your local sports development team for details. The Lawn Tennis Association publishes free guides giving contacts for private clubs and public courts listed by borough or county, along with contact details for local development officers; it also holds details of tennis holidays available.

Hackney City Tennis Clubs

Clissold Park Mansion House, Stoke Newington Church Street, N16 9HJ (7254 4235/www.hackneycitytennisclubs.co.uk). Stoke Newington rail/73 bus. **Open** *Mar* 10am-5.30pm Mon-Fri; 9am-5.30pm Sat, Sun. *Apr-Sept* 10am-7.30pm Mon-Fri; 9am-7.30pm Sat, Sun. *Oct, Nov* 10am-4.30pm Mon-Fri; 9am-4.30pm Sat, Sun. *Dec-Feb* 10am-3.30pm Mon-Fri; 9am-3.30pm Sat, Sun. **Court hire** £5.50/hr; £2.50 under-16s (9am-5pm Mon-Fri). Phone to check availability.

Part of a nationwide LTA programme to make inner-city tennis facilities cheaper and easier to find, this is Britain's first City Tennis Club (with courts in Clissold Park, London Fields and Millfields). Sessions for three- to 16-year-olds are offered during term time (one hour per week costs from £25 for five weeks' of lessons), with free racquets and balls; holiday courses are also available. There are additional CTCs in Highbury Fields (Islington) and Eltham Park South (Greenwich).

David Lloyd Leisure

0870 888 3015/www.davidlloydleisure.co.uk All David Lloyd centres are family-friendly, if not exactly cheap, and the courts and equipment are excellent. Check out the website or phone for your nearest venue.

Islington Tennis Centre

Market Road, N7 9PL (7700 1370/www. aquaterra.org). Caledonian Road tube. **Open** 7am-11pm Mon-Thur; 7am-10pm Fri; 8am-10pm Sat, Sun. **Court hire** *Non-members* Indoor £20/hr; £9/hr 5-16s. Outdoor £9/hr; £4.40/hr 5-16s.

Developed under the LTA's Indoor Tennis Initiative, the centre offers subsidised coaching. It also runs half-hour coaching sessions for three- to five-year-olds.

Redbridge Sports & Leisure Centre

Forest Road, Barkingside, Essex IG6 3HD (8498 1000/www.rslonline.co.uk). Fairlop tube. **Open** 6.30am-11pm Mon-Fri; 8am-9pm Sat; 8am-10pm Sun. **Court hire** prices vary; phone for details.

An independent charitable trust runs this outstanding sports centre. There are eight indoor and 18 outdoor courts to use as a member or 'pay as you go'. There are holiday activities for six- to 14-year-olds, 'fun play' sessions and a short tennis club for under-eights.

Sutton Tennis Academy

Rose Hill Recreation Ground, Rose Hill, Sutton, Surrey SM1 3HH (8641 6611/www. sjtc.org). Morden tube/Sutton Common rail. **Open** 7am-11pm Mon-Fri; 7am-9pm Sat, Sun. **Court hire** *Indoor* £19; £14 under-18s. *Outdoor* £8; £6 under-18s. *Clay* £13; £9 under-18s.

Frenchman Erich Dochterman, who has taught various ATP and WTA-ranked players, is head coach at this acclaimed tennis school. There are residential courses for players seeking professional status and a scholarship scheme linked to Cheam High School. Children can be steeped in tennis culture from the age of three with Tiny Tots classes, mini tennis and holiday programmes. Facilities include six red clay, ten acrylic and 11 indoor courts.

Westway Tennis Centre

1 Crowthorne Road, W10 6RP (8969 0992/ www.westway.org). Latimer Road tube. **Open** 8am-10pm Mon-Fri; 8am-8pm Sat; 10am-10pm Sun. **Court hire** *Indoor* £16-£22.50; £10 5-16s. *Outdoor* £8-£9; £5-£7 5-16s.

The Westway, another product of the LTA's Indoor Tennis Initiative, follows a similar model to Islington (*see p216*): it's excellent for subsidised coaching and courses, short tennis and transitional tennis. There are eight indoor and four outdoor clay courts for kids to play on.

TENPIN BOWLING

Tenpin bowling has become the evening pursuit of choice for many a hip Londoner, but families get a look-in during the daytime. Many centres have ramps, bumpers and lightweight balls to make things easier for small children.

Admission to the following centres averages around £6 per game, including the hire of soft-soled bowling shoes. Phone for details of children's party packages.

Acton Tenpin

Royale Leisure Park, Western Avenue, W3 0PA (0871 873 3150/www.megabowl.co.uk). Park Royal tube. **Open** noon-12.30am Mon-Thur; noon-3am Fri; 10am-3am Sat; 10am-1pm Sun. **Credit** MC, V.

1st Bowling Lewisham

11-29 Belmont Hill, SE13 5AU (0870 118 3021). Lewisham rail/DLR. **Open** noon-11pm Mon, Thur, Sat, Sun; 10am-11pm Tue, Wed, Fri. **Credit** MC, V.

Funland

Trocadero Centre, 1 Piccadilly Circus, W1D 7DH (7292 3642/www.funland.co.uk). Piccadilly Circus tube. **Open** 10am-1am daily. **Credit** MC, V.

Hollywood Bowl Finchley

Great North Leisure Park, Chaplin Square, off Finchley High Road, N12 0GL (8446 6667/ www.hollywoodbowl.co.uk). East Finchley tube, then 263 bus. **Open** 10am-midnight Mon-Thur, Sun; 10am-1am Fri, Sat. **Credit** MC, V.

Hollywood Bowl Surrey Quays

Mast Leisure Park, Teredo Street, SE16 7LW (7237 3773/www.hollywoodbowl.co.uk). Canada Water DLR. **Open** 10am-11.30pm Mon-Thur, Sun; 10am-midnight Fri, Sat. **Credit** MC, V.

Queens

17 Queensway, W2 4QP (7229 0172/www. queensiceandbowl.co.uk). Bayswater or Queensway tube. **Open** 10am-11pm daily. **Credit** MC, V.

Rowans Tenpin Bowl

10 Stroud Green Road, N4 2DF (8800 1950/ www.rowans.co.uk). Finsbury Park tube/rail. **Open** 10.30am-12.30am Mon-Thur, Sun; 10.30am-2.30am Fri, Sat. **Credit** MC, V.

London Palace Superbowl

Elephant & Castle Shopping Centre, 2 Elephant & Castle, SE1 6TE (7252 6677/ www.palacesuperbowl.com). Elephant & Castle tube. **Open** 11am-11pm daily. **Credit** MC, V.

WATERSPORTS

London is a river city, so there are plenty of opportunities to take to the water in canoes, dinghies or rowing boats, and meander down the Thames. It's also worth checking out the city's many reservoirs.

Ahoy Centre

Borthwick Street, SE8 3JY (8691 7606/ www.ahoy.org.uk). Deptford rail/Cutty Sark DLR.

This is the place to come for sailing, rowing and (for older children and teens) powerboating on the Thames, and in Surrey and Victoria Docks. Members help run the centre, which keeps prices down and fosters a community spirit.

BTYC Sailsports

Birchen Grove, NW9 8SA (8205 0017/ www.btycsailsports.org.uk). Neasden or Wembley Park tube/rail.

Dinghy sailing, windsurfing, basic training and RYA courses on the Welsh Harp reservoir.

Canalside Activity Centre

Canal Close, W10 5AY (8968 4500/www.rbkc. gov.uk). Ladbroke Grove tube/Kensal Rise rail/ 52, 70, 295 bus.

Utilising the resource of the Grand Union canal, this centre offers canoeing lessons, as well as water safety classes.

Anyone for a paddle?

Canoeing and kayaking are two of the most exhilarating, healthy ways of having fun outdoors. Beware though; one session and you'll be hooked. There are plenty of opportunities to get afloat in the capital, with clubs on the Thames from Putney to further inland catering for everyone from complete novices to aspiring Olympians.

For beginners, a taster at **Wimbledon Park Watersports Centre** *(see p218)*, on a reassuringly placid lake, is a good start. Kayaks are based on Inuit designs and have you sitting with your legs out in front. Canoes, originally used by north American Indians, have you kneeling or perched on a seat. Fears that each wobbly stroke might capsize the boat are soon allayed – kayaks are more stable than they look. Within minutes you'll be racing through the waves. A quick warning: taking spare clothes is advisable as water from the paddles does have a habit of dripping down your legs.

Unlike a municipal park rowing boat, the light, plastic kayaks use a double-ended blade cannily angled so that even those with minimal co-ordination soon get it right. It's almost impossible to get it wrong, but safety measures are in place

in case. Life jackets are compulsory, and all activities are accompanied by qualified instructors. Cautious parents may prefer two-seaters, but most children can't wait to go solo.

Anyone from age eight upwards can take part in the centre's organised games and activities. The thrill-filled paddlesports sessions take in racing and water polo, and you can even play 'It' on the lake while swans, geese and ducks follow you around hoping to join in. The dual attractions of communing with nature and gliding along on the water make it strangely addictive.

Younger children will like the idea of games, while teenagers may swiftly want to take it more seriously. For anyone interested in competing in the London Youth Games, there are slalom lessons and sprint courses.

Britain has a long history of excelling on the water in the Olympics, which is something of a sore point in the boating fraternity, who see athletics getting the glory even though watersports regularly pick up more gold doubloons. However... trophies or none, boating is certainly fun. *For more information on canoeing, visit www.bcu.org.uk*

Activities

Docklands Sailing & Watersports Centre

Millwall Dock, 235A Westferry Road, E14 3QS (7537 2626/www.dswc.org). Crossharbour DLR. **Membership** £110/yr adult; £20/yr under-17s; £220/yr family (2+3).
This watersports centre offers canoeing, dragon-boat racing, windsurfing and dinghy sailing for over-eights. Non-members can also take part in open sessions; phone for details.

Globe Rowing Club

Trafalgar Rowing Centre, 11-13 Crane Street, SE10 9NP (www.globerowingclub.co.uk). Cutty Sark DLR/Maze Hill rail.
A friendly, Greenwich-based rowing club that offers competitive as well as recreational rowing and sculling on a stretch of river from Tower Bridge to the Thames Barrier.

Lea Rowing Club

Spring Hill, E5 9BL (Club house 8806 8282/ www.learc.org.uk). Clapton rail.
Rowing and sculling classes, and holiday courses for children aged ten or above who can swim at least 50m.

Royal Victoria Dock Watersports Centre

Gate 5, Tidal Basin Road, off Silvertown Way, E16 1AD (7511 2342/www.royaldockstrust. org.uk). Royal Victoria Dock DLR. **Membership** £88/6mths; £53/6mths 8-18s.
Dinghy sailing and RYA beginners' courses take place in Victoria Dock. A scholarship scheme offers free tuition.

Wimbledon Park Watersports Centre

Home Park Road, SW19 7HX (8947 4894/www.merton.gov.uk/sport). Wimbledon Park tube.
This centre offers sailing, canoeing and kayaking for children aged eight and above.

Stoke Newington West Reservoir Centre

Green Lanes, N4 2HA (8442 8116/ www.gll.org). Manor House tube/141, 341 bus.
Environmental education and watersports centre for dinghy sailing.

Surrey Docks Watersports Centre

Greenland Dock, Rope Street, SE16 7SX (7237 4009/www.fusion-lifestyle.com). Canada Water tube.
Eights and over can learn sailing, windsurfing and canoeing in this sheltered dock during the holidays. RYA courses are also available.

Westminster Boating Base

136 Grosvenor Road, SW1V 3JY (7821 7389/ www.westminsterboatingbase.co.uk). Pimlico tube/Vauxhall tube/rail.
This canoeing and sailing club for over-tens asks for donations rather than fees.

YOGA

Yoga is a great way to maintain children's co-ordination, flexibility and concentration, but do pick an approved and registered course. The biggest name in yoga for kids is **YogaBugs** (www.yogabugs.com). The company teaches three- to seven-year-olds at a variety of venues, using a mix of storytelling and songs to capture children's attention. Yoga'd Up is the next step, offering classes for eight- to 12-year-olds.

The **Special Yoga Centre** (*see below*) is a registered charity which offers a programme of one-to-one sessions for infants with disabilities.

The following centres run regular classes for children; check websites for details.

Holistic Health

64 Broadway Market, E8 4QJ (7275 8434/ www.holistichealthackney.co.uk). London Fields rail/26, 48, 55, 106, 236 bus.

Iyengar Institute

223A Randolph Avenue, W9 1NL (7624 3080/www.iyi.org.uk). Maida Vale tube.

Sivananda Yoga

Vedanta Centre, 51 Felsham Road, SW15 1AZ (8780 0160/www.sivananda.co.uk). Putney Bridge tube/Putney rail.

Special Yoga Centre

The Tay Building, 2A Wrentham Avenue, NW10 3HA (8968 1900/www.specialyoga. org.uk). Kensal Rise rail.

Triyoga

6 Erskine Road, NW3 3AJ (7483 3344/ www.triyoga.co.uk). Chalk Farm tube.

Yoga Junction

The Old Flower Shop, 93A Weston Park, N8 9PR (8347 0000/www.yogajunction.co.uk). Harringay rail/ W5 bus.

Activities

Consumer

Eating

Food for the brood.

Whether it's down to crusading chefs (step forward Jamie and Hugh), the organic boom, or increasingly choosy parents, more and more of London's restaurants have realised that a children's menu of nuggets, burgers, chicken and chips no longer cuts the mustard. It's not about phasing out old favourites, just upping the quality: chunky, freshly cut chips and home-made fish cakes beat limp, from-the-freezer fish fingers and fries any time. After all, sometimes, the simplest grub is the best: we're as partial to a bowl of tomato pasta or macaroni cheese as the next man, and you can't beat a heaped plate of sausages and mash.

That said, the capital's dining scene also offers plenty to entice children away from their usual favourites. One small bite can expand their culinary horizons no end: dim sum at **Royal China** (*see p235*), a black bean and cheese taco at **Wahaca** (*see p247*) or a prawn-stuffed rice paper roll at **Sông Quê Café** (*see p252*) are appealing enough to tempt the most doubtful of young diners.

We've tried to pick a range of cafés and restaurants to suit all tastes and budgets, from laid-back cafés and ice-cream parlours to special-occasion eateries. Some serve a dedicated children's menu, while others are happy to serve scaled-down grown-up mains for kids. Entertainment ranges from colouring sheets and pencils to well-stocked toy boxes and organised activities, giving parents the chance to put their feet up: lunch at an establishment like the **Brilliant Kids Café & Arts Centre** (*see p224*) is a rest cure for beleaguered parents.

BRASSERIES

Banners

21 Park Road, N8 8TE (8292 0001). Finsbury Park tube/rail, then W7 bus. **Meals served** 9am-11.30pm Mon-Thur; 9am-midnight Fri; 10am-4pm, 5pm-midnight Sat; 10am-4pm, 5-11pm Sun. **Main courses** £9.25-£14.75. **Set lunch** £6.95 1 course. **Credit** MC, V.
The menu (with a cover drawn by Louis, age 13) ranges from Sri Lanka to the Caribbean via good old Blighty, and is complemented by a list of specials. Smoothies and floats are popular with children, and there's a long list of cocktails plus decent Argentinian chardonnay by the glass for parental pick-me-ups. Jerk chicken burger didn't look appealing but tasted delicious, with beautifully tender slices of nicely-spiced bird, and we liked the skin-on chips. Local mums and dads return time and time again, drawn by the laid-back, hip feel, while even fussy kids are bound to be tempted by something on the menu. *Buggy access. Children's menu (£2.95-£4.75). Crayons. High chairs. Toys.*

Chapters

43-45 Montpeller Vale, Blackheath Village, SE3 0TJ (8333 2666/www.chaptersrestaurants. com). Blackheath rail. **Breakfast served** 8-11.30am Mon-Fri; 8am-noon Sat; 9am-noon Sun. **Lunch served** noon-3pm Mon-Sat; noon-4pm Sun. **Tea served** 3-6pm Mon-Sat; 4-6pm Sun. **Dinner served** 6-11pm Mon-Sat; 6-9pm Sun. **Main courses** £7.50-£22.95. **Credit** MC, V.
Families with children in tow are subtly ushered to the first floor at this Blackheath brasserie, leaving couples and adult groups in peace downstairs. Exposed brickwork, wooden flooring, banquette seating and scatter cushions create a relaxed, informal setting. The all-day dining strapline translates to a menu that spans eggs benedict and cream teas to delicate fish dishes and hearty traditional roasts. Children can choose between macaroni cheese, sausage and mash or fish and chips, and there's ice-cream for pudding. *Buggy access. Children's menu (£3.95-£4.50). Disabled access: toilet. High chairs. Nappy-changing facilities.*

National Café.

Depot

Tideway Yard, 125 Mortlake High Street, SW14 8SN (8878 9462/www.depotbrasserie. co.uk). Barnes Bridge or Mortlake rail/209 bus. **Brunch served** 9.30am-12.30pm Sat. **Lunch served** noon-3pm Mon-Fri; 12.30-3.30pm Sat; noon-4pm Sun. **Dinner served** 6-11pm Mon-Sat; 6-10.30pm Sun. **Main courses** £9.95-£15. **Set meal** (noon-3pm Mon-Fri) £12.50 2 courses, £15.50 3 courses. **Credit** AmEx, DC, MC, V.

This smart brasserie is always full of youngsters, from toddlers to teens. The setting – a courtyard by the Thames – is a big part of the draw, but the food is similarly appealing. There are exotic salads (jerusalem artichoke, salsify, russet apple and french bean with hazelnut), alongside fish (tuna sashimi, roast cod) and meat dishes (slow roast pork belly, roast beef salad), many of which can be ordered as starters or mains. The kids' menu includes pasta, fish cakes, chicken strips and Sunday roasts; for pud, there's ice-cream. A monthly colouring-in competition awards the winner and two guests a free meal. *Buggy access. Children's set meal (£5.75). Crayons. High chairs. Nappy-changing facilities. Tables outdoors (11, courtyard).*

Giraffe

Units 1&2, Riverside Level 1, Royal Festival Hall, SE1 8XX (7928 2004/www.giraffe.net). Waterloo tube/rail. **Meals served** 8am-10.45pm Mon-Fri; 9am-10.45pm Sat; 9am-10.15pm Sun. **Main courses** £7.95-£14.95. **Set dinner** (5-7pm Mon-Fri) £7.25 2 courses. **Credit** AmEx, MC, V. **Map** p317 M8.

Pleasant staff at this South Bank branch of Giraffe welcome lots of families during the daytime. On a sunny day, try for a table on the riverside patio and order up a giddy giraffe (one of Giraffe's perkily-named but tempting smoothies). This chain is the same whichever branch you go to; the colour is orange, the soundtrack is world music and the murals are full of happy, smiling faces. The kids' menu is lengthy and offers a cooked breakfast (sausage, eggs, beans and toast, or a veggie version) until 4pm. Options for later in the day include grilled chicken with fries, mash or vegetables, or vegetarian pizza, pasta or falafel. For the adults, substantial salads offer a healthy alternative to the excellent burgers and noodle dishes. Desserts are on the small side, though the warm chocolate brownie with hot chocolate sauce is always a treat. *Balloons. Buggy access. Children's set meal (£5.50 noon-3pm Mon-Fri). Crayons. Disabled access: toilet. High chairs. Nappy-changing facilities. Tables outdoors (40, terrace). Takeaway service.* **Branches** throughout town.

National Café

East Wing, National Gallery, Trafalgar Square, WC2N 5DN (7747 5942/www.the nationalcafe.com). Charing Cross tube/rail. **Breakfast served** 8-11.30am, **lunch served** noon-5pm daily. **Dinner served** 5.30-11pm Mon-Sat. **Tea served** 3-5.30pm daily. **Meals served** 10am-6pm Sun. **Main courses** £8.50-£16.50. **Set dinner** (5.30-7pm) £14.50 2 courses, £17.50 3 courses. **Credit** MC, V.

The glossy black woodwork, soaring ceilings and red leather seating in this grown-up dining room might seem off-putting, but families looking for a treat are well catered for. Children get their own menu, which includes mini macaroni cheese, burger and chips and chicken and steamed broccoli, but would probably be far happier with an ice-cream sundae (something of a speciality here), especially the absurdly extravagant 'National Catastrophe'. Adults can choose from classic brasserie mains like steamed sea bass with braised fennel and grown-up burger and chips, or opt for one of the charcuterie or cheese platters. It's a great place to get away from the tourist throngs for a while.
Buggy access. Disabled access: toilet. High chairs. Children's menu (£4.50-£6). Nappy-changing facilities.

Tate Modern Café: Level 2
2nd Floor, Tate Modern, Sumner Street, SE1 9TG (7401 5014/www.tate.org.uk). Southwark tube/London Bridge tube/rail/Blackfriars rail. **Meals served** 10am-6pm Mon-Thur, Sat, Sun; 10am-10pm Fri. **Main courses** £10.50-£12.95. **Credit** AmEx, MC, V.
It's no wonder Tate Modern is a popular venue for a family day out – and a recent winner of the Time Out Best Family Restaurant award. With a morning of artistic appreciation in the bag, it's a relaxed spot to settle for a delicious meal and an enthusiastic welcome. When an adult orders a main and second course, an accompanying child can feast on a three-course menu of superior fare, free of charge. Kids can choose soup, salad or garlic bread to start, followed by fresh fish fingers, pasta bolognese or macaroni cheese, then ice-cream, jelly or fruit salad. Floor-to-ceiling windows framing the Thames provide passing entertainment, but there are also art and literacy activities on the kids' menus to keep idle hands busy. It's top-quality food, with an emphasis on quality over quantity; ingredients are carefully sourced and seasonal wherever possible. Get here by 12.30pm at the latest if you want to be led straight to a table.
Buggy access. Children's set menu (£5.95 11am-3pm daily). Disabled access: lift, toilet. High chairs. Nappy-changing facilities.

CAFÉS

Boiled Egg & Soldiers
63 Northcote Road, SW11 1ND (7223 4894). Clapham Junction rail. **Meals served** 9am-6pm Tue-Sat; 9am-4pm Sun. **Main courses** £5-£10. **Credit** MC, V.

Unassuming and cosy, this café in oh-so-trendy Clapham is the perfect enclave for a quick lunch or tea and cake with the children. It serves plain and simple infant-friendly breakfast staples such as the eponymous egg and soldiers alongside more parent-appropriate 'Hangover Cures', including Virgin Mary mocktails, fresh smoothies and wholesome baguettes and jacket potatoes. The relatively compact premises soon fill up with buggies, but if the weather's nice there are always a few tables on the street outside. It's possibly not ideal for a big family sit-down meal, but spot-on for an afternoon mothers' meeting and a milkshake.
Buggy access. Children's menu (£3.50-£4.50). High chairs. Tables outdoors (3, pavement; 8, garden). Takeaway service.

Blue Mountain
18 Northcross Road, SE22 9EU (8299 6953/ www.bluemo.co.uk). East Dulwich tube. **Meals served** 9am-6pm Mon, Tue; 9am-10pm Wed-Sat; 10am-6pm Sun. **Main courses** £4.50-£8. **Credit** AmEx, MC, V.
Blue Mountain was an East Dulwich institution long before the arrival of Bugaboos and loft conversions, and continues to draw the crowds with its quality all-day breakfasts and calorific cake selection. The perennial best seller is the Full Monty: herby butcher's sausage, bacon, beans, portobello mushroom, grilled tomato, chunky toast, a choice of eggs and a cup of tea. More interesting, and better value, are the lunchtime specials, which on our visit featured panfried haddock with capers and sun-dried tomatoes (£7.45) and stuffed pepper with aubergine, chickpeas in Moroccan sauce and couscous (£5.65); the jerk chicken (served with plantain) is also highly recommended. The funky mosaic patio, made by local artists, is a sunny spot to observe the bustle of Northcross Road (particularly its Saturday market), and is packed with families and freelancers during the week. Long the envy of neighbouring up-and-coming enclaves such as Honor Oak, Blue Mountain now has a branch in Sydenham.
Buggy access. Children's menu (£2.45-£3.65). Disabled access: toilet. High chairs. Nappy-changing facilities. Toys.
Branch 260 Kirkdale, SE26 4RG (8659 6016).

Brew House
Kenwood, Hampstead Lane, NW3 7JR (8341 5384/www.companyofcooks.com). Bus 210, 214. **Meals served** Oct-Mar 9am-dusk daily. Apr-Sept 9am-6pm daily (7.30pm on concert nights). **Main courses** £6.95-£11.95. **Credit** (over £10) MC, V.

The Brew House is a self-service café run by Company of Cooks in the wonderful setting of Kenwood House (*see p58*). It would be hard to find a more picturesque, sheltered terrace on which to sit and dine in the sunshine. Breakfasts are hearty with huge sausages, scrambled eggs, very good bacon, field mushrooms and tomatoes; on bright weekend mornings, be here by 10am to stake out a table. For lunch, there's a choice of quiche and salad, a generous meat dish or soup with various accompaniments. Children can have smaller portions of the day's dishes, or a bowl of macaroni cheese that's enough to fill an adult. The queuing system takes a while to get used to, and at busy times the hot food service can seem interminably slow. Somehow, none of this matters once the food is on the table – and it's impossible to come away and not feel as if you've had lunch in the countryside.
Buggy access. Children's menu (£2.75-£4). High chairs. Nappy-changing facilities. Tables outdoors (40, garden). Takeaway service.

Brilliant Kids Café & Arts Centre

8 Station Terrace, NW10 5RT (8964 4120/ www.brilliantkids.co.uk). Kensal Green tube. **Meals served** 8am-6pm Mon-Fri; 9am-5pm Sat. Closes 2pm Sat during birthday parties. **Main courses** £6.95-£7.50. **Credit** MC, V.

With the North London Line's Kensal Green station just opposite Brilliant Kids Café & Arts Centre, there's no reason why locals should be the only ones to appreciate this great venue. The food alone is worth travelling for, but any parent with a newspaper to read or some work to catch up on will be delighted by Brilliant's next-door studio, which offers supervised art workshops for children (*see p184*). Substantial all-day breakfasts come with thick bacon rashers and sausage, and the daily lunch special is always superb (all meat comes from Devon Rose Organics). Mums' coffee mornings are fuelled by great cappuccinos and lattes and some fine pastries and cakes (our favourite is the raspberry crème anglais tart). Also on the board are salads, bagels and sandwiches, all made with fresh and imaginative ingredients. Children can have smaller portions of anything that's chalked up, but are also tempted by special treats such as miniature rainbow-sprinkled fairy cakes and gorgeous sausage rolls. The owner goes out of her way to be welcoming and helpful (on our last visit, the café was just closing, but took us in nonetheless), and its friendly atmosphere makes Brilliant a laid-back place to linger.
Birthday parties (2-5pm Sat, Sun). Buggy access. Crayons. Disabled access: toilet. High chairs. Tables outdoors (3, garden). Play area. Takeaway service.

A haven on the heath: Hampstead's **Brew House**. *See p223.*

Café On The Rye

Peckham Rye, SE15 3UA (8693 9431).
Peckham Rye rail. **Meals served** 9am-
5.30pm daily. **Main courses** £3.50-£7.
No credit cards.
From the moment this café opened in late 2007
it has done a roaring trade. Tactically
positioned next to the One O'Clock Club, it's the
perfect location for parents who have just had a
hectic swing-pushing workout. The food is
wholesome, organic and delicious, ranging from
full breakfasts to toasted ciabatta stuffed with
camembert, mushrooms, lemon and thyme, and
Angus beefburgers with caramelised onion,
bulgar wheat and salad – and don't overlook the
sweets and sticky cakes. The owners are also
applying for an alcohol licence. The architecture
is pretty tasty too: the circular wooden frontage
faces the vast green expanse of Peckham Rye,
and there are chairs to sit on outside and enjoy
the scenery. On the day we visited, though, most
of the under-fives were too busy rolling down
the nearby grassy slope to take in the view.

Cibo

Mamas & Papas, 256-258 Regent Street,
W1B 3AF (01484 438476/www.mamasand
papas.com). Oxford Circus tube. **Meals**
served 10am-8pm Mon-Wed, Fri; 10am-9pm
Thur; 9am-8pm Sat; noon-6pm Sun. **Main**
courses £6.75-£9.95. **Set dinner** (4-7.30pm
Mon-Fri) £9.95 3 courses. **Credit** MC, V.
Map p314 J6.
Carefully tailored to the needs of pregnant
women and small children, this café provides a
peaceful haven from the West End tourist
overload outside. Set at the back of the first floor
of the flagship Mamas & Papas store, there's
plenty of space for buggies and a very warm
welcome from the predominantly Italian staff.
The food on our last visit could have done with
more seasoning, but the menu is generally
healthy and appealing. The breakfast section
offers organic toast, bagels and salmon and
scrambled eggs, along with lunchtime
smoothies, sandwiches, salads and hot meals.
Children's dishes include organic burgers and
fries, organic salmon fish cake and ketchup,
pasta dishes and ice-cream.
Buggy access. Children's menu (£3.25-£4.50).
High chairs. Nappy-changing facilities.
Takeaway service. Toys.

Coffee & Crayons

915 Fulham Road, SW6 5HU (3080 1050/
www.coffeeandcrayons.co.uk). Putney Bridge
tube. **Meals served** 7.30am-6pm daily.
Main courses £2.65-£7.95. **Credit** MC, V.

If you want to entertain your children with a
clear conscience, this is definitely the place.
Coffee & Crayons banks with the Co-op and uses
organic and fair trade produce where possible.
For those simply interested in refuelling, there
are snacks and pastries: the pies come highly
recommended. As the name suggests, this light,
funky café caters for both the thirsty parent and
their artistic offspring, with a range of hot
drinks and smoothies upstairs and a supervised,
arts and crafts-focused playroom downstairs
where children can unleash their inner Picasso
(there's a charge, but you can stay as long as you
like). There are also regular organised events,
ranging from dressing-up and music sessions to
fairy school. There's plenty of room to park your
buggies inside; if you can trust your toddlers
not to make a beeline for the King's Road with
your credit card, there are seats out front too.
Buggy access. Children's menu (£1.50-£4.25).
Disabled access: toilet. High chairs. Nappy-
changing facilities. Play area (£4 18mths-
9yrs; £3.50 under 18mths). Tables outdoors
(3, pavement). Takeaway service.

Common Ground

Wandsworth Common, off Dorlcote Road,
SW18 3RT (8874 9386). Wandsworth
Common rail. **Meals served** 9am-5.30pm
Mon-Fri; 10am-5.30pm Sat, Sun. **Main**
courses £3.50-£9. **Credit** MC, V.
Who needs fancy decor when the views from the
window are so glorious? With cricket pitches on
one side and a pristine bowling green on the
other, this former lodge building keeps things
simple. There are wooden floors and wooden
tables in the conservatory, a generous patio with
tables outside, and a cosier room with sofas and
buckets of toys where parent and toddler
groups meet on weekdays. The food is tastier
than its simple presentation might suggest, with
a children's menu that includes home-made
chicken goujons or locally-made sausages
served with mash or chips and broccoli or peas.
There are also simple sandwiches and tasty
cakes. The only thing disturbing the peace are
locals' dogs, tied up and yapping outside while
their owners take refreshment.
Buggy access. Children's menu (£2.25-£3.95).
High chairs. Nappy-changing facilities. Play
area. Takeaway service.

Crumpet

66 Northcote Road, SW11 6QL (7924 1117/
www.crumpet.biz). Clapham Junction rail.
Meals served 8.30am-6pm Mon-Sat; 9.30am-
6pm Sun. **Main courses** £4.20-£7.50. **Credit**
AmEx, MC, V.

Pizza perfection at **Franco Manca**. *See p229.*

Located in the middle of south London's nappy valley, this café knows its well-heeled clientele and strives to make it as comfortable as possible. The owners have thought of everything, from the well-stocked play corner and bookshelf to the vast children's menu. There's a large space to park buggies, and even the toilets feature free nappies and a child-size loo. Lunches for adults suffer from slightly zealous portion control, but the children's plates are piled with steaming veg and a choice of salmon fingers, sausages, cottage pie, chicken fingers and more. Babies are catered for with purées for three different age groups. Proper teas, with scones, imaginative sandwiches and cakes baked by local mums are also a Crumpet speciality. Everything's organic and free-range where possible, naturally.
Buggy access. Children's menu (£1.20-£4.50). Crayons. Disabled access: toilet. High chairs. Nappy-changing facilities. Play area (under-5s). Tables outdoors (2, pavement). Takeaway service.

Deep Blue Café
Science Museum, Exhibition Road, SW7 2DD (7942 4488/www.sciencemuseum.org.uk). South Kensington tube. **Meals served** 11.30am-3pm daily. **Main courses** £7.25-£8.95. **Credit** MC, V.

It's certainly an education getting to the Science Museum's Deep Blue Café. From the Exhibition Road entrance you pass an Apollo lunar module, a Model T Ford and Stephenson's Rocket. Once there, the café is true to its name. The subdued lighting is such a powerful shade of blue you risk losing sight of your kids if they go walkabout. The food is not especially inventive, but it is filling. An eclectic menu ranges from scrumptious sausages to sizzling stir fries, via the ubiquitous panini and salads. The children's menu offers a good range of sophisticated pizza, pasta and chip-based meals, then pudding. It's best for well-behaved little Einsteins though; service can be slow, and those with energy to burn might prefer packed lunches.
Buggy access. Children's set meal (£5.50). Disabled access. High chairs. Nappy-changing facilities.

Esca
160 Clapham High Street, SW4 7UG (7622 2288/www.escauk.com). Clapham Common tube. **Meals served** 8am-9pm Mon-Fri; 9am-9pm Sat, Sun. **Main courses** £3.95-£8.35. **Credit** MC, V.

Esca's light, roomy design features banks of communal, blond wood tables to encourage sociable dining. Catering for vegetarians and vegans as well as those of a carnivorous bent, the menu includes dishes such as grilled halloumi and pumpkin with flaked almonds, honey-roasted gammon and poached salmon, all within a price range that doesn't set alarm bells ringing. Among other delights, Esca offers a 'make your own' breakfast selection, and so enticing a range of salads, pies and pastas that ordering can involve a serious amount of deliberation. Dishes also come in smaller starter portions, which are great for children and toddlers. What really stands out, though, is the eye-catching display of cakes and tarts; chocolate brownies sit alongside layered cream sponges and generous slabs of cheesecake. Complete with a Victorian library-style moving ladder, the attached deli stocks a vast array of jams, fancy biscuits, chocolates and gifts, much of it shipped in from Italy.
Buggy access. Disabled access: toilet. High chairs. Nappy-changing facilities. Takeaway service.

Fait Maison
Ravenscourt Park, Paddenswick Road, W6 0UG (8563 9291/www.fait-maison.co.uk). Ravenscourt Park tube. **Meals served** 8am-6pm daily. **Main courses** £3.95-£7.50. **No credit cards.**

Rainforest Cafe

A WILD PLACE TO SHOP AND EAT®

Rainforest Cafe is a unique venue bringing to life the sights and sounds of the rainforest.

Come and try our fantastic menu!
With a re-launched healthy kids menu, including gluten free, dairy free and organic options.

15% DISCOUNT
off your final food bill*

Offer valid seven days a week.
Maximum party size of 6.

020 7434 3111

20 Shaftesbury Avenue, Piccadilly Circus, London W1D 7EU
www.therainforestcafe.co.uk

*Please show this advert to your safari guide when seated.
Cannot be used in conjunction with any other offer.

Field day

tomatoes and cucumbers. After an afternoon's toil, hard workers can be treated to ice-cream at the farm shop; you can also buy local honey and fresh cream to take home.

Once back at base, you can set the children to work turning their tray of produce into simple dishes such as a vegetable tart or fruit crumble, or they can help you make jams and pickles for winter. Food tastes so much better when you've picked it yourself. And after all that fresh air and hard work, a sound night's sleep is guaranteed.

Parkside Farm is open June-Oct, 9am-5.30pm Tue-Sun.

Despite the emergence of farmers' markets and the slow food movement, supermarkets still dominate the British food scene, and fruit and vegetables often arrive in the home pre-washed and vacuum packed, with little hint of their earthy origins. Pick your own is the perfect antidote; a cost-effective and fun way of providing children with their five-a-day. They will relish the opportunity to get their hands dirty and work for their food. And for the green-conscious, no food-miles, no packaging and supporting the local economy into the bargain means PYO ticks all the eco-friendly boxes.

Parkside Farm (Hadley Road, Enfield, Middlesex, EN2 8LA, 8367 2035, www.parksidefarmpyo.co.uk), just north of Enfield and easily accessible from the M25, is a family-run business set in beautiful countryside. Exclusively pick your own, the farm produces about 20 different crops. From the beginning of June to the beginning of October you can pick whatever is in season, from soft fruit to vegetables – including broad beans,

Consumer

From the outside, Fait Maison looks like an unappealing council carbuncle, but the interior prompts a speedy re-evaluation. Collapse on to an inviting sofa and tuck into supersized croissants and mega-meringues. On the day of our visit, dish of the day was spicy meatballs and rice (£6.50), which came in a portion that would feed an entire family; at £3.50 a slice, the freshly cooked pizzas also looked good value. The atmosphere is cheerful and chilled: park your pram by your table and grab a high chair, or head for the outdoor seating. If you've been on the swings, racing round the park, or tackling the shops in nearby Hammersmith, this is the ideal place to recover. Fait Maison means 'home-made', and this feels like a home-from-home. *Buggy access. Children's menu (£3.90). Disabled access: toilets. Tables outdoors (6, park). Takeaway service.* **Branches** 3 Stratford Road, W8 6RQ (7937 2777); 245 Goldhawk Road, W12 8EU (8222 8755).

Feast on the Hill
46 Fortis Green Road, N10 3HN (8444 4957). Highgate tube, then 43, 134 bus. **Meals served** 8am-6pm Mon, Tue; 8am-10pm Wed-Sat; 9am-5pm Sun. **Main courses** £4.95-£12.50. **Credit** MC, V.

This appealing establishment was formerly known as Café On The Hill; having joined forces with the neighbouring Feast Delicatessen, it has adjusted its name accordingly. A transitional phase had visitors that wanted cake having to trot next door to the deli to choose; thankfully, the café now has a small selection on display in-house. All-day breakfasts are Feast's main event, with full English, vegetarian and free-range eggs benedict among the many options available. A short lunch menu, served from 11am to 4pm, offers paninis, salads and a few heartier platefuls like beef lasagne or steak-frites. Dishes sound simple but are cooked with loving attention to detail. The children's menu was being rewritten on our last visit, but usually includes variations on the adult breakfasts and no-nonsense classics such as spaghetti bolognese. Popular with all age groups, the café is always busy. Smiley service is charged at ten per cent. *Buggy access. Children's menu (£2.20-£4.95). High chairs. Tables outdoors (6, pavement). Takeaway service.*

Franco Manca
4 Market Row, Electric Lane, SW9 8LD (7738 3021/www.francomanca.co.uk). Brixton tube. **Meals served** noon-5pm Mon-Sat. **Main courses** £4-£5.90. **Credit** MC, V.

Franco Manca is a thinking man's pizzeria. The sourdough is left to rise for 20 hours before baking, and its ingredients are largely organic. Pizzas (some with simple toppings like tomato, basil and mozzerella, some with more unusual combinations such as ricotta and pork) are disarmingly good. This place may not look like much from the outside – a handful of café tables and a couple of shared wooden pews – but families could do worse than stock up here and take the booty over to Brockwell Park (*see p112*). *Buggy access. Disabled access: toilet. Tables outdoors (6, pavement). Takeaway service.*

Frizzante at City Farm
1A Goldsmith's Row, E2 8QA (7739 2266/ www.frizzanteltd.co.uk). Bus 26, 48, 55. **Meals served** 10am-5.30pm Tue, Wed, Fri-Sun; 10am-5.30pm, 7-10pm Thur. **Main courses** £4.50-£10.40. **Credit** MC, V.

With its colourful oilcloth-covered tables and make-and-mend style, Frizzante is like an outsized farmhouse kitchen. Work up an appetite for the hearty portions by meeting the pigs, chickens, geese, sheep and goats in the farmyard outside. Visitors tend to opt for the daily specials if they're not tucking into one of the legendary breakfasts, so it's worth arriving early before dishes sell out. Kids tend to plump for no-nonsense, populist pasta dishes such as spaghetti bolognese or macaroni cheese; for afters, there are incredibly good home-made ice-creams and cakes. Babies with forgetful mums can purloin a tube of Ella's Kitchen purée from the shelves, although the chef was a bit grumpy about heating up some mush in tupperware on our last visit. Generally, however, the welcome is warm and the atmosphere delightfully laid-back. The only downside is having to order at the till, where there's invariably a queue (the person taking the orders also makes teas and coffees). Still, for a café with so much to offer, including outside seating for warm days, it would be churlish to complain. *Buggy access. Children's menu (£2.25-£4.25). Disabled access: toilet. High chairs. Nappy-changing facilities. Tables outdoors (12, garden). Takeaway service.*

Garden Café
Inner Circle, Regent's Park, NW1 4NU (7935 5729/www.thegardencafe.co.uk). Baker Street or Regent's Park tube. Oct-Apr **Breakfast served** 9-11am, **lunch served** noon-4pm daily. May-Sept **Breakfast served** 9-11am, **lunch served** noon-4pm, **dinner served** 5-8pm daily. **Main courses** £8.50-£12.50. **Credit** MC, V.

The first time we tried the Garden Café on a Sunday, we were laughed out of the building for not having booked. The staff weren't much friendlier on a second visit, although we did manage to get a table this time. Garden Café is run by Company of Cooks, who do a much more persuasive job at Kenwood's Brew House (*see p223*). Still, on a sunny day, the tables in the garden are a lovely place to sit and watch the world go by, and the food is a cut above the average. Classics such as risotto are given imaginative touches like using barley instead of rice, although a very small slice of savoury tart with a few lettuce leaves seemed expensive at £8.50. Children are offered a limited menu, but it's home-made and topped off by ice-creams from north London's legendary purveyor of glacé, Marine Ices.

Buggy access. Children's set meal (£6). Disabled access: toilet. Nappy-changing facilities. Tables outdoors (40, park).

Golders Hill Park Refreshment House

North End Way, NW3 7HD (8455 8010). Golders Green or Hampstead tube/210, 268 bus. **Meals served** *Summer* 9am-6.30pm daily. *Winter* 9am-dusk daily. **Main courses** £3-£7. **Credit** (over £10) AmEx, MC, V.

There has been a tea room here since the 19th century. Sadly, the old building was demolished after being damaged in World War II, but the pavilion style café that stands here now is a lovely place to sit and eat; there are views over the well-manicured park from indoors and outdoors on the large south-facing terrace, where elderly Jewish local residents talk like they're in a Woody Allen movie, *sans* New York accent. The food is on an Italian theme, with assorted tasty pasta dishes. The cakes don't look terribly inviting, but the ice-cream is very good (also sold from the kiosk at the side of the building in summer), as is the coffee.

Buggy access. Children's menu (£3-£5). Disabled access: toilet. High chairs. Nappy-changing facilities. Tables outdoors (25, terrace). Takeaway service.

Gracelands

118 College Road, NW10 5HD (8964 9161/ www.gracelandscafe.com). Kensal Green tube. **Meals served** 8.30am-5pm Mon-Fri; 9am-5pm Sat; 9.30am-3.30pm Sun. **Main courses** £3.95-£11.95. **Credit** MC, V.

An indoor play area and the chance of an interesting workshop in Gracelands Yard next door means this airy, family-focused café is permanently packed. There's little sense of order, though, and service can be utterly chaotic, even when staff numbers appear to equal the number of customers. On our last visit, meals were going around the café, garden and pavement tables several times before finding their destination. That said, when our large mixed salad platters finally arrived they were highly imaginative and lovingly assembled; highlights included grated beetroot and celeriac in lemon juice, crushed potatoes with chives, perfectly roasted pepper and butternut squash and black beans in zingy dressing. The all-day breakfast menu, lunchtime specials, cakes and pastries are also made with attention to detail. Children's pasta portions are enormous and can put off reluctant eaters or leave greedier kids with tummy ache, so order one to share. All in all, a great local resource – but one that knows it's got a captive market.

Buggy access. Children's set meal (£3.50). High chairs. Nappy-changing facilities. Play area. Tables outdoors (4, pavement; 11, garden). Takeaway service. Toys.

Hummingbird Bakery

47 Old Brompton Road, SW7 3JP (7584 0055/www.hummingbirdbakery.com). South Kensington tube. **Open** 10.30am-7pm daily. **Credit** MC, V.

After braving the crowds of yummy mummies with kiddies on a sugar high, settle down among tasteful shades of pink and brown in the small café, or nab one of the coveted outdoor tables. American-style sweets are the order of the day, with cupcakes being the star attraction. Get to this chichi South Ken bakery early to avoid the frustrating queues and spotty service or, better yet, take one for the road.

Buggy access. Tables outdoors (4, pavement). Takeaway service.
Branches 133 Portobello Road, W11 2DY (7229 6446)

Inn The Park

St James's Park, SW1A 2BJ (7451 9999/ www.innthepark.com). St James's Park or Westminster tube. **Meals served** 8am-11pm Mon-Fri; 9am-9.30pm Sat; 9am-6pm Sun. *Winter* times vary; phone for details. **Main courses** £10.50-£18.50. **Credit** AmEx, MC, V. **Map** p317 K8.

The setting for Oliver Peyton's timber-clad, glass-fronted posh park café couldn't be more idyllic. The tables on the terrace overlook St James's Park and the picturesque Duck Island; even the indoor tables have lovely views, thanks to floor-to-ceiling windows. Most families head straight to the self-service area, as the restaurant is heart-stoppingly expensive (there is a children's menu, but it'll set you back £7.50 and doesn't include dessert); more modestly priced self-service offerings include soups, sandwiches, pies and cakes. If it's a special occasion, you can book a summer barbecue for a party (minimum 25 people).

Buggy access. Children's menu (£7.50). Disabled access: toilet. High chairs. Nappy-changing facilities. Tables outdoors (40, patio). Takeaway service.

Mudchute Kitchen

Mudchute Park & Farm, Pier Street, E14 3HP (7515 5901/www.mudchutekitchen.org). Mudchute DLR/D6, D7, D8 bus. **Meals served** 9am-4pm Tue-Sun. **Main courses** £3.50-£8.50. **Credit** MC, V.

This lovely spot in the middle of Mudchute City Farm *(see p134)* is well used by locals. Inside, the wax tablecloths and toys give the spacious hut a homely air. Outside, children love to sit in the large courtyard and watch the horses nodding their heads over the stable doors. Service at the counter is a bit casual (we had to call into the kitchen both times we wanted to order), but this is a community hub, not a fine dining establishment. The fresh, seasonal menu isn't extensive, but it's all own-made. The menu usually features a few hot dishes (Moroccan meatballs, lentil soup or pasta with mushrooms and cream, for example), and there's an all-day breakfast menu. Children might turn their noses up at Mudchute's version of baked beans on toast (made with butter beans and homemade tomato sauce), but grown-ups will be seriously impressed. The cakes are a highlight; poppy seed and ginger are both moist and delicious, while the delectable carrot cake is worth the trip alone. Wash it down with a very strong cup of coffee before heading off to look at the animals.

Buggy access. Children's menu (£2.50-£3.50). Disabled access: toilet. High chairs. Nappy-changing facilities. Tables outdoors (15, courtyard). Takeaway service.

Parlour

167 Stoke Newington Church Street, N16 0UL (7923 0654). Stoke Newington rail/tube. **Meals served** 8am-6.30pm daily. **Main courses** £2.25-£4.40. **Credit** MC, V.

This Stokey café specialises in gluten-, wheat- and dairy-free grub for hungry people of all ages. A wide selection of fillings are available on various different breads, or inside jacket potatoes. Freshly squeezed juices and fruit smoothies are a healthy and delicious option, and the own-made waffles a real treat –

especially slathered with banana, toffee and whipped cream. Relaxed, friendly staff and shabby-but-almost-chic decor complement the rustic food. There is a shady courtyard and a playroom stacked full of toys, books and games.

Buggy access. Disabled access. High chairs. Nappy- changing facilities. Play area. Tables outdoors (3, garden). Takeaway service. Toys.

Pavilion Café, Dulwich

Dulwich Park, off College Road, SE21 7BQ (8299 1383/www.pavilioncafedulwich.co.uk). North Dulwich or West Dulwich rail. **Meals served** *Summer* 9am-6.30pm daily. *Winter* 9am-4pm daily. **Main courses** £3.50-£6.95. **Credit cards** MC, V.

Busy on weekdays and positively heaving at weekends, this is the park café by which all others should be judged. The well-balanced menu has serious child appeal, offering grilled chicken, penne pasta, Scotch beefburgers, chunky chips and sandwiches. There's also organic baby food, Innocent smoothies and garishly coloured ice drinks, plus raisins, crisps, fruit and crayons (obviously not for eating). For afters, there's ice-cream – also sold through a side hatch in summer. Daily specials for grown-ups are overshadowed by the all-day breakfasts of top-quality sausages and bacon, free-range eggs and chunky toast (white or wholemeal). Food is sourced locally (Borough Market for veg, William Rose for meat and Moxon's for fish), cakes are home-made and, where possible, food is prepared fresh on site. As well as serving great food, the café has also become a social hub, providing information on local events, a colourful play corner, baby changing facilities and clean toilets, and bird food for feeding the ducks; it can also cater for birthday parties. Outdoor tables offer verdant views in summer; in winter, it's a cosy spot to warm up over a hot chocolate (with a shot of rum for the grown-ups). If you don't like children, you may want to give this place a wide berth; if you have some of your own, it's a lifesaver.

Buggy access. Children's menu (£1.50-£3.95). Disabled access: toilet. High chairs. Nappy-changing facilities. Play area. Tables outdoors (12, terrace). Takeaway service.

Pavilion Café, Highgate

Highgate Woods, Muswell Hill Road, N10 3JN (8444 4777). Highgate tube. **Meals served** 9am-1hr before park closing daily. **Main courses** £6-£10. **Credit** AmEx, MC, V.

Set in a clearing amid the trees, the Pavilion Café's leafy setting makes it a firm favourite with families. Whatever the time of day, week

or year, there's sure to be buggies in evidence. Indoor space is limited to seven tables, but a covered area provides shade in summer and shelter in winter. Open-air outdoor tables are in ready supply, and are completely enclosed by bushes and a fence – ideal for letting the kids have a wander while the adults order coffees. While the main menu is Mediterranean-influenced, the children's dishes are more straightforward: burger and chips and pasta are the favourites. Save room for pudding: the ice-cream is very good indeed, as is the warm, densely moist brownie. On our last visit, the chef came round with samples of a lemon polenta cake that he'd just taken out of the oven. Service is presided over by the ever-attentive head waiter, whose charm puts a twinkle in local mums' eyes.
Buggy access. Children's set meal (£3.50). Crayons. Disabled access: toilet. High chairs. Nappy-changing facilities. Tables outdoors (30, garden). Takeaway service.

Pavilion Tea House
Greenwich Park, Blackheath Gate, SE10 8QY (8858 9695). Blackheath rail/Greenwich rail/DLR. **Meals served** 9am-5.30pm Mon-Fri; 9am-6pm Sat, Sun. **Main courses** £4.95-£6.60. **Credit** MC, V.
Weekdays are the best time to visit this hexagonal park café; at weekends, the painfully slow service means the queue is always enormous. The menu is full of appealingly hearty fare, with meaty specials, generously filled sandwiches and a good value all-day breakfast menu. It's licensed, so you can wash your lunch down with a glass of wine. Options for children include pasta dishes and baked beans on toast, but limited indoor space means parents are requested to leave pushchairs outside. If you're not too full after the large main courses, the own-made cakes are very good.
Buggy access. Children's menu (£2.25-£2.95). Disabled access: toilet. High chairs. Nappy-changing facilities. Tables outdoors (20, patio).

Petitou
63 Choumert Road, SE15 4AR (7639 2613). Peckham Rye rail. **Meals served** 9am-5.30pm Mon-Sat; 10am-5.30pm Sun. **Main courses** £4.35-£6.95. **Credit** AmEx, MC, V.
This charming local café serves wholesome fare, overlaid with an appealing dash of nostalgia. Located at the leafier end of Peckham, it attracts an arty crowd alongside the bourgeois buggy wielders. All-day breakfasts range from childhood favourites such as scrambled egg, English muffins and toast with peanut butter or marmalade to (love 'em or hate 'em) cheesy marmite crumpets. Salads and quiches are made from locally sourced ingredients, cakes are homely, juices are freshly squeezed, herbal teas plentiful, and almost everything is prefixed with 'organic'. The furniture is a junk shop pot-pourri, with an old-fashioned coat stand and mismatched wooden chairs. Community notices and posters for local events cover the walls, while the radio hums Classic FM. The relaxed atmosphere, cheery interior and shady front patio make this a perfect lunch spot for families.
Buggy access. Disabled access: toilet. High chairs. Tables outdoors (4, pavement).

Ragged Canteen
Beaconsfield, 22 Newport Street, SE11 6AY (7582 6465/www.beaconsfield.ltd.uk). Lambeth North tube. **Meals served** 11am-5pm Tue-Sun. **Main courses** £3.50-£4.80. **No credit cards.**
The café at this former Victorian Ragged School, now a contemporary art venue, is not, on the face of it, an attractive prospect for weary parents with kids in tow. First, you need to buzz your way in through a side street door behind the railway tracks, then negotiate two small flights of steps and a narrow doorway to get to a basement space with a flagstone floor, white walls, arty flyers and little else. The friendliness of the staff soon makes up for the stark interior, though. A box of toys and colouring-in pads are available, with free Wi-Fi and weekend papers for adults. The healthy eating credentials can't be faulted either, with seasonal vegetarian dishes, fair trade and home-baked cakes, all at reasonable prices. A spicy potato and red chard curry, with chana masala and cucumber raita (£4.80) was refreshing and filling. Good food, without the Giraffe-style gaiety (*see p222*).
Buggy access. Crayons. Disabled access (call ahead): toilets. Nappy-changing facilities. Toys.

S&M Café
4-6 Essex Road, N1 8LN (7359 5361/ www.sandmcafe.co.uk). Angel tube/19, 38 bus. **Meals served** 7.30am-11pm daily. **Main courses** £6.50-£9.95. **Credit** AmEx, MC, V.
Loud blue Formica tables and dinky red leather chairs make for a cramped but jovial atmosphere at this anglo diner. But the look of the place is more authentic than the food. There aren't any workmen to be found in here; the portions wouldn't be enough for them. In fact, the sausage and mash (£6.50) is hardly enough for an adult of any professional persuasion. Even the children looked forlornly at their single sausage on a blob of mash. That said, the ambience almost makes up for it, and the food

all tastes good. The eponymous sausage and mash isn't the only option – there's an all-day breakfast menu and the blackboard promotes heartier Sunday lunch-type meals.

Buggy access. Children's set meal (£3.95). Crayons. High chairs. Nappy-changing facilities. Takeaway service. Toys. **Branches** throughout town.

That Place on the Corner

1-3 Green Lanes, N16 9BS (7704 0079/ www.thatplaceonthecorner.co.uk). Highbury & Islington tube/rail/Canonbury rail/21, 73, 141, 276, 341, 476 bus. **Meals served** 9.30am-7pm Mon-Thur; 9.30am-8pm Fri; 10am-6pm Sat, Sun. **Main courses** £4.85-£8.25. **Credit** MC, V.

This light-flooded café on the corner of Newington Green is run by two local mothers, and is very popular with the N16 buggy set. It's easy to see why. TPOTC is a rare refuge in London where parents have no worries about annoying their table neighbours – adults aren't allowed in unless they're with a child. There's a buggy park by the door and an inviting play corner with brightly coloured cushions, a well-stocked book shelf and a large dressing-up cupboard. The tiny 'creativity room' has now been taken over by the kitchen, so the daily music, arts and crafts sessions are held in the main café – a definite improvement. Cakes are bought in and weren't very exciting on our last visit, although at least the kids' cupcakes are a sensible size and the coffee's good. The children's menu is a run-down of old favourites like sausage and mash, pasta, pizza (kids can put the toppings on themselves), burgers and cottage pie, all home-made and served with a portion of veg. Babies are also catered for with a daily organic vegetable purée, available in different textures for those with and without teeth.

Buggy access. Children's menu (£4.50-£5.25). Crayons. Disabled access: toilet. High chairs. Nappy-changing facilities. Play area.

Tide Tables

2 The Archways, Riverside, Richmond, Surrey TW9 1TH (8948 8285). Richmond tube/rail. **Meals served** 9am-6pm daily. **Main courses** £2.60-£6.25. **No credit cards.**

Nestled inside the last archway under Richmond Bridge before it spans the Thames, this café's biggest draw is its location. On fine-weather days, customers sip organic coffee out on the gravelled terrace while overlooking the river. The café is patronised by pumped-up joggers stopping by for an energy drink as well as more laid-back dog-walkers; parents, meanwhile, praise its toddler-friendly outdoor space and welcoming attitude to children. New mothers also flock here in droves, attracted by the comfy sofas and wholehearted support of breast-feeding. Offering toothsome vegetarian fare with a North African influence, as well as the usual

Cupcake-fuelled crafts await inside **That Place on the Corner**.

pastries and muffins, the menu rates highly in terms of nutrition and variety. Regulars are treated like old friends, while newcomers are charmed by the affable owners.
Buggy access. Children's menu (£2.60). Disabled access. High chairs. Takeaway service.

Upper Deck

London Transport Museum, The Piazza, WC2E 7BB (7598 1356/www.ltmuseum.co.uk). Covent Garden tube. **Meals served** 10am-7pm Mon-Sat; 10am-6pm Sun. **Main courses** £3.10-£8. **Credit** AmEx, MC, V. **Map** p317 L7.

Situated on an airy mezzanine floor above the London Transport Museum's entrance and shop, this is an exciting place to sit and watch goings-on down below and out in Covent Garden's piazza. Kids will also be mesmerised by the huge set of traffic lights suspended from the ceiling. Buggies are parked on arrival and highchairs magically appear, courtesy of the incredibly accommodating staff. Children can have a half-price, half-portion version of most of the adult meals, which include burger and chips, beans on toast, pasta, panini and soup. (Adults will also appreciate the good-looking cocktail menu.) You don't have to be visiting the museum (*see p84*) to dine here.
Buggy access. Disabled access: lift, toilet. High chairs. Nappy-changing facilities.

V&A Café

Victoria & Albert Museum, Cromwell Road, SW7 2RL (7942 2000/www.vam.ac.uk). South Kensington tube. **Meals served** 10am-5.15pm Mon-Thur, Sat, Sun; 10am-9.30pm Fri. **Main courses** £6-£10. **Credit** MC, V.

Lined with glittering tiles, the V&A's main café is like a giant jewellery box, with two quieter, smaller rooms to each side. Even kids that aren't impressed by the baroque tiling will probably like the huge ball chandeliers – especially if they're given a little something from the luscious cake selection. A three-layered chocolate sponge with marbled icing, perhaps? There's a good selection of savouries too, with a hot food counter serving crispy roasts (from pork and apple to pesto-drizzled aubergine) and an adventurous sandwich bar. Kids' portions (for the under-tens) are available from both counters for £4.95, it's buggy-friendly and high chairs are provided. The staff's somewhat laconic attitude doesn't matter as the café is self-service. As a good-weather option, there are tables outside in the peaceful red sandstone courtyard; fountains bubble in the shallow lake at the centre.
Buggy access. Disabled access: toilet. High chairs. Nappy-changing facilities.

CHINESE

Dragon Castle

100 Walworth Road, SE17 1JL (7277 3388/ www.dragoncastle.co.uk). Elephant & Castle tube/rail. **Meals served** noon-11.30pm Mon-Sat; 11.30am-10.30pm Sun. **Main courses** £5.50-£25. **Set meals** £14.80-£32.80 per person (minimum 2) 2-3 courses. **Credit** AmEx. MC, V.

Residents of this unloved corner of Elephant & Castle are over the moon about this place. It's a commendable attempt to recreate an authentic Hong Kong-like dining experience, complete with carp ponds, gilt dragons and a menu that runs to duck tongues and poached eels. Come for dim sum in the daytime, as these savoury morsels will really appeal to children. We loved the simple, steamed corn-fed chicken in a lightly spicy root ginger stock, and an enormous serving of glossy, green morning glory in XO chilli sauce. Service runs from bossy-boots to nice-as-pie, but it's all pretty much on the ball.
Buggy access. Disabled access: toilet. High chairs. Takeaway service.

Joy King Lau

3 Leicester Street, WC2H 7BL (7437 1132). Leicester Square or Piccadilly Circus tube. **Dim sum served** noon-5pm Mon-Sat; 11am-5pm Sun. **Meals served** noon-11.30pm Mon-Sat; 11.30am-10.30pm Sun. **Main courses** £6.80-£20. **Set meal** £10-£35 per person (minimum 2). **Credit** AmEx, MC, V. **Map** p317 K7.

The atmosphere is always family-friendly in this ground-floor dining room, which tries to offset the lack of natural light with lime and pink wall panels. Its menu is comprehensive, but Joy King Lau is best known for the dim sum that draws a high proportion of Chinese punters. Tender squid rings in mild curry sauce, juicy char sui croquettes and prawn and chive dumplings will delight the more adventurous youngster. The sweet dim sum is just as good; feather-light hot sponge cake (butter ma-lai ko) and crisp, deep fried custard buns are among the highlights.
Buggy access. Disabled access. High chairs. Takeaway service.

Royal China

30 Westferry Circus, E14 8RR (7719 0888/ www.royalchinagroup.co.uk). Canary Wharf tube/DLR/Westferry DLR. **Dim sum served** noon-4.45pm daily. **Meals served** noon-11pm Mon-Thur; noon-11.30pm Fri, Sat; 11am-10pm Sun. **Dim sum** £2.65-£4.20. **Main courses** £7-£50. **Set meal** £30 per person (minimum 2). **Credit** AmEx, DC, MC, V.

Perfect pizza

You can't beat a pizza, hot from the oven – but which of the city's chains are best for families? We've chosen a few chains and listed the good and bad points about each.

ASK

160-162 Victoria Street, SW1E 5LB (7630 8228/www.askcentral.co.uk). Victoria tube/rail. **Meals served** noon-11pm Mon-Sat; noon-10.30pm Sun. **Main courses** £5.60-£8.45. **Credit** AmEx, MC, V.

While it rarely wows with its cooking, there is plenty to like about ASK, including the amiable staff, comfy furnishings and attention to detail (such as proper chilled glasses for Peroni). Adults who don't fancy one of the 14 pizzas can opt for pasta, risottos and salads; the so-so desserts aren't really worth saving room for.

Total number of branches 22.
What's in it for the kids? The £5.95 kids' menu comes with colouring-in and wax crayons and gives sprogs a choice of ten pastas and pizzas, garlic bread, salad and a scoop of ice-cream or a banana split.
Buggy access. Children's set meal (£5.95). Disabled access. Crayons. High chairs. Nappy-changing facilities. Takeaway service.

Pizza Express

Benbow House, 24 New Globe Walk, SE1 9DS (7401 3977/www.pizzaexpress.com). London Bridge tube/rail. **Meals served** noon-11pm Mon-Thur; noon-midnight Fri, Sat; noon-10.30pm Sun. **Main courses** £5.90-£10.95. **Credit** AmEx, DC, MC, V.

Pizza Express now offers four different styles of pizza – regular, Romana (thinner, crisper bases), Leggera (less calories, salad on top) and posh, rectangular Theo Randall numbers. And guess what? The cheaper Fiorentinas, Diavolos and American Hots you've been ordering for years taste just as good as the new models. This chain is pretty reliable, though quality does vary with individual staff and you can get the odd soggy base, stingy topping or overcooked pizza.

Total number of branches 122.
What's in it for the kids? The Piccolo menu offers three courses for £5.95, with pasta options including bolognese, a creamy version of napoletana and carbonara with mushrooms. A choice

of sundaes and a cup of Bambinoccino finish the feast in sophisticated style. Plum organic baby food (£1.70) is also available. Staff are friendly enough, but waiting times during busy periods can mean little feet get itchy.
Buggy access. Children's set meal (£5.65). Crayons. Disabled access (ground floor): toilet. High chairs. Nappy-changing facilities. Tables outdoors (12, riverside). Takeaway service.

Pizza Paradiso

61 The Cut, SE1 8LL (7261 1221/www.pizzaparadiso.co.uk). Southwark tube/Waterloo tube/rail. **Meals served** noon-midnight Mon-Sat; noon-11pm Sun. **Main courses** £6.10-£17.95. **Credit** AmEx, MC, V.

There's a friendly, neighbourhood trattoria vibe to this small family chain. Kids will be happy with dough balls and starter-sized portions of spaghetti napoletana, bolognese or carbonara. Some of the pasta is homemade, including the gnocchi and filled ravioli. As well as pizzas, there are meat and fish dishes (salmon with pink peppercorn sauce, veal scallopine) and specials for those happy to spend more. The own-made ice-cream is terrific.

Total number of branches 4.
What's in it for the kids? Staff will discount a quid off some pasta dishes sold in child sizes.
Buggy access. High chairs. Tables outdoors (6, pavement). Takeaway service.

La Porchetta

74-77 Chalk Farm Road, NW1 8AN (7267 6822). **Lunch served** noon-3pm Mon-Fri. **Dinner served** 6-11pm Mon-Sat. **Main courses** £5.90-£11.50. **Credit** MC, V.

Portions are vast: pizzas threaten to fall off the plates, which in turn threaten to fall off the tiny tables, so consider sharing. A lengthy menu takes in all the classic pizza toppings; alternatively, there are good-looking bowls of pasta and meat and fish dishes. On our last visit, pizzas were undercooked at the centre, though the toppings tasted fine. We liked frutti di mare and messicana (Italian sausage and chilli). No-nonsense black-clad Italian staff work the room, but getting their attention can be difficult during peak times.

Consumer

Total number of branches 6.
What's in it for the kids? Children can order a half portion of pasta at a reduced price, or share one of the huge pizzas. *Buggy access. High chairs. Takeaway service.*

Prezzo

17 Hertford Street, W1J 7RS (7499 4690/ www.prezzoplc.co.uk). Green Park or Hyde Park Corner tube. **Meals served** noon-11.30pm Mon-Sat; noon-11pm Sun. **Main courses** £6.25-£9.95. **Credit** AmEx, MC, V.
There's nothing very Italian about the dark oak panelling and moody lighting in the Mayfair branch of this chain. Unfortunately, the food isn't especially Italian either – on our last visit the pizza was undercooked, meanly topped and light on the love. Still, prices are keen for such a swish location by Hyde Park. There's a selection of salads, meat dishes and risottos; puds can be disappointing for the price.
Total number of branches 18.
What's in it for the kids? Staff perk up when children are around, and serve the kids' menu with panache: a choice of three pizzas/pastas, ice-cream and squash. *Buggy access. Children's set meal (£4.50). High chairs. Takeaway service.*

Strada

29 Kensington High Street, W8 (7938 4648/www.strada.co.uk). High Street Kensington tube. **Meals served** 11.30am-11pm Mon-Sat; 11.30am-10.30pm Sun. **Main courses** £6.95-£16.50. **Credit** AmEx, MC, V.
Strada's pizzas range from a simple margherita to more complex offerings, like the formaggio di capra (goat's cheese, walnuts, balsamic onions, celery cress, tomato sauce and mozzarella). There's five-or-so of everything else: salads, pasta, risotto, fish and meat dishes. Desserts (*panettone al forno, torta della nonna*) are respectable and come with excellent ice-cream. We love that Strada puts free chilled, bottled and filtered water on every table.
Total number of branches 28.
What's in it for the kids? Not all branches offer the kids' menu, so check ahead. Where it is available, children can choose between spaghetti pomodoro, penne bolognese, pizza margherita and grilled chicken, with pannacotta or ice-cream for pudding, plus a soft drink. *Buggy access. Children's set meal (£4.50). Disabled access. High chairs. Takeaway service.*

Zizzi

73-75 Strand, WC2R 0DE (7240 1717/ www.zizzi.co.uk). Covent Garden or Embankment tube/Charing Cross tube/ rail. **Meals served** noon-11.30pm Mon-Sat; noon-11pm Sun. **Main courses** £6.25-£11.95. **Credit** AmEx, DC, MC, V.
Ingredients on the main menu at Zizzi (buffalo milk ricotta, santos tomatoes, cotta ham) suggest thoughtful sourcing not readily apparent at other chains, while the Bambini menu offers three courses for a mere £5.95. You can also check online for allergen and other dietary information on each dish. More on-the-ball service would be nice though; each of our recent visits has had us vowing never to return.
Total number of branches 25.
What's in it for the kids? The kids' menu offers breadsticks, a choice of seven pizzas and pasta dishes, then ice-cream. *Buggy access. Children's set meal (£5.95). Disabled access: toilet. High chairs. Nappy-changing facilities. Takeaway service.*

Consumer

Royal China remains consistently dependable for good quality cooking and excellent dim sum, and the fact that this branch overlooks the Thames makes it a good choice for families visiting Docklands for the day. Staff glide discreetly among guests, ensuring a smooth service and providing helpful recommendations. We were delighted by unctuous braised pork belly with preserved cabbage, silky steamed cod with dried yellow bean sauce and a perfect dish of Chinese broccoli in ginger juice. A vast menu means there's something to appeal to all tastes. *Booster seats. Buggy access. Disabled access: toilet. Nappy-changing facilities. Tables outdoors (23, terrace). Takeaway service.* **Branches** 40 Baker Street, W1U 7AB (7487 4688); 13 Queensway, W2 4QJ (7221 2535); 805 Fulham Road, SW6 5HE (7731 0081).

FISH

Belgo Noord
72 Chalk Farm Road, NW1 8AN (7267 0718/ www.belgo-restaurants.com). Chalk Farm tube. **Lunch served** noon-5pm daily. **Dinner served** 5-11pm Mon-Thur; 5-11.30pm Fri, Sat; 5-10.30pm Sun. **Main courses** £8.95-£15.95. **Set lunch** £6.50 1 course. **Credit** AmEx, MC, V.

Beer, mussels and chips made this chain famous, but if it seems a strange choice of venue for children, read on. The menu also includes a decent array of alternatives. The sausage with stoemp mash, beer-basted rotisserie chicken or Hoegaarden beer battered haddock and frites reflect the prominent Belgian theme – as do the staff, who are quirkily dressed in traditional Trappist monks' habits. Food is served in cool, industrial surroundings with an open kitchen; noisy but cheerful. The other great reason to bring children here is that they qualify for a free two-course menu when an adult orders a main from the à la carte menu. Helpful, speedy service means you can be in and out of the door in under an hour, but the kids' menu has plenty of puzzles and colouring if parents prefer to linger. *Buggy access. Crayons. Disabled access (call ahead): toilet. Children's menu (free). High chairs. Nappy-changing facilities. Tables outside (4, pavement).* **Branches** throughout town.

Costas Fish Restaurant
18 Hillgate Street, W8 7SR (7727 4310). Notting Hill Gate tube. **Lunch served** noon-2.30pm, **dinner served** 5.30-10.30pm Tue-Sat. **Main courses** £5.90-£8.40. **No credit cards.**

Two brothers; two neighbouring restaurants. One serves Greek food, the other is this classic English fish and chip joint, albeit with Greek touches (starters include taramasalata or houmous and pitta). Walk past the fryers into the restaurant out back and it's like a set from *Life On Mars*, all maroon leatherette chairs, brown tables and dodgy Greek landscapes on the walls. It doesn't look as if much has changed since this place opened in 1981, but that doesn't matter when the fish and chips are this good (and anyway, it's nice to know the gentrification of Notting Hill hasn't swept through every nook and cranny). Juicy, freshly fried fish and great chips – fluffy on the inside, crispy on the outside – will go down well with children of any age. Adults wanting a lighter option should avoid the unimaginative salads (iceberg lettuce, thick slices of cucumber and tomato with the faintest drizzle of dressing) and skip supper instead. *Buggy access. Tables outdoors (2, pavement). Takeaway service.*

fish!
Cathedral Street, Borough Market, SE1 9AL (7407 3803/www.fishdiner.co.uk). London Bridge tube/rail. **Meals served** 11.30am-11pm Mon-Thur; noon-11pm Fri, Sat; noon-10.30pm Sun. **Main courses** £9.95-£26.95. **Credit** AmEx, MC, V. **Map** p317 M8.

This smart glass pavilion overlooking Borough Market and Southwark Cathedral doesn't look terribly family-friendly from the outside, especially on weekdays when it's full of suits and well-heeled tourists. Nonetheless, staff are very welcoming to the high chair set and the acoustic racket inside means a tantrum would go unnoticed. And after all, what child doesn't like fish and chips? Adults can choose from the extensive fish list and decide whether they want it steamed or grilled, or indulge in a comfortingly rich fish pie or classic cod or haddock and chips. The mushy peas are among the finest we've ever tasted. Families on a budget will prefer to get takeaway fish and chips from the kiosk to the side of the restaurant for half the price. *Buggy access. Children's set meal (£6.95). Crayons. Disabled access: toilet. High chairs. Nappy-changing facilities. Tables outdoors (24, terrace). Takeaway service.* **Branch** fish! kitchen 58 Coombe Road, Kingston-upon-Thames, Surrey KT2 7AF (8546 2886).

North Sea Fish Restaurant
7-8 Leigh Street, WC1H 9 (7387 5892). Russell Square tube/Euston or King's Cross tube/rail/68, 168 bus. **Lunch served**

noon-2.30pm, **dinner served** 5.30-10.30pm Mon-Sat. **Main courses** £8.95-£19.95. **Credit** MC, V. **Map** p315 L3/4.

This traditional fish and chip restaurant is quite a grown-up sort of place (single malt whiskies line up along the counter, while grilled sea bass features on the menu) but staff are cheerful and there are plenty of fried goodies to satisfy the nippers. Forget the bigger portions altogether: you'll find 'normal' sized battered cod or haddock with chips easily big enough to share. *Buggy access. Disabled access. High chairs. Takeaway service.*

Olley's

65-69 Norwood Road, SE24 9AA (8671 8259/ www.olleys.info). Herne Hill rail/3, 68 bus. **Lunch served** noon-3pm, **dinner served** 5-10.30pm Tue-Sun. **Main courses** £8.45-£18.45. **Set lunch** £7 1 course. **Credit** AmEx, MC, V.

The best chippy in south London is famous for its specials. The Cilla Black Experience involves haddock and chips with interesting sides. The Guy Dimond Experience (named after *Time Out* magazine's food critic) is battered lemon sole fillet with chips and a lemon wedge. Olley's has always been one for diversification; there are various exotic varieties of fish on offer, which can be steamed or grilled for batter-phobes. High chairs are clingfilm-wrapped (!) for each use so your child won't be picking up the last kid's peas. The children's menu consists mainly of the usual 'nuggets and chips' options, but there are also calamares and prawns. The staff will also bring small portions of the steamed dishes on request. The creamy mushy peas are among the best in London, and the chips also deserve a mention, being blanched before frying. *Buggy access. Children's menu (£4-£4.50). Crayons. Disabled access: toilet. High chairs. Tables outdoors (12, pavement). Nappy-changing facilities. Takeaway service.*

Rock & Sole Plaice

47 Endell Street, WC2H 9AJ (7836 3785). Covent Garden or Leicester Square tube. **Meals served** 11.30am-10.30pm Mon-Sat; noon-9.30pm Sun. **Main courses** £9-£12. **Credit** MC, V. **Map** p315 L6.

Tourists in search of classic British cuisine and nearby office workers needing comfort food seek out this small corner chippy, near Covent Garden. The plaice is good and juicy, but order the less popular rock and you'll get it fried to order. Seaside setting and newspaper wrapping aside, this is fish and chips the way it ought to be. It's best for families with older children, as the restaurant doesn't have high chairs and there's very little space for pushchairs, unless it's warm enough to eat outside. *Tables outdoors (7, pavement). Takeaway service.*

Toff's

38 Muswell Hill Broadway, N10 3RT (8883 8656/www.toffsfish.co.uk). Highgate tube, then 43, 134 bus. **Meals served** 11.30am-10pm Mon-Sat. **Main courses** £7.95-£17.50. **Set lunch** £8.95 1 course. **Credit** AmEx, DC, MC, V.

At frying time, there's always a long queue of customers at this acclaimed Muswell Hill chippy (note the unusually high number of certificates and accolades on the door, collected over the past 40-odd years). Behind the bustling takeaway counter at the front, through a pair of saloon-style swing doors (which children love), the restaurant offers more serenity. Toff's large choice of fish can be ordered in plain or matzo-meal batter, or grilled for a healthier alternative – a rarity in most chippies. There's also a well-executed children's menu featuring proper fish and own-made chips. If you can squeeze anything else in, there are salads (tomato and red onion, olive-topped coleslaw, Greek), soups, deep-fried camembert and traditional British puds, served in veritable ponds of custard. *Buggy access. Children's menu (£3.50-£3.95). Crayons. Disabled access: toilet. High chairs. Takeaway service.*

FRENCH

Belvedere

Holland House, off Abbotsbury Road, in Holland Park, W8 6LU (7602 1238/www. whitestarline.org.uk). Holland Park tube. **Lunch served** noon-2.15pm Mon-Sat; noon & 2.30pm Sun. **Dinner served** 6-10pm Mon-Sat. **Main courses** £12-£22. **Set meal** (Sat, Sun) £24.95 3 courses. **Credit** AmEx, MC, V.

This art deco gem in the middle of the park is run by Marco Pierre White. With its white tablecloths, leather chairs and smart period features, it certainly doesn't look very child friendly at first glance. But looks can be deceptive; staff couldn't be more welcoming, and this is a superb place to have a special family lunch with the grandparents, especially on a Sunday when the three-course set menu and pianist attract lots of families with young children in tow. There's no designated children's menu, but the chef will whip up a range of child-friendly classics (pasta, sausage and mash, meat and vegetables without the rich sauces) at a reduced price on request. With the park and adventure playground just outside, it's a family day out that everyone will remember. *Buggy access. Disabled access (ground floor, call ahead). High chairs. Tables outdoors (5, terrace).*

Le Cercle

1 Wilbraham Place, SW1X 9AE (7901 9999/ www.lecercle.co.uk). Sloane Square tube. **Lunch served** noon-3pm, **dinner served** 6-11pm Tue-Sat. **Set lunch** £15 3 dishes, £19.50 4 dishes. **Set dinner** (6-7pm) £17.50 3 dishes, £21.50 4 dishes. **Tapas** £6-£16. **Credit** AmEx, MC, V.

Le Cercle is part of the Gascon family of restaurants, and offers refined French regional dishes. The entrance, on a side road off Sloane Street, is easily missed, so there's not much passing trade. But word of mouth provides the cavernous basement restaurant with a steady stream of customers. There are no high chairs, so it's not great for toddlers. However, the big draw is that, at lunchtime, children under 12 can eat free from a fixed menu of five smaller dishes when an adult eats too. The food comes in tapas-style portions and rewards adventurous palates. Each small dish was delicious, vividly coloured and intensely flavoured, satisfying through variety rather than quantity. Staff surreptitiously seat parties with children away from other diners, but couldn't be more helpful and friendly. *Buggy access. Disabled access: lift, toilet. Children's menu (free Tue-Sat lunch).*

Roussillon

16 St Barnabas Street, SW1W 8PE (7730 5550/www.roussillon.co.uk). Sloane Square tube. **Lunch served** noon-2.30pm Mon-Fri. **Dinner served** 6.30-10.30pm Mon-Sat. **Set lunch** £35 3 courses. **Set dinner** £55 3 courses. **Set meal** £65-£75 8 course tasting menu. **Credit** AmEx, MC, V.

Roussillon suits all manner of gourmands: families, elderly couples, friends out for a quiet dinner. It isn't cheap at £55 for three courses, but the food is sublime and with solicitous service and subdued decor, the restaurant manages to maintain the air of a friendly family local (although you'd have to be very well-heeled to actually live around here). The menu changes with the seasons and vegetarians have their own eight-course tasting menu. But what is there to appeal to children? Those with an enthusiastic interest in food will love the mini gastronomes menu, offering six small but perfectly formed courses starring such delights as scallops, truffle ravioli and smoked eel. *Buggy access. Children's set meal (£20 lunch).*

Gastropub fodder and proper pints at the **Clissold Arms**.

GASTROPUBS

Clissold Arms

115 Fortis Green, N2 9HR (8444 4224).
East Finchley tube. **Open** noon-11pm Mon-Fri;
noon-midnight Sat; noon-10.30pm Sun. **Lunch
served** noon-4.30pm Mon-Sat. **Dinner
served** 6-10pm Mon-Sat. **Meals served**
noon-9pm Sun. **Main courses** £11-£18.50.
Credit MC, V.
Muswell Hill definitely needed a great
gastropub like this. The decor could be more
characterful, but the staff are friendly and
enthusiastic, so it's no surprise that the Clissold
has become a huge hit with local families. Our
favourite is the Sunday roast with Yorkshire
puddings for all, and the puddings aren't bad
either. It's refreshing to find a pub that's
comfortable with children, but recognises that
parents want a treat too – and one where the
pint pullers have been trained in the fine art of
proper pouring.
*Buggy access. Disabled access: toilet. High
chairs. Nappy-changing facilities. Tables
outdoors (15, terrace; 25, garden).*

Lansdowne

*90 Gloucester Avenue, NW1 8HX (7483 0409/
www.thelansdownepub.co.uk). Chalk Farm tube.*
Open noon-11pm Mon-Sat; noon-10.30pm
Sun. **Lunch served** noon-4pm, **dinner
served** 6-10pm Mon-Fri. **Meals served**
12.30-10pm Sat; 12.30-9.30pm Sun. **Main
courses** £9.50-£16.50. **Credit** MC, V.
This pleasant pub in the middle of Primrose
Hill is always heaving with families in the
downstairs bar (customers wanting a more
polished experience can make their way
upstairs to the dining room). Happily, it hasn't
sacrificed its 'local pub' vibe in favour of gastro
pomp, though it has all the requisite features;
the decor is tasteful, if a little worn at the edges,
and food takes pride of place with a huge
blackboard chalked up with the day's menu. The
additional pizza menu makes an appealing,
child-friendly alternative to the more expensive
gastro fare. Adults can choose from six or seven
starters encompassing an array of salads,
seafood and soups. Sloppiness can creep in, but
the demands of maintaining a menu that
changes daily may account for that. Service can
be somewhat slow, but with the pub's cheerful
vibe, you won't mind hanging round a little
longer than usual before heading off for a
bracing walk or kite-flying foray.
*Buggy access. Disabled access: toilet. High
chairs. Tables outdoors (4, pavement).
Takeaway service.*

Prince Regent

*69 Dulwich Road, SE24 0NJ (7274 1567/
www.theprinceregent.co.uk). Brixton tube/rail/
Herne Hill rail.* **Open** noon-11pm Mon-Thur;
noon-midnight Fri, Sat; noon-10.30pm Sun.
Lunch served noon-3pm Mon-Sat; noon-5pm
Sun. **Dinner served** 7-10pm Mon-Sat; 6-9pm
Sun. **Main courses** £8.85-£16. **Credit** MC, V.
At weekends, the downstairs of this friendly pub,
with its elegant original features, is bouncing
with toddlers. Especially on Sundays, when the
locally (in)famous 'family lunch' can get a bit
wild. There's plenty of space to park prams by
the tables, a selection of games and books lying
around, and an excellent beer selection for the
adults. There's no child-specific menu, but the
chef is willing to serve up items from the
excellent brunch menu (eggs, smoked salmon,
bacon), or small portions of selected gastro
classics, such as sausage and mash or fish and
chips. The puddings are worth saving room for,
and children love the playful presentation, quality
ice-creams and custard. The atmosphere here is
as warm as the welcome; parties without children
are led upstairs to escape. Note that children must
be out by 7pm.
*Buggy access. Disabled access: toilet. High
chairs. Nappy-changing facilities. Tables
outdoors (12, terrace).*

Stein's

*Richmond Towpath, rear of 55 Petersham
Road, Richmond, Surrey TW10 6XT (8948
8189/www.stein-s.com). Richmond tube/rail.*
Meals served *Summer* noon-10pm Mon-Fri;
10am-10pm Sat, Sun. *Winter* noon-10pm Sat,
Sun. Times vary depending on weather, call
to check. **Main courses** £7.90-£14.90. **Set
lunch** (noon-4pm Mon-Fri) £5.99 1 course
incl soft drink. **Credit** MC, V.
Stein's is an unusual proposition; a riverside
Bavarian beer garden with views over Richmond
Bridge and Richmond Hill. Customers sit
outdoors on the long tables with bench seating,
having picked up their food from the timber-clad
kiosk. There's no indoor seating, but gas heaters
provide warmth on chilly days. Watch those
clouds though; at the slightest sign of rain, Stein's
closes. The menu is 100% German, with wursts
(sausages) at its core, but there are other Bavarian
specialities like roasted pork shoulder with
dumplings and pork meatloaf. Bratkartoffeln –
potatoes sautéed with bacon, onion and spices
– is a good choice for children: simple, own-
made comfort food. The kitchen also rustles up
some mean breakfasts and a vast array of
strudel desserts. As you might expect, German
beer flows freely and the Almdudler, an apple-

Consumer

Ottolenghi: bold flavours, fresh produce and terribly tempting cakes.

flavoured herbal lemonade from Austria, is lovely. There is a safe, small area where under-fives can play and the picturesque, enclosed riverside location means families love it. *Buggy access. Crayons. Disabled access. High chairs. Nappy-changing facilities. Play area. Tables outdoors (28, towpath). Takeaway service.*

ICE-CREAM

Don't miss **Marine Ices** (*see p244*), the gelateria/caff that has been fattening up Chalk Farm residents since the 1920s.

Gelateria Danieli

16 Brewers Lane, Richmond, Surrey TW9 1HH (8439 9807/www.gelateriadanieli.com). Richmond tube/rail. **Open** *Summer* 10am-10pm daily. *Winter* 10am-6pm daily. Times may vary, phone to check. **Ice-cream** £2/scoop. **Credit** MC, V.

Squeezed into a narrow shopping arcade, marked at one end by two jolly guardsmen standing to attention outside a chocolate shop, this small gelateria dishes out superior sorbets and ice-creams to be savoured around Richmond Green. Wooden floorboards and a couple of chairs inside make it cosy in winter but rather

cramped in summer, when queues stretch out of the door. When they're not rushed off their feet, friendly staff invite you to try before you buy. *Buggy access. Takeaway service.*
Branches Bentalls Centre, Wood Street, Kingston-upon-Thames, Surrey KT1 1TX (8141 5098); 47 Queenstown Road, SW8 3RG (7720 5784, open summer only).

Gelato Mio

138 Holland Park Avenue, W11 4UE (7727 4117/www.gelatomio.co.uk). Holland Park tube. **Open** 7.30am-10pm Mon-Thur, Sun; 8.30am-11pm Fri, Sat. **Ice-cream** £2.50/scoop. **Credit** MC, V.

Still only in its second summer, this stylish, orange-hued parlour already has a second branch in Charing Cross. We were given an enthusiastic, typically Italian welcome and invited to have a taste, before plumping for a gorgeous strawberry sorbet with sharp fruity flavours. There's seating inside; alternatively, take your ice to nearby Holland Park (*see p116*). The ever-changing menu may include nocciola (hazelnut), stracciatella (chocolate chip) and arrancia (orange sorbet). *Buggy access. Delivery service. Tables outdoors (2, pavement). Takeaway service.*
Branch 45 Villiers Street, WC2N 6NE (7930 5961).

Gelateria Valerie

*9 Duke of York Square, SW3 4LY (7730
7978/www.patisserie-valerie.co.uk). Sloane
Square tube.* **Open** 8am-7pm Mon-Sat;
10am-7pm Sun. **Ice-cream** £1.75/scoop.
Credit AmEx, MC, V.
A cone's throw away from the Saatchi Gallery,
this glass-walled branch of the ever-expanding
Valerie chain is a shining island in the heart of
Chelsea's prime retail site. There's plenty of
outside seating looking over the fountains in
summer, while stools lining the glass shop front
are perfect for people watching. Rum baba, wild
berry yoghurt and the alarmingly coloured
banana blue are among the flavours.
*Buggy access. Disabled access. Tables outdoors
(20, Duke of York Square). Takeaway service.*
Branches throughout town.

Oddono's

*14 Bute Street, SW7 3EX (7052 0732/www.
oddono.co.uk). South Kensington tube.* **Open**
11am-11pm Mon-Thur, Sun; 11am-midnight
Fri, Sat. **Ice-cream** £2.50/scoop. **Credit** MC, V.
With its minimalist interior and retro seating,
this place is all about quality; the focus is on
premium ingredients and classic flavours. Even
on a grey day, regulars troop in for their fix of
vaniglia, made from Madagascan vanilla pods.
The pistachio was the best we've ever tasted,
with generous sprinkles of the namesake nut.
*Buggy access. Disabled access. Takeaway
service. Tables outdoors (2, pavement).*

Scoop

*40 Shorts Gardens, WC2H 9AB (7240 7086/
www.scoopgelato.com). Covent Garden tube.*
Open 11am-9pm daily. Times vary, phone to
check. **Ice-cream** £2.50/scoop. **Credit** MC, V.
A required stop if you're out and about in
Covent Garden. One very generous dollop of
intensely dark chocolate ice-cream spilled over
the sides of the cone, and required some hastily-
executed licking. Sugar-, gluten- and milk-free
varieties are available for the diet conscious, and
the daily baked pastries are worth a visit alone.
Look out for summertime special events
promoting unusual flavours and ingredients.
*Buggy access. Delivery service. Takeaway
service.*

INDIAN

Masala Zone

*80 Upper Street, N1 0NU (7359 3399/www.
masalazone.com). Angel tube.* **Lunch served**
12.30-3pm, **dinner served** 5.30-11pm Mon-
Fri. **Meals served** 12.30-11pm Sat; 12.30-
10.30pm Sun. **Main courses** £6.50-£9.
Thalis £7.80-£10.70. **Credit** MC, V.
Bright and breezy premises, with mural-daubed
walls and a laid-back buzz, make Masala Zone
an appealing pit-stop for families. The kitchen
draws its influences from across India, with a
focus on zesty street snacks: adventurous kids
will enjoy sampling chickpea purée-stuffed dahi
puri, crunchy chicken samosas and spicy *aloo
tikki chat* – chilli-laced potato cakes, served with
yoghurt and chutney. Thalis are another draw;
steel platters of little bowls, filled with different
dishes; the scaled-down versions on the kids'
menu are great value. Curries, spicy burgers and
chilli-flecked noodles complete the menu.
*Buggy access. Children's set meal (£4.15).
Disabled access. High chairs. Takeaway service.*
Branches throughout town.

Tamarind

*20-22 Queen Street, W1J 5PR (7629 3561/
www.tamarindrestaurant.com). Green Park
tube.* **Lunch served** noon-2.45pm Mon-Fri,
Sun. **Dinner served** 5.30-11pm Mon-Sat; 6-
10.45pm Sun. **Main courses** £12.95-£24.75.
Set lunch £14.95 2 courses, £18.95 3 courses.
Set dinner (5.30-6.45pm, 10.30-11pm) £25
3 courses. **Credit** AmEx, DC, MC, V.
Serving north-west Indian cuisine, Tamarind
offers an attractive Sunday lunch deal. Under-
tens can eat a three-course tasting menu for free,
if they're with two or more adults eating from the
main menu. Starters include spiced potato cakes
and Indian style fish fingers; for mains, there's
grilled chicken, monkfish, or paneer in masala
sauce, served with veg and rice. Pudding is ice-
cream with fruit. The open kitchen means kids
can watch the chefs working with the Tandoor
oven. Note that children must be out by 7pm.
*Buggy access. Children's set meal (£12.50, free
under-10s, Sun lunch). High chairs. Takeaway
service.*

INTERNATIONAL

Ottolenghi

*287 Upper Street, N1 2TZ (7288 1454/
www.ottolenghi.co.uk). Angel tube/Highbury
& Islington tube/rail.* **Meals served** 8am-
11pm Mon-Sat; 9am-7pm Sun. **Main courses**
£8-£10. **Credit** AmEx, MC, V.
A long communal table dominates this white
deli-style space, all the better to frame the
fabulously colourful food; tables à deux line
either side. Ottolenghi's cooked breakfasts are
among the best in town and there's also granola

and pastries. Counter salads, which double as eat-in starters or takeaways, are a vibrantly hued riot of fresh ingredients. Children will love the display of extravagant cakes piled up in the window, but be prepared to bat away pleas to try absolutely everything. To make a meal, the menu suggests ordering three of the starter-sized dishes per person, but a robust adult appetite requires at least four. *Buggy access. Disabled access. High chairs. Tables outdoors (2, pavement). Takeaway service.* **Branches** 63 Ledbury Road, W11 2AD (7727 1121); 1 Holland Street, W8 4NA (7937 0003); 13 Motcomb Street, SW1X 8LB (7823 2707).

Rainforest Café

20 Shaftesbury Avenue, W1D 7EU (7434 3111/www.therainforestcafe.co.uk). Piccadilly Circus tube. **Meals served** noon-10pm Mon-Thur; noon-8pm Fri; 11.30am-8pm Sat; 11.30am-10pm Sun. **Main courses** £12.25-£18.90. **Credit** AmEx, MC, V. **Map** p317 K7.
This jungle themed basement restaurant, populated by animatronic wildlife, is the closest thing to Disneyland in London. It's hideously expensive, but worth it for the experience. The unchallenging global menu of meze, pasta, seafood, ribs, steaks and burgers isn't up to much, although it does offer organic sausages, organic salmon and pasta for children alongside the more predictable burgers, goujons and pizza. Children's set meals comprise two courses; puddings are a range of extremely sweet and sticky bowlfuls. It's worth paying an extra £3 for the Adventure Meal, as it comes with a fantastic gift pack with mask, purse, stationery and sticker book. Score a table upstairs to sit amid the fish, elephants and gorillas; downstairs has far fewer animals and is far less thrilling for the children. Take a camera with a flash as it's incredibly dark inside. Bookings are not accepted. *Buggy access. Children's set meal (£11.50). Crayons. Entertainment: face painting, weekends & school hols. High chairs. Nappy-changing facilities.*

Shish

313-319 Old Street, EC1V 9LE (7749 0990/ www.shish.com). Old Street tube/rail. **Meals served** 11.30am-11.30pm Mon-Fri; noon-11.30pm Sat; noon-10.30pm Sun. **Main courses** £4-£10.80. **Credit** AmEx, MC, V.
This place is generally thronged, and it's easy to see why. The food is fresh and reasonably priced, the staff friendly and efficient. Kids are offered a great meal deal; for a main course they can choose from chicken, fish cake, falafel

or a cold meze selection, served with rice, pitta, chips, couscous or salad; for pudding, it's own-made ice-cream or sorbet – and all for £4.25. *Buggy access. Children's menu (£4.25). Crayons. Delivery service. Disabled access: toilet. High chairs. Nappy-changing facilities. Tables outdoors (5, pavement). Takeaway service.* **Branch** 2-6 Station Parade, NW2 4NH (8208 9290).

ITALIAN

Carluccio's Caffè

Reuters Plaza, E14 5AJ (7719 1749/www. carluccios.com). Canary Wharf tube/DLR. **Meals served** 7am-11.30pm Mon-Fri; 9am-11.30pm Sat; 10am-10.30pm Sun. **Main courses** £6.95-£13.95. **Credit** AmEx, MC, V. **Map** p314 J6.
Carluccio's understands that children want something to happen as soon as they sit down. And lo and behold; grissini, a soft drink and some paper and crayons appear at the table. The clattering acoustics common to most branches isn't exactly soothing, but the warmth of the service, tasty grub, great smell of coffee and shelves of aspirational deli items keep enticing the customers back. This branch is popular with the suited and booted office folk of Docklands, but the waiters save a bit of extra twinkle and charm for babies. Children can choose from a selection of pasta shapes and sauces, or there's chicken and potatos, stuffed ravioli and lasagne. To finish, the little darlings get an individual tub of Carluccio's lovely Italian ice-cream. *Buggy access. Children's set meal (£5.95). Crayons. Disabled access: toilet. High chairs. Nappy-changing facilities. Tables outdoors (25, piazza). Takeaway service.* **Branches** throughout town.

Marco Polo

Eastfields Avenue, SW18 1LP (8874 7007/ www.marcopolo.uk.net). East Putney tube/ Wandsworth Town rail. **Open** noon-11pm Mon-Thur; noon-11.30pm Fri, Sat; noon-10.30pm Sun. **Main courses** £7.50-£21.50. **Set lunch** £9.95 1 course, £11.95 2 courses. **Credit** MC, V.
There's a fine range of dishes to appeal to adults at this modish eaterie, while children love the £4.95 pasta dishes and large, pleasantly thin pizzas, with a bowl of ice-cream to follow. A useful patch of grass beside the numerous outdoor tables means children can stretch their legs with impunity. No wonder it's packed out by Wandsworth family groups all year round.

Marine Ices.

Buggy access. Children's menu (£4.95-£6.95). Disabled access. High chairs. Tables outdoors (60, terrace). Takeaway service.

Marine Ices

8 Haverstock Hill, NW3 2BL (7482 9003/ www.marineices.co.uk). Chalk Farm tube/ 31 bus. **Lunch served** noon-3pm, **dinner served** 6-11pm Tue-Fri. **Meals served** noon-11pm Sat; noon-10pm Sun. **Main courses** £6.50-£13.60. **Credit** MC, V.

Family-run and fiercely popular, Marine Ices is little changed since it opened in 1928. This retro ice-cream parlour has a slightly strange aquatic theme, but remains a great place to bring your children for a takeaway or eat-in ice-cream, or for a good value Italian meal. Service is no frills but friendly, and the food is simple. Pizzas are the best option – huge crispy bases, heaped with toppings, that spill over the edge of your plate. Pasta is decent too; diners select a pasta shape, then choose a sauce to match. House specials are tempting (home-made Neopolitan fennel sausage with red wine, tomato and lentil sauce, for instance), as are the meat and seafood options, but it's worth saving yourself for pudding. There's a splendid selection of ice-creams, from toffee crunch to maple walnut, along with a choice of fruity sorbets. The location is handy for the Roundhouse and Camden Market (*see p108* **Great Days Out**). *Buggy access. Disabled access. High chairs. Takeaway service.*

JAPANESE

Benihana

100 Avenue Road, NW3 3HF (7586 9508/ www.benihana.co.uk). Swiss Cottage tube. **Lunch served** noon-3pm daily. **Dinner served** 5.30-10.30pm Mon-Sat; 5-10pm Sun. **Set lunch** £11-£19. **Set dinner** £18-£48. **Credit** AmEx, MC, V.

The key to this Japanese restaurant chain's popularity with families isn't crayons and toys – it's making the food itself entertaining. All hot dishes are prepared on a teppan, a hot plate at centre stage at each table. And what a stage it is; here, cooking is theatre. On our last visit we were lucky enough to have head chef Andrew, whose tricks and banter were vastly superior to that of some of his younger colleagues at surrounding tables. First, there's an explosion of fire as the teppan is cleaned. Our chef started with an onion, which soon became a volcano and then a steam train. The rice was a beating heart. The chicken was a caterpillar. The salt and pepper pots did somersaults around our heads before landing on the top of the chef's hat. And all that with accompanying jokes: 'Watch this butterfly' said the chef, as he catapaulted some butter on to the grill. Butter. Fly. Geddit? It's a natty way of charging a lot for what's essentially a pretty average stir fry, but the kids will be talking about it for weeks afterwards. On a Sunday lunchtime, they'll also go home with balloon animals made by the resident clown. *Buggy access. Children's menu (£9.50-£13.50). Entertainment: clown Sun lunch. High chairs. Takeaway service.* **Branches** 37 Sackville Street, W1S 3DQ (7494 2525); 77 King's Road, SW3 4NX (7376 7799).

Yo! Sushi

The Brunswick, WC1N 1AE (7240 1883/ www.yosushi.com). Russell Square tube. **Meals served** noon-11pm Mon-Sat; noon-10.30pm Sun. **Dishes** £1.70-£5. **Credit** AmEx, MC, V.

Children adore watching Japanese delicacies gliding round on Yo! Sushi's conveyor belt. The deal is simple: they grab 'em and you pay for 'em, according to the item's price code. Purists may quibble at the food's authenticity, but it's an event as much as a meal. There's plenty for vegetarians as well as raw fish fans, and you can also order hot food (grilled chicken or salmon, and various rice or noodle dishes). *Buggy access. Delivery service. Disabled access: toilet. Nappy-changing facilities. Takeaway service.* **Branches** throughout town.

Consumer

Send in the clowns

Benihana.

These days, crayons and a menu to colour in are the very least that mini gourmands expect with their babycinos. Many cafés and restaurants, particularly beyond the Circle line, have developed a package that offers children a lot more than just a plate of food. Play dens, book corners, slides and activities could be on the menu, with restaurateurs keen to grab a slice of the lucrative family market.

In south London's nappy valley on Northcote Road, **Crumpet** (*see p225*) has a small playroom and shelves of books for children to enjoy. **Common Ground** (*see p225*), beside the cricket pitches and bowling green of Wandsworth Common, has a cosy playroom at the back with regular music sessions for the under-fives. Children are also kept busy in Fulham's **Coffee & Crayons** (*see p225*), where they can paint, sign up for fairy school, or join in with music sessions.

Moving north, Newington Green's **That Place on the Corner** (*p234*) offers classes as well as a large dressing-up wardrobe and cosy reading corner. Families around Kensal Green are spoilt for choice, with two great venues on their doorstep. **Brilliant Kids Café & Arts Centre** (*see p224*) is our favourite, keeping parents happy with great coffee

and indecently good cakes while their offspring enjoy imaginative activities next door in the studio. Nearby, **Gracelands** (*see p230*) is more chaotic, but also offers creative workshops as well as a compact play area. Exciting new venues are opening all the time. Look out for the **Papered Parlour**, just off Clapham High Street (*see p195*), whose café hadn't opened when we went to press.

Kids also like being entertained at their table. At Japanese chain **Benihana** (*see p245*), the chefs make cooking lunch into theatre, tossing utensils around and making the food come alive right in front of their eyes. There's also a clown who wanders from table to table. **Smollensky's on the Strand** (*see p250*) has clowns and magicians at weekend lunchtimes between noon and 3pm.

The delights of **TGI Friday's** (*see p250*) aren't always appreciated by parents, but kids love the comfort food and face painting during weekend lunches. And if the real animals at **Frizzante** (*see p228*) and **Mudchute Kitchen** (*see p231*) aren't exciting enough, how about trying the **Rainforest Café** (*see p244*), with its animatronic attractions – the nearest thing to Disneyland this side of the Channel Tunnel?

MEXICAN

Wahaca

66 Chandos Place, WC2N 4HG (7240 1883/www.wahaca.co.uk). Covent Garden or Leicester Square tube. **Meals served** noon-11pm Mon-Sat; noon-10.30pm Sun. **Main courses** £3.25-£9.95. **Credit** AmEx, MC, V.
Children often want a meal earlier in the day than adults, and in this case that's no bad thing; at peak times, Wahaca invariably has queues snaking out of the door. Get here at noon or at 5pm, however, and you should be shown straight to a table. The surroundings are cheerful and colourful, the staff knowledgeable and friendly. There's no children's menu as such, but ordering is easy thanks to a range of street food options – tacos, tostadas and quesadillas – that come in small portions at reasonable prices. Puddings include doughnuts with chocolate sauce, ice-cream and mango sorbet.
Buggy access. Disabled access: toilet. High chairs. Nappy-changing facilities. **Branch** Southern Terrace, Westfield Shopping Centre, W12 7GB (8749 4517).

MODERN EUROPEAN

Ambassador

55 Exmouth Market, EC1R 4QL (7837 0009/ www.theambassadorcafe.co.uk). Angel tube/ Farringdon tube/rail/19, 38 bus. **Breakfast/ lunch served** 9am-3pm Mon-Fri; 11am-3.30pm Sat, Sun. **Dinner served** 6-11pm Mon-Sat; 6-10pm Sun. **Main courses** £9.50-£17. **Set meal** (noon-3pm, 6-11pm Mon-Fri) £12.50 2 courses, £16 3 courses. **Credit** AmEx, MC, V.
The food takes centre stage at this quietly accomplished brasserie, with its understated decor and easy-going charm. Leisurely weekend brunches are particularly popular with families; parents ponder the papers while kids concentrate on the colouring books. The children's menu is a one-dish affair (generally fish and chips, with a chocolate and banana milkshake to wash it down), but there's plenty to tempt them on the main brunch menu too, from waffles with caramel bananas to scrambled eggs on sourdough toast. The kitchen are also happy to cook up child-sized versions of mains wherever possible, at half the menu price. In summer, tables spread on to the street – a traffic-free thoroughfare that's perfect for people-watching.
Buggy access. Children's menu (£1.50-£3.50 Sat, Sun brunch). Crayons. High chairs. Tables outdoors (10, pavement). Toys.

Bumpkin

209 Westbourne Park Road, W11 1EA (7243 9818/www.bumpkinuk.com). Westbourne Park tube. **Lunch served** noon-3pm Mon-Fri; 11am-3.30pm Sat, Sun. **Dinner served** 6-11pm daily. **Credit** MC, V.
Downstairs, the setting is country chic with distressed wood furniture and mismatched chairs – though it's clear the look came from a design studio rather than second-hand shops. Wooden crates, sheaves of wheat and miscellaneous sacks nestling under the butcher's block waiter station are a little twee, but the overall effect is as cosy as a country kitchen and has a welcoming, convivial feel. The daily changing menu is seasonal and modern, with many ingredients sourced in the UK. There's something to suit all ages and palates, from comforting macaroni cheese to excellent ribeye steak with béarnaise sauce. There's a more sedate dining room upstairs for special occasions.
Buggy access. Crayons. Disabled access: toilet. High chairs. Nappy-changing facilities. **Branch** 102 Old Brompton Road, SW7 3RD (7341 0802).

NORTH AMERICAN

Big Easy

332-334 King's Road, SW3 5UR (7352 4071/www.bigeasy.uk.com). Sloane Square tube, then 11, 19, 22 bus. **Meals served** noon-11.15pm Mon-Thur, Sun; noon-12.15am Fri, Sat. **Main courses** £8.85-£27.50. **Set lunch** (noon-5pm Mon-Fri) £7.95 2 courses. **Credit** AmEx, DC, MC, V. **Map** p313 E12.
The children's menu at this somewhat raucous restaurant offers the likes of beefburgers, hot dogs and chicken dippers, all served with chips and a drink (ice-cream sodas, fresh fruit juices, milk). Avoid dining here in the evening with small children, as the after-work crowd soon packs it out. The draw for adults consists of huge steaks, enormous, juicy burgers, vast seafood platters and racks of ribs. Steaks are tender and well priced, Alaskan king crab and lobster are house specialities and side dishes are carefully done.
Buggy access. Children's menu (£5.95). Crayons. Disabled access. High chairs. Nappy-changing facilities. Tables outdoors (3, pavement). Takeaway service.

Bodean's

10 Poland Street, W1F 8PZ (7287 7575/www. bodeansbbq.com). Oxford Circus or Piccadilly Circus tube. **Lunch served** noon-3pm,

Spicy but nice **Wahaca**. *See p247.*

dinner served 5.30-11pm Mon-Fri. **Meals served** noon-11pm Sat; noon-10.30pm Sun. **Main courses** £8-£16. **Credit** AmEx, MC, V.

The main event here is barbecued meat, served in large portions; Bodean's 'signature' dish is a mighty rack (or a half rack for wusses) of baby back ribs. Then there are steaks, burgers and fiery chicken wings. It's obviously not a vegetarian-oriented sort of place, although the sweet baked beans and fries are good. Children eat free between noon and 5pm at the weekend when accompanied by an adult; options include barbecue chicken breast or slices of smoked beef, turkey or ham with fries or mash, with ice-cream to follow. At other times, the children's menu costs £5. Big screens showing sporting fixtures can make conversation tricky, but staff do thoughtful things like bringing jugs of iced tap water without being asked, and giving extra scoops of ice-cream to older siblings, which make us feel warm about this place nonetheless. *Buggy access. Children's menu (£5, free noon-5pm Sat, Sun). High chairs. Nappy-changing facilities. Takeaway service.* **Branches** throughout town.

Dexter's Grill

20 Bellevue Road, SW17 7EB (8767 1858/ www.tootsiesrestaurants.co.uk). Wandsworth Common rail. **Meals served** 11am-10.30pm Mon-Fri; 10am-11pm Sat; 10am-10pm Sun. **Main courses** £6.85-£16.95. **Credit** AmEx, MC, V.

Chilled-out staff at this chain are happy to make a fuss of the nippers, who are treated to their own mini smoothies and shakes, beef bolognese with five hidden vegetables, burgers, individual fish pies and ice-cream in sundae glasses. While the decor might look grown-up, like its rival Tootsies, Dexter's is primarily aimed at the family market. Most diners opt for the burgers, which come with their own trays of relishes, mustards and sauces and are far superior to those served up by the 'gourmet' chains. Breakfasts and brunches are also popular, and can be as healthy (fruit salad) or unhealthy (pancakes with maple syrup, full English) as you like. Arrive by 12.15pm to guarantee a table. *Buggy access. Children's menu (£3.75-£5.50). Crayons. Disabled access: toilet. High chairs. Nappy-changing facilities. Tables outdoors (8, terrace). Takeaway service.* **Branches** throughout town.

Gourmet Burger Kitchen

44 Northcote Road, SW11 1NZ (7228 3309/ www.gbkinfo.co.uk). Clapham Junction rail. **Meals served** noon-11pm Mon-Fri; 11am-11pm Sat; 11am-10pm Sun. **Main courses** £5.45-£7.40. **Credit** MC, V.

The influx of customers with discount vouchers (when is there not a special offer on at the moment?) certainly puts staff under pressure, but the burgers at this growing chain are highly reliable. While everyone has their favourites, superior classics like chilli or blue cheese tend to be more satisfying than the more outré variants. The satay burger, for example, is very rich, but we wouldn't order it again. Organic buffalo, wild boar and pork and leek burgers from Laverstoke Park Farm are a welcome addition to the menu; there's also a decent choice for vegetarians. Smaller burgers (beef, chicken, puy lentil) are offered for kids, and customers watching their waistlines.
Buggy access. Children's menu (£3.45-£3.95). Disabled access. High chairs. Tables outdoors (4, pavement). Takeaway service.
Branches throughout town.

Haché
24 Inverness Street, NW1 7HJ (7485 9100/ www.hacheburgers.com). Camden Town tube. **Meals served** noon-10.30pm Mon-Sat; noon-10pm Sun. **Main courses** £6.95-£12.95. **Credit** AmEx, MC, V.
Any gourmet burger bar should be able to shine on basic burgers, and Haché truly excels. The portions are large and the meat first-rate, with good-quality extra toppings (flavoursome bacon dry-cured in brine, proper cheese, huge mushrooms). It looks a cut above your average gourmet burger joint too, with art on the walls and muted lighting; nonetheless, it's warmly welcoming to children. There's a wide range of burgers to choose between, from beef, duck, lamb and venison to a welcome vegetarian selection; chips, meanwhile, can be frites-style, skinny or fat. Crêpes have recently been added to the dessert options, but the brownies are the thing to have.
Buggy access. High chairs. Takeaway service.
Branch 329-331 Fulham Road, SW10 9QL (7823 3515).

Hard Rock Café
150 Old Park Lane, W1K 1QR (7629 0382/ www.hardrock.com). Hyde Park Corner tube. **Meals served** 11.30am-12.30am Mon-Thur, Sun; 11am-1am Fri, Sat. **Main courses** £9.95-£15.95. **Credit** AmEx, MC, V. **Map** p316 H8.
Music blasts at impressive levels and rock memorabilia covers the walls at this famous themed chain restaurant, which is more suitable for older children and teenagers than anyone arriving in a buggy. Hamburgers and sides are the order of the day, piled high on plates carried

by waitresses in teeny-tiny uniforms. Also on the menu are classic salads, barbecue dishes and nachos. Fortunately, all this noise doesn't mask the fact that the food is pretty darn good. Burgers are satisfyingly juicy, the nachos gooey, the salads a decent size and the ice-cream sundaes excellent. Further attractions include face painting at certain times, a children's menu with pizza, pasta and burgers, and occasional themed activities.
Booking advisable. Buggy access. Children's set meal (£6.95). Crayons. Disabled access: toilet. Entertainment: face painting (check website). High chairs. Nappy-changing facilities. Tables outdoors (10, terrace).

Lucky 7
127 Westbourne Park Road, W2 5QL (7727 6771/www.lucky7london.co.uk). Royal Oak or Westbourne Park tube. **Meals served** 10am-11pm Mon-Thur; 9am-11pm Fri, Sat; 9am-10.30pm Sun. **Main courses** £4.50-£15.95. **Credit** MC, V.
Tom Conran's cosy American diner and neighbourhood hang-out is one for families with older children to enjoy. The green booths and tin ceiling are effortlessly stylish, the vibe laidback as staff banter with the regulars. Although there are a few salads and sandwiches on the menu, the choice is basically between breakfasts and burgers. There's no kids' menu, but pretty much everything will appeal to youngsters, from buttermilk pancakes or huevos rancheros to the various burger options (kids get the same size burger as adults, but it automatically comes with fries). With shakes, coke floats, ice-creams and home-made pecan pie on offer too, what's not to like about this place?
Takeaway service.

Planet Hollywood
57-60 Haymarket, SW1Y 4QX (7437 7639/ www.planethollywoodlondon.com). Piccadilly Circus tube. **Meals served** 11am-1am daily. **Main courses** £10.45-£21.95. **Credit** AmEx, DC, MC, V. **Map** p317 K7.
Movie memorabilia floor to ceiling, swinging klieg lights (just like in LA) and blasting film soundtracks might be overstimulating for tinies, but older children love it. The food is everything they approve of too; burgers, rôtisserie chicken, fajitas and steaks, accompanied by fries and washed down with shakes and pop.
Booking advisable. Buggy access. Children's menu (£8-£9). Crayons. Disabled access: toilet. Entertainment: DJs Mon-Fri dinner; all day Sat, Sun, school hols. High chairs. Nappy-changing facilities.

Consumer

Smollensky's on the Strand

105 Strand, WC2R 0AA (7497 2101/www.smollenskys.com). Embankment tube/Charing Cross tube/rail. **Meals served** noon-10pm Mon-Wed, Sun; noon-11pm Thur-Sat. **Main courses** £9.95-£23.95. **Credit** AmEx, MC, V. **Map** p317 L7.

This basement steakhouse is a warm, inviting place to hole up in winter, with children's entertainment every Saturday and Sunday lunchtime; there's also a TV and Playstation at their disposal. The menu is full of simple, sturdy ribstickers, with an emphasis on steaks – which arrive with good chips and a choice of sauces. The children's menu is divided into two sections: one category for under-sevens (who are deemed only to want fried food – burgers, chicken and fish – bar one vegetarian pasta dish) and one for 'mini adults' (who are treated to the likes of steak or jambalaya). Mains can be variable, but we've no complaints about the puds: moreish chocolate mousse and memorable Mississippi mud pie.

Booking advisable. Children's menu (£3.95-£7.95). Crayons. Entertainment: clown, magician, noon-3pm Sat, Sun. High chairs. Nappy-changing facilities. **Branch** 1 Reuters Plaza, E14 5AG (7719 0101).

TGI Friday's

6 Bedford Street, WC2E 9HZ (7379 0585/www.tgifridays.co.uk). Covent Garden or Embankment tube/Charing Cross tube/rail. **Meals served** 11am-11.30pm Mon-Thur; 11am-midnight Fri, Sat; noon-11pm Sun. **Main courses** £8.29-£17.99. **Credit** AmEx, MC, V. **Map** p317 L7.

We would recommend lunchtime visits at this busy Covent Garden branch of TGI Friday's, as the bar gets very crowded in the evenings. The immensely cheery, overwhelmingly child-friendly staff here hand out balloons and activity packs to children, who are chatted to sweetly and even entertained on certain days (see the website for details). The food is varied, with an emphasis on sticky barbecues and tasty Tex-Mex dishes as well as the inevitable burgers and fries. The children's menu has all the fried regulars too, but side dishes can be exchanged for healthier options – crudités, corn on the cob or vegetables. All that good will be undone at the pudding stage, when dirt and worm pie (for chocolate and fudge fiends), sundaes and cheesecakes are the order of the day. Free Heinz baby food is provided for babes of four to ten months accompanying a dining adult.

Buggy access. Children's set meal (£2.99-£4.99). Crayons. Disabled access: lift, toilet. Entertainment: face painting Sat, Sun lunch. High chairs. Nappy-changing facilities. **Branches** throughout town.

Tootsies Grill

120 Holland Park Avenue, W11 4UA (7229 8567/www.tootsiesrestaurants.com). Holland Park tube. **Meals served** 10am-11pm Mon-

Hotdog heaven at **Lucky 7**. *See p249.*

Thur; 10am-11.30pm Fri; 9am-11.30pm Sat, Sun. **Main courses** £6.95-£16.95. **Credit** AmEx, MC, V.
Families love this burger chain, which has always taken the vagaries of tot behaviour in its stride. Parents can feel reassured by the knowledge that children's nutritional expert Annabel Karmel designed the children's menu, while kids just love the fact they're getting everything they most like to eat; burgers, hot dogs, ribs or pasta, with drinks and a build-your-own sundae option for pudding. They are also plied with wax crayons and colouring-in while they wait. Waiting staff couldn't be friendlier, and each branch is designed to be light, bright and spacious, so there's plenty of room for buggies
Buggy access. Children's menu (£3.75-£5.50). Crayons. High chairs. Nappy-changing facilities. Tables outdoors (3, pavement). Takeaway service.
Branches throughout town.

ORIENTAL

Wagamama
11 Jamestown Road, NW1 7BW (7428 0800/ www.wagamama.com). **Meals served** noon-11pm Mon-Sat; noon-10pm Sun. **Main courses** £6.35-£12.95. **Credit** AmEx, DC, MC, V.
This popular chain continues to provide tasty and wholesome oriental fast food at a fair price. The Camden branch is particularly good for families as there is plenty of space to accommodate buggies. There's something to appeal to everyone among the noodle and rice dishes; children will also love the chicken katsu (chicken breast fried in breadcrumbs) with dipping sauce and the gyoza (steamed then grilled dumplings). Developments in recent years include unusually flavoured desserts such as tamarind and chilli pavlova. To drink there's saké, juices and free green tea.
Buggy access. Children's menu (£2.75-£4.25). Crayons. Disabled access: toilet. High chairs. Nappy-changing facilities. Takeaway service.
Branches throughout town.

PORTUGUESE

Nando's
57-59 Goodge Street, W1T 1TH (7637 0708/www.nandos.com). **Meals served** 11.30am-11pm Mon-Thur; 11.30am-11.30pm Fri, Sat; 11.30am-10.30pm Sun. **Main courses** £5.80-£10.60. **Credit** MC, V.

For a quick, straightforward meal, especially if you've got kids, this chain smacks the Burger Kings of this world clear out the water. The appeal of Portuguese-inspired Nando's lies, like most restaurant franchises, in its simplicity, lack of ceremony and keen prices. With proper wooden tables and chairs and a menu that centres around freshly grilled chicken, it's not quite a fast food restaurant – but it's not a million miles away (meal deals, bottomless refills on drinks and a super-casual vibe). Chicken served with spicy peri peri sauce of varying degrees of fierceness is the mainstay, and it's worth sticking to – grilled halves and quarters are crisp skinned and juicy inside, while sides dishes (flavoursome corn on the cob, thick cut, slightly school canteen-style chips) make for a filling, decent value meal. Vegetarian options (halloumi and roast portobello mushroom wraps, say, or bean burgers) are also available, and tasty enough. Staff on our last visit were chirpy and efficient.
Buggy access. Children's set meal (£3.95). Disabled access: toilet. Crayons. High chairs. Nappy-changing facilities. Tables outdoors (1, pavement).

THAI

Blue Elephant
4-6 Fulham Broadway, SW6 1AA (7385 6595/ www.blueelephant.com). Fulham Broadway tube. **Lunch served** noon-2.30pm Mon-Sat; noon & 2.30pm Sun. **Dinner served** 6.30-11.30pm Mon-Sat; 6.30-10.30pm Sun. **Main courses** £11.90-£28. **Set buffet** (Sun lunch) £25; £12.50 under-11s. **Credit** AmEx, DC, MC, V.
Smiling staff are dressed in traditional costume and welcome diners into an unusual setting. With its palms, topiary, ponds full of koi carp, waterfalls and walkways, it's not difficult to see why this restaurant is so popular with well-off local families. Adults may be disappointed that the kitchen tempers the authentic Thai fieriness, but it's good for the little ones. Even the fussiest eater usually succumbs to the platter of classic starters (mostly deep-fried offerings such as spring rolls). The extensive menu, featuring all the mainstays of Thai cuisine as well as lesser known dishes, offers several set options that are good for those on a budget. Families flock here on Sunday lunchtimes, when children eat for half price and are entertained by face painters (note that there are two sittings).
Booking advisable (Sun lunch). Buggy access. Crayons. Delivery service. Disabled access:

Consumer

toilet. Entertainment: face painting Sun
lunch. High chairs. Nappy-changing facilities.
Takeaway service.

TURKISH

Gallipoli Again
120 Upper Street, N1 1QP (7226 8099/
www.cafegallipoli.com). Angel tube/Essex Road
rail. **Meals served** noon-11pm Mon-Thur;
10.30am-midnight Fri, Sat; 10.30am-11pm Sun.
Main courses £6.95-£10.95. **Credit** MC, V.
The infectious party atmosphere and Turkish
decor appeals to the children, while adults love
the reasonable pricing. The long, narrow
restaurant has a rosy glow and a throbbing beat,
and is generally packed with diners sharing
delicious bowls of food. Chewy pide bread with
mixed meze is a good bet for starters (everyone
loves to dip), while falafel, kofte and filling
moussaka make for appealing mains. Staff in
silver-monogrammed black shirts are extremely
graceful considering how busy they are.
Buggy access. Crayons. High chairs. Tables
outdoors (8, garden; 2, pavement). Takeaway
service.
Branches Gallipoli Café Bistro, 102 Upper
Street, N1 1QN (7359 0630); Gallipoli Bazaar,
107 Upper Street, N1 1QN (7226 5333).

Mangal II
4 Stoke Newington Road, N16 8BH (7254
7888/www.mangal2.com). Dalston Kingsland
rail/76, 149, 243 bus. **Meals served** 3pm-
1am Mon-Thur; 2pm-1am Fri, Sat; 2pm-
midnight Sun. **Main courses** £8.45-£15.99.
Credit MC, V.
The grilled meats and fish here are superb,
which accounts for Mangal II's huge popularity
with families of all nationalities. It also helps
that the service is so friendly and efficient. For
mains, the adana kebab (alternating patties of
minced lamb and slices of aubergine grilled on
a skewer) is excellent; children particularly
relish the grilled chicken and pide and saç bread.
Buggy access. High chairs. Takeaway service.

Tas
22 Bloomsbury Street, WC1B 3QJ (7637 4555/
www.tasrestaurant.com). Tottenham Court
Road tube. **Meals served** noon-11.30pm
daily. **Main courses** £6.95-£12.45. **Set**
meze £8.65-£18.65 per person (minimum 2).
Credit AmEx, MC, V.
Much of the menu will appeal to little ones at
this cheerfully busy eaterie near the British
Museum, from meze favourites such as

houmous and piping-hot borek (little filo parcels,
stuffed with feta cheese) to pasta with tomato
sauce. For adults, there are almost 40 starters,
then a comprehensive choice of fish and rice
dishes, pasta and casseroles, in addition to the
expected grills. Even the fussiest of eaters will
find something they're happy to order, and staff
are adept at dealing with family groups.
Buggy access. Disabled access: toilet. High
chairs. Tables outdoors (14, pavement).
Branches throughout town.

VIETNAMESE

Namô
178 Victoria Park Road, E9 7HD (8533 0639/
www.namo.co.uk). Mile End tube, then 277 bus.
Lunch served noon-3.30pm Fri-Sun. **Dinner**
served 5.30-11pm Tue-Sun. **Main courses**
£6.90-£8.90. **Credit** MC, V.
This pleasant little café is sister of the excellent
Huong Viet in Dalston, but has a much more
polished feel. The decor is stripped down and
stylish, with a modish little terrace at the back
for warmer weather. Children love assembling
and scoffing the crispy duck pancakes and
chicken and prawn banh xeo (Vietnamese
pancakes); spring rolls, chicken satay and wok-
fried crispy noodles might also appeal.
Alternatively, they can choose from their own
special menu.
Buggy access. Children's set meal (£4.50).
Crayons. Disabled access. High chairs. Tables
outdoors (4, patio). Takeaway service.
Branch Huong-Viet, 12-14 Englefield Road,
N1 4LS (7249 0877).

Sông Quê Café
134 Kingsland Road, E2 8DY (7613 3222).
Bus 26, 48, 55, 67, 149, 242, 243. **Lunch**
served noon-3pm, dinner served 5-11pm
Mon-Sat. **Meals served** 11am-11pm Sun.
Main courses £5-£7. **Credit** MC, V.
Eternally popular (and invariably packed) Song
Quê is a bustling, canteen-style Vietnamese
restaurant on the corner of Kingsland Road and
Pearson Street. The menu is mind-bogglingly
vast, but children generally opt for steaming
bowls of *phô* (noodle soup) or delicately-
fashioned rice paper rolls stuffed with prawns,
vegetables or chicken; orders are hastily
scrawled on the paper tablecloth, and appear
with astonishing alacrity. Devotees consider the
rich, fragrant beef *phô* the best in the city; the
little parcels of beef wrapped in betel leaves are
also deliciously moreish.
Buggy access. High chairs. Takeaway service.

Shopping

From essential nursery equipment to pocket-money purchases, the city's shops have it all.

Whether you're in search of sensible school shoes, essential baby equipment or delightful fripperies, the capital's teeming shopping scene is guaranteed to deliver. Though shopping expeditions can test children's and parents' tempers to the limit, London's savvier shops are adept at keeping fractious children sweet with toy boxes, face-painting and colouring tables.

The big names remain as popular as ever, with a jaunt to **Hamleys** (*see p280*) or a trip to see Santa at **Harrods** (*see p253*) or **Selfridges** (*see p271*) sending most kids into a frenzy of excitement. Less excitable grown-ups tend to prefer the city's smaller independents, where sturdy wooden toys, hand-knitted bootees and sprigged cotton frocks press all the right buttons; it's hard to resist the nostalgic appeal of shops like **Honeyjam** (*see p281*) and **Olive Loves Alfie** (*see p269*). It's well worth supporting the city's smaller bookshops, too – establishments such as **Tales on Moon Lane** (*see p260*), where you can snuggle up for a good old-fashioned storytelling session, appeal to all ages.

ALL-ROUNDERS

Blue Daisy
13 South End Road, NW3 2PT (7681 4144/ www.blue-daisy.com). Belsize Park tube/ Hampstead Heath rail. **Open** 9.30am-5.30pm Mon-Fri; 10am-5.30pm Sat. **Credit** AmEx, MC, V.
When you first walk in to this baby boutique, it can seem as if there's not much here. But look a little closer and the minimalist presentation hides a wealth of great products to make parenting just that bit easier and more stylish. The shop stocks prams, toys, slings, organic lotions, nappies and changing accessories, clothes, potties, plastic crockery and a lot more besides. The layout has been thoughtfully designed with a play alcove for small children and a nappy changing room, while the generous floor space means it's also easy bringing buggies inside. *Buggy access. Mail order. Nappy-changing facilities. Play area.*

Born
168 Stoke Newington Church Street, N16 0JL (7249 5069/www.borndirect.com). Bus 73, 393, 476. **Open** 9.30am-5.15pm Tue-Fri; 9.30am-5.30pm Sat; noon-5pm Sun. **Credit** MC, V.
Natural, organic and fair trade pregnancy products, baby equipment and clothes fill the shelves at Born, from cotton nappies and babygros to brightly-painted toys and sturdy little scooters (fashioned from sustainable rubberwood, naturally). Practical gear includes Ergo's super-soft cotton baby slings and sleek buggies from the likes of Phil & Teds and Bugaboo, alongside chemical-free toiletries and baby wipes and the shop's own brand of pregnancy massage oils. The shop is a joy to visit with children in tow: there's ample space to play, and a sofa for breastfeeding mothers. Born is incredibly attentive when it comes to customer service, and its network of support even extends to recommending complementary health practitioners and birthing pool suppliers. *Buggy access. Delivery service. Disabled access: ramp. Mail order. Nappy-changing facilities. Play area.*

Harrods
87-135 Brompton Road, SW1X 7XL (7730 1234/www.harrods.com). Knightsbridge tube. **Open** 10am-8pm Mon-Sat; noon-6pm Sun. **Credit** AmEx, DC, MC, V. **Map** p313 F9.
The fourth floor is the one to head for at Harrods, with room after room devoted to uniforms, party clothes, nursery gear, books and babygros. Toy Kingdom (7225 6781) is a child's dream come true, with its jolly demonstrators and immense range of toys. Clothes begin with beautiful babywear, including ranges from Christian Dior and Roberto Cavalli, and go through ultra-smart

Bags of potential East Dulwich

The buggies began rolling into this suburban patch of south London in the 1990s, when the first wave of upwardly mobile young families started moving in. The sprog scene centres around residential Northcross Road, home of original trendsetter the **Blue Mountain Café** (*see p223*), then spills out on to Lordship Lane. Although local favourite the Never Ending Story Bookshop has sadly now, er, ended, there's still plenty to catch the eye and lighten the wallet.

One new arrival is swish shoe boutique **Jolie à Pied** (*see p269*), stocking a small range of high-end footwear for toddlers and private-schooled princesses from the likes of Spanish label Maá. The more established **Oranges & Lemons** provides chic maternity and baby wear (*see p273*), while further down Northcross Road, the

wonderful **Hope & Greenwood** (20 Northcross Road, SE22 9EU, 8613 1777, www.hopeandgreenwood.co.uk) lures you in with '40s dance tunes on the wireless and shelves stacked with glass jars of flying saucers, gobstoppers and lemon bonbons.

Back on Lordship Lane, the Dulwich branch of **Soup Dragon** (*see p259*) is an Aladdin's cave of groovy clothes, toys and the ubiquitous micro scooters. Above the shop, children's yoga and baby massage sessions take place at the **Family Natural Health Centre** (8693 5515). The south London branch of the **JoJo Maman Bébé** mini-chain sits at one end of the high street (*see p255*); further down, the sensible **John Barnett** (*see p276*) makes sure little feet have something practical and hard-wearing to put on.

Hope & Greenwood.

tweedy garb from the Harrods label (think proper winter coats with velvet collars and silk and tulle party frocks). School uniforms from London's smarter educational establishments are also stocked. Couture childrenswear from international designers includes mini togs by Burberry, Missoni, Miss Blumarine, Ralph Lauren and Armani; Bunny London's exquisitely embellished dresses are also sold here. Footwear is by One Small Step One Giant Leap (*see p276*). There's face-painting, haircutting and lots of interactive fun in the holidays and at special events and launches. The nursery department carries all the famous pram and buggy, cot, bed and high chair brands. *Buggy access. Café. Car park. Delivery service. Disabled access: lift, toilet. Hairdressing. Mail order. Nappy-changing facilities.*

Igloo

300 Upper Street, N1 2TU (7354 7300/ www.iglookids.co.uk). Angel tube/Highbury & Islington tube/rail. **Open** 10am-6.30pm Mon-Wed; 10am-7pm Thur; 9.30am-6.30pm Fri, Sat; 11am-5.30pm Sun. **Credit** AmEx, MC, V.

Quirky toys, clothes and accessories, often from lesser-known labels, have made Igloo a mecca for chic north London parents. The premises are small but well-stocked, with shelves of toys reaching to the ceiling – an enticing mix of sticker books, puppet-making kits, puzzles and skipping ropes, along with pedal cars, tipis and trikes. Racks of clothes cater for newborns to ten-year-olds, with a stellar selection of labels (don't miss the fresh floral prints from Room Seven and hand-smocked frocks from I Love Gorgeous). The spacious shoe corner has plenty of seating and some top-notch brands (Start-rite, Crocs, Camper, Angelus and Naturino, alongside some nifty dinosaur and bee wellies). All bases are covered: there's a mirrored parlour for children's haircuts, a table for reading and drawing and a gift-wrapping service. *Buggy access. Delivery service. Disabled access. Hairdressing. Mail order.*
Branches 80 St John's Wood High Street, NW8 7SH (7483 2332); 227 King's Road, SW3 5EJ (7352 4572).

John Lewis

278-306 Oxford Street, W1A 1EX (7629 7711/www.johnlewis.co.uk). Bond Street or Oxford Circus tube. **Open** 9.30am-8pm Mon-Wed, Fri; 9.30am-9pm Thur; 9.30am-7pm Sat; noon-6pm Sun. **Credit** AmEx, DC, MC, V. **Map** p314 H6.

Good old John Lewis is always a dependable port of call. Follow the stream of parents heading up to the fourth floor, dedicated to all things child-related, and take advantage of its knowledgeable staff and seriously good service. As an all-rounder it's hard to beat, stocking everything from school uniforms, clothes and sportswear to toys, nursery furniture and essentials; the down-to-earth buying-for-baby advice is a lifesaver for bemused first-time parents, and there's a free car-seat fitting advisory service. The toy department overflows with of-the-moment toys, educational games and old classics, with plenty left out for younger shoppers to test. The real jewel in the store's crown, though, is its bustling shoe department (Clarks, Start-rite, Kangaroo, Timberland), saving parents' sanity with its orderly computerised ticketing system and distracting their reluctant offspring with computer games, CBeebies on the telly and free face-painting sessions in the pre-September peak. *Buggy access. Cafés. Delivery service. Disabled access: lift, toilet. Mail order. Nappy-changing facilities.*
Branches Brent Cross Shopping Centre, NW4 3FL (8202 6535); Wood Street, Kingston, Surrey KT1 1TE (8547 3000).

JoJo Maman Bébé

68 & 72 Northcote Road, SW11 6QL (maternity 7228 0322/baby & children 7223 8510/www.jojomamanbebe.co.uk). Clapham Junction rail. **Open** 9.30am-5.30pm Mon-Sat; 11am-5pm Sun. **Credit** MC, V.

Launched in 1993 as an inexpensive maternity and babywear company, JoJo has expanded into a sizeable empire. While it's still primarily a catalogue-based retailer (larger items are ordered from the book), a network of boutiques has sprung up in London's nappy valleys, displaying some of its vast stock of clothes, equipment and furniture. Its own-label clothing lines are relaxed and affordable, with everything from maternity bras, yoga wraps and workwear for expectant mothers to swim nappies, stripy all-in-ones and sturdy dungarees for kids. The company adheres to a strong ethical code – a spirit exemplified by the organic cotton sleepsuits and the Polartec fleeces, made from recycled plastic bottles. JoJo also supports the Nema Foundation, which runs community projects in Mozambique. *Buggy access. Delivery service. Disabled access. Mail order. Nappy-changing facilities.*
Branches 101 Westbourne Grove, W2 4UW (7727 3578); 3 Ashbourne Parade, 1259 Finchley Road, NW11 0AD (8731 8961); 82 Turnham Green Terrace, W4 1QN (8994 0379); 6 Lordship Lane, SE22 8HN (8693 2123); 30 Putney Exchange, Putney High Street, SW15 1TW (8780 5165).

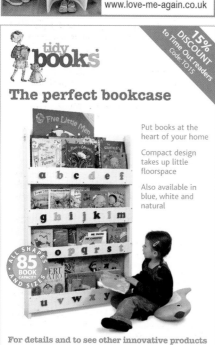

Little White Company
*90 Marylebone High Street, W1U 4QZ
(7486 7550/www.thewhitecompany.com).
Baker Street or Bond Street tube.* **Open**
10am-7pm Mon-Sat; 11am-5pm Sun.
Credit AmEx, MC, V. **Map** p314 G5.
All is calm, orderly and impossibly pretty at
the Little White Company, promising salvation
to stressed-out parents. Snowy cotton soft
furnishings and crisp bedlinen are neatly
arrayed alongside sweetly traditional nightwear
and clothes (little smocks with matching
bloomers and seersucker gingham pyjamas
epitomise the LWC look), and there's
an equally attractive range of white-painted
nursery furniture. Not everything's white, of
course; striped towelling beach hoodies in
fuchsia and navy, floral quilts and lengths of
pastel-hued bunting add a splash of colour.
Prices are reasonable considering the quality,
with demure linen/cotton best summer dresses
starting at around £20.
Buggy access. Delivery service. Mail order.
Branch 261 Pavillion Road, SW1X 0BP
(7881 0783).

Mamas & Papas
*256-258 Regent Street, W1B 3AF (0845 268
2000/www.mamasandpapas.co.uk). Oxford
Circus tube.* **Open** 10am-8pm Mon-Wed, Fri;
10am-9pm Thur; 9am-8pm Sat; noon-6pm Sun.
Credit AmEx, MC, V. **Map** p314 J6.
Amid the chaos of Regent Street, the flagship
outpost for this buggy brand is a spacious,
air-conditioned oasis of calm. There are large
changing rooms for bump and buggy
manoeuvres, and assistants are at hand to advise
on sartorial matters. As well as inexpensive baby
clothes, maternity fashion and lingerie, there's a
dizzying array of Mamas & Papas prams,
pushchairs and car seats – the company's stock
in trade. The first floor, meanwhile, is devoted to
interiors, with a series of 'dream nursery' rooms
displaying cots, changing tables, wardrobes and
storage systems in all shapes and sizes. The first-
floor Cibo café (*see p225*) serves nutritious
homemade fare for mothers-to-be and a
straightforward children's menu.
*Buggy access. Café. Delivery Service. Mail
order. Nappy-changing facilities.*
Branches Brent Cross Shopping Centre,
NW4 3FL (0845 268 2000); Level 1, Westfield
Shopping Centre, W12 7GF (0845 268 2000).

Mini Kin
*22 Broadway Parade, N8 9DE (8341 6898).
Finsbury Park tube/rail, then W7 bus.* **Open**
9.30am-5.30pm Mon-Sat; 10.30am-4.30pm Sun.
Credit MC, V.

Bags of potential
Hampstead

Shopping in Hampstead is like browsing
in a very exclusive market town. But
although money practically oozes out
of the brickwork up here, the area
manages to retain something of the
bohemian, creative community that has
been attracted here for generations.
Play spot the actor as you take a stroll
down Flask Walk, with its old world
charm, and let the shopping begin.

Mystical Fairies (*see p281*) is sheer
heaven for those who like anything pink,
sparkly and otherworldly; unfortunately,
beautiful children's clothes shop Humla,
which used to be opposite, has closed
down. Pregnant women may miss the
Hampstead branch of Formes, also
now closed – although the stylish
and somewhat cheaper **Séraphine**
(*see p275*), just north of the tube,
affords some consolation.

For children needing to be shod, it
would be hard to find a better shoe
shop than the small but very well
stocked **Cubs** (*see p276*) on Heath
Street. Down Rosslyn Hill is toy shop
Happy Returns (*see p281*) which caters
for parties and presents for zero to
fives. And at a lower gradient still, on
South End Green near the Royal Free
Hospital, there's the fantastic **Blue
Daisy** (*see p253*), which stocks just
about every accessory a baby or its
parent could possibly want.

The kids will love the special reading
room at **Daunt Books** (*see p260*);
once you've picked up a linen bag full
of literary goodies, the whole family can
head to neighbouring Hampstead Heath
to let off some steam.

Small but perfectly formed, Mini Kin combines
a modishly stocked children's clothing boutique
with a hairdressing salon. An impeccably chic
array of clothes includes the unusual colours
and pretty patterns of Imps & Elfs, frothy
frocks from Noa Noa and nautical stripes
from Bonnie Baby, and there are fragrant
salves, creams, oils and lotions by Burt's Bees,
Green People and Earth Friendly Baby. Out
back there is the hairdressing salon, decorated
to look like a mythical forest with trailing ivy
and branches; animal-painted chairs and

Best of the web **Clothes & toys**

Ladybird Prints.

CLOTHES

www.alexandalexa.com
If it's stylish, it's stocked here, from classics such as Cacharel to hip new names like Japanese brand Muchacha.

www.belleanddean.co.uk
Distinctive, etching-style animal drawings adorn the organic cotton sleepsuits, tank tops and T-shirts; prices are a steal.

www.dandystar.com
Dandy eschews brash, lurid slogan Ts in favour of sweet, '70s-style designs with a worn-in, vintage look.

www.littlefashiongallery.com
Labels on this cult kid's fashion site range from Paul & Joe and Little Marc to lesser-known names: check out Swedish brand Mini Rodini's guitar-print Ts.

www.nippaz.com
One of the original purveyors of edgy, motto-print T-shirts.

www.noaddedsugar.co.uk
Best known for its bold slogan prints, No Added Sugar now offers more subtle lines: the ruffled, floral dresses are exquisite.

www.nordickids.com
Some of the best childrenswear in the world hails from Scandinavia. Check out the cream of the crop, with Plastisock, Mini Rodini, Smafolk and more.

www.snuglo.com
Lisa Quinn's range is typified by hip, grown-up colours and bold type: 'I want chips, chocolate and cake' is a best-seller.

TOYS

www.brightminds.co.uk
Sparky ideas that make learning fun, from flowering magic gardens to 'explosive experiment' kits and slime laboratories.

www.bumpto3.com
Traditional toys (baby walkers, first bike, mini easels) and fun newcomers – like the ingenious build-your-own saxoflute.

www.gltc.co.uk
Everything from simple flower-pressing kits and bubble-makers to spectacular galleon-shaped climbing frames and toy kitchens.

www.ladybirdprints.com
Choose an image from Ladybird Books' archive and order it as a print or canvas; Peter and Jane peering from a wigwam or the cover of *Ned the Lonely Donkey* are perfect for nostalgia-tinged nurseries.

www.lapinandme.co.uk
Lapin & Me sells the sweetest toys we've ever seen: tin tea sets, colour-in sticker sets and reprinted '40s storybooks.

www.larkmade.com
A small but sweet range of fair trade gifts and soft toys, including quirky cupcake- and doughnut-shaped knitted rattles.

www.ptolemytoys.co.uk
Fabulous toys, baby products, dressing-up clothes and educational goodies.

www.sparrowkids.co.uk
Gorgeous felt kits for crafty children aged five and up: patterns range from bird-shaped bags to rocket pencil cases.

Consumer

charming staff conspire to coax recalcitrant tots into the hotseat. Haircuts start at £10.95. *Buggy access. Disabled access. Hairdressing. Nappy-changing facilities. Play area.*

Mothercare
526-528 Oxford Street, W1C 1LW (7629 6621/www.mothercare.com). Marble Arch tube. **Open** 10am-8pm Mon-Sat; noon-6pm Sun. **Credit** AmEx, MC, V. **Map** p314 G6.
Two floors house all manner of baby-related paraphernalia. It's great for bulk-buy basics such as muslins and plain rompers, and the maternity wear section yields some unexpected finds. *Buggy access. Delivery service. Disabled access: lift, toilet. Mail order. Nappy-changing facilities.* **Branches** throughout town.

Soup Dragon
27 Topsfield Parade, Tottenham Lane, N8 8PT (8348 0224/www.soup-dragon.co.uk). Finsbury Park tube/rail, then W7 bus. **Open** 9.30am-6pm Mon-Sat; 11am-5pm Sun. **Credit** AmEx, MC, V.
This cavernous grotto of a shop is piled high with colourful clothes and toys for little magpies to find. It's an excellent spot to pick up imaginative but relatively inexpensive kids' clothes; the own-brand striped knits are great value. For lovers of bold prints, there are vibrant designs from Danish labels Katvig and Minymo, while the Kidorable in the Rain range is fun and practical. In addition to the everyday clothes, there's a great selection of party wear and fancy dress. On the toy front, dollhouses, castles, farms and pirate ships fire up children's imaginations; there's also a dinky mini kitchen play area where kids can bang pots and pans about. Sign up to the mailing list for details of the regular warehouse sales. *Buggy access. Disabled access. Mail order. Play area.* **Branch** 106 Lordship Lane, SE22 8HF (8693 5575).

Pure Baby
208 Fulham Road, SW10 9PJ (7751 5544/ www.purebaby.co.uk). Fulham Broadway or South Kensington tube, then 14, 414 bus. **Open** 10am-6.30pm Mon-Wed, Fri, Sat; 10am-7pm Thur; 11am-5pm Sun. **Credit** AmEx, MC, V.
Located in a strategic spot near Chelsea & Westminster Hospital's Maternity Unit, Pure Baby is as smart and sleek as its well-heeled clientele. Cashmere cardigans and bootees, Bugaboo prams and embroidered changing bags are among the goodies on offer. *Buggy access. Delivery service.*

EDUCATIONAL

Books
Several toy shops (*see pp260-263*) also stock children's picture books.

Big Green Bookshop
Unit 1, Brampton Park Road, N22 6BG (8881 6767/www.biggreenbookshop.com). Turnpike Lane or Wood Green tube. **Open** 9.30am-6pm Mon-Sat; noon-5pm Sun. **Credit** AmEx, MC, V.
Opened in 2008, this friendly local bookshop has an excellent children's section, where young readers can relax with their favourite tome. Writers pop in to read and talk to the children and there's also a monthly book club for nine to 13s. *Buggy access. Mail order.*

Bookseller Crow on the Hill
50 Westow Street, SE19 3AF (8771 8831/ www.booksellercrow.com). Gypsy Hill rail. **Open** 10am-7pm Mon-Fri; 9.30am-6.30pm Sat; 11am-5pm Sun. **Credit** AmEx, MC, V.
Run by the Crow family, this shop is a laid-back place to while away an afternoon, with a wealth of books for children and grown-ups alike. All of the classics are present and correct, and there's a splendid selection of picture books. *Buggy access. Mail order. Play area.*

Bookworm
1177 Finchley Road, NW11 0AA (8201 9811/ www.thebookworm.uk.com). Golders Green tube. **Open** 9.30am-5.30pm Mon-Sat; 10am-1.30pm Sun. **Credit** MC, V.
The shelves at this independent children's bookshop are packed with treasures. Storytelling sessions for under-fives take place on Tuesdays and Thursdays (2pm) when badges and stickers are handed out, while author visits give children the chance to meet their literary heroes. *Buggy access. Disabled access. Mail order.*

Children's Bookshop
29 Fortis Green Road, N10 3HP (8444 5500). Highgate tube, then 43, 134 bus. **Open** 9.15am-5.45pm Mon-Sat; 11am-4pm Sun. **Credit** AmEx, MC, V.
Clued-up staff and peaceful surrounds make this relaxing place to pick up some new reading material. There's a children's corner with child-sized chairs and picture books at floor level, plus Thursday morning storytelling sessions for preschoolers, kicking off at 11am. Other book-related events, including regular author signings, are publicised in the shop's quarterly newsletter. *Buggy access. Mail order.*

Daunt Books

51 South End Road, NW3 2QB (7794 8206/
www.dauntbooks.co.uk). Belsize Park tube/
Hampstead Heath rail. **Open** 9am-6pm
Mon-Sat; 11am-6pm Sun. **Credit** MC, V.
There's a cosy, welcoming reading room for
children in the back of this branch of the well-
loved independent, with seats where adults can
read to children without fear of disturbing other
customers. The room is decorated with fields and
farm animals and has a good shelf of books.
Just outside is the children's book section, which
offers a very good choice of titles for all ages.
Buggy access. Mail order. Play area.
Branches 193 Haverstock Hill, NW3 4QL
(7794 4006); 83 Marylebone High Street, W1U
4QW (7224 2295); 112-114 Holland Park
Avenue, W11 4UA (7727 7022); 158-164
Fulham Road, SW10 9PR (7373 4997).

Golden Treasury

29 Replingham Road, SW18 5LT (8333 0167/
www.thegoldentreasury.co.uk). Southfields tube.
Open 9.30am-6pm Mon-Fri; 9.30am-5.30pm
Sat; 10.30am-4.30pm Sun. **Credit** MC, V.
The sprawling premises of this brilliant
children's bookshop house a host of titles, from
books on pregnancy to teen fiction. In the unlikely
event that you can't find what you're after, staff
are happy to order it in. There's also an excellent
programme of author events; past visitors
include Judith Kerr (*The Tiger Who Came to Tea*)
and Emma Chichester Clarke (*Blue Kangaroo*).
Buggy access. Mail order. Play area.

Lion & Unicorn

19 King Street, Richmond, Surrey TW9 1ND
(8940 0483/www.lionunicornbooks.co.uk).
Richmond tube/rail. **Open** 9.30am-5.30pm
Mon-Fri; 9.30am-6pm Sat; 11am-5pm Sun.
Credit MC, V.
Opened in 1977 (the late, great Roald Dahl was
the guest of honour), this venerable bookshop
has kept up with the times. 'The Roar', its
quarterly online newsletter, is invaluable for
book reviews and details of signings and special
events. Staff are happy to advise on the diverse
stock crammed into every nook and cranny.
Buggy access. Mail order.

Owl Bookshop

209 Kentish Town Road, NW5 2JU
(7485 7793). Kentish Town tube. **Open**
9.30am-6pm Mon-Sat; noon-4.30pm Sun.
Credit AmEx, MC, V.
A colourful collection of children's books take
pride of place in the window at this tranquil
independent bookshop; inside, titles are sorted

by age and interest. The shop also hosts
readings by local children's authors; for details,
sign up to the mailing list.
Buggy access. Mail order.

Tales on Moon Lane

25 Half Moon Lane, SE24 9JU (7274 5759/
www.talesonmoonlane.co.uk). Herne Hill rail/3,
37, 68 bus. **Open** 9am-5.45pm Mon-Fri; 9.30am-
6pm Sat; 10.30am-4pm Sun. **Credit** MC, V.
Beloved by local families, this award-winning
children's bookshop is a delight. Bright, airy
premises and enthusiastic staff encourage long
visits, as does the wide range of books. The
storytelling sessions are very popular (turn up
early for a place on the sofa), and there's the odd
puppet show. Check online for author events.
Buggy access. Mail order.
Branch 9 Princess Road, NW1 8JN (7722 1800).

Victoria Park Books

174 Victoria Park Road, E9 7HD (8986 1124/
www.victoriaparkbooks.co.uk). London Fields
rail then 277 bus. **Open** 10am-5.30pm daily.
Credit MC, V.
With its book club, wall of book reviews from
schoolchildren and popular patio area, this place
oozes community spirit. Books are categorised
by look and feel as well as content – there's a
section for interactive titles, and children can get
their hands on cloth, bath and buggy books.
Other stock is divided into user-friendly sections:
history, art, dinosaurs, reference, a Ladybird
corner and more. Teenagers and adults are also
catered for. Authors visit regularly and there are
drop-in story sessions at 11am on Fridays.
Buggy access. Mail order. Play area.

Educational toys & games

Education Interactive

10 Staplehurst Road, SE13 5NB (8318 6380/
www.education-interactive.co.uk). Hither Green
rail. **Open** 9.30am-1.30pm Mon-Fri (by
appointment weekday afternoons). **Credit**
MC, V.
As its name suggests, this place specialises in
toys and games to expand the grey matter.
Polydron building blocks and Times Table Lotto
are among the artfully educational offerings.
Buggy access. Mail order.

Fun Learning

Bentall Centre, Clarence Street, Kingston-
upon-Thames, Surrey KT1 1TP (8974 8900/
www.funlearning.co.uk). Kingston rail. **Open**
9am-6pm Mon-Wed, Fri, Sat; 9am-8pm Thur;
11am-5pm Sun. **Credit** MC, V.

Consumer

Big Green Bookshop. See p259.

You're encouraged to try before you buy at this independent retailer, which sells all manner of puzzles, computer games, art and craft activities and science experiment sets. It's a wonderful place for unusual Christmas presents (a paint-your-own chair, say), but there are affordable pocket money items too, ranging from balloon-making gunk kits to hatching dinosaur eggs. *Buggy access. Disabled access. Mail order.* **Branch** Brent Cross Shopping Centre, NW4 3FP (8203 1473).

Musical instruments

Chappell of Bond Street

152-160 Wardour Street, W1F 8YA (7432 4400/www.chappellofbondstreet.co.uk). Oxford Circus or Tottenham Court Road tube. **Open** 9.30am-6pm Mon-Fri; 10am-5.30pm Sat. **Credit** AmEx, MC, V. **Map** p314 J6.

Chappell's three-storey premises showcase a gleaming array of instruments. It's a Yamaha piano and keyboard specialist. Some instruments (typically flutes, saxes, clarinets, trumpets) may be available on a rent-to-buy scheme, but quarter- and half-size instruments must be purchased. *Buggy access. Delivery service. Mail order.*

Dot's

132 St Pancras Way, NW1 9NB (7482 5424/ www.dotsonline.co.uk). Camden Town tube/ Camden Road rail. **Open** 9am-5.30pm Mon-Sat. **Credit** MC, V.

Run by an experienced music teacher, Dot's is a wonderfully friendly establishment. The shop sells new instruments – mostly stringed and wind – from, say, £8.45 for a recorder, £40 for a guitar and £75 for a violin. There's a rent-to-buy scheme too. Check the website for tuition and second-hand instruments. *Mail order. Repair service.*

Dulwich Music Shop

9 Upland Road, SE22 9EE (8693 1477/ www.dulwichmusic.com). East Dulwich rail/ 40, 185, P13 bus. **Open** 9.30am-5.30pm Mon, Tue, Thur-Sat. **Credit** AmEx, MC, V.

A vast array of stringed, woodwind and brass instruments are stocked here, with hire and buy-back options. Accessories and classical sheet music are also sold, and there's a repairs service. *Buggy access. Mail order. Repair service.*

Northcote Music

155C Northcote Road, SW11 6QB (7228 0074). Clapham Junction rail, then 319 bus. **Open** 10.30am-6pm Mon-Fri; 10am-5pm Sat. **Credit** MC, V.

Bags of potential
Walton Street

Walton Street, SW3, has long been home to a clutch of upmarket nursery shops. **Nursery Window**, **Blue Almonds** and **Dragons of Walton Street** (*for all, see p267*) continue to furnish smart nurseries with traditional painted wooden furniture, voile-trimmed moses baskets and matching blankets and cushions. Yet while the south side may still be dominated by traditional shops, the north has developed a cooler reputation in recent years.

Blossom Mother & Child (*see p275*) has led the way with its high-fashion, contemporary maternity wear and deliciously fragrant pampering products. For chic children's attire, meanwhile, there's **Marie Chantal** (*see p273*). Here, sugary prints are eschewed in favour of far more sophisticated designs; some of the little smocks and beautifully cut coats could've come straight from the catwalk. Finally, retro **Guys & Dolls** (*see p269*) is positively cool, with its cache of designer names and funky decor.

This friendly little music shop is tucked away next to QT Toys, somehow squeezing string, percussion and wind instruments (which you can rent or buy) into the tiny space, as well as brass and digital equipment. In the remaining space are the music books and sheet music, some of which are appropriate for younger children (including nursery rhymes for the piano and group sing-along pieces). It's deservedly popular, so try to avoid the after school rush. *Buggy access. Delivery service. Mail order. Repair service.*

Robert Morley

34 Engate Street, SE13 7HA (8318 5838/ www.morleypianos.com). Lewisham DLR/rail. **Open** 9.30am-5pm Mon-Sat. **Credit** MC, V.

To see if a child is serious about playing the piano, Morley's will hire one out, charging £250 for initial payment and delivery, then a monthly charge starting from £30. If, after a year, the child is still piano-friendly, you can buy it, and get half the rental payments off the price, plus the delivery charge. Morley's also builds early keyboards such as clavichords, harpsichords and virginals. *Buggy access. Delivery service.*

EQUIPMENT & ACCESSORIES

Gifts

Bob & Blossom
*140 Columbia Road, E2 7RG (7739 4737/
www.bobandblossom.com). Old Street tube/rail/
55 bus.* **Open** 9am-3pm Sun. **Credit** MC, V.
Despites its restricted opening hours (coinciding
with Sunday's famous flower market), B&B
does a roaring trade in crochet-knit toys, retro
spinning tops and wooden Noah's Ark sets.
The boutique also sells the brand's trademark
T-shirts, hats and sleepsuits, emblazoned with
cheeky mottos.
Buggy access. Mail order.

Finnesse Lifestyle
*453 Roman Road, E3 5LX (8983 9286/
www.finnesselifestyle.com). Bethnal Green
tube, then 8 bus.* **Open** 9.30am-6pm Mon-Sat.
Credit AmEx, MC, V.
Alongside its collections of organic and
fairtrade womenswear, accessories and home
furnishings, Finnesse has an interesting
selection of children's clothes and toys from
around the world. Marimekko, Hug and
Organics for Kids are among the labels; Pia
Wallen's snug little woollen slippers (£20) would
make a lovely gift for a newborn.
Buggy access. Mail order.

Goody Gumdrops
*128 Crouch Hill, N8 9DY (8340 3484/
www.goodygumdrops.co.uk). Finsbury Park
tube/rail then W7 bus/Crouch Hill rail.*
Open 10am-5.30pm Mon-Sat; noon-4.30pm
Sun. **Credit** MC, V.
Decorated with shiny stars, this shop stocks a
mixture of mainstream and quirky toys and
clothes for all ages. It's great for contemporary
crafts, such as the Buttonbag range of sew your
own toys, and for beautiful gifts. Clothes
includes puffy fairy dresses and more stylish
offerings from Ellie & Olla and Albetta. There's
a large table in the middle, stacked with tins of
pocket money buys, and a drop-in story corner
on Friday mornings from 10am.
Buggy access.

Green Baby
*345 Upper Street, N1 0PD (7359 7037/
www.greenbaby.co.uk). Angel tube/Highbury
& Islington tube/rail.* **Open** 9.30am-5.30pm
Mon-Fri; 10am-5pm Sat; 11am-5pm Sun.
Credit MC, V.

Eco-friendly basics are Green Baby's forte, with
adorable organic cotton playsuits for summer
babies and long, striped baby gowns for winter,
made by a community project in India. The
company also sells organic sheets, strokably
soft pastel-hued sheepskins, washable nappies,
Tripp Trapp high chairs, pop-up baby beds,
Huggababy slings and the ever-reliable Baby
Björn Active Carrier. Nappy balms and baby
lotions based on pure lanolin, sweet almond oil
and cocoa butter occupy the remaining space.
Anything too bulky to fit in the shop can be
ordered from the website or catalogue.
*Buggy access. Delivery service. Mail order
(0870 240 6894).*
Branches 5 Elgin Crescent, W11 2JA (7792
8140); 4 Duke Street, Richmond, Surrey TW9
1HP (8940 8255); 52 Greenwich Church Street,
SE10 9BL (8858 6690).

O Baby
*126 Fortis Green Road, N10 3DU (8444
8742). Highgate tube, then 43, 134 bus.*
Open 9.30am-5.30pm Mon-Sat. **Credit** MC, V.
This small shop sells fair trade and organic
bedding, toys and clothes for babies and
toddlers, natural skincare products and runs a
baby list service.
Buggy access.

Semmalina-Starbags
*225 Ebury Street, SW1W 8UT (7730 9333/
www.starbags.info). Sloane Square tube.* **Open**
9.30am-5.30pm Mon-Sat. **Credit** MC, V.
Semmalina-Starbags specialises in bespoke
party bags. Wrapped in crackling cellophane
and garlanded with bright ribbons, the bags can
be filled with all sorts of trinkets – from the
neon-lit sweetie selection to bubbles, potty putty,
bouncy balls, hair bobbles, stationery and more.
Delivery service. Mail order.

So Tiny London
*64 Great Titchfield Street, W1W 7QH (7636
2501/www.showroom64.com). Oxford Circus
tube.* **Open** 11am-6pm Mon-Fri. **Credit**
AmEx, MC, V.
There are beautiful presents for newborns to be
unearthed at this compact shop, ranging from
Bonnie Baby's sumptuous cashmere cardies to
tongue-in-cheek Rolling Stones and Led Zeppelin
babygros. Tiny Mary Jane sock sets (£20) and
knitted bonnets cater to more traditional tastes.
The selection of new baby cards is also excellent,
with some lovely hand-printed designs. Clothes
sizes go up to eight-years-old; don't miss the sale
rail, which often offers generous reductions.
*Buggy access. Mail order. Nappy-changing
facilities.*

Bags of potential
Crouch End

This bohemian, middle-class and family friendly neighbourhood has oddly been the home of a number of fantasy authors. Even Stephen King has visited; in his short story 'Crouch End', the area acts as an inter-dimensional portal. Meanwhile, a great range of independent toy and clothing shops encourages children to use their imaginations and to enter into their own fantasy worlds.

The original, happy, hippy, infant all-rounder **Soup Dragon** (*see p259*) continues to enchant children with its range of dollshouses, pirate ships and castles. Girls will love **Goody Gumdrops** (*see p264*), both for its tempting pocket-money purchases and stylish clothes. For gorgeous gifts, bohemian **Aravore Babies** (*see p268*) produces organic and handcrafted items such as sweet little linen dresses with crochet trims.

For the best pram and buggy advice in the area, head to **Rub a Dub Dub** (*see p266*) and pick up all the other child essentials you need at the same time. Finally, feet can be properly fitted into comfy shoes at **Red Shoes** (*see p277*) and hair groomed to perfection at **Mini Kin** (*see p257*).

Goody Gumdrops.

Tiny Impressions

176 Northcote Road, SW11 6RE (7585 1115/ www.tinyimpressions.co.uk). Clapham Junction rail, then 319 bus. **Open** 10am-6pm Mon-Sat; by appointment Sun. **Credit** MC, V.

An impressive array of upper-end nursery furniture, high chairs, prams, car seats and accessories are tucked away in this smart boutique. Sets of wheels run from ultra-light Micralite and Maclaren strollers to hardwearing Phil & Teds and Mountain Buggy three-wheelers, while chic changing bag brands include Storksac and New York's Skip Hop. There's a small range of toys (including a miniature piano), christening presents and some pretty baby clothes.

Buggy access. Delivery service. Mail order.

Bikes

Chamberlaine Cycles

75-77 Kentish Town Road, NW1 8NY (7485 4488/www.chamberlainecycles.co.uk). Camden Town tube. **Open** 8.30am-6pm Mon-Sat. **Credit** AmEx, MC, V.

Outside, ranks of gleaming, polished bikes line the pavement; inside there are even more to choose from, along with baby seats, trailer bikes, lights and the all-important locks.

Buggy access. Delivery service. Disabled access. Mail order. Repair service.

D2 Leisure

143 Stoke Newington Road, N16 8BP (7254 3380/www.d2leisuregroup.co.uk). Rectory Road rail/67, 76, 149, 243 bus. **Open** 9am-5.30pm Mon-Fri; 9am-5pm Sat. **Credit** MC, V.

The bike shop formerly known as Daycock's has a great range of cycles in the kids' showroom, though staff are not always overly helpful. Most bikes can be ordered online via the website.

Buggy access. Disabled access. Mail order. Repair service.

Branches 201-203 Roman Road, E2 0QY (8980 4966); 70-72 Loampit Vale, SE13 7SN (8297 0225).

Edwardes

221-225 Camberwell Road, SE5 0HG (7703 3676). Elephant & Castle tube, then 12, 68, 176, P3 bus. **Open** 8.30am-6pm Mon-Sat. **Credit** MC, V.

A reliable general bike shop, Edwardes also stocks mounts for two to 12s (brands include Pro Bike, Bronx and Giant) and accessories such as bike seats, helmets, trailers and tag-alongs.

Buggy access. Delivery service. Disabled access. Mail order. Repair service.

Consumer

Bags of potential
Northcote Road

In stark contrast to the peaceful suburbia that surrounds it, Northcote Road is a buzz of activity. A steady stream of prams and pushchairs trundle along the pavements – so it comes as no surprise to find that the street is bursting with quality children's shops. Located between Wandsworth and Clapham Commons, the area lays claim to a mix of upmarket clothes shops such as Jigsaw and Whistles, but also to traditional butchers and bakers and small Italian cafés.

Upmarket children's brands such as **Petit Bateau** (*see p274*), **Fat Face Kids** (*see p274*), **Jigsaw Junior** (*see p274*) and shoe-retailing mini-chain **One Small Step One Giant Leap** (*see p276*) have all set up shop here, catering to well-heeled Nappy Valley dwellers, alongside a host of imaginative independents.

One of the old-timers is the friendly **QT Toys** (*see p282*); along the road, **Northcote Music** (*see p263*) has long supplied local children with their first recorder. Newer arrivals selling upmarket kids' clothing and glossy equipment include **Quackers** (*see p270*) and **Tiny Impressions** (*see p265*), while an outpost of **JoJo Maman Bébé** (*see p255*) covers all the basics.

Northcote Music.

Two Wheels Good
143 Crouch Hill, N8 9QH (8340 4284/ www.twowheelsgood.co.uk). Finsbury Park tube/rail, then W7 bus. **Open** 8.30am-6pm Mon-Fri; 9am-6pm Sat. **Credit** AmEx, MC, V.
Although there isn't a wide range of children's bikes on the floor of this shop (known for its excellent repair service), the incredibly friendly and helpful staff are more than happy to offer recommendations on bikes you can order in from the Gary Fisher and Trek websites.
Buggy access. Disabled access. Mail order. Repair service.
Branch 165 Stoke Newington Church Street, N16 0UL (7249 2200).

Prams & accessories
See also p254-259.

Babyworld
239 Munster Road, SW6 6BT (7386 1904). Fulham Broadway tube, then 211, 295 bus. **Open** 10am-6pm Mon-Wed, Fri; 10am-5.30pm Sat. **Credit** AmEx, MC, V.
The premises may look small but Babyworld crams lots in. Specialising in essential equipment for zero to fours, its stock includes stairgates, prams, pushchairs, high chairs, breast pumps and toys from an impressive range of manufacturers (Medela, Tomy, Maclaren, Bugaboo and Mountain Buggy among them).
Buggy access. Mail order.

Pram Shop
57 Chepstow Road, W2 5BP (7313 9969/ www.thepramshopnottinghill.co.uk). Notting Hill Gate tube, then 28, 328 bus. **Open** 10am-5pm Mon, Fri, Sat; 10am-5.30pm Tue-Thur. **Credit** AmEx, MC, V.
Staff really know their stuff at the Pram Shop – a major distributor for Sweden's Emmaljunga brand, alongside Bugaboo, Phil & Teds and Mountain Buggy. Accessories, such as foot muffs, rain covers and transport bags, are also sold, along with Start-rite shoes.
Buggy access. Delivery service.

Rub a Dub Dub
15 Park Road, N8 8TE (8342 9898). Finsbury Park tube/rail then W7 bus. **Open** 10am-6pm Mon- Sat; noon-4pm Sun. **Credit** MC, V.
All the biggest brands are present and correct at this welcoming, well-stocked shop, from playfully-hued Bugaboos to more rugged Mountain Buggy, Out 'N' About and Phil & Teds three-wheelers. Along with Tripp-Trapp high chairs, travel cots, muslins and various UV-protecting pushchair covers, there are fun

mouse, tiger and ladybird shaped Wheelybugs for whizzing round the house, and plenty of toys. Eco-friendly nappy brands include Bambo and Nature Babycare, and there's a sweet-smelling array of chemical-free babywipes. *Buggy access. Delivery service. Disabled access. Mail order. Nappy-changing facilities. Play area.*

The nursery

Aspace
140 Chiswick High Road, W4 1PU (8994 5814/www.aspaceuk.com). Turnham Green tube. **Open** 10am-6pm Mon-Sat; 11am-5pm Sun. **Credit** AmEx, MC, V.
The understated range at Aspace includes children's beds of every description, from white-painted four posters to solid oak bunks. Handsome wardrobes, sturdy chests of drawers, and tasteful soft furnishings – mattresses, quilts, throws, curtains and cushions – complete the collection.
Buggy access. Delivery service. Mail order (0845 872 2400).

Blue Almonds
79 Walton Street, SW3 2HP (7584 8038). South Kensington tube. **Open** 10am-6pm Mon-Fri; 10.30am-5pm Sat. **Credit** MC, V.
The wooden nursery furniture in this old-fashioned shop is prolifically painted with flowers and woodland creatures. Tartin et Chocolat blankets and cuddly toys are soft and sweet, while the cool African print range makes a refreshing change if you're tired of conventional pastel prints.
Buggy access. Delivery service. Mail order.

Chic Shack
77 Lower Richmond Road, SW15 1ET (8785 7777/www.chicshack.net). Putney Bridge tube, then 14, 22 bus. **Open** 9.30am-6pm Mon-Sat. **Credit** MC, V.
Inspired by 18th-century French and Swedish antiques, Chic Shack's largely white-painted furniture and soft furnishings are delightfully elegant. Pretty without being sickly-sweet, the range includes cots, chests, toy boxes, wardrobes and pastel-pink or blue floral- and stripe-upholstered chairs.
Buggy access. Delivery service. Mail order.

Dragons of Walton Street
23 Walton Street, SW3 2HX (7589 3795/ www.dragonsofwaltonstreet.com). Knightsbridge or South Kensington tube. **Open** 9.30am-5.30pm Mon-Fri; 10am-5pm Sat. **Credit** AmEx, MC, V. **Map** p313 E10.

This Walton Street landmark has spawned a host of imitations. Its wooden furniture is hand-painted with bunnies and boats, soldiers and fairies; alternatively, you can come up with your own design. Beatrix Potter and Paddington Bear lampshades and bedspreads are in abundance, and handsome traditional toys are also stocked. *Buggy access. Delivery service. Mail order.*

Natural Mat Company
99 Talbot Road, W11 2AT (7985 0474/ www.naturalmat.com). Ladbroke Grove tube. **Open** 9am-6pm Mon-Fri; 10am-4pm Sat. **Credit** MC, V. **Map** p310 A5.
Behind a window hung with prints of children's illustrations is a range of solid nursery furniture, with a choice of organic mattresses and bedding. Knowledgeable staff can help you decide between the different materials; organic coir, latex straight from a rubber tree and mohair for mattresses, along with goose down and lambswool-stuffed cot bed covers and duvets. There are also baby jumpers in soft lambswool, cashmere blankets and cotton Breton-striped babygros.
Buggy access. Delivery service. Mail order.

Nursery Window
83 Walton Street, SW3 2HP (7581 3358/ www.nurserywindow.co.uk). Knightsbridge or South Kensington tube. **Open** 10am-6pm Mon-Sat. **Credit** AmEx, MC, V. **Map** p313 E10.
This supremely traditional nursery shop stocks solid wooden cots and cribs, and all the blankets and quilts you could ever need to cover them. Prints are nostalgic and romantic, and despite the dry-clean only label, Sue Hill's cashmere knits are lovely. Waffle blankets with pink or blue satin trim (£24.95) are a fail-safe buy for any new arrival.
Buggy access. Delivery service. Mail order.

FASHION

Amaia
14 Cale Street, SW3 3QU (7590 0999/ www.amaia-kids.com). Sloane Square or South Kensington tube. **Open** 10am-6pm Mon-Sat. **Credit** MC, V. **Map** p313 E11.
There's an appealingly nostalgic feel to the baby clothes and childrenswear at Amaia, from the knitted all-in-ones and T-bar shoes to the ruffled cotton sundresses. Boys' clothes are equally classic, with cotton shorts, cords and linen shirts – no brash slogans or scratchy synthetics here. Prices are middling to expensive; expect to pay upwards of £50 for a little girl's day dress.
Buggy access. Mail order.

Small is beautiful at **Notsobig**.

Consumer

Aravore Babies
*31 Park Road, N8 8TE (8347 5752/
www.aravore-babies.com). Highgate tube/
Crouch Hill rail/41, 91, W5, W7 bus.* **Open**
10am-5.30pm Mon-Sat; noon-4.30pm Sun.
Credit AmEx, MC, V.
This luxury brand for babies and under-fives
has some covetable pieces, all made from fairly-
traded organic cotton and super-soft merino
wool. At its small shop, gorgeous hand-knitted
coats, dresses, bootees and dungarees nestle
alongside delicate shawls and cot blankets. It
also stocks other like-minded brands such as
Bamboo Baby, Lille Barn, Tatty Bumpkin and
the Erbaviva skincare range.
Buggy access. Mail order.

Biff
*41-43 Dulwich Village, SE21 7BN (8299
0911/www.biffkids.co.uk). North Dulwich rail/
P4 bus.* **Open** 9.30am-5.30pm Mon-Fri; 10am-
6pm Sat. **Credit** MC, V.
Occupying two shops, with a café next door, Biff
has become a hub for local mummies. At No.41
there's an enormous selection of shoes from the
likes of Lelli Kelly, Converse, Crocs, Geox and
Start-rite, and an equally broad range of clothing
brands for boys and girls aged all the way from
two to 16. Labels include Catamini, Pepe Jeans,
Powell & Craft, Bench, Roxy, Tartin et Chocolat,

Quiksilver and Noa Noa. Next door caters to
smaller fry, with baby gifts, Grobags, first shoes,
swimwear and clothes for two-and-unders.
*Buggy access. Disabled access. Mail order.
Play area.*

Bonpoint
*15 Sloane Street, SW1X 9NB (7235 1441/
www.bonpoint.com). Knightsbridge tube.*
Open 10am-6pm Mon-Sat. **Credit** AmEx,
MC, V. **Map** p313 F9.
Describing itself as a 'French childrenswear
couture house', Bonpoint brings Gallic panache
and exquisite workmanship to the world
of children's fashion. Charming bloomers,
sundresses, linen shorts and jumpers are hard
to resist, though the hefty price tags may make
you think twice; the fragrant, well-heeled
regulars don't bat an eyelid, *naturellement.*
Buggy access. Mail order.
Branches 256 Brompton Road, SW3 2AS
(3263 5057); 197 Westbourne Grove,
W11 2SE (7792 2515); 17 Victoria Grove,
W8 5RW (7584 5131).

Burberry Children
*199 Westbourne Grove, W11 2SB (7221
3688/www.burberry.com). Notting Hill Gate
tube.* **Open** 10am-6pm Mon-Sat; noon-6pm
Sun. **Credit** AmEx, MC, V.
This airy, glamorous new flagship store on
Westbourne Grove houses clothes with the same
unusual twists on British classics offered by
the adult Burberry line, only in miniature. The
range goes from three months to 12 years,
with a separate special occasion collection
which features girls' skirts with gold-mesh
petticoats and smart blazers for boys. With their
immaculate detailing and signature checked
lining, the macs are hardest on parental credit
cards, costing around £260 depending on age.
T-shirts, bags and shoes are less expensive, but
you'll struggle to find much for under £30.
*Buggy access. Mail order. Nappy-changing
facilities. Play area.*

Caramel Baby & Child
*77 Ledbury Road, W11 2AG (7727 0906/
www.caramel-shop.co.uk). Notting Hill Gate or
Westbourne Park tube.* **Open** 10am-6pm Mon-
Sat; noon-5pm Sun. **Credit** AmEx, MC, V.
Map p310 A6.
Caramel's clothing range (0-12s), designed by
Eva Karayiannis, is wonderfully idiosyncratic
and effortlessly chic. Ribbon-strap floral
sundresses, crisp smocks and beautifully-cut
woollen coats have serious fashion appeal. As
you'd expect, it's not cheap; check washing
instructions, too, as some pieces are made from

silk and cashmere. A small selection of vintage-inspired toys are displayed downstairs, and there's a hair salon (book ahead).
Buggy access. Hairdressing. Mail order.
Branches 259 Pavillion Road, SW1X 0BP (7730 2564); 291 Brompton Road, SW3 2DY (7589 7001).

Frère Jacques
121 Stoke Newington Church Street, N16 0UH (7249 5655). Finsbury Park tube/rail, then 106 bus/73, 393, 476 bus. **Open** 11am-6pm Tue-Sat; noon-6pm Sun. **Credit** AmEx, MC, V.
Giving equal weight to boys' and girls' clothes (zero to eights), this place is a great little all-rounder. The emphasis is on stylish and durable design, with shelves of classic clothes from the likes of Petit Bateau and Danish label Minymo. Colourful animal-themed mackintoshes and brightly patterned wellies from Kidorable are big sellers, along with quality shoes from Pedi Ped, Robeez and Superfit.
Buggy access.

Guys & Dolls
172 Walton Street, SW3 2JL (7589 8990/ www.guysanddollsuk.com). Knightsbridge or South Kensington tube. **Open** 10am-6pm Mon-Sat. **Credit** AmEx, MC, V.
This impossibly cool shop displays its wares on a smooth, curving rail and brightly coloured plastic pods. Each item on display is unique, with pieces arranged according to age (up to 12 years). There are designer and street labels, including the likes of Sonia Rykiel and Little Marc – Mr Jacobs' covetable children's line; shoes are by Simonetta. Kids can lounge on beanbags as their elders make use of their credit cards.
Buggy access. Nappy-changing facilities. Play area (garden).

Jakss
469 Roman Road, E3 5LX (8981 2233/ www.jakss.co.uk). Bethnal Green tube, then 8 bus. **Open** 10am-5.30pm Tue-Sat. **Credit** AmEx, MC, V.
Founded in 1977, Jakss is a treasure trove of children's designer togs, ranging from all-in-ones for newborns to cutting-edge looks for 16-year-olds. The list of labels is endless: Ralph Lauren, Armani, Jottum, Burberry, DKNY, CP Company, Oilily and Stone Island fill the rails, along with children's and adult's Birkenstocks.
Buggy access. Mail order.

Jolie à Pied
82 Lordship Lane, SE22 8HF (8693 4509). East Dulwich rail. **Open** 10am-6pm Mon-Sat. **Credit** MC, V.

Rebranded last year, this chic boutique is still relatively new to East Dulwich, and stocks a selection of baby and kids shoes definitely not designed for splashing about in puddles. There are soft leather pumps from Tip Toey Joey, perfect for growing baby feet, and pretty, sparkling creations from Maá.
Buggy access.

Notsobig
31A Highgate High Street, N6 5JT (8340 4455). Archway or Highgate tube. **Open** 10am-6pm Mon-Sat; 11am-5pm Sun. **Credit** MC, V.
An eclectic blend of labels and designers make Notsobig's shelves a pleasure to peruse. Swishy party dresses from I Love Gorgeous and Cacherel rub shoulders with cool casuals from American Outfitters and hip Parisian label Eva & Oli; look out, too, for Little Linens' light, airy shirts and trousers. Dressing-up clothes from Bandicoot Lapin, tulle-skirted tutus sourced from Los Angeles, hand-made jewellery and a sterling selection of shoes round off the stock: Elephantito's silver Mary Janes are a hot seller.
Buggy access. Delivery service. Mail order.

Olive Loves Alfie
84 Stoke Newington Church Street, N16 0AP (7241 4212/www.olivelovesalfie.co.uk). Finsbury Park tube/rail then 106 bus/73, 393, 476 bus. **Open** 9am-5.30pm Mon-Fri; 10am-6pm Sat; noon-5pm Sun. **Credit** AmEx, MC, V.
This design-led boutique stocks an inspired mix of clothing for children of all ages. Gorgeous and reasonably priced, its collection is full of nautical stripes, bright paisley patterns and bold, graphic prints. Pieces by hugely popular Scandinavian designer Katvig fly out of the shop, as does Danish label Ziestha's limited edition range. Artfully arranged gifts and toys include painted wooden animals, hand-knitted cuddly toys and a washing line strung with hats; mothers-to-be will love the comfy cotton kimonos and organic bath products.
Buggy access. Mail order.

Petit Aimé
34 Ledbury Road, W11 2AB (7221 3123/ www.aimelondon.com). Notting Hill Gate tube. **Open** 10am-6.30pm Mon-Sat. **Credit** AmEx, MC, V. **Map** p310 A6.
An offshoot of the acclaimed womenswear boutique next door, owned by French-Cambodian sisters Val and Vanda Heng-Vong, this white-painted boutique dresses newborns to 12-year-olds with the crème de la crème of Gallic labels: Isabel Marant, BonTon, Aymara and Antik Batik among them. Kitsch blankets,

cushions and brightly coloured bedspreads from Petit Pan are a great way to liven up a nursery, and the hand-knitted rabbits will enchant younger children.
Buggy access. Mail order.

Quackers
155D Northcote Road, SW11 6QB (7978 4235). Clapham Junction rail, then 319 bus. **Open** 9.30am-5.30pm Mon-Fri; 10am-5.30pm Sat. **Credit** MC, V.

Bags of potential
Stoke Newington

Despite significant gentrification over the past decade or so, 'Stokey' still clings to its bohemian identity. Second-hand books and products with green credentials are easy to find round here; on Saturdays, there's a very good farmers' market in the grounds of William Patten Primary School.

In an area that's famed for its high concentration of young families, shopping for children couldn't be easier. Most of the action is centred around the pleasant, café-dotted stretch of Church Street, making for a restful afternoon's lunching and browsing.

Toy shop **Route 73 Kids** (*see p283*) is a little less chichi now that Woolies on the High Street has closed, and has a great range of toys and games for under-tens. A few doors away, the immaculate window display of boutique **Olive Loves Alfie** (*see p269*) is a showcase for the hottest childrenswear designers. **Frère Jacques** (*see p269*) offers distinctive and reasonably priced children's clothes and shoes, and also dispenses haircuts. One of the best children's shops in London is all-rounder **Born** (*see p253*), well-stocked with clothes, prams, accessories, green nappies and more. Church Street is also home to a friendly branch of bike shop **Two Wheels Good** (*see p266*), although savvy parents will make for **D2 Leisure** (*see p265*) on the High Street for cheaper prices.

Down the road on Newington Green, **Three Potato Four** (*see p272*) – selling children's clothes, toys, books and offering haircuts – has recently opened next to kids' café **That Place on the Corner** (*see p234*).

Kids can root through the box of toys while their parents browse the rails. There's a healthy crop of Danish designers to choose from: Minymo, Molo Kids, Phister & Philina and Louie Louis among them. Modish little cotton dresses and tiered skirts by Hilly Chrisp are superb summer buys, and there are playfully printed Hatley raincoats for autumn showers. Toys include floppy favourites by Moulin Roty and attractive wooden pull-alongs and trikes.
Buggy access.

Rachel Riley
82 Marylebone High Street, W1U 4QW (7935 8345/www.rachelriley.com). Baker Street or Bond Street tube. **Open** 10am-6.30pm Mon-Sat; 10am-5.30pm Sun. **Credit** AmEx, MC, V. **Map** p314 G5.
There's a wonderfully wholesome, 1950s feel to Rachel Riley's designs, handmade in her atelier in the Loire Valley. Cherry-print poplin frocks, beruffled bloomers and pleated pinafores are traditional without being stuffy; for the chaps, there are anchor- and aeroplane-print shirts and smart striped pyjamas. The ruched, rose-print swimsuit (£49) is a classic.
Buggy access. Delivery service. Mail order.
Branch 14 Pont Street, SW1X 9EN (7259 5969).

Ralph Lauren Children's Store
143 New Bond Street, W1S 2TP (7535 4600/www.polo.com). Bond Street tube. **Open** 10am-6pm Mon-Wed, Fri, Sat; 10am-7pm Thur; noon-5pm Sun. **Credit** AmEx, MC, V. **Map** p314 H6.
Ralph Lauren's beautifully made but eye-wateringly expensive outfits are displayed in suitably stately surrounds (mahogany panelling, sepia prints and strategically arranged rocking horses). There's more to the brand than polo shirts: the baby dresses and cashmere cable-knit cardigans, in particular, are gorgeously pretty.
Buggy access. Delivery service. Mail order.
Branch 139-141 Fulham Road, SW3 6FD (7761 0310).

Roco
6 Church Road, SW19 5DL (8946 5288). Wimbledon tube/rail. **Open** 10am-6pm Mon-Sat; noon-5pm Sun. **Credit** MC, V.
A stylish boutique for newborns to ten-year-olds, this double-fronted store is bursting with bright and colourful clothes. The lower area of the split-level premises is devoted to sales bargains, while the main space houses new stock from a clutch of international brands: Marie Chantal, Charabia, Pepe Jeans, Tutto Piccolo and DKNY, to name just a few.

Consumer

Three Potato Four. *See p272.*

Buggy access. Play area (garden).
Branch Coco, 27A Devonshire Street,
W1G 6PN (7935 3554).

Sasti

*8 Portobello Green Arcade, 281 Portobello
Road, W10 5TZ (8960 1125/www.sasti.co.uk).
Ladbroke Grove tube.* **Open** 10am-6pm Mon-
Sat. **Credit** AmEx, MC, V.
Bold designs and colours ensure Sasti's clothes
stand out from the crowd, whether you're
investing in a pair of cowboy-meets-Indian
jeans with tan fringing down the side or a
leopard-print all-in-one. Everything is made
in the UK, and prices are competitive, starting
at around £12 for fleeces and long-sleeved
T-shirts. The collection of kitsch accessories
also make great presents for cool kids.
*Buggy access. Delivery service. Mail order.
Nappy-changing facilities. Play area.*

Selfridges

*400 Oxford Street, W1A 1AB (0800 123400/
www.selfridges.com). Bond Street tube.* **Open**
9.30am-8pm Mon-Wed, Fri, Sat; 9.30am-9pm
Thur; noon-6pm Sun. **Credit** AmEx, DC, MC,
V. **Map** p314 G6.
The sprawling third floor is chock-full of well
known children's brands to browse through –
predominantly clothes, although there are a few
toy ranges (including Hello Kitty and VTech).
All the major designers are represented,
including Armani, Dior, D&G, Chloé, Little Marc
and Tommy Hilfiger. Sonia Rykiel's range for
girls features bright pink dresses with attached
fabric flowers; for boys, John Galliano's jeans,

khaki jackets and print T-shirts have lots of
attitude. Slightly cheaper, and a favourite with
fashionista parents, French brand Finger in the
Nose's range includes rock 'n' roll essentials
such as bootcut jeans and acid wash T-shirts.
There's also a large shoe department, featuring
Step2wo, and fancy dress costumes. Although
there is no specific play space, there's plenty of
room for children to run around; look out, too,
for seasonal events such as Easter egg hunts.
*Buggy access. Cafés. Delivery service. Disabled
access: lift, toilet. Mail order. Nappy-changing
facilities.*

Their Nibs

*214 Kensington Park Road, W11 1NR (7221
4263/www.theirnibs.com). Ladbroke Grove or
Notting Hill Gate tube.* **Open** 10am-6pm Mon-
Sat; noon-5pm Sun. **Credit** AmEx, MC, V.
Their Nibs is known for its whimsical,
distinctive clothes, featuring 1950s-esque prints
and unusual colours. Signature prints include a
toadstool fairy pattern for girls' blouses and
dresses, and a pirate design for boys' shirts.
More elaborate party frocks cost up to £55,
but there's plenty that's a good deal cheaper;
the raincoats go for £20. The vintage emporium
at the back includes dollhouses, clothes and
prams, and there's a small range of Stokke
cribs and high chairs. Kids can play with the
blackboard, mini-kitchen and books or have a
haircut while you browse.
*Buggy access. Hairdressing. Mail order.
Play area.*
Branch 79 Chamberlayne Road, NW10 3ND
(8964 8444).

Consumer

Three Potato Four

Alliance House, Newington Green, N16 9QH (7704 2228). Canonbury rail/73 bus. **Open** 10am-5.30pm Mon-Fri; 9.30am-6pm Sat; 11am-5pm Sun. **Credit** MC, V.

Overlooking Newington Green, this recently opened boutique is already enticing customers inside with its nautically-themed window display. The compact collection of clothing includes vibrant coloured pieces by Dutch designer Kik Kid, and there are gifts galore: books, old-fashioned toys and Science Museum games. A fairly reasonably priced children's hair salon occupies a corner of the shop, and there are a couple of train tracks to keep the little ones occupied while you shop.

Buggy access. Disabled access. Hairdressing. Nappy-changing facilities. Play area.

Trotters

34 King's Road, SW3 4UD (7259 9620/ www.trotters.co.uk). Sloane Square tube. **Open** 9am-7pm Mon-Sat; 10.30am-6.30pm Sun. **Credit** AmEx, MC, V. **Map** p313 F11.

With clothes, toys, accessories, toiletries, shoes and books, Trotters is a one-stop shop for beleagured parents. Exclusive designs from the Chelsea Clothing Company include Liberty-print dresses and nicely-cut smocks, while boys look shipshape in Petit Breton's stripy tops and cotton shorts. There's a hairdressing station with a big fish tank to distract the littl'uns during their fringe trim; first-timers get a certificate and a lock of hair for fond parents to treasure. Stocked with Converse, Pom d'Api and Start-rites, the shoe section also gives out 'first shoe' certificates. Other useful bits and bobs include organic sunscreens, insulated lunchboxes and Nitty Gritty headlice treatments.

Buggy access. Delivery service. Hairdressing. Mail order. Nappy-changing facilities.

Branches 127 Kensington High Street, W8 5SF (7937 9373); 86 Northcote Road, SW11 6QN (7585 0572); 84 Turnham Green Terrace, W4 1QN (8742 1195).

Others

Catimini

52 South Molton Street, W1Y 1HF (7629 8099/www.catimini.com). Bond Street tube. **Open** 10am-6.30pm Mon-Wed, Fri, Sat; 10am-7pm Thur; 11am-5pm Sun. **Credit** AmEx, MC, V. **Map** p314 H6.

Startlingly bright colours and vibrant patterns are Catimini's signature style, with crocheted cardigans, patchwork cotton separates, sweet baggy shorts and striped T-shirts.

Buggy access. Disabled access. Mail order. Play area.

Branch 33C King's Road, SW3 4LX (7824 8897).

Felix & Lilys

3 Camden Passage, N1 8EA (7424 5423/ www.felixandlilys.com). Angel tube. **Open** 10am-6pm Mon-Sat; 11am-5pm Sun. **Credit** AmEx, MC, V.

This tucked-away boutique sells colourful designer togs for babies and children, including some chic Scandinavian brands (Ej Sikke Lej, IdaT and Katvig), plus old favourites like Bob & Blossom and Toby Tiger. Look out, too, for the quirky Ella & Otto sleeping bags. Toys include wooden food and pull-along pals, along with robust trainer bikes.

Buggy access. Mail order.

Frogs & Fairies

69A Highbury Park, N5 1UA (7424 5159). Highbury & Islington tube/rail. **Open** 10am-5.30pm Mon-Sat; 10am-4pm Sun. **Credit** AmEx, MC, V.

This friendly shop is an excellent place for shoe-shopping, with footwear from Start-rite, Converse, Lelli Kelly, Geox and Crocs. More of interest to children are the toys: goodies by Playmobil, Lego and Galt, plus the ubiquitous micro-scooters. There's also a modest range of clothes for zero to fives, with lines from Petit Bateau and Katvig. An ever-changing selection of cards, gift wrap, party bag-fillers and pocket money toys rounds things off nicely.

Buggy access.

I Love Gorgeous

52 Ledbury Road, W11 2AJ (7229 5855/ www.ilovegorgeous.co.uk). Notting Hill Gate or Westbourne Park tube. **Open** 10am-6pm Mon-Sat. **Credit** MC, V.

Stocking girls' clothes from newborn to 15 years, the rails of this small boutique are full of wonderfully tactile fabrics such as romantic georgette and soft cotton voile. Some of the designs are quite funky, like the hot pink star prints and lurex cardigans; others are much more innocent, with broderie anglaise trims and muted colours. There's a pretty collection of bridesmaid dresses downstairs, with shades to match most nuptial colour schemes.

Buggy access. Mail order.

Jakes

79 Berwick Street, W1F 8TL (7734 0812/ www.jakesofsoho.co.uk). Oxford Circus tube. **Open** 11am-7pm Mon-Sat. **Credit** AmEx, MC, V. **Map** p314 J6.

Gallic chic for kids at **Catimini**.

Jake is a boy with cerebral palsy, and a percentage of the profits from this shop go towards his future. Kidswear consists of distinctive 'Lucky 7' slogan T-shirts (£12.50), and sweatshirts.
Buggy access. Mail order.

Litkey Kids
2A Devonshire Road, W4 2HD (8994 4112). Turnham Green tube. **Open** 10am-5.30pm Mon-Fri; 10am-6pm Sat; 11am-4pm Sun. **Credit** MC, V.
A boutique stocking clothes for newborn to 13s, with traditional designs from Hungarian company Litkey and Spanish label Mayoral.
Buggy access.

Marie Chantal
148 Walton Street, SW3 2JJ (7838 1111/ www.mariechantal.com). Knightsbridge or South Kensington tube. **Open** 10am-6pm Mon-Sat. **Credit** AmEx, MC, V.
Immaculate detailing, smart cuts and expensive fabrics, as you'd expect from a range designed by the eponymous Crown Princess of Greece. The collection includes some very high-fashion items such as jumpsuits, though there's plenty to suit more staid tastes; tweed jackets and braces for the boys, for example.
Buggy access. Mail order.
Branches 61A Ledbury Road, W11 2AA (7243 0220); 133A Sloane Street, SW1X 9AX (7730 8662).

Membery's
1 Church Road, SW13 9HE (8876 2910/ www.memberys.com). Barnes Bridge rail. **Open** 10am-5pm Mon-Sat. **Credit** AmEx, MC, V.
Membery's stocks a good, solid range of baby gifts and quality clothing for small boys and girls up to six years old. The range includes everything from nightwear to special-occasion outfits; it's also particularly good for children's wedding wear.
Buggy access. Delivery service. Play area.

Oranges & Lemons/ Pretty Pregnant
61 Northcross Road, SE22 9ET (8693 9010/ www.prettypregnant.co.uk). East Dulwich rail. **Open** 9.30am-5.30pm Mon-Sat; 11am-5pm Sun. **Credit** MC, V.
This sister branch to the Pretty Pregnant maternity brand (a new store recently opened on the King's Road) stocks tiny outfits by Petit Bateau and funky Dutch designer Kik Kid, along with animal-motif appliqué T-shirts by Lipfish and some sweet toys. Reggie the Big Eyed Dummy (£16) makes a change from the usual fluffy rabbits.
Buggy access. Mail order.
Branches 102 Northcote Road, SW11 6QW (7924 4850); 13-15 Chiltern Street, W1U 7PG (7486 2531); 186 King's Road, SW3 5XP (7349 7450).

Consumer

Tots Boutique

*39 Turnham Green Terrace, W4 1RG
(8995 0520). Turnham Green tube.* **Open**
10am-6pm Mon-Sat; noon-5pm Sun. **Credit**
AmEx, MC, V.
Across the road from Snap Dragon (*see p283*),
Tots crams in a broad range of designer gear
for babies and children. The frequently
changing cache might include the likes of
Mini A Ture, Lili Gaufrette, Ralph Lauren
and Catimini, with casualwear courtesy of
Quiksilver and Roxy. A drawing table and
various toys keep the kids sweet as you shop.
Buggy access. Mail order. Play area.

Chain stores

Adams

www.adams.co.uk
A good bet for inexpensive playwear, babywear
and school uniforms.

Fat Face

www.fatface.com
Sporty, surf-inspired casualwear including a
small range of tops, bottoms, dresses and shirts
in muted colours for girls and boys.

Gap Kids

www.gap.com
The pastel-hued babywear makes a safe gift for
new parents, while the childrenswear is
hardwearing and popular with all ages.

H&M

www.hm.com
Cheap-as-chips and up-to-the-minute designs for
babies, children and grown-ups.

Jigsaw Junior

www.jigsaw-online.com
The branch at 190-192 Westbourne Grove, W11
2RH (7727 0322) has a silver slide instead of
stairs to the basement.

Monsoon

www.monsoon.co.uk
Collections for boys and girls, ranging from
simple puff-sleeved T-shirts and turn-up jeans
to lavish, sequin-sprinkled party frocks.

Petit Bateau

www.petit-bateau.com
Classic French cotton baby clothes, in floral,
plain and trademark milleraies striped designs.

Purls of wisdom

Crafts of all kinds boomed along with
the economy a few years back as jaded
materialists sought out the retro pleasures
of artisanal chic; now they're booming
again thanks to a new enthusiasm for
anything bracingly low-cost. Trends may
come and go, but the city's knitters click
away regardless – among them Central
St Martins-trained textile artists Rachael
Matthews and Louise Harries.

The pair's Bethnal Green shop, **Prick
Your Finger** (260 Globe Road, EC2 0JD,
8981 2560, www.prickyourfinger.com), is
a haven of woolly delights, adorned with
their off-the-wall creations – including a
crocheted toilet and handbasin – and,
of course, lots of beautiful materials.

At weekends, they teach yarn crafts to
both adults and children, and (crucially)
they do it with infinite patience and
cheerfulness. There's nothing like getting
to grips with a fiddly new activity to make
even the most poised individual feel
cack-handed, but with Louise and Rachael
declaring all our efforts brilliant, our
confidence grew along with our ability.

Having harboured a mysterious yet
fervent desire to learn knitting for some
time, our nine-year-old tester, Ivy, set
to work with the kind of determination
and concentration we can only dream
of during maths homework sessions.
Soon we were knitting and purling,
casting on and off, increasing and
decreasing – and discovering that you
knit your personality into your work along
with the yarn. Ivy's vigorous creativity
has never expressed itself on a miniature
scale, and she was soon flinging out row
after row of loose, freeform work; by
contrast, my neater efforts seemed
a little uptight.

But how wonderful, above all, to find
something you and your child can learn
together, on an equal footing. Buoyed
up by the praise lavished on our humble
successes, we left with our own needles,
yarn, and bags of pride and enthusiasm
for our newfound skill. And we're both
still knitting.

*Classes cost £30 for adults, £15 for
children; see the website for details.*

Consumer

Zara

www.zara.com
The Spanish high street giant offers unusual childrenswear and some bright and beautiful dresses for girls.

Maternity

Blossom Mother & Child

*164 Walton Street, SW3 2JL (7589 7500/
www.blossommotherandchild.com). South
Kensington tube.* **Open** 10am-6pm Mon-Sat;
noon-5pm Sun. **Credit** AmEx, MC, V.
Map p313 E10.
Only the most stylish maternity labels make it on to the hallowed shelves at this über-chic boutique. The own-label range offers flattering, perfectly-cut dresses, separates and lingerie, hanging alongside pieces by the likes of Missoni, Antik Batik and Clements Ribeiro; the denim bar offers bump-accommodating jeans from the hottest brands (True Religion, Citizens of Humanity, J Brand). Amazing bargains can sometimes be found in the website's sale section.
Buggy access. Mail order.
Branches 69 Marylebone High Street, W1U
5JJ (7486 6089); 31 Wimbledon High Street,
SW19 5BY (8947 7106).

Elias & Grace

*158 Regent's Park Road, NW1 8XN (7449
0574/www.eliasandgrace.com). Chalk Farm
tube.* **Open** 10am-6pm Mon-Sat; noon-6pm
Sun. **Credit** MC, V.
Perfectly at home amid Primrose Hill's many chichi boutiques, Elias & Grace stocks a stylish combination of high fashion, luxury accessories and gifts. As well as hip labels for mothers-to-be (See by Chloé, Vivienne Westwood, J Brand), there's an international array of brands for babies and under-tens, among them Maan, Bonton, I Love Gorgeous and Quincy. Toys and accessories include bags and dolls from Madame Mo and quirky Sparrowkids craft sets. A relaxed atmosphere, with plenty of room for pushchairs, a mini play area and friendly assistants make for hassle-free browsing.
*Buggy access. Mail order (7483 4334).
Play area.*

Séraphine

*58-62 Heath Street, NW3 1EN (7937 3156/
www.seraphine.com). Hampstead tube.* **Open**
10.30am-6pm Mon-Wed, Fri; 10.30am-7pm
Thur; 10am-6.30pm Sat; noon-5pm Sun.
Credit MC, V.

This Hampstead boutique looks expensive but stocks surprisingly reasonably priced pregnancy wear from French designer Cécile Reinaud. The emphasis is on co-ordinated smart casual items for yummy mummies, in block colours. A small range of newborn baby clothes and nice Boo Boo smellies for baby and Mama Mio products for mothers mean it's good for presents too. Upstairs is a nursery furniture showroom with decorative white cots, wardrobes and chests of drawers.
Buggy access. Mail order (0870 609 2602).
Branch 28 Kensington Church Street,
W8 4EP (7937 3156).

HAIRDRESSING

Several shops listed elsewhere in this chapter incorporate a children's salon, with haircuts available on certain days of the week. See **Harrods** (*see p253*), **Caramel** (*see p268*), **Mini Kin** (*see p257*), **Trotters** (*see p272*); **Their Nibs** (*see p271*) and **Igloo** (*see p255*). For the ultimate in children's barnet styling, however, have a **Tantrum** (*see below*).

Tantrum

*398 King's Road, SW10 0LJ (7376 3966/
www.yourtantrum.com). Sloane Square tube,
then 11, 19, 22, 319 bus.* **Open** 10am-6pm
Tue-Fri; 9am-6pm Sat; 10.30am-4.30pm Sun.
Credit AmEx, MC, V.
Billing itself as 'a revolutionary new concept in children's hairdressing', Tantrum spoils its young clients rotten with all sorts of bells and whistles. Aimed at an eight- to 14-year-old clientele, the basement area features a juice bar and games room, while the ground floor keeps the under-sevens amused with its buzzing locomotives and starry skies, as well as a general play area. In both areas, each styling chair is equipped with a flat screen TV and DVDs. The premises can also host children's parties; call for details.
Buggy access. Play area.

SAMPLE SALES

Junior Style

7689 3925/www.juniorstylesales.co.uk
Sharp-eyed shoppers are rewarded by discounts of up to 75% off designer labels at these regular sample sales. Sizes run from newborn to 12, while the featured designers might include the likes of Replay, Cavalli, Evisu, Kenzo, Simonetta, Imps & Elfs and Ralph Lauren.

Consumer

SECOND-HAND

Merry-Go-Round
12 Clarence Road, E5 8HB (8985 6308).
Hackney Central rail. **Open** 10am-5pm Mon-
Sat; 11am-5pm Sun. **Credit** MC, V.
This environmentally friendly agency trades on
behalf of its clients in second-hand clothing,
toys and baby equipment. Expect to find lots of
high chairs, pushchairs, clothes, books and
more, allowing budget- and eco-conscious
families to be entirely kitted out with recycled
goods. Go prepared for some serious browsing
and buying; visitors generally leave with
armfuls of purchases. All stock is clean and
carefully checked; no missing puzzle pieces or
bobbly jumpers here.
Buggy access. Nappy-changing facilities.
Play area.

Merry Go Round
21 Half Moon Lane, SE24 9JU (7737 6452).
Herne Hill rail. **Open** 9.15am-5pm Mon-Sat.
Credit MC, V
No relation to its Hackney namesake (above),
this place is a fertile hunting-ground for second-
hand children's clothes and school uniforms,
along with maternity fashion and brand new
stock from top-notch names such as Catimini,
Molo and Grobags.
Buggy access.

SHOES

Brian's Shoes
2 Halleswelle Parade, Finchley Road, NW11
0DL (8455 7001/www.briansshoes.com).
Finchley Central or Golders Green tube.
Open 9.15am-5.15pm Mon-Sat; 10.30am-
1.30pm Sun. **Credit** MC, V.
Founded in 1970, Brian's has kitted out
generations of kids and is known for its expert
fittings. D&G and Ricosta are stocked alongside
more sober Start-rite and Hush Puppies.
Buggy access.

Cubs
42 Heath Street, NW3 6TE (7431 0018).
Hampstead tube. **Open** 10am-6pm Mon-Sat;
noon-6pm Sun. **Credit** AmEx, MC, V.
This compact shoe shop, just opposite the
Everyman cinema, has an impressive range
of shoes for babies and children. Staff are
friendly and patient, calmly measuring feet and
fetching numerous pairs out of the storeroom
until they are satisfied with the fit. Brands
include Start-rite, Ricosta, Babybotte, Geox and

Ralph Lauren, and there are plenty of wellies
too. Children are enticed into being good with
the promise of a free balloon.
Buggy access.

John Barnett
137-139 Lordship Lane, SE22 8HX (8693
5145). East Dulwich rail. **Open** 9.30am-5.30pm
Mon-Sat; 11am-5pm Sun. **Credit** MC, V.
This long-established Dulwich shoe shop has
a great section for children. Brands include
Clark's, Ecco, Skechers, Dr Martins and Kickers.
Buggy access. Disabled access.

Little Me
141 Hamilton Road, NW11 9EG (8209
0440). Brent Cross tube. **Open** 10.30am-
6.15pm Mon-Thur; Fri phone to check;
11am-4pm Sun. **Credit** MC, V.
A wide range of continental children's shoes,
fitted with a precision shoe-measuring system.
Buggy access.

Merlin Shoes
44 Westow Street, SE19 3AH (8771 5194/
www.merlinshoes.com). Crystal Palace rail.
Open 9.30am-6pm Mon-Sat. **Credit** MC, V.
Experienced, patient shoe fitters and a wide
range of footwear make this place a firm
favourite with families.
Buggy access. Disabled access.

One Small Step One Giant Leap
3 Blenheim Crescent, W11 2EE (7243 0535/
www.onesmallsteponegiantleap.com). Ladbroke
Grove or Notting Hill Gate tube. **Open** 10am-
6pm Mon-Fri; 9am-6pm Sat; 11am-5pm Sun.
Credit MC, V.
Live near an outpost of this award-winning
children's shoe shop and you'll never have to
choose between comfort and style. Summer
sandals, gumboots, Crocs, football boots, trainers
and school sensibles are all present and correct.
The Bannock gauge is used for measuring, and
staff take time to ensure a proper fit. A
thoughtfully assembled range of labels runs the
gamut from practical (Start-rite, Ecco, Ricosta)
to playful (Lelli Kelly, Pom d'Api).
Buggy access. Mail order.
Branches throughout town.

Papillon
43 Elizabeth Street, SW1W 9PP (7730 6690/
www.papillon4children.com). Sloane Square
tube/Victoria tube/rail. **Open** 10am-6pm
Mon-Fri; 10am-5pm Sat. **Credit** MC, V.
Ballet-style pumps in a rainbow of colours and
prints feature largely here, but there are also
school shoes and beach sandals for boys and

girls, flip flops, moccasins and bridesmaids shoes. Hunter gumboots, socks and tights are also sold, along with tiny, ribbon-tie baby shoes. *Buggy access. Mail order.*

Red Shoes

30 Topsfield Parade, N8 8QB (8341 9555). Finsbury Park tube/rail, then 41, W7 bus. **Open** 10am-5.30pm Mon-Sat; noon-4.30pm Sun. **Credit** MC, V.
Fit and comfort are the key words at this child-friendly shoe shop, where children can match their parents with fashionable big brands such as Crocs, Birkenstock, Ecco and Camper. *Buggy access.*

Shoe Station

3 Station Approach, Kew, Surrey TW9 3QB (8940 9905/www.theshoestation.co.uk). Kew Gardens tube. **Open** 9am-6pm Mon-Sat. **Credit** MC, V.
Run by two mothers, the Station is a cheery little independent, staffed by trained Start-rite fitters. Children's shoes for every occasion are available, from child's size 2 to adult size 7. Brands include Start-rite (of course), Ricosta, Aster, Naturino, Babybotte, TTY, Giesswein, Mod8, Pom d'Api, Geox, Nike, Puma, Birkenstock, Primigi, Freed and Daisy Roots. Football boots, ballet shoes, slippers and wellies are also stocked. *Buggy access.*

Stepping Out

106 Pitshanger Lane, W5 1QX (8810 6141/ www.steppingoutshoes.co.uk). Ealing Broadway tube, then E2, E9 bus. **Open** 10am-5.30pm Mon-Fri; 9.30am-5.30pm Sat. **Credit** MC, V.
The experienced fitters are Start-rite trained, and specialise in advice on shoes for children with mobility problems. Shoes by Naturino, Start-rite, Geox, Umi and Ricosta line the shelves, along with wellies, plimsolls, slippers, trainers and baby shoes; there's also a quirky selection of toys and pressies at the back. *Buggy access. Play area.*

Vincent Shoe Store

19 Camden Passage, N1 8EA (7226 3141/ www.vincentsshoestore.com). Angel tube. **Open** 11am-6pm Tue, Thur, Fri; 10am-6pm Wed, Sat; noon-4pm Sun. **Credit** MC, V.
Launched in 1999, this Swedish company prides itself on its affordable, colourful kids' footwear. The range includes appealing gumboots (check out the flamingo print beauties), leather daisy-dotted baby shoes and patent Mary Janes. *Buggy access. Mail order.*
Branch Westfield Shopping Centre, W12 7SL (8743 9730).

Pick and mix

Covent Garden's famous **Bead Shop** (21A Tower Street, WC2H 9NS, 7240 0931, www.beadshop.co.uk) provides children with hours of creative fun. The shop has two floors, with trays upon trays of multicoloured beads lying in wait for kids to get their mitts on. Pick up a little plastic container and sift your way through the collection of more than 5,000 different beads. Choose from chunky wooden spheres, shiny bugle beads and glowing glass baubles; for the indecisive, there's a mixed bag or the kids' pre-made kit. Prices start at 2p a bead, though for those with more pocket money than sense there are Swarovski crystals, semi-precious or sterling silver beads. It's surprising how much you could spend.

Staff are happy to help out, and there are free instruction sheets on how to create your own beaded beauties. If you can't make it in to central London, you can order on the website and get the kids making things as soon as they arrive. The site is easy to use; among the vast array of treasures to choose from, there's also tips and techniques, colour tools, care and repair info and a how-to-library. It won't just be the kids that'll be keen to start creating.

SPORT

Ace Sports & Leisure

341 Kentish Town Road, NW5 2TJ (7485 5367). Kentish Town tube. **Open** 9.30am-6pm Mon-Sat. **Credit** AmEx, MC, V.

Set just opposite Kentish Town tube station, Ace has footwear for all sports, as well as junior rackets, bats and swimming equipment. Brands include Puma, Adidas, Reebok and Nike. There are also small baseball mitts and footballs in all sizes, first cricket bats and balls, ping-pong balls and bats in all colours, tracksuits, swim nappies, goggles, earplugs and nose clips – everything, in fact, to get kids active.
Buggy access. Disabled access.

David J Thomas

8 Croxted Road, SE21 8SW (8766 7400). West Dulwich rail. **Open** 9.15am-5.15pm Mon-Sat. **Credit** MC, V.

A school uniform and sports kit specialist with a great line in cheap equipment in junior sizes.
Buggy access.

Decathlon

Canada Water Retail Park, Surrey Quays Road, SE16 2XU (7394 2000/www.decathlon. co.uk). Canada Water tube. **Open** 10am-9pm Mon-Fri; 9am-7pm Sat; 11am-5pm Sun. **Credit** MC, V.

The French sporting giant's London outpost occupies two enormous hangars by Surrey Quays, crammed with a huge range of gear. There are hard hats, jodhs, crops and grooming kits for riders, snow-proof gear in all sizes for skiers, bikes, fishing rods, no-nonsense walking boots, trainers of every description, footballs, golf equipment and more. Decathlon has 12 own brands, including the affordable and hard wearing Quechua (for hiking, mountaineering and snowboarding). You'll also find Nike, Reebok and Adidas. The young, often French staff are bright and enthusiastic. Services include racquet restringing and ski maintenance. Children generally enjoy coming on an expedition here, as there's always plenty of scope to play – trying out gym equipment, bouncing balls and testing bikes.
Buggy access. Disabled access. Mail order. Repair service.

Lillywhites

24-36 Lower Regent Street, SW1Y 4QF (0870 333 9600/www.sportsdirect.com). Piccadilly Circus tube. **Open** 10am-9pm Mon; 10am-9.30pm Tue-Sat; noon-6pm Sun. **Credit** AmEx, MC, V.

A fixture on Piccadilly since 1925, Lillywhites is good for mainstream sports gear, concentrating on urban activities, especially football.
Buggy access. Disabled access. Mail order.

Ocean Leisure

11-14 Northumberland Avenue, WC2N 5AQ (7930 5050/www.oceanleisure.co.uk). Embankment tube. **Open** 10am-7pm Mon-Fri; 10am-5pm Sat. **Credit** MC, V.

Hidden away under the arches by Embankment, this watersports emporium sells all manner of sailing, scuba and surfing gear. Some of the stock – including wetsuits, swimwear, Reef sandals and neoprene Aquashoes – comes in very small sizes. There are also baby life-jackets, fins, masks and snorkels; specialist children's scuba equipment can be ordered in.
Buggy access. Disabled access. Mail order.

Slam City Skates

16 Neal's Yard, WC2H 9DP (7240 0928/ www.slamcity.com). Covent Garden tube. **Open** 11am-7pm Mon-Sat; noon-5pm Sun. **Credit** AmEx, MC, V.

A well-stocked source of skateboards, sneakers of the moment, rucksacks and accessories, beloved by teen aficionados.
Mail order (0870 420 4146).

Soccerscene

56-57 Carnaby Street, W1F 9QF (7439 0778/ www.soccerscene.co.uk). Oxford Circus tube. **Open** 10am-7pm Mon-Wed, Fri, Sat; 10am-8pm Thur; noon-6pm Sun. **Credit** AmEx, MC, V. **Map** p314 J6.

Scaled-down replica kits, socks, goalie gloves and more, plus footie and rugby themed gifts and accessories.
Delivery service. Mail order.
Branches 156 Oxford Street, W1D 1ND (7436 6499); 49-50 Long Acre, WC2E 9JR (7240 4070).

Speedo

41-43 Neal Street, WC2H 9PJ (7497 0950/ www.speedo.com). Covent Garden tube. **Open** 10am-7pm Mon-Wed, Sat; 10am-8pm Thur, Fri; noon-6pm Sun. **Credit** AmEx, MC, V. **Map** p315 L6.

Swimming costumes, shorts and nappies, alongside all manner of aquatic accessories: armbands, snorkels, goggles and caps that match your swimsuit.
Buggy access. Disabled access. Mail order.

Wigmore Sports

39 Wigmore Street, W1U 1QQ (7486 7761/ www.wigmoresports.co.uk). Bond Street tube.

Consumer

Bags of potential
Notting Hill

The leafy streets of Ladbroke Grove and Notting Hill are the original stamping ground of the yummy mummies and their offspring. Here, organic cotton-clad babies recline in expensive three-wheelers while their parents stroll around the shops; the streets leading off Portobello Road are sprinkled with brilliant boutiques and specialist shops, stocking all the smartest brands alongside trendsetting lesser-known labels.

For stylish children's clothing, there's no end of choice; start at the Ladbroke Grove (and cheaper) end of Portobello Road with **Sasti** (*see p271*) for hardwearing, 1970s-inspired designs. Girls will adore the romantic day dresses and party frocks at **I Love Gorgeous** (*see p272*), made from deliciously floaty fabrics; to ensure your child doesn't look out of place on the Riviera, **Petit Aimé** (*see p269*) stocks the best French childrenswear designers.

Their Nibs (*see p271*) also continues to enchant both parents and children with its vintage-inspired designs and quirky prints; pirate-printed shirts and pyjamas for the chaps, and a sweet fairy design for girls.

Old-fashioned toys and games can be found at the charming **Honeyjam** (*see p281*) on Portobello Road, run by two fabulously fashionable friends. If you're in need of a more substantial set of wheels than its chunky wooden cars and pull-along animals, the **Pram Shop** (*see p266*) is the best place to go for considered advice and top of the range baby transport options.

Honeyjam.
See p281.

Open 10am-6pm Mon-Wed, Fri, Sat; 10am-7pm Thur; 11am-5pm Sun. **Credit** AmEx, MC, V. **Map** p314 G6.

Junior stock at London's premier racquet sports specialist (tennis, squash, badminton and more) includes footwear by brands such as K-Swiss, Adidas, Asics and Nike; shorter racquets and softer balls are a speciality. Staff are committed to the tennis cause and are keen to match youngsters up with the right racquet. There's a 'try before you buy' practice wall, which children love when it's not being used by some hard-bitten hitter. Raquet restringing is also offered.

Buggy access. Delivery service. Disabled access. Mail order.

TOYS & GIFTS

Art Stationers/
Green's Village Toy Shop

31 Dulwich Village, SE21 7BN (8693 5938). North Dulwich rail. **Open** 9am-5.30pm Mon-Sat. **Credit** MC, V.

The shop at the front is an Aladdin's cave of arts and crafts-related bits and pieces: pipe cleaners, beads, pompoms, stick on jewels, sequins and beads, along with paints, pastels, stationery, clay and other materials. That's just half the story, though. A big sign bearing the legend TOYS has the children cantering down the passage for the booty: Brio, Sylvanian Families,

Consumer

Sylvanian Families.
See p283.

Playmobil, Crayola, Lego, Warhammer and other big brands. Lesser-spotted companies such as Tantrix and Wow are also represented. The enormous pocket money-priced range goes from a rubber goldfish (25p) to a £2.25 magnetic car racer.
Buggy access.

Disney Store
360-366 Oxford Street, W1N 9HA (7491 9136/www.disneystore.co.uk). Bond Street tube. **Open** 9am-9pm Mon-Sat; noon-6pm Sun. **Credit** AmEx, MC, V.
Children make a beeline to this bright, brash shrine to all things Disney, which sells figurines, stationery, toys, costumes and all manner of merchandise. Enduring favourites are the character dolls, lunch-boxes, costumes and classic DVDs.
Buggy access. Disabled access. Mail order.
Branches 10 The Piazza, WC2E 8HD (7836 5037); 22A & 26 The Broadway Shopping Centre, W6 9YD (8748 8886).

Early Learning Centre
36 King's Road, SW3 4UD (7581 5764/ www.elc.co.uk). Sloane Square tube. **Open** 9.30am-7pm Mon-Fri; 9.30am-6pm Sat; 11am-6pm Sun. **Credit** AmEx, MC, V.
A presence on British high streets since the 1970s, ELC has stuck to its ethos of encouraging imaginative play for babies and young children. Everything is sturdy, brightly

coloured and reasonably priced; on Tuesday mornings (10am-noon), kids can get hands-on with the toys or try some craft activities at the weekly drop-in play sessions.
Buggy access. Delivery service. Mail order (08705 352352).
Branches throughout town.

Fagin's Toys
84 Fortis Green Road, N10 3HN (8444 0282). East Finchley tube, then 102, 234 bus. **Open** 9am-5.30pm Mon-Sat; 10am-3pm Sun. **Credit** MC, V.
Along with toys from the likes of Galt, Orchard, Brio, Lego, Playmobil, Meccano and Sylvanian Families, Fagin's has a central table of penny dreadfuls for party bags. Have fun choosing between little rubber fish and stretching aliens, powerballs, pots of slime, magic screens, colouring sets and silk purses; prices run from 15p for a fortune-telling fish to £1.69 for a pack of magnetic marbles.
Buggy access. Disabled access. Play area.

Hamleys
188-196 Regent Street, W1B 5BT (0870 333 2455/www.hamleys.com). Oxford Circus tube. **Open** 10am-8pm Mon-Fri; 9am-8pm Sat; noon-6pm Sun. **Credit** AmEx, DC, MC, V.
Arranged on seven noisy, bustling floors, with perky demonstrators showing off selected wares, Hamleys has become a prime tourist draw. Most must-have toys are here – though

Consumer

more modern toys by Jellycat; there's a big Sylvanian Families collection, plus toys by Galt, Schleich and Playmobil, doll's house accessories by Plan and jolly, chunky plastics by Wow Toys. *Buggy access.*

Honeyjam
267 Portobello Road, W11 1LR (7243 0449/ www.honeyjam.co.uk). Ladbroke Grove tube. **Open** 9.30am-5.30pm Mon-Sat; 11am-4pm Sun. **Credit** MC, V.
Spinning tops, skipping ropes and traditional wooden toys from companies like Bigjigs and Le Toy Van delight nostalgia-hungry parents, while children deliberate over the pocket-money purchases. You'd need to save for longer to afford the bigger pieces: the best-selling mini wooden Aga (£350), for example, which is exclusive to the shop. In the dressing-up section, boys can be transformed into knights and pirates, while little girls are enchanted by the reversible costumes: Snow White on one side and the Sleeping Beauty on the other, or Cinderella in her ballgown and rags. There's a small collection of baby and infant clothes and an ever- expanding range of fair trade and eco-friendly products.
Buggy access. Disabled access.

Just Williams
18 Half Moon Lane, SE24 9HU (7733 9995). Herne Hill rail. **Open** 9.30am-6pm Mon-Sat. **Credit** MC, V.
A bright blue-painted child's paradise, Williams has some top names in toys, with plenty of goodies from Brio, Sylvanians, Schleich and Playmobil. Traditionalists will approve of the wooden playthings from Bigjigs, Plan Toys, Pintoy and Santas, while Warhammer enthralls more bloodthirsty boys.
Buggy access.

Little Rascals
140 Merton Road, SW19 1EH (8542 9979). South Wimbledon tube. **Open** 9am-5.30pm Mon-Sat. **Credit** AmEx, MC, V.
Aimed at under-fives, this friendly, family-run local shop is full of appealing toys and gifts. Check out the handmade wooden book ends and money-boxes and colourful greetings cards; for younger babies, there are snug Grobag sleeping bags and Taggies comforter blankets.
Buggy access.

Mystical Fairies
12 Flask Walk, NW3 1HE (7431 1888/ www.mysticalfairies.co.uk). Hampstead tube. **Open** 10am-6pm Mon-Sat; 11am-6pm Sun. **Credit** MC, V.

Hamleys isn't immune to that pre-Christmas panic when the cult toy of the moment becomes scarce. Down in the basement are the gadgets and construction toys, while the ground floor is devoted to soft toys and magic tricks. Floor one is games, science kits and sweets, two is for preschoolers, three is girls' stuff, four hobbies, models and remote control toys, and five is boys' toys and a nice little café. Though racing round the store is thrilling enough for most children, large-scale family events are held on site throughout the year. Check the schedule to find out who's planning to pop in; Scooby-Doo, perhaps, or SpongeBob SquarePants. In-store parties are also offered – although at £7,000 for ten kids, the Hamleys Sleepover is possibly best left to young billionaires.
Buggy access. Café. Delivery service. Disabled access. Mail order. Nappy-changing facilities. Play areas.

Happy Returns
36 Rosslyn Hill, NW3 1NH (7435 2431). Hampstead tube. **Open** 10am-5.30pm Mon-Fri; 10am-6pm Sat; noon-5.30pm Sun. **Credit** MC, V.
This fairly small toy shop doesn't have bags of choice, but the range is a clever mix of products with prices to suit everyone. Aimed at the zero to five age group, the shop is geared largely towards parties. Stock up on the celebration essentials then go hunting for presents. Look out for classics like glow stars or Etch-A-Sketch, or

Consumer

From beans to bar

Notting Hill's boutique chocolatier, **Melt**, (59 Ledbury Road, W11 2AA, 7727 5030, www.meltchocolates.com) nestles amid an enclave of luxury outlets at the ritzier end of Westbourne Grove. This is where the posh set get their sweeties – bonbons in palate-tickling designer flavours such as salted caramel (the top seller); thick chocolate bars made from the finest blends; butterfly lollipops worked in rich, jewel-like colours.

The open kitchen is set at the back of the shop, which means that customers can witness the entire production process, masterminded by charming head chocolatier Chika Watanabe. Twice a week, Chika also hosts small workshops where you can learn the secrets of the cocoa bean and have a go at making a few goodies under her watchful eye.

Starting with a chat about the countries where cocoa is grown and the impact of the 'terroir' on the finished flavour, Chika then brings out some samples (snapping the kids' focus back nicely) and lets her pupils compare different beans, blends and techniques.

After that, it's down to the hands-on business, heating up the chocolate, tempering it on a marble surface to preserve its silky shine, then brushing and piping the delicious stuff into various moulds. To finish, we all went crazy decorating giant lollipops with nuts, coconut, jellied orange and the like.

The two nine-year-old girls in our group loved every second and left clutching large goodie bags heaped high with their creations, plus a few extras (including their own chocolate-making tools). Be warned, though, that younger kids with wandering attention spans might not get the most out of the experience: ideally, this should be a chance to absorb some fascinating, indeed award-winning, expertise, rather than a mere excuse to scoff chocs.

With a superhuman effort of will, we managed to restrain ourselves until we hit the pavement, then stuffed our faces all the way back to the tube station. Yum.

Children's courses run Mon-Sat, last an hour and cost £35 (£25 on Wed).

There are several thousand small and pretty things in this shop, at least half of them hanging from silver branches overhead. Most of the merchandise is pink or sparkly and features princesses, ballerinas, flower fairies, pixies and elves. The back of the shop is an Aladdin's cave of costumes (mostly for girls, though there are some token wizard and pirate outfits). Mystical Fairies is a shop that's hard to leave empty-handed; it's full of tea sets, trinkets, books, sticker sets, stationery, slippers, dressing gowns, pyjamas and duvet covers, wands, wings, craft sets and jewellery. Staff also run parties in the shop's fairy light-decked Enchanted Garden (the basement). Check the website for details of the regular fairy schools.
Buggy access. Mail order.
Branch Bluewater Shopping Centre, Greenhithe, Kent, DA9 9ST (01322 624997).

Patrick's Toys & Models

107-111 Lillie Road, SW6 7SX (7385 9864/ www.patrickstoys.co.uk). Fulham Broadway tube. **Open** 9.30am-5.30pm Mon-Sat.
Credit MC, V.
One of London's biggest toy and model shops, Patricks is a major service agent for Hornby and Scalextric, attracting adult enthusiasts as well as kids. The model department specialises in rockets, planes, cars, military and sci-fi, while the general toy department has traditional wooden toys, board games, soft toys and doll's houses.
Buggy access. Delivery service (local). Disabled access. Mail order.

Postmark

59 Northcross Road, SE22 9E7 (8693 1133/www.postmarkonline.co.uk). East Dulwich rail. **Open** 10am-5.30pm Mon-Sat; 11.30am-4.30pm Sun. **Credit** MC, V.
Unable to live up to its name, the Never Ending Story Bookshop closed last year. Its former premises are now occupied by this cheerful card shop, which has a small back room full of models, games and toys of an educational bent.
Buggy access.
Branch 123 Balham High Road, SW12 9AR (8675 7272).

QT Toys

90 Northcote Road, SW11 6QN (7223 8637/ www.qttoys.co.uk). Clapham Junction rail. **Open** 9.30am-5.30pm Mon-Sat; 9.30am-5pm Sun. **Credit** MC, V.

Consumer

Snap Dragon

56 Turnham Green Terrace, W4 1QP (8995 6618). Turnham Green tube. **Open** 9.30am-6pm Mon-Sat; 11am-5pm Sun. **Credit** AmEx, MC, V.

A good general toy shop for big brands, Snap Dragon stocks a bit of everything: Lego, Playmobil, Brio and Sylvanian Families are among the biggest sellers, along with other games and jigsaws from Orchard Toys as well as stacks of cuddly toys. For rainy days, there's an abundance of classic board games, from Buckaroo to Boggle. There are generally a few sandpits and goalposts on the shop floor, while bulkier trampolines and wooden climbing frames by TP Toys can be ordered in on request.
Buggy access. Delivery service.

Sylvanian Families

68 Mountgrove Road, N5 2LT (7226 1329/ www.sylvanianfamilies.com). Finsbury Park tube/rail. **Open** 9.30am-5.30pm Mon-Fri; 9am-6pm Sat; 10am-4pm Sun. **Credit** MC, V.

Scores of neatly-attired woodland critters line the shelves at this tucked-away emporium of all things Sylvanian, along with every conceivable accessory. Here you can buy your favourite dressed-up animals from the numerous families, along with their homes, wardrobes, hospitals, schools, cars and furniture.
Buggy access. Mail order.

Toy Station

6 Eton Street, Richmond, Surrey TW9 1EE (8940 4896). Richmond tube/rail. **Open** 10am-6pm Mon-Fri; 9.30am-6pm Sat; noon-5pm Sun. **Credit** (over £8) MC, V.

This bastion of traditional, good-quality toys has two storeys filled with model animals, knights and soldiers, forts and castles, remote-control vehicles and more traditional wooden playthings.
Buggy access. Disabled access.

Toys R Us

760 Old Kent Road, SE15 1NJ (7732 7322/ www.toysrus.co.uk). Elephant & Castle tube/rail then 21, 56, 172 bus. **Open** 9am-8pm Mon-Fri; 9am-7pm Sat; 11am-5pm Sun. **Credit** AmEx, MC, V.

The American retail giant generally has industrial quantities of the toy of the moment amid its mighty stockpile, though it can be hard to find an assistant.
Buggy access. Car park. Delivery service. Disabled access. Nappy-changing facilities.
Branches throughout town.

From ever-popular Lego and Sylvanian Families sets to tubs of luridly-hued Play Doh, it's all here. There are also some educational games, craft and modelling kits and stationery for older kids.
Buggy access. Disabled access. Mail order. Nappy-changing facilities.

Route 73 Kids

92 Stoke Newington Church Street, N16 0AP (7923 7873/www.route73kids.co.uk). Bus 73, 393, 476. **Open** 10am-5.30pm daily. **Credit** MC, V.

Named after the bendy bus that chugs along Stoke Newington Church Street, this jolly toyshop caters to all budgets. A party-bag-tastic table full of pocket money toys takes centre stage, and there's a great selection of traditional names such as Brio and Galt. It's geared towards parents looking for quality wooden toys rather than tacky plastic goods; Plan Toy's eco-friendly rubberwood designs are particularly popular. Then there are books, puzzles, jigsaws, word games, craft packs, Jellycat animals and Starchild's soft leather baby shoes. The train and racing car tables are there to be played with, along with a bike and scooter to whizz about on.
Buggy access. Disabled access.

Traditional toys

Benjamin Pollock's Toyshop
*44 The Market, WC2E 8RF (7379 7866/
www.pollocks-coventgarden.co.uk). Covent
Garden tube.* **Open** 10.30am-6pm Mon-Sat;
11am-4pm Sun. **Credit** AmEx, MC, V.
One of the capital's most charming toy shops,
Pollock's is best known for its three-dimensional
toy theatres. These cost from £6.95 for the basic
Pollock's Diorama, though more elaborate models
cost up to £85. Other charming finds include
cardboard jumping Jacks, wind-up music boxes,
china tea sets, glove puppets and spinning tops.
Mail order.

Compendia Traditional Games
*10 The Market, SE10 9HZ (8293 6616/
www.compendia.co.uk). Cutty Sark DLR/
Greenwich rail.* **Open** 11am-5.30pm Mon-Fri;
10am-6pm Sat, Sun. **Credit** MC, V.
No games requiring plugs or batteries are sold
at Compendia. Instead, you can invest in timeless
board games (Ludo, backgammon, dominoes,
Scrabble, Snakes & Ladders) or investigate more
obscure games from around the world, such as
the fast-flicking, furious-paced carrom.
Buggy access. Disabled access. Mail order.

Enchanted Forest
*6 Lichfield Terrace, Sheen Road, Richmond,
Surrey TW9 1AS (0870 420 8632/
www.enchantedforest.uk.com). Richmond
tube/rail.* **Open** 9.30am-5.30pm Mon-Sat;
11am-4pm Sun. **Credit** MC, V.
All manner of imaginative toys vie for kids'
attention: sturdy farm sets and animals from the
likes of John Crane and Schleich, dolls, soft toys,
jigsaws, spectacular science kits, pirate costumes,
Lego and Meccano sets. It's also a brilliant place
to pick up party essentials, from helium balloons
and pinatas to invites and party bags.
Buggy access.

Farmyard
*63 Barnes High Street, SW13 9LF (8878
7338/www.thefarmyard.co.uk). Barnes or
Barnes Bridge rail.* **Open** 10am-5.30pm
Mon-Fri; 9.30am-5.30pm Sat. **Credit** MC, V.
Handpainted, personalised toddler's chairs and
wooden toys for newborns to eight-year-olds are
the mainstay here, alongside nursery gifts, toys
and dressing-up kit. There's lots you can buy for
under a tenner: paint-your-own piggybanks and
tea sets make inexpensive birthday presents.
Staff are also happy to assemble ribbon-tied
party bags with your choice of contents.
Buggy access. Delivery service.

Kristin Baybars
*7 Mansfield Road, NW3 2JD (7267 0934).
Kentish Town tube/Gospel Oak rail/C2, C11 bus.*
Open 11am-6pm Tue-Sat. **No credit cards.**
This place isn't for sticky-mitted, curious
toddlers or buggies, but older children with an
interest in doll's houses and miniatures will be
enraptured by the thousands of tiny treasures.
Although many of the items are cheap (tiny
bottles of Coke are just 25p), plenty of the doll's
houses and their contents are valuable, and the
items displayed in drawers and cabinets deeper
inside the shop are for serious collectors only.

Never Never Land
*3 Midhurst Parade, N10 3EJ (8883 3997/
www.never-never-land.co.uk). East Finchley
tube.* **Open** 10am-5pm Tue, Wed, Fri, Sat.
Credit MC, V.
The self-proclaimed 'biggest little toy shop in
London' abounds in old-world delights, including
imposing kit-build and ready-made doll's houses
(from £99) and miniatures. Reasonably priced
wooden toys include a sweet little foldaway
cooker and a splendid castle and siege set, while
babies are provided for with all sorts of brightly
painted pram toys. Pocket money purchases
include felt craft kits and teeny-tiny teddy bears.
Buggy access. Mail order.

Petit Chou
*15 St Christopher's Place, W1U 1NR (7486
3637/www.petitchou.co.uk). Bond Street tube.*
Open 10.30am-6.30pm Mon-Sat; noon-5pm
Sun. **Credit** AmEx, MC, V.
Hard-wearing, aesthetically pleasing wooden
toys are the focus at this pricey boutique, from
a cherry-red London bus to a resplendent ride-
on fire engine. Skittle sets, shape-sorters and
pull-alongs are equally easy on the eye, along
with mechanical music boxes, wall hangings
and classic building block-filled baby walkers.
Buggy access.

Puppet Planet
*787 Wandsworth Road, SW8 3JQ (7627
0111/07900 975276/www.puppetplanet.co.uk).
Clapham Common tube.* **Open** 9am-4pm Tue-
Sat, phone to check; also by appointment.
Credit AmEx, MC, V.
All sorts of puppets inhabit Lesley Butler's
specialist shop, from classic Pelham characters to
traditional Czech, Indian and African marionettes,
Balinese shadow puppets, vintage carved puppets
and felt hand puppets. Some are collectors'
items, but there's plenty that's affordable.
*Buggy access. Delivery service. Disabled access.
Mail order.*

Directory

Directory

GETTING AROUND

PUBLIC TRANSPORT

The prices listed for transport and services were correct at the time of going to press, but bear in mind that some prices (especially those of tube tickets) are subject to a hike each January.

Public transport information

Full details can be found online at www.thetube.com and www.tfl.gov.uk, or by phoning 7222 1234.

Transport for London (TfL) also runs Travel Information Centres that provide maps and information about the tube, buses, Tramlink, riverboats, Docklands Light Railway (DLR) and national rail services within the London area. You can find them in Heathrow Airport, as well as in Liverpool Street and Victoria stations.

London TravelWatch
6 Middle Street, EC1A 7JA (7505 9000/ www.londontravelwatch.org.uk). **Open** *Phone enquiries* 9am-5pm Mon-Fri.
This is the official, campaigning watchdog monitoring customer satisfaction with transport.

Fares, Oyster cards & Travelcards

Tube and DLR fares are based on a system of six zones stretching 12 miles (20 kilometres) out from the centre of London. A cash fare of £4 per journey applies across the tube for zones 1-6 (£3.20 excluding zone 1); customers save up to £2.40 with Oyster pay-as-you-go (*see below*). Beware of £25 on-the-spot fines for anyone caught without a ticket.

Children aged under 11 travel free on buses, DLR and the tube. If you are using only the tube, DLR, buses and trams, Oyster pay-as-you-go will always be cheaper than a Day Travelcard (*see below*). If you are using National Rail services, however, the Day Travelcard may best meet your needs (children travelling with you can buy a Day Travelcard for £1). Under-16s get free travel on buses.

Travelcards, valid for tubes, buses, DLR and rail services, can be the cheapest way of getting around. Travelcards can be bought at stations, London Travel Information Centres or newsagents.

Day Travelcards
Peak Day Travelcards can be used all day Monday to Friday (except public holidays). They cost from £7.20 (£3.60 for under-16s) for zones 1-2, with prices rising to £14.80 (£7.40 for under-16s) for zones 1-6. Most people use the off-peak Day Travelcard, which allows you to travel from 9.30am Monday to Friday and all day Saturday, Sunday and public holidays. They cost from £5.10 for zones 1-2, rising to £7 for zones 1-6. Up to four children pay £1 each when accompanied by an adult with a Travelcard.

Oyster card
The Oyster card is a travel smart-card that can be charged with Pre-Pay and/or 7-day, monthly and longer-period (including annual) travelcards and bus passes. Oyster cards are currently available to adults and under-16 photocard holders when buying a ticket. Tickets can be bought from www.oystercard.com, at tube station ticket offices, London Travel Information Centres, some National Rail station ticket offices and newsagents. A single tube journey in zone 1 using Oyster to pay-as-you-go costs £1.60 at all times (80p for under-16s, children under 11 go free).

Children
Under-16s can travel free on buses and trams; under-11s travel free on the tube at off-peak hours and at weekends with an adult with a valid ticket. Children aged 14 or 15 need a child – or 11-15 – photocard to travel at child rate on the tube, DLR and trams.

Children who board National Rail services travelling with adult-rate 7-day, monthly or longer travelcard holders can buy a day travelcard for £1. An under-16 Oyster photocard is required by children aged 11-15 years to pay as they go on the Underground or DLR, or to buy 7-day, monthly or longer period travelcards.

Three-day Travelcards
If you plan to spend a few days charging around town, you can buy a 3-Day Travelcard. The peak version can be used for any journey that starts between the ticket start date and 4.30am on the day following the expiry date, and is available for £18.40 (zones 1-2) or £42.40 (zones 1-6). The off-peak travelcard, which can be used from 9.30am, costs £21.20 (zones 1-6).

Children aged 5-15 and New Deal Photocard holders pay £9.20 for zones 1-2 and £21.20 for zones 1-6 (peak), or £6 (off-peak, zones 1-6).

London Underground

The tube in rush hour (8-9.30am and 4.30-7pm Monday-Friday) is not pleasant, so it is best to travel outside these hours with children, if possible.

Using the system

Tube tickets can be purchased or Oyster cards (*see p287*) topped up from a ticket office or self-service machine. Ticket offices in some stations close early (around 7.30pm); it's wise to carry a charged up-Oyster card to avoid being stranded.

To enter and exit the tube using an Oyster card, touch it to the yellow reader that will open the gates. Make sure you touch the card when you exit the tube, otherwise you may be fined.

There are 12 Underground lines, colour-coded on the tube map for ease of use; we've provided a full map of the London Underground on the back page of this book. Note that the East London line is closed until 2010.

Timetable

Tube trains run daily from around 5.30am (except Sunday, when they start later). The only exception is Christmas Day, when there is no service. During peak times the service should run every two or three minutes.

Times of last trains vary, but they're usually around 11.30pm-1am daily, and 30 minutes to an hour earlier on Sunday. Debates continue as to whether to run the tube an hour later at weekends. The only all-night public transport is by night bus.

Fares

The single fare for adults within zone 1 is £4 (Oyster fare £1.60); for zones 1-2 it's £4 (Oyster fare £2.20 or £1.60). For zones 1-6 it's £4 (Oyster fare £3.80 or £2.20). The single fare for 11-15s in zone 1-6 is £2 (Oyster fare 55p with a valid 11-15 Oyster photocard), £1.60 for zones 2-6 (Oyster fare 55p). Children under 11 travel free at all times.

Docklands Light Railway (DLR)

The DLR (7363 9700, www.dlr.co.uk) runs trains from Bank or Tower Gateway, close to Tower Hill tube (Circle and District lines), to Stratford, Beckton and the Isle of Dogs, then south of the river to Greenwich, Deptford and Lewisham. Trains run 5.30am to 12.30am Monday to Saturday and 7am to 11.30pm Sunday.

Fares

The single fare for adults within zone 1 is £4 (Oyster fare £1.60). For zones 1-2 it's £4 (Oyster fare £2.20 or £1.60). The zones 1-6 single fare is £4 (Oyster fare £3.80 or £2.20). To travel by DLR only, zones 2-3 is £1.60 (£1.10 Oyster). Children under 11 travel free. Children aged 11-15 pay £2

(Oyster fare 55p) or £1.60 for zones 2-6 (Oyster fare 55p) DLR only, while zones 2-3 for children is 80p (55p Oyster).

One-day 'Rail & River Rover' tickets combine unlimited DLR travel with hop-on, hop-off boat travel on City Cruises between Greenwich, Tower, Waterloo and Westminster piers. Tickets cost £12 for adults, £6 for kids and £28 for a family pass; under-5s go free.

Buses

New buses, with low floors for wheelchair and buggy users, and bendy buses with multiple-door entry and the 'pay before you board' schemes now make up much of the fleet. Buses in central London also require you to have an Oyster card or buy a ticket before boarding from pavement ticket machines. Be sure to have a ticket or swiped Oyster card on you while travelling: inspectors can slap a £25 fine on fare-dodgers. Of the famous open-platform Routemaster fleet, only Heritage routes 9 and 15 remain in central London.

Using an Oyster card (*see p287*) to pay as you go costs £1 at all times; the most you will pay a day is £3.30 on buses and trams. Paying by cash at the time of travel costs £2 per trip. A one-day bus pass gives unlimited bus and tram travel at £3.80. Children under 16 and students up to age 18 and resident in London travel free on buses. New Deal and 16+ Oyster fare is half-price (50p) for those in education outside London.

Night buses

Many night buses run 24 hours a day, seven days a week, and some special night buses with an 'N' prefix to the route number operate from about 11pm to 6am. Most services run every 15 to 30 minutes, but many busier routes have a bus around every ten minutes. Travelcards and Bus Passes can be used on night buses until 4.30am on the day after they expire. Oyster Pre-Pay and bus Saver tickets are also valid on night buses.

Green Line buses

Green Line buses (0870 608 7261, www.greenline.co.uk) serve the suburbs and towns within a 40-mile (64km) radius of London. Their main departure point is Ecclestone Bridge, SW1 (Colonnades Coach Station, behind Victoria).

Coaches

National Express (0871 781 8181, www.nationalexpress.com) runs routes to most parts of the country; coaches depart from **Victoria Coach Station**, a five-minute walk from Victoria rail and tube stations.

Victoria Coach Station

164 Buckingham Palace Road, SW1W 9TP (0871 781 8181/www.tfl.gov.uk/vcs). Victoria tube/rail. **Map** p316 H1.
National Express, which travels to the Continent as Eurolines, is based at Victoria Coach Station.

Rail services

Independently run services leave from the main rail stations. Travelcards are valid on services within the right zones. The very useful London Overground line, run by TFL (0845 601 4867, www.tfl.gov.uk/rail) goes through north London from Richmond to North Woolwich, via Kew, Kensal Rise, Gospel Oak, Islington, Stratford and City Airport.

If you've lost property at an overground station or on a train, call 0870 000 5151; an operator will then connect you to the appropriate station.

Family & Friends Railcard

www.family-railcard.co.uk.
This is worth buying if you make even a couple of long rail journeys per year with the children, as the discounts it gives are substantial. The card costs £24 and lasts one year. Valid across Britain, it gives travellers with children one year of discounts from standard rail fares (a third off adult fares, 60 per cent off child fares, £1 minimum fare). Under-fives travel free. Up to two adults can be named as cardholders – they do not have to be related. The minimum group size is one cardholder and one child aged five to 15; maximum group size with one cardholder is four adults and four children. To pick up a form for the Family & Friends Railcard, visit your local staffed station.

London's mainline stations

Charing Cross *Strand, WC2N 5HS.* **Map** p317 L7.
For trains to and from south-east England (including Dover, Folkestone and Ramsgate).
Euston *Euston Road, NW1 1BN.* **Map** p315 K3.
For trains to and from north and north-west England and Scotland, and a line north to Watford.
King's Cross *Euston Road, N1 9AP.* **Map** p315 L2.
For trains to and from north and north-east England and Scotland, and suburban lines to north London.
Liverpool Street *Liverpool Street, EC2M 7PD.* **Map** p319 R5.
For trains to and from the east coast, Stansted airport and East Anglia, and services to east and north-east London.
London Bridge *London Bridge Street, SE1 2SW.* **Map** p319 Q8.
For trains to Kent, Sussex, Surrey and south London suburbs.
Paddington *Praed Street, W2 1HB.* **Map** p311 D5.
For trains to and from west and south-west England, South Wales and the Midlands.
Victoria *115 Buckingham Palace Road, SW1W 9SJ.* **Map** p316 H10.

For fast trains to and from the channel ports (Folkestone, Dover, Newhaven); for trains to and from Gatwick Airport, and suburban services to south and south-east London.
Waterloo *York Road, SE1 7NZ.* **Map** p319 M9.
For fast trains to and from the south and south-west of England (Portsmouth, Southampton, Dorset, Devon), and suburban services to south London.

Tramlink

Trams run between Beckenham, Croydon, Addington and Wimbledon. Travelcards and bus passes taking in zones 3-6 can be used on trams; cash single fares cost £2 (Oyster fare £1 or 50p for 16- to 17-year-old photocard holders). A one-day bus pass gives unlimited tram and bus travel at £3.80 for adults.

Water transport

The times of London's assortment of river services vary, but most operate every 20 minutes to hourly between 10.30am and 5pm, with more frequent services in summer. Call the operators for schedules, or see www.tfl.gov.uk. Travelcard holders can expect one-third off scheduled riverboat fares. Thames Clippers (0870 781 5049, www.thamesclippers.com) runs a commuter boat service. Clippers stop at all London piers, including Embankment, Blackfriars, Bankside, London Bridge and Tower (near Tower Bridge). The names in bold below are the names of piers.

Royal Arsenal Woolwich – **Greenwich** (15mins) – **Masthouse Terrace** (3mins) – **Greenland Dock** (4mins) – **Canary Wharf** (4mins) – **Tower** (8mins) – **London Bridge** (4mins) – **Bankside** (5mins) – **Blackfriars** (3mins) – **Embankment** (4mins); Thames Clippers (*see above*).
Westminster – **Embankment** (5 mins) – **Festival** (5mins) – **London Bridge** (10mins) – **St Katharine's** (5mins); Crown River 7936 2033, www.crown river.com.
Westminster – **Greenwich** (1hr); Thames River Services 7930 4097, www.westminsterpier.co.uk.
Westminster – **Kew** (1hr 30mins) – **Richmond** (30mins) – **Hampton Court** (1hr 30mins); Westminster Passenger Service Association 7930 2062, www.wpsa.co.uk.
Westminster – **Tower** (30mins); City Cruises 7740 0400, www.citycruises.com.

TAXIS

Black cabs

Licensed London taxis are known as black cabs – even though they now come in a wide variety of colours – and are a

Directory

quintessential feature of London life. Drivers of black cabs must pass a test called the Knowledge to prove they know every street in central London and the shortest route to it. If a taxi's yellow 'For Hire' sign is switched on, it can be hailed. If a taxi stops, the cabbie must take you to your destination, provided it's within seven miles. Expect to pay slightly higher rates after 8pm on weekdays and all weekend.

You can book black cabs in advance. Both Radio Taxis (7272 0272, www.radio taxis.co.uk) and Dial-a-Cab (cash bookings 7253 5000, credit card bookings 7426 3420, www.dialacab.co.uk) run 24-hour services for black cabs (there's a booking fee in addition to the regular fare). Enquiries or complaints about black cabs should be made to the Public Carriage Office (www.tfl.gov.uk).

Minicabs

Be sure to use only licensed firms and avoid minicab drivers who tout for business on the street. There are plenty of trustworthy and licensed local minicab firms around, including Lady Cabs (7272 3300, www.ladyminicabs.co.uk), which employs only women drivers, and Addison Lee (0844 800 6677, www.addisonlee.com). Whoever you use, always ask the price when you book and confirm it with the driver when the car arrives.

DRIVING

Congestion charge

Everyone driving in central London – an area defined as within King's Cross (N), Old Street roundabout (NE), Aldgate (E), Old Kent Road (SE), Elephant & Castle (S), Vauxhall, Chelsea, South Kensington (SW), Kensington, Holland Park, North Kensington, Bayswater, Paddington (W), Marylebone and Euston (N) – between 7am and 6pm Monday to Friday, has to pay an £8 fee. Expect a fine of £60 if you fail to do so (rising to £120 if you delay payment). Passes can be bought from newsagents, garages and NCP car parks; the scheme is enforced by CCTV cameras. You can pay by phone or online any time during the day of entry, even afterwards, but it's an extra £2 after midnight on the day following the day of travel. Payments

are accepted until midnight on the next charging day after a vehicle has entered the zone. Note that in spring 2010, the Western extension of the Congestion Charge zone (covering Chelsea, Kensington, Knightsbridge, Bayswater and Notting Hill) is due to be scrapped.

For information, phone 0845 900 1234 or go to www.cclondon.com. The Congestion Charge zone is marked on the Central London by Area map, *see p308*.

Parking

Central London is scattered with parking meters, but finding a vacant one can take ages. When you do, it'll cost you up to £1 for every 15 minutes to park there, and you'll be limited to two hours on the meter. Parking on a single or double yellow line, a red line or in residents' parking areas during the day is illegal. In the evening (from 6pm or 7pm in much of central London) and at various times at weekends, parking on single yellow lines is legal and free. If you find a clear spot on a single yellow line during the evening, look for a sign giving the regulations. Meters are also free at certain times during evenings and weekends.

NCP 24-hour car parks (0845 050 7080, www.ncp.co.uk) in and around central London are numerous but expensive. Fees vary, but expect to pay £10-£55 per day. NCP car parks can be found at Drury Lane, Parker Street, Parker Mews, and Upper St Martins Lane, WC2; and 2 Lexington Street, W1.

Driving out of town

Check your route for possible delays and roadworks. Try the route-planner service available from the RAC (www.rac.co.uk) or the AA (www.theaa.com).

CYCLING

Parents who want to find out more about cycle training can visit www.bikeforall.net for info, or log on to he websites below. Most local authorities include Safe Routes to Schools schemes in their local transport plans. Check the Sustrans website for details (www.sustrans.org.uk). London Cycle Guide maps are available from some stations and bike shops, or the Travel Information Line (7222 1234).

London Cycle Network
www.londoncyclenetwork.org.uk.
This 560-mile (900km) network of routes for
cyclists will be completed in 2009/10.

London Cycling Campaign
7234 9310/www.lcc.org.uk.
Looks after the city's pedallers.

WALKING

The least stressful way to see London is on
foot. A selection of street maps covering
central London is on pp308-319 but you'll
need a separate map of the city: both the
standard Geographers' *A–Z* and Collins's
London Street Atlas are very easy to use.

The Guy Fox *London Children's Map* is
comprehensive and packed with colourful
illustrations of city landmarks; buy it at
www.guyfox.co.uk at £2.95 or bookshops
and tourist attractions.

RESOURCES

Councils

Barnet *8359 2000, www.barnet.gov.uk.*
Brent *8937 1200, www.brent.gov.uk.*
Camden *7278 4444, www.camden.gov.uk.*
Corporation of London *7606 3030,
www.cityoflondon.gov.uk.*
Ealing *8825 5000, www.ealing.gov.uk.*
Greenwich *8854 8888, www.greenwich.gov.uk.*
Hackney *8356 3000, www.hackney.gov.uk.*
Hammersmith & Fulham *8748 3020,
www.lbhf.gov.uk.*
Haringey *8489 0000, www.haringey.gov.uk.*
Hounslow *8583 2000, www.hounslow.gov.uk.*
Islington *7527 2000, www.islington.gov.uk.*
Kensington & Chelsea *7361 3000,
www.rbkc.gov.uk.*
Lambeth *7926 1000, www.lambeth.gov.uk.*
Lewisham *8314 6000, www.lewisham.gov.uk.*
Merton *8274 4901, www.merton.gov.uk.*
Newham *8430 2000, www.newham.gov.uk.*
Richmond upon Thames *8891 1411,
www.richmond.gov.uk.*
Southwark *7525 5000, www.southwark.gov.uk.*
Tower Hamlets *7364 5000,
www.towerhamlets.gov.uk.*
Waltham Forest *8496 3000,
www.walthamforest.gov.uk.*
Wandsworth *8871 6000, www.wandsworth.gov.uk.*
Westminster *7641 6000, www.westminster.gov.uk.*

Education

Advisory Centre for Education (ACE) *0808 800
5793/exclusion advice line 7704 9822/www.ace-
ed.org.uk.* **Open** 9am-5pm Mon-Tues, 10am-5pm
Wed-Fri.
Phone the centre for advice about your child's
schooling; the advice line is for parents whose
children have been excluded from school, have

been bullied, or have special educational needs.
School admission appeals advice is also available.
British Association for Early Childhood Education
*136 Cavell Street, E1 2JA (7539 5400/www.early-
education.org.uk).* **Open** *Phone enquiries* 9am-5pm
Mon-Fri.
A charitable organisation that provides information
on infant education from birth to eight years.
Gabbitas Educational Consultants *Carrington
House, 126-130 Regent Street, W1B 5EE (7734
0161/www.gabbitas.co.uk).* **Open** 9am-5.30pm
Mon-Fri.
The consultants at Gabbitas give advice to parents
and students on choosing an independent school.
Home Education Advisory Service *PO Box 98,
Welwyn Garden City, Herts AL8 6AN (01707
371854/www.heas.org.uk).* **Open** *Phone enquiries*
9am-5pm Mon-Fri.
Call for information if you want to educate your
child at home. An introductory pack costs £2.50,
a year's subscription £15.
ISC Information Service London & South-East
7766 7070/www.iscis.uk.net. **Open** *Phone enquiries*
9am-5pm Mon-Fri.
The Independent Schools Council Information
Service works to help parents find out about
independent schools.
Kidsmart *www.kidsmart.org.uk.*
Kidsmart is an internet safety awareness
programme run by Childnet International, funded
by the DFES and Cable & Wireless. Its guide is
available to all primary schools.
National Association for Gifted Children *Suite
14, Challenge House, Sherwood Drive, Bletchley,
Milton Keynes, Bucks MK3 6DP (0845 450 0295/
www.nagcbritain.org.uk).* **Open** *Phone enquiries*
9am-4pm Mon-Fri.
Support and advice on education for gifted kids.
Parenting UK *Unit 431, Highgate Studios, 53-79
Highgate Road, NW5 1TL (7284 8370/www.
parenting-forum.org.uk).* **Open** *Phone enquiries*
9.30am-5.30pm Mon-Fri.
Information about parenting classes and support
for parents. It was set up for people who work
with parents, but parents can call as well.
Pre-School Learning Alliance *Fitzpatrick Building,
188 York Way, N7 9AD (7697 2500/www.pre-
school.org.uk).* **Open** *Phone enquiries* 9am-5pm
Mon-Fri.
A leading educational charity specialising in
the early years. It runs courses and workshops
in pre-schools around the country for parents of
children under the age of five.

Fun & games

Activity camps
Barracudas Young World Leisure Group *Bridge
House, Bridge Street, St Ives, Cambs PE27 5EH
(0845 123 5299/www.barracudas.co.uk).*
School holiday camps based in schools in outlying
countryside. Children aged five to 16 are welcome.
Cross Keys *48 Fitzalan Road, N3 3PE (8371
9686/www.xkeys.co.uk/www.miniminors.co.uk).*
Day camps in Finchley for kids aged 12 or under
and rural week-long camps in Norfolk, for children
aged up to 17.
EAC Activity Camps *45 Frederick Street,
Edinburgh, EH2 1EP (0131 477 7570/
www.eacworld.com).*

Day and residential camps for children aged five to 16 in countryside sites.

PGL *Alton Court, Penyard Lane, Ross-on-Wye, Herefordshire HR9 5GL (08700 551 551/ www.pgl.co.uk).*
Sport and activity camps for children aged seven to 16 in the UK and Europe.

Wickedly Wonderful *Russett Cottage, Itchenor, West Sussex PO20 7DD (0794 123 1168/ www.wickedlywonderful.com).*
A holiday company that runs weekly buses from London down to the beach during the summer holidays.

Indoor play

Crêchendo *8772 8100/www.crechendo.com.*
Active play classes for babies and pre-school kids.

Gymboree Play & Music *0800 092 0911/ www.gymboreeplayuk.com.*
A parent-and-child play organisation for children aged 16 months to four-and-a-half years.

National Association of Toy & Leisure Libraries *(NATLL) 68 Churchway, NW1 1LT (7255 4600/ helpline 7428 2286/www.natll.org.uk).*
Open *Helpline* 9am-5pm Mon-Tues, Thur.
For information on more than 1,000 toy libraries.

Toys Re-united *www.toys-reunited.co.uk.*
Check the website to see if a missing plaything might have been found.

TumbleTots *0121 585 7003/www.tumbletots.com.*
Open *Phone enquiries* 9am-5.30pm Mon-Fri.
Phone to find out about TumbleTots play centres in your area.

Health

Asthma UK *0800 121 6255/www.asthma.org.uk.*
Open *Helpline* 9am-5pm Mon-Fri.
Advice and help if you or your child has asthma.

Contact-A-Family *7608 8700/helpline 0808 808 3555/www.cafamily.org.uk.* **Open** *Helpline* 10am-4pm, Mon-Fri.
Support for parents of children with disabilities. This organisation is a valuable resource for those who feel isolated while caring for their disabled children.

Euro Pair Agency *8421 2100/www.euro-pair.co.uk.*
An au pair agency that specialises in French candidates.

Family Natural Health Centre *106 Lordship Lane, SE22 8HF (8693 5515).* **Open** 9.30am-9.30pm Mon-Thur; 9.30am-6pm Fri-Sat; 11am-5pm Sun.
A wide range of alternative therapies, from acupuncture to osteopathy, are practised here. French classes, sing and sign classes, children's yoga and art therapy are also offered.

Family & Parenting Institute *430 Highgate Studios, 53-79 Highgate Road, NW5 1TL (7424 3460/www.familyandparenting.org).* **Open** *Phone enquiries* 9.30am-5.30pm Mon-Fri; 24hr answerphone other times.
A resource centre that produces factsheets covering all aspects of parenting.

Food for the Brain Foundation *8788 3801/ www.foodforthebrain.org*
The Food for the Brain schools project is designed to help parents throughout the UK make the right food choices to help improve their children's brain function, behaviour and intelligence. A

downloadable leaflet, the 'Smart Food Smart Kids Shopping Guide', accompanies the scheme.

Greatcare *www.greatcare.co.uk.*
A useful resource for those looking for childcare. Greatcare has 20,000 registered users, including nannies, au pairs, babysitters, mothers' helps and maternity nurses.

NHS Direct Helpline *0845 4647/www.nhsdirect. nhs.uk.* **Open** *Helpline* 24hrs daily.
Confidential information and health advice; an invaluable resource.

WellChild Helpline *0808 801 0330/ www.wellchild.org.uk.*
This national charity offers practical and emotional support to sick children and their families.

Help & support

Bestbear *0870 720 1277/www.bestbear.co.uk.*
Open 9am-6pm Mon-Fri; 24hr answerphone other times.
Information about childcare agencies.

Childcare Link *0800 234 6346/www.childcare link.gov.uk.* **Open** *Phone enquiries* 9am-5pm Mon-Fri.
Provides a list of childcare organisations in your area.

ChildLine *0800 1111/www.childline.org.uk.*
Confidential 24-hour helpline for young people in the UK. The counsellors are trained to listen and help with all kinds of issues, from bullying and abuse to drugs and STDs. Sometimes they put callers in touch with someone who can help further.

Daycare Trust *21 St George's Road, SE1 6ES (7840 3350/helpline 0845 872 6251/www.daycare trust.org.uk).* **Open** 10am-1pm, 2-5pm Mon-Tue, Thur-Fri; 2-5pm Wed.
A national charity that works to promote high-quality, affordable childcare. If you are a parent or carer paying for childcare, the www.paying forchildcare.org.uk site provides easy-to-read introductions to each of the main types of benefits, grants and subsidies that are available to help ease the financial burden of paying for childcare.

4Children *7512 2112/information line 7512 2100/ www.4children.org.uk.* **Open** *Phone enquiries* 9am-5pm Mon-Fri.
4Children is the national children's charity for children and young people aged up to 19. It works with government, local authorities, primary care trusts, children's service providers, and children and parents to ensure joined-up support for all children and young people in their local community.

Kids *6 Aztec Row, Berners Road, N1 0PW (7359 3635/www.kids.org.uk).* **Open** *Phone enquiries* 9.30am-5.30pm Mon-Fri.
An organisation that seeks to enhance the lives of disabled children, through play, leisure, education, family support, information, advice and training, with a view to empowering them in society.

Kidscape *2 Grosvenor Gardens, SW1W 0DH (7730 3300/helpline 08451 205204/ www.kidscape.org.uk).* **Open** *Helpline* 10am-8pm Mon, Tue; 10am-4pm Wed-Fri.
Established by the indomitable child psychologist and mum Dr Michele Elliott, this was the first charity in the UK set up specifically to prevent bullying and child abuse in the family as well as at school. The helpline is for the use of parents, guardians or concerned relatives and friends of bullied children.

London Mums *www.londonmums.org.uk.*
A group of new mums based in London who support each other by sharing views and tips online and organising activities for mums (and dads) and babies, such as trips to view exhibitions at the National Gallery, movies at the local cinema and nature walks.

London Au Pair & Nanny Agency *www.londonnanny.co.uk.*
Matches families with child carers.

Nannytax *PO Box 988, Brighton, East Sussex BN1 3NT (0845 226 2203/www.nannytax.co.uk).*
Open *Phone enquiries* 9am-5pm Mon-Fri.
For £254 a year, Nannytax registers your nanny with the Inland Revenue, organises National Insurance payments and offers advice.

Night Nannies *7731 6168/www.nightnannies.com.*
Night Nannies provides a list of qualified carers who may be able to offer respite from sleepless nights.

Parent Company *6 Jacob's Well Mews, W1U 3DY (0845 094 4220/www.theparentcompany.co.uk).*
Open *Bookings* 9am-3pm Mon-Fri.
The company runs first aid training courses for parents and carers of babies and children. The courses are delivered by paediatric nurses, either in the home or workplace.

Parent Courses *Holy Trinity Brompton, Brompton Road, SW7 1JA (7581 8255/www.htb.org.uk).* **Open** *Phone enquiries* 9.30am-5.30pm Mon, Wed-Fri; 10.30am-5.30pm Tue.
Runs Parenting Course for parents with children under the age of 12, and Parenting Teenagers, for parents of children aged 13-18. Each course costs £30 and takes place over five weeks once a year.

Parentline Plus *Helpline 0808 800 2222/ www.parentlineplus.org.uk.* **Open** *Helpline* 24hrs daily.
Organises nationwide courses on how to cope with being a parent. For more details, call the free helpline.

Parents for Inclusion *Helpline 0800 652 3145/ www.parentsforinclusion.org.* **Open** 10am-noon, 1-3pm Mon, Wed.
Organises workshops for parents of disabled children as well as providing training for teachers who want to develop inclusion in their schools.

The Parent Practice *Bookings 8673 3444/ www.theparentpractice.com.*
A support and training group that promises to endow parents with the skills for transforming family life. It also produces CDs (£18.50; £33/pair) that provide harrassed mums and dads with practical strategies to make family life calmer, happier and more rewarding.

Parent Support Group *72 Blackheath Road, SE10 8DA (Helpline 8469 0205).* **Open** *Helpline* 10am-8pm Mon-Thur; 24hr answerphone other times.
As well as the helpline, staff run one-to-one support sessions and offer courses on parenting skills to the parents and carers of adolescents who are acting in an antisocial or criminal manner.

Post-Adoption Centre *5 Torriano Mews, Torriano Avenue, NW5 2RZ (7284 0555/Advice Line 7284 5879/www.postadoptioncentre.org.uk).*
Open *Advice Line* 10am-1pm Mon-Wed, Fri; 5.30-7.30pm Thur.
Registered charity providing advice, support and information for anyone affected by adoption, including adoptive/foster parents and their children, adopted adults, birth relatives and the professionals who work with them.

Simply Childcare *www.simplychildcare.com.*
If you're seeking a nanny, check this website.

Sitters *0800 389 0038/www.sitters.co.uk.* **Open** *Phone enquiries* 8am-7pm Mon-Fri; 9am-1pm Sat.
A babysitting agency with locally based nurses, teachers and nannies on its books.

FURTHER REFERENCE

Websites

BBC London *www.bbc.co.uk/london.*
London-focused news, weather, travel and sport.

Children First *www.childrenfirst.nhs.uk.*
Run by Great Ormond Street Hospital and children's charity WellChild, this website has information on all aspects of healthy living, with special sections about going into hospital.

Department for Education and Skills *www.parentscentre.gov.uk.*
The DfES website gives parents advice on schools and other aspects of children's education.

Hidden London *www.hiddenlondon.com.*
The city's undiscovered gems.

Learning Partnership *www.thelearningpartnership.com.*
The Learning Partnership's online guide to parenting, Top Tips for Tiny Tots (www.tt4tt.co.uk), provides new parents with essential information on pregnancy, birth and early development in one easy-to-use downloadable course.

London Active Map *www.uktravel.com.*
Click on a tube station and find out which attractions are nearby. A useful resource for families who are unfamiliar with the city.

London Parks & Gardens Trust *www.parkexplorer.org.uk.*
A website designed to help Key Stage 2 children learn more about the parks, gardens and open spaces of London.

London Underground Online *www.thetube.com.*
Use the journey planner to find the quickest routes to your destination, and check for any disruptions or delays. The planner can also find you cycling routes.

Meteorological Office *www.metoffice.gov.uk.*
The most accurate source of weather forecasts.

Parent Pages *www.parentpages.co.uk*
A useful listings site for families with children and professionals working with children.

The River Thames Guide *www.riverthames.co.uk.*
Interesting places to stay, eat, drink and play, all along the riverbank.

Street Map *www.streetmap.co.uk.*
Grid references and postcodes.

Time Out *www.timeout.com.*
Up-to-the-minute listings, features and reviews, plus critics' recommendations.

Transport for London *www.tfl.gov.uk.*
The official website for travel information about buses, DLR and river services, as well as travel times and cycle routes.

Visit London *www.visitlondon.com.*
The official tourist board website, full of information and special offers.

Walkit *www.walkit.com/london.*
Type in your setting off point and destination, and find out how long it'll take to walk it. It'll even find you the route with the lowest pollution levels.

Yellow Pages Online *www.yell.com.*
The best online resource for numbers and addresses.

Directory

Advertisers' Index

Please refer to relevant sections for addresses / telephone numbers

A-Z Indez

A-Z Index

A-Z Index

Area Index

Index

Index

Make the most of London life

Maps

Place of interest and/or entertainment ...	
Hospital or college	
Railway station	
Park	
River	
Motorway	=
Main road	
Main road tunnel	
Pedestrian road	
Airport	✈
Church	✛
Synagogue	✡
Congestion charge zone	C
Underground station	⊖
Area name	SOHO

See p316

London Overview

© Copyright Time Out Group 2009

Central London
by Area

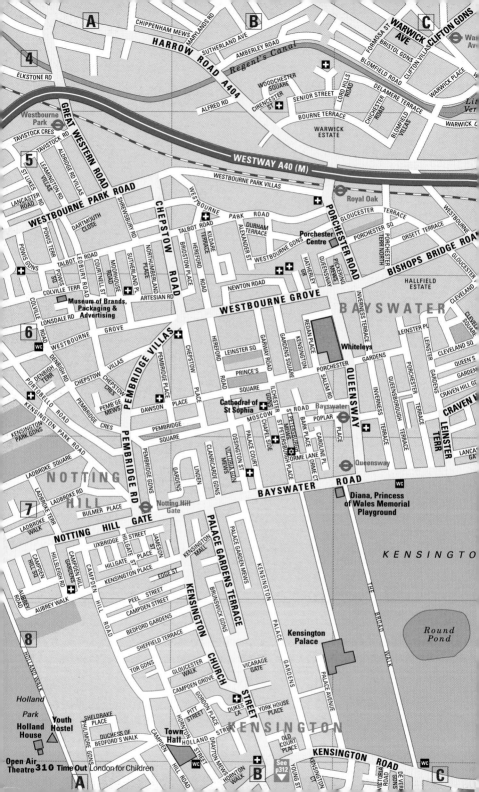

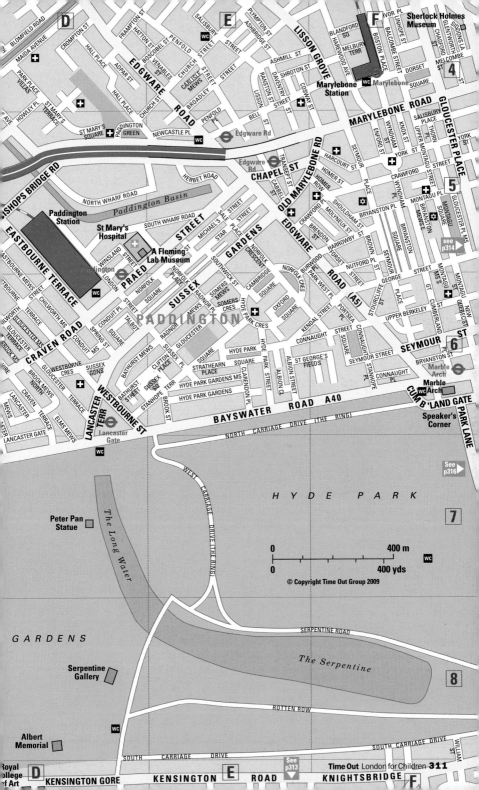

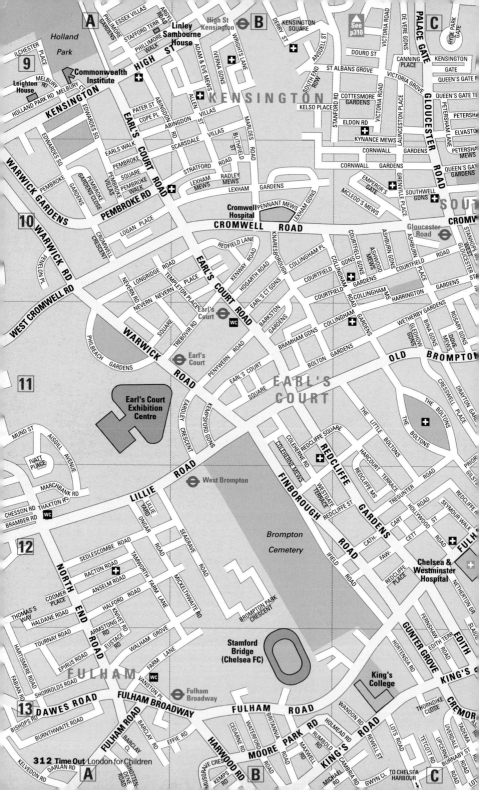

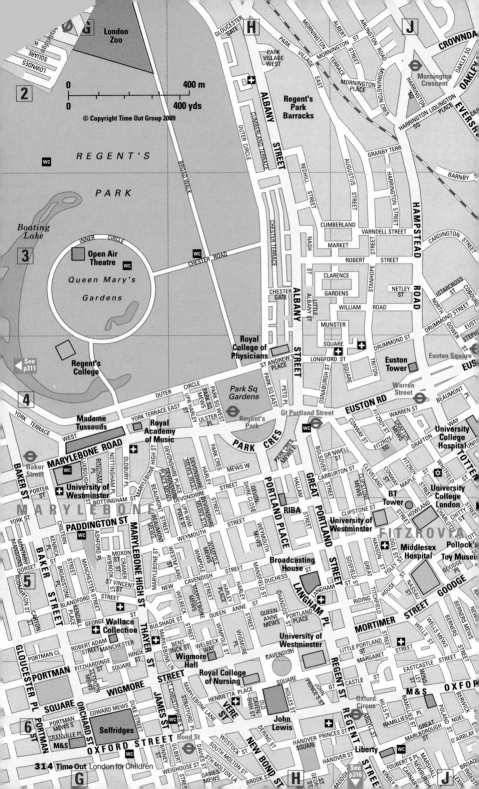

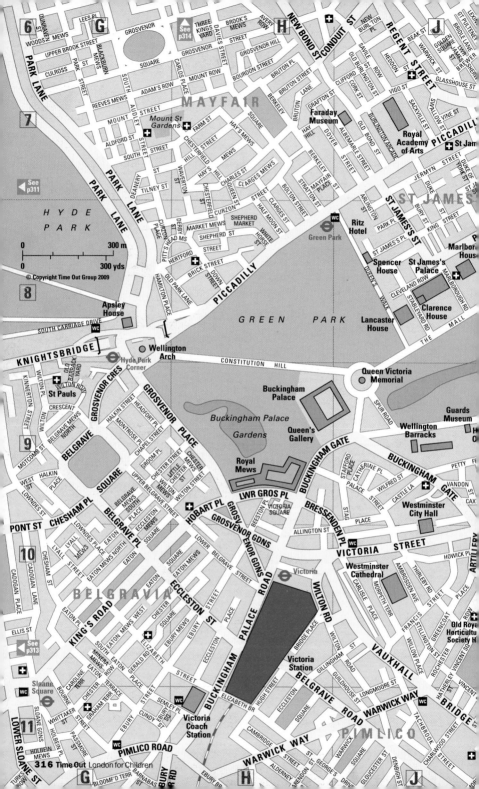

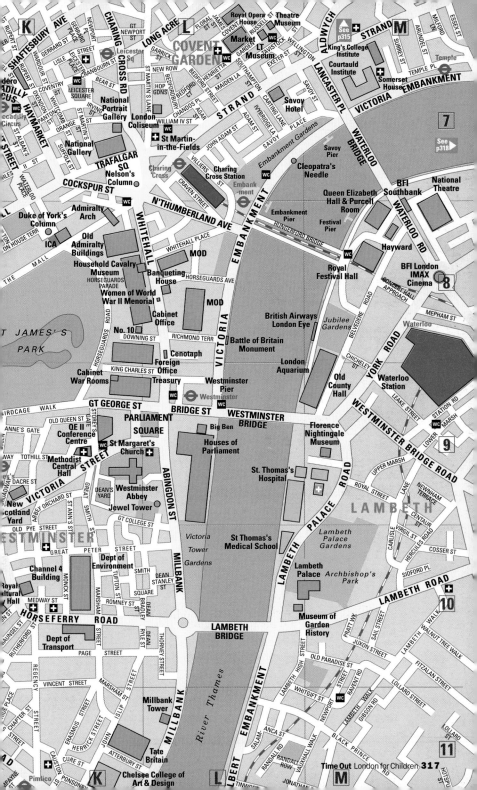

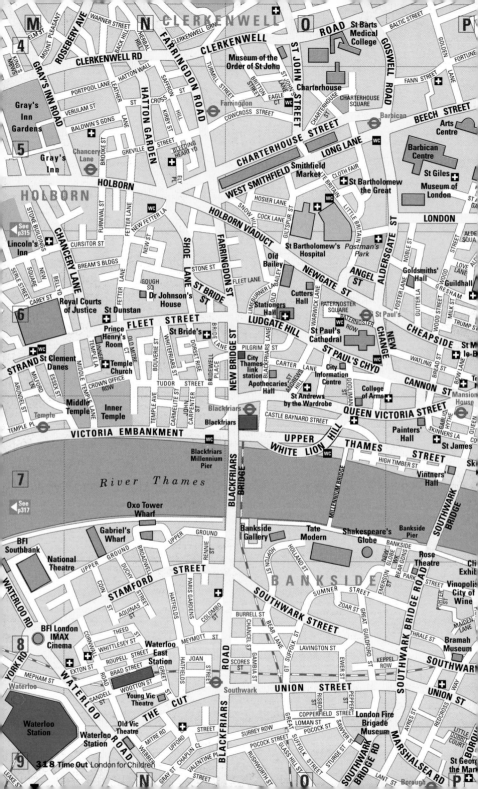

© Copyright Time Out Group 2009

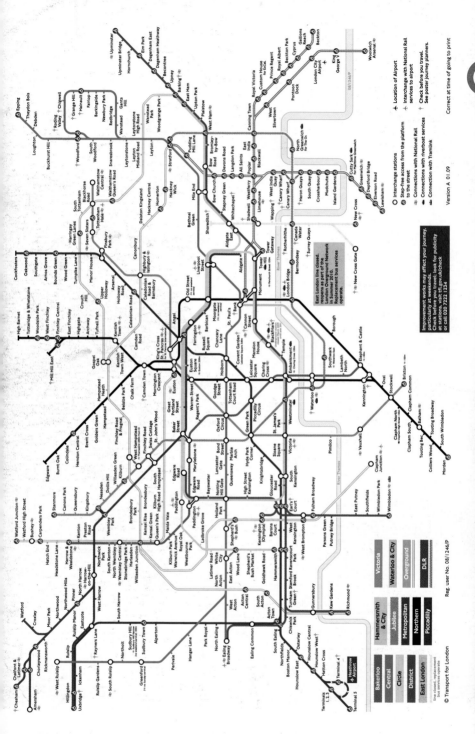

Version A. 01.09

Correct at time of going to print

Improvement works may affect your journey, particularly at weekends. Check before you travel, look for publicity at stations, visit tfl.gov.uk/check or call 020 7222 1234

East London line closed, reopens as part of the London Overground Network in Summer 2010. Replacement bus services operate.

○ Interchange stations
Ⓓ Step-free access from the platform to the street
✚ Connections with National Rail
⚓ Connections with riverboat services
⬛ Connection with Tramlink

✈ Location of Airport
✦ Interchange with National Rail services to airport
✦ Check before you travel.
See poster journey planners.

Reg. user No. 08/1246/P

Bakerloo
Central
Circle
District
East London
line closed, replacement bus services operate

Hammersmith & City
Jubilee
Metropolitan
Northern
Piccadilly

Victoria
Waterloo & City
Overground
DLR

Ⓣ Transport for London